2006

COACH OF THE YEAR CLINICS
FOOTBALL MANUAL

Edited by Earl Browning

www.coacheschoice.com

ISBN: 1-58518-969-3

Library of Congress Control Number: 2006925215

Telecoach, Inc. Transcription: Earl Browning, Jr., Kent Browning, Tom Cheaney, Bill Gierke, Dan Haley

Diagrams: Steve Haag

Book layout and cover design: Studio J Art & Design

Front and back cover photos of Mack Brown: Courtesy of the University of Texas

Back cover photo of Joe Paterno: Craig Melvin/Getty Images

Special thanks to the Nike clinic managers for having the lectures taped.

Coaches Choice
P.O. Box 1828
Monterey, CA 93942
www.coacheschoice.com

Contents

Contents

LINEBACKER DRILLS AND TECHNIQUES

Miami University

Thank you. It is a real pleasure to be here with you today. I want to talk about linebacker drills and techniques today, and I want you to refer to the handout I gave you as we go along.

The first thing we always talk about at Miami University when we talk about linebackers is tackling. As a defense, we feel that if we tackle well, everything will come together, so we strive for good tackling and we try to emphasize it. We will do 10 minutes of various tackling drills every day and we start defensive practice that way.

TACKLING DRILLS

The first drill is a Form Tackling Drill. At the beginning, especially for our freshmen, we just walk through form tackling. Of course, they can tackle when they come in, but not all of them tackle correctly, so we are just going to walk them through it at first.

We place two players two yards away from each other and start by teaching them to get into a good football position. By that, I mean we want them to bend their knees, and keep their backs flat, heads up, and arms ready to strike. We want their weight on the balls of their feet. That, to us, is good football position.

When we talk about having the arms ready to strike, we talk about "shooting them from the holster." We see on film that when our tacklers get their arms all the way out they have a tendency to duck their heads, so we tell them to keep their arms right by their hips, or keep them in their holsters.

After we get our players in a good football position, we take them through the drill by using a cadence. The ballcarrier stands there with a slight body lean, and our first command is "toes!" On this command, the tackler will run up and step on the toes of the ballcarrier. Then, on the command "ball!" the tackler will put his head on the side where the ball is held. The more we get our helmet on the football, the more likely it is that we will cause a fumble, so we coach them to put their head to the side of the ball.

Once we give them "toes," where they step "on the toes," and "ball" where they turn their heads to the football, we will give them a "hips" call. On the "hips" call, they bring their hips up into the ballcarrier and club their arms through his armpits.

To review, we start the drill by saying "stance." We take them through toes, ball, hips, and then they run their feet. If we are putting our face to the football and we are bringing our arms up through the ballcarrier's armpits, then we are getting more things on the football before we run our feet.

Next, we will get them at five yards and give them the same cadence. This will make them have to come under control. Too many guys want to go for the head shots and just go nail the ballcarrier, so we try to teach them to come under control, step on the toes, ball, hips—boom! Make a good form tackle and run their feet. That is our first tackling drill.

Our next drill is our One-Man Sled Drill. The one-man sled is essentially a tackling dummy that allows us to go through the same techniques as the form tackle without having to use another player. In this drill, we will not give them the toes-ball-hips cadence. We will just start them on the whistle. The key coaching point on the one-man sled drill is to bring the arms through the armpits of the dummy, and the second point of emphasis is hip rotation that puts their waist right on that pad. Of course, we always finish by running our feet at shoulder width and controlling the sled.

We follow that drill with the Shed and Tackle Drill. On this drill, we will put a ballcarrier behind the one-man sled and then use the sled as a blocker. We will punch off of the sled and then make the form tackle on the ballcarrier, to whichever side he goes. It just teaches the complete sequence of getting off of the block, reading the ballcarrier, and making the tackle.

We have an Angle Tackle Drill in which we place two players two yards away from each other. The offensive guy will go at a 45-degree angle with the ball in his outside arm. The teaching points are the same as before. We want to step on his toes, stay inside of him, and we really emphasize getting the head across the body. We usually run this drill to the sideline to help teach the tackler to stay inside the ballcarrier and use the sideline as an extra defender. We will use our hips, bring up our arms, and run our feet five yards out of bounds.

After these basic form tackling drills, we will move to our Open-Field Tackling Drill. Like everyone else, we have trouble with the open-field tackle because we are out in space, so we try to emphasize coming under control. We start the drill with two players 10 yards apart, and we tell the tackler that we want him to go, but come under control. Now, we do not want them coming under control at seven or eight yards. We want them to go full speed until they are within four or five yards of the ballcarrier and then start breaking down, but they should never stop their feet. Too many players want to stop their feet when they break down, and then they are in cement when the running back makes a move.

We may actually start the drill by having the defender just break down at four or five yards, keep his feet moving, and then finish the drill from there. The ballcarrier may continue at 45 degrees or he may turn right into him, and he would finish with the proper tackle. Again, open-field tackling is difficult, so this is a drill that we practice a lot.

We do a Sideline Drill, which is really just an extension of the Angle Tackle Drill, but we put our guys out in space to start it. We will have a quarterback swing the ball to a back who wants to catch the ball and turn up the sideline. Our primary coaching point in this drill is to stay inside the football and do not overrun it. Take the proper angle, go downhill, and attack the ballcarrier—do not wait on him. Finish the tackle with the head across the bow and drive him out of bounds. That is the design of our whole 4-3 defense, to go downhill and attack the football.

I will show you all of these drills on film, but let us go on now to the next drill that we use, the Eye-Opener Drill (Diagram #1). We place three bags in a line about three yards apart, representing holes for the ballcarrier to run through. We place a running back on one side and a linebacker on the other. The running back starts out and picks which hole he will run through, and the linebacker slides along with him and makes the tackle when he turns up through the hole. The key teaching points for the linebacker include getting into a good football position to start with, staying inside of the football, starting to shuffle by coming downhill, and keeping the shoulders square. Once the running back picks a hole to go through the linebacker will execute a proper form tackle. This is a great drill to get practice started.

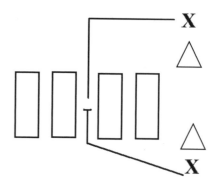

Diagram #1. Eye-Opener Drill

We also use a Box Drill, which we set up on the sideline with four cones or dots in a five-yard square (Diagram #2). There are two on the sidelines and two inside the football field. We will start an offensive guy on one of the cones and a defensive guy on the other cone. The offensive guy is going to run to the sideline at 45 degrees, aiming at the cone that is diagonal from him. The defender will close on the ballcarrier, but will stay inside the football. You will have to tell the ballcarrier to run directly at that cone every single time, full speed, and then it is just a straight sideline tackle by the defender. We emphasize staying inside, getting the head across, and running the feet.

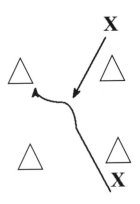

Diagram #2. Box Drill

TACKLING CIRCUIT

We do a tackling circuit every single week. It is something to get the guys going and we will do it first thing when we split up offense and defense. We set up the One-Man Sled Drill, the Sideline Drill, and what we call the Cut-Cut Drill. We do this for five minutes or whenever Coach Johnson gets sick of us tackling. This is what we always try to do first to speed up the tempo of practice.

The players are on the sideline and in the end zone grouped in threes. We have two people on the sideline and one in the end zone. We do the One-Man Sled Drill as I previously described it, just working on technique. The Sideline Drill will be run towards the sideline, and the last one is the Cut-Cut Drill.

We use two medicine balls, which we throw at the tackler in the Cut-Cut Drill. We want our tackler to keep his outside leg back and strike the first medicine ball while bending his knees and keeping his back flat. We break on the first medicine ball,

strike, push it back, and get downhill to the next medicine ball, which is then thrown at us. We strike it, play off of it, and finish with a form tackle on the ballcarrier.

Now they are working three separate tackling drills in this circuit. We will give them a minute and a half in each drill and then they have to sprint to the next drill. Let me show some film of our guys doing these tackling drills. (Film)

One other tackling drill that we like to do, which I do not have on film, is the Cup Drill. Now, you need a tough guy to carry the ball in this drill. We have a coach where the quarterback would be when the ball is on the hash, and he will just pitch the ball to the ballcarrier into the sideline. We will have a defensive back, a linebacker, and a defensive lineman in their approximate positions, and we want them all to take proper angles to the football. The defensive back will take three steps back and then drive up for outside leverage. The linebacker will go right now with the pitch, and the defensive lineman will execute an up-down and then take his angle to the ball. We get the defensive back on the outside, the linebacker staying inside on the ball, the defensive lineman taking his proper angle, and we have a true cup drill.

TURNOVER DRILLS

I want to get to our turnover drills now, which we consider as key to our success as our tackling drills, and we emphasize them just as much. We were fifth in the country this past year in creating turnovers with 34, and we did not even get any the last game, so we felt pretty good about what we did turnover-wise.

The first one I want to talk about is the Strip Drill. We will start the defensive player and the ballcarrier on the same side at two yards apart. The ballcarrier will take off at three-quarter speed with the ball in his right hand. The defender will run and secure the tackle with his left arm along the waist of the ballcarrier. That is the key to the drill. If he strips the ball but does not secure the tackle, 90 percent of the time the offensive guy who recovers the ball is the guy who fumbled it, so we tell the defender he must secure the tackle before he does anything else—whether it is strip or punch.

On the strip technique, after securing the tackle, he clubs his arm down on the ball as violently as he can. Once the ball is out, now he can go scoop and score, and at Miami we want to scoop and score everything.

The other one is the Punch Drill. If we are on the same side, we come with the strip, but if we are on the opposite side, we come with the punch. On the punch, we again secure the tackle first, and then we are going to punch through his armpit. We think that the key thing here is seeing where the ball is. When he sees where it is, he will bring his arm like an uppercut, but he must secure the tackle first. When the ball is out, we want to get upfield, scoop, and score—always scoop and score.

We usually get 20 minutes of individual time in practice before getting into group work, and I try to spend five minutes in a tackling drill and five minutes in a turnover drill. Every single day I have some kind of tackling drill and some kind of turnover drill.

The next turnover drill we do is a simple Interception Drill. We place a guy at 15 yards and the coach will throw the ball at him. The key coaching points include making a diamond with thumb and forefinger, looking the ball in, and always catching the ball in the hands. We always do the drill full speed so that the player looks the ball in, secures the catch, and runs it right back to the coach.

We go "low ball", where they actually bend their knees and scoop the ball, and then "high ball," where we want them to catch the ball at the highest possible point. In both cases, we then want them to rip the football into their body and secure it.

The last turnover drill we do is the Fumble Recovery Drill. We place three bags in the vicinity of the 10-yard line and the players have to work over them. When we flip the ball on the ground, they have to go downhill over the bags, bend their knees when they get to the ball, then scoop and score. They should always grab the ball with two hands,

secure it into their body, and get into the end zone. Always finish the drill, sprint back to the coach, and hand him the football.

If they cannot scoop and score, we want them to recover the ball. We still have the three bags, they are still getting downhill, and they are picking the ball with two hands. The key here is to not roll over because the ball could fly up in the air. We tell them to grab it with two hands, secure it, and then just go into a fetal position. If they wind up on their right side, they should bring their left leg up over the ball, and vice versa. Let me show you some film on these turnover drills. (Film)

AGILITY DRILLS

I want to get into our agility drills. Linebackers have to be able to bend their knees and play football. They cannot be stiff in the hips and they need to be flexible, so we will do agility drills every single day. The first one we do to loosen up their hips is a Hip Turn Drill. We have them make three turns on the drill (Diagram #3). We are a 4-3 defense, so our first three linebackers will pop out, all on a line, facing the coach. The coach gives them a "ball" call and points the ball to one side. The players all turn their hips to that side while still facing the coach. Then, when the coach points the ball to the other side, the players respond by flipping their hips to that side while continuing to face the coach.

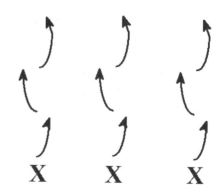

Diagram #3. Hip Turn Drill

Pad level is a key coaching point in this drill. They start from a good football position, drop as in pass coverage, and I will give them three turns, but they must maintain good pad level throughout the drill. They will finish by driving to the hash mark.

We like to reroute receivers at Miami University, so we do a 45-Degree Angle Drill (Diagram #4). We get them in a good football position and I start them straight down the line with a "ball" call, one way or the other. Once they get about five yards they will push off, turn, and flip their hips. Then, when they get back to the original line they were on, they will push off as if they were rerouting a receiver. Then they turn again, flip their hips, and go at a 45-degree angle. We do so much rerouting of receivers that we have to constantly do drills in which our players reroute, push, and extend their arms.

and simulate defeating a cut block. We keep our chest up, our eyes up, and we go down and make three hits as hard as we can. We want to keep the outside leg back because all running backs are taught to aim for the outside leg when they cut block.

We do the Pro Agility Drill just as everyone else does, and of course, we time the drill (Diagram #5). The player starts in the middle of a 10-yard area, touches five yards to each side, and returns to his original starting position while not turning his back on the coach. The key coaching point is to really plant off of that outside foot, accelerate back to the opposite line, and finish the drill by exploding an extra two yards past the finish.

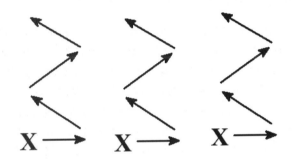

Diagram #4. 45-Degree Angle Drill

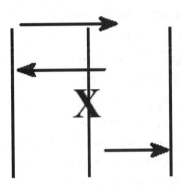

Diagram #5. Pro Agility Drill

The next agility drill we do is the Rat-Tit-Tat-Tat Drill. Players get in one line, on, say the 30-yard line, and, basically, their feet are just going over the line. They try to do it quickly. Again, they start from a good football position, bend their knees, maintain pad level, keep their eyes up, and be quick.

We do a Slow Shuffle Drill in which we move down a straight line by shuffling our feet while staying low in a good football position. We tell them not to click their heels as they shuffle, so they will keep a good base. Along with that drill, we also do a Quick Lateral Shuffle Drill, in which our players move in and out of a straight line while shuffling back and forth. We are just trying to improve their foot speed.

We are now facing so many offenses that cut block that we have to train for it, so we do what we call a Three Touches Drill. We will shuffle down the line, keeping our outside leg back, bending our knees,

Our W Drill is a "plant and break" drill. We do three linebackers at a time. I give them a pass read and they will turn, flip their hips, and go. When I show the ball, they will plant their back foot and accelerate off it back to me as if it was a draw play. Then I raise the ball again and take them through the same sequence a second time, emphasizing good football position and techniques.

One other drill we do as a warm-up is the Quick Carioca Drill that I am sure you have all done. We cross over our legs quickly one at a time as we work down a line. We do it in directions, emphasizing quickness, and trying to loosen our hips. I have most of these agility drills on film here, along with a couple of others. (Film)

BAG DRILLS

We have several bag drills that we do to get our players going in the individual part of practice. The first one is called the One-Foot Drill. We will put four or five bags out and they will just work down the line and go "one in the hole." We want them to get in a good football position, bend their knees, keep their eyes up, and always go full speed.

They will progress to the Two-Foot Drill, which is essentially the same except they are putting two feet in the hole, and then we go on to the Rapid-Fire Drill, where thy chop four times in each hole and then finish.

We also work over the bags with a Shuffle/Lateral Shuffle Drill. In this drill, we shuffle in between the bags with eyes up on the coach. To keep eyes up, I throw a football at them. They have to catch the ball and flip it back as they go "rapid fire" through the drill.

Our Typewriter Drill is more of a discipline drill used when I am a little upset with the players. In this drill, the players are still working through the bags as in the Shuffle Drill, but they have to take short choppy steps. I make them do this until their quads really burn, and it gets their attention quickly. The points of emphasis are the same regarding bent knees, pad level, eyes, and good football position.

I want the linebackers to go through a Backpedal Drill similar to what the defensive backs do. They will backpedal through the first space, plant the back foot, explode forward, and backpedal through the next space, until they finish the drill. To ensure their eyes stay up, I throw a ball at them. The primary point of emphasis in teaching the backpedal technique is to keep your "nose over your toes," so when you plant you can explode off that back foot and go.

The last bag drill we do is the Flip Drill. It is a lot like the Backpedal Drill, but when they sprint up to the front of the bag they have to plant and flip their hips at 90 degrees. They have to do a right plant, left plant, right plant, and left plant, just turning and flipping their hips. Now let us look at the bag drills on film. (Film)

KEY DRILLS

In our base 4-3 defense, our linebackers key the tailback. If the quarterback is under center and a running back is behind him, then we will key that running back and no one else. Whatever steps he takes, we will mirror him. If he steps with his right foot, we will step with our left, and that step is a six-inch power step going downhill. We begin teaching this with our Mirror Drill.

In this drill, if I have 15 guys. I put five guys five yards in front of me, another five behind them, and another five behind them, where they can still see me. I tell them to get into a good stance and I take a step to my right, which they mirror by taking a step with their left. Then go over all the basic steps for four or five minutes, and then I will add to that the favorite runs of our opponent for that week and we will progress to the Downhill Drill.

We watch film of our opponent's steps, and on Tuesdays we will work the Downhill Drill. When the players mirror my steps and get downhill for five yards, they will call out what play it is, because we will know the steps by then. If they know that the power step is just a slide step, and they are getting downhill on it, they will call it out when I give them that slide step—"Power!"—and they will get downhill. We will study all of their steps, and all the things they do best, and that is what we work on in this drill.

We move from the mirror drills to the Run Reads Drill. I get the kickers and some of the extra guys, and we will put together an offensive line along with tight ends and running backs. Coach Johnson, our defensive coordinator, will be our quarterback, and we align our linebackers in their alignments against various offensive sets that we expect to see. Then we go through all the run plays we expect to see and how we fit to those run plays.

We "spill" everything at Miami except on fire zones, where we "box" everything. By spilling, I mean that we are going to take away the inside of your numbers and make everything bounce, or "spill," outside. We do that because the weakness of our defense is structurally in the middle.

Once we tell them what their run fits are, they know that they have to take away their blocker's inside number. It is the same concept as "wrong arming," but we do not use that term. They seem to equate wrong arming with taking themselves out of the play, so we just ask them to take away the inside part of their number. That works better for us.

We may start the run read drill at a walk-through pace, using four garbage cans for defensive linemen. I might also say that it takes some time to plan with the offensive group so they will give good "looks," and do what we want them to do. The key part of this is to show our guys where they fit on each play.

Finally, when I say that our linebackers key the tailback only, I still want them to have "big vision." By this, I mean that they have to be able to feel what else is going on in front of them, including the flow of the other offensive players, or something that maybe is going against that flow. We want to know when the guards are pulling on the counter play for example, and to call it out to each other. We want communication among our linebackers, and we do not want tunnel vision.

Gun Reads are a little different. We still have the offensive line and backs in the drill, but now we have receivers out there and we will get them in a bunch of different formations. Now it is shotgun reads. Now, we have to totally change our concept.

We do not key the tailback anymore in our shotgun reads. Now we are going to key the offensive linemen. That means that if you are an outside backer who is removed and out of the box, you will key that offensive tackle to your side. Even if they are in the box, the outside backers will always key the tackles. Now, the Mike backer can either key the guard or the center, whichever is better for him, but if he is removed to a 30 alignment, he will just key the guard.

Offensive linemen never lie in the shotgun, so if they have "high hat" we are probably getting pass, or possibly draw. We would play the pass and rally to the draw. If it is a run-blocking scheme, we see it at once, so we can get ourselves into the box and try to make a football play. If we see an offensive tackle pulling, then we know it is probably going to be a run. That is what we key in shotgun. Those are

our gun reads. Here are the films of our key drills. (Film)

BLOCK DESTRUCTION DRILLS

The first technique that we teach when we engage blockers is very simple. It is the rip move, and we teach it in our Rip Drill, which our linebackers like doing the most (Diagram #6). We actually do a bunch of different drills where they are ripping off a one-man sled or where they have a partner. We start with two players standing two to five yards apart. When the offensive player releases in a zone scheme, we attack him by getting downhill and bending our knees, with our eyes on him, and we want to have great pad level.

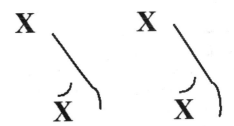

Diagram #6. Rip Drill

We want to be lower than the offensive player. When he extends his arms to block, we will rip our arm in an upward motion, club right through his arms, and finish the drill by squaring up in a good football position. A big key is pad level, so we tell them to drop their hips and bend their knees.

The next one is the Punch Drill. It is just "punch the offense player in the chest." We will get about two yards from the blocker in a good football position and just punch the guy. We teach our people to put their thumbs up when they punch because we will get injuries to the wrist when we punch with our palms. We want to come from the holsters and punch the chest plate with thumbs up and arms locked out so we can gain separation. Offensive linemen will always hold, so we are not worrying about it. We just have to lock out on them so we can gain separation.

Now for the Jam Drill (Diagram #7). If our guy feels the offensive lineman is going to beat him to his gap responsibility, he will jam him. By jamming, I mean we are going to punch through him and push him all the way back into the hole. It is essential to be in a good football position to have the leverage needed to do this to a big old 300-pound lineman. We are a very simple defense and the reads are easy, so we expect our guys to attack downhill and get into their gaps. They either beat that guy or they jam him.

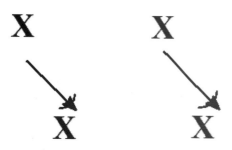

Diagram #7. Jam Drill

We also run the Jam and Rip Drill (Diagram #8). We place a dummy in front of the blocker. We want the linebacker to jam the blocker and use the rip technique to get past the block.

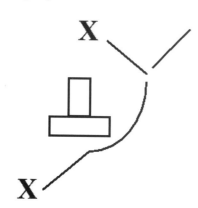

Diagram #8. Jam and Rip Drill

We do a Cut Drill, which is really an extension of the Three Touches Drill. When the back starts to the outside and shows his intention to cut you, you have to punch him in the helmet and near shoulder pad while keeping your outside leg back. His aiming point will be your outside hip to knee area, so when he declares that he is going to try to cut you, we say your hand placement should be to his helmet, but

we mean that we want you to knock that guy's head off. Your other hand should be on his shoulder pad to help stop his momentum and keep your legs free.

The Slip Drill is a drill we use to teach our guys another way to defeat the block when the offensive lineman beats us to our gap responsibility. We expect our guy to be where he is supposed to be, but sometimes he is just going to be late. When that happens, he will allow the offensive player to think he is trying to get past him and then at the last moment he will drop his hips, bend his knees, and slip right behind him. We want him to be butt to butt with the blocker when he does this, with no air between them.

The last drill we do to teach playing off blocks is the Three Way Drill (Diagram #9). We place three blockers about three yards apart with a ballcarrier behind them and line our defender up head on the first one. The defender has to rip off the first blocker, work to the second blocker, and rip off him, and then to the third blocker, and finally he will finish with a form tackle on the ballcarrier.

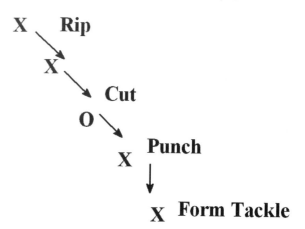

Diagram #9. Three Way Drill

We do the Three Way Drill different ways and we do it a lot. We can use medicine balls instead of blockers, and we can work on all of our rip, cut, or punch techniques as we work across to the football. Here are our block destruction drills on the film. (Film)

DEFENSIVE ADJUSTMENTS VS. MULTIPLE FORMATIONS

Duke University

Thank you. It is great to be here today. I hope I can give you some ideas and thoughts that will help you in your program.

The package I am going to present is something I keep in my hip pocket. Offenses today are all multiple-formation teams. On first and second down, we get three and four wideout packages. We also get two tight ends and two wideout formations a great deal of the time.

In college football, the ball is on the hash mark most of the time. The basic philosophy in our scheme is to play "cloud support" into the boundary. If the ball is on the hash mark, the shortest throw is into the boundary. We want to play cloud support that way.

Into the wide side of the field, we play with a strong safety down in the coverage and the field corner plays a quarter-coverage concept. Our basic coverage is quarter-quarter-half.

In our front, we play with a Sam linebacker–type character on the tight end. We have a Mike or middle linebacker in our scheme. We have a Will or weakside linebacker, who plays the weakside of our defense.

In our defensive line, we play with an E, N, T, and an R. We align them depending on the call. Everyone on the defense except for the corners has a name. The reason we do that is to establish a relationship among our defensive players.

The Sam and Mike linebacker, the end, and the noseguard travel together in our scheme. The tackle, rush, and Will linebacker travel together. We can flip-flop our defense either way on the line of scrimmage.

The first example I will show you is boundary Okie. By making that call, we tell the front seven defenders where to align. The tackle, rush, and Will linebacker go into the boundary on this call. The end, noseguard, and the Mike and Sam linebackers go opposite. If we reverse the call and call field Okie, the defenders line up to the other side.

This defense is not a formation defense. We set the defense according to the field. In a pro formation with a tight end and flanker into the wide side of the field, we declare our 3-technique tackle to the split end or boundary side of the defense (Diagram #1). The rush end aligns on the offensive tackle to that side.

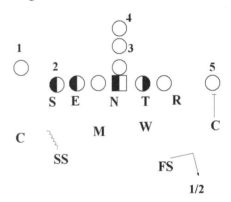

Diagram #1. Boundary Okie

The noseguard aligns in a strongside shade on the center. The end lines up in a 5-technique on the offensive tackle, and the Sam linebacker aligns in a 9-technique on the outside shoulder of the tight end.

The fieldside corner is an inside-leverage corner playing quarter coverage. The strong safety by definition is a quarter defender, but we drop him into the box on a run track. The Mike and Will linebackers align inside and the boundary corner aligns on the split end. The other man in the defense is the half-field safety.

In our defense, there are no coverage checks. On first and 10, I do not want to give up an out cut into the sideline because that is the shortest throw. If the offense throws the quick out, it is into the wide side of the field. That is a long throw for the quarterback.

We number the receivers from the wide side to the boundary. The widest receiver to the fieldside is the number 1 receiver. From that point, we number each eligible receiver 2, 3, 4, and 5 going to the boundary. If the Will linebacker has to walk out of the box because the 4-receiver moved, he cannot cover the A gap (Diagram #2). If the number 4 receiver goes in motion to the weakside, the Will linebacker has to cover him.

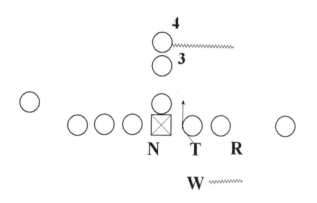

Diagram #2. Motion Weak

The tailback on the back of the I formation is the number 4 receiver. If he goes in motion to the weakside, the Will linebacker has to walk out of the box to cover him. He cannot defend the number 4 receiver on the vertical if he has the A gap. When the Will linebacker has to leave the box, we spike the 3-technique tackle.

In the pass cover, we roll the corner. The Will linebacker has the seam to vertical, and the safety plays half cover over the top. The fieldside plays quarter-quarter coverage.

The Will linebacker cannot play the A gap and cover the 4-receiver on the vertical, but he can play the B gap and cover the seam. At Duke, when you are in situations as we are, you do not have the option of playing man coverage. Their players run 4.2 in the 40-yard dash and our players are much slower.

If we bring the motion the other way toward the field, the Sam linebacker has to walk (Diagram #3). As the number 4 receiver goes in motion to the strongside, he becomes the number 3 receiver. The Sam linebacker has to be in the divide position between the number 2 and number 3 receivers. The defensive line has to bang toward the tight end.

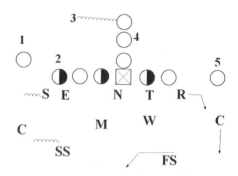

Diagram #3. Motion Strong

The 5-technique end widens to a 7-technique on the tight end. The 7-technique is an inside leverage on the inside shoulder of the tight end. The noseguard moves from the strong shade on the center to a 2i position on the offensive guard. That is also an inside leverage position on the guard. The backside does not move. They play 3- and 5-techniques to the backside.

The strong safety backs out of the box and makes a solid check as the motion comes. The corner plays the seam between the number 1 and number 2 receivers and is the deep defender. The strong safety plays the seam between the number 2 and number 3 receivers. The Sam linebacker plays the first player to the flat. The Mike linebacker plays the first part of the vertical and helps on the curl.

Here is what our players are thinking: If Will walks, we spike the 3-technique tackle. If Sam walks, we bang the front and play solid. The coverage concept stays the same in both situations.

The next formation is the twin-receiver formation to the field. The defensive alignment does not change. We play boundary Okie (Diagram

#4). The 3-technique tackle aligns on the outside should of the guard. The rush linebacker widens to a 7-technique on the tight end. To the fieldside, the nose is in the shade on the center and the end plays a 5-technique on the openside tackle.

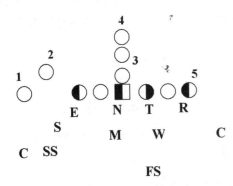

Diagram #4. Twin Set

The width of the split in the twin set determines the alignment of the Sam linebacker and the strong safety. One of those players has to be the run-support player in the B gap. If the offense runs an isolation play at the Mike linebacker, he has to spill the ball to someone. The splits will determine that player.

We base it all on the split of the number 2 receiver in the twin set. If the number 2 is closer to the tackle than to the number 1 receiver, the strong safety plays the B gap. If the number 2 receiver is closer to the number 1 receiver than to the tackle, the Sam linebacker is the B gap player. We do not want the twin set to get us out of the extra man in the box.

If the strong safety is the support player in the B gap, he can also play the number 2 receiver on the vertical (Diagram #5). The Sam linebacker plays heavy on the number 2 receiver from an outside alignment. He knocks the crap out of the vertical and turns him over to the strong safety. If the number 2 receiver widens, the Sam linebacker goes into the box and the strong safety goes outside and plays the vertical by number 2.

If there is motion from the twin set, we have to adjust. In this diagram, the number 2 receiver is

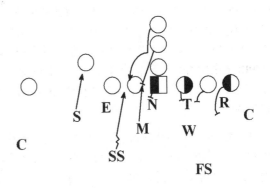

Diagram #5. Isolation Left

closer to the number 1 receiver (Diagram #6). That alignment means the strong safety is out and the Sam linebacker is in the box. The rules are the same as the pro set. If the Will linebacker has to walk, we spike the 3-technique tackle into the A gap. If the motion goes the other way, the Sam linebacker walks and we play solid on the three-receiver set. There is no lead back threat on the Mike linebacker and he plays the B gap.

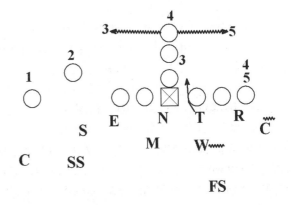

Diagram #6. Twin Motion

The twin set with the split receiver is no different as far as our base rules for alignment (Diagram #7). The alignments for the down linemen and the linebackers are the same. We play 35-techniques into the boundary and shade and a 5-technique to the fieldside. The adjustment to the twin set is no different from the previous set. The strong safety or Sam linebacker has to stay in the box, depending on the split of the number 2 receiver. If the Sam linebacker calls "top," the strong safety is in the box.

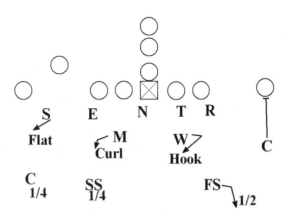

Diagram #7. Split Twin

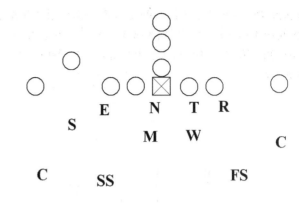

Diagram #8. Detroit

If the motion goes to the twin side, we play solid. If the motion goes the other way, the Will linebacker walks out in the two-by-two set. Before he walks, he spikes the defensive tackle into the A gap.

This sounds simple, but it is okay to be simple. We cannot keep up with the offensive genius in the other room. They draw stuff up at night. I cannot worry about them. I have to make sure our players know what they are doing.

The next thing I want to talk about are the double and triple sets. We play zone on all those multiple formations. I do not want our players to be confused in their coverage on these sets. Therefore, I group them into double or triple categories and name the formation for the players. When I get into a situation, I can blitz the formation by giving a call.

We name any double formation with a "D" word. The first double set is Detroit (Diagram #8). Detroit is a double-slot formation. If the offense comes out in a double-slot formation, it is hard to play boundary Okie in a first- and second-down situation. Our Will linebacker cannot handle the number 4 receiver in a double-slot formation.

We like to play quarter-quarter-half coverage, which we call cover 6, against all sets. However, we have trouble playing cover 6 in the double slot. We call boundary Okie, cover 6, Detroit, and a tag to go with the formation. If the offense comes out in any other formation we play cover 6. If the offense comes out in a double-slot formation, we play the tagged defense against Detroit. I am doing this for a

purpose. I do not want to be stuck in a defense I cannot play.

The next double set is Denver (Diagram #9). Denver is a two-tight-end-and-two-wide-receiver set. We can play our base defense against this formation. The place we have problems is the backside zone play. The Will linebacker walks out in his alignment and we have trouble with the rush end getting cut off. We can run a tagged stunt that helps us in this formation.

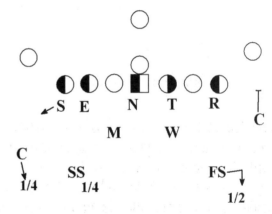

Diagram #9. Denver

The three-wide-receiver-and-one-tight-end set is Dallas (Diagram #10). This puts the twin set into the wide side of the field and the tight end and single receiver into the boundary. We match up well against this set in our base defense. However, there are some problem areas on the backside.

The last double set is Dolphin (Diagram #11). That is the same formation as Dallas, except that the twin is into the boundary and the tight end and flanker are to the wide side. We have the same problem with Dolphin as we do with Detroit. We have our Will linebacker matched on their best receiver.

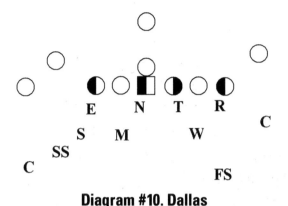

Diagram #10. Dallas

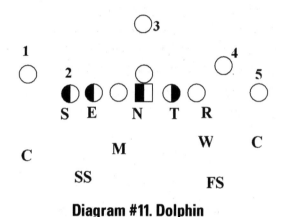

Diagram #11. Dolphin

The double sets are named with a D-word. I am at Duke so I have to come up with an interesting concept. Our triple sets start with the letter "T." The tight end set with three wide receivers, with an openside to the backside, is called trey open (Diagram #12).

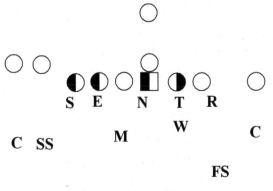

Diagram #12. Trey Open

If the tight end is to the backside and the three wide receivers are together, that is trips (Diagram #13). If there is no tight end in the set, it is called trips open.

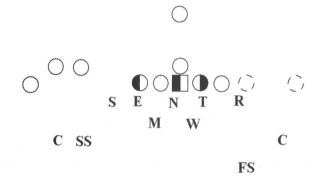

Diagram #13. Trips and Trips Open

In each of these formations, we can call the base defense, but by using a tag, we improve the defense.

We want to do two things in the base package. In the base package, we want to be able to bring a fourth and a fifth rusher. In our base scheme, if I want to bring the fourth rusher from the boundary, we call North. On a North call, the rush end becomes the fourth rusher.

To bring the fifth rusher we call tornado. The tornado brings the Sam linebacker from the fieldside of the defense. Tornado is one call for the fifth rusher. When we run the tornado, we general run it with two 3 techniques and play man-free coverage behind it. The Sam linebacker blitzes from the outside, so the defensive end does not have containment responsibility. He moves down into a 3 technique on the guard or spikes inside on the snap. We have others blitzes we can use.

We want to be able to zone pressure out of the same basic package. There are millions of zone-pressure schemes. They are simple for us from a coverage standpoint. We have three ways to bring zone pressure. We can bring it from the field zone, boundary zone, or middle zone. In our zone-blitz package, there are scrapes, screws, crashes, and sabers. We run them from the field or the boundary equally well.

The next thing we want do is rush three. I never thought in my life, I would say that aloud. That takes away my masculinity. There are times when we rush three and drop eight into coverage.

This is my menu for this package. If we want to bring the fourth rusher, we call it North (Diagram #14). We like to bring five against the Denver formation. We call North-6, which is the quarter-quarter-half coverage with the rush end coming off the edge. To that call, we add the term Denver-tornado. That brings the fifth rusher from the other side. The tornado call is a zone blitz coming from the field. If the formation is a Denver set, we run the tornado blitz. If the set is any other set, we play North-6.

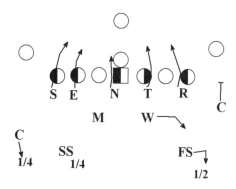

Diagram #14. North-6 Denver-Tornado

We have zone pressures that we like to run from the fieldside of the formation. Against the Detroit formation, we like to run a zone field blitz, because there is no tight end. We do not like that zone pressure if the offense gives us a tight end into the field.

When we zone blitz, we try to disguise the defense so it looks the same as the base front. We want the offense to think the fourth rusher is coming from the rush end. We play tornado and what we call 18-free, which is our loose man-free concept.

The field corner comes down into coverage and plays bump man-to-man coverage. The strong safety drops down into the box. We want the offense to think he comes down to play in the quarter scheme. He comes down to play man

coverage on the tight end. We do not press on our man coverage.

The Mike linebacker has the number 3 receiver in the backfield. The Will linebacker has the number 4 receiver in the backfield and the backside corner has the number 5 receiver. The free safety is free.

We always tag something for the end, nose, and tackle based on the protection scheme. In our twist games, we want penetration from the end, nose, or tackle going toward the slide of the protection and the loopers going away from the slide. If the running back sets to the defensive left, the penetrating defenders work to the right and the looping defenders work to the left.

You can be creative in what you do with the end, nose, and tackle. You can move them all in the same direction or twist them in some scheme.

If the defensive call is North-6, Dallas, tornado, we have a five-man rush against the Dallas formation. We bring the rush end and blitz the Sam linebacker off the openside. If the offense comes out in any other formation, we play base defense.

The formation does not dictate as much in the check game as the surface to the field (Diagram #15). For us, there are only two surfaces. There is a two-man side or a three-man side. If the formation to the field has no tight end, that is a two-man surface. We tag that alignment with an "alert" call. If we use the term "alert" with tornado, any two-man surface to the field is a zone blitz with the Sam linebacker.

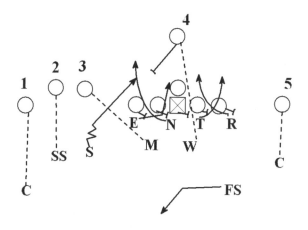

Diagram #15. Alert

The "alert" call applies to the formations. Detroit, Dallas, and trips all have a two-man side to the field. In each of those formations with an alert call, we blitz from the field. If we call trim, it tells the players to look for three-man surfaces to run a stunt.

If the offense is in a three-man surface to the field, we do not like to blitz the Sam linebacker to that look. We like the match-up on the tackle or running back. If the call is alert and there is a three-man surface to the field, the blitz is off. However, if the tight end were to shift or trade to the other side, the tornado is back on. These types of adjustments let us eliminate some bad defenses and match-up problems.

There are situations in a game when we have the advantage. That is the time we must have the proper blitz or defense called.

When we do our game-planning on Sunday evenings, I want to know the running plays the offense runs to the three-man surface of the field. If you know the runs, you know what the scheme will be.

The second thing I need to know is the offensive running plays to the two-man surface of the field. If the offense runs no gap scheme to the two-man side, that is the information I need. These one-back offensive geniuses have nothing to run to the two-man side. You can line up with a 3 technique and a rush end like my sister and they have nothing to attack that side.

They have one scheme. They have some form of G-run that way and that is it. You will not know that unless you look into their surface tendencies. It great to have that information, but I have to figure a way to get that to my players without blowing their brains out. They do not have to know all the information. They know if they have an alert call, they run whatever word track that follows the call to the two-man surface.

I want to take on of the double formation and show you how we defend it. The first on is Detroit (Diagram #16). Detroit is the double-slot formation.

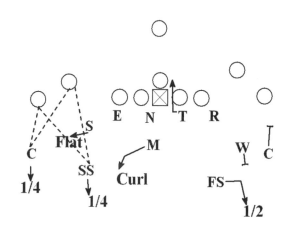

Diagram #16. Base Against Detroit

In our base set the call is North-6. We have to walk out with the Sam and Will linebackers. The noseguard bumps into a 2i position on the guard and the 3 technique tackle spikes into the A gap. In the secondary, we have cloud cover to the boundary and quarters to the field.

The problem in this defense is our Will linebacker cannot handle their slot receiver. The adjustment we make is boundary screw (Diagram #17). On screw, the Will linebacker comes off the edge from the outside. The 3 technique spikes into the A gap and the rush end slants into the B gap. The free safety comes down on the slot and the strong safety rotates into the middle. The Sam linebacker matches up on the slot and the Mike linebacker takes the number 3 receiver in the backfield.

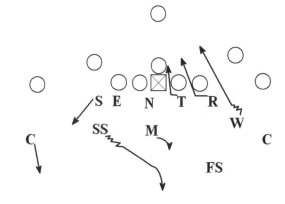

Diagram #17. Boundary Screw

Everyone has to move late so as not to tip the stunt and coverage to the offense.

The offensive set is four wide receivers and the huddle call is Okie. We can bring the fourth rusher from either side. If we want the fourth rusher to come from the boundary, we call North. If we want the fourth rusher to come from the field, we call South (Diagram #18). On the South call, the Sam linebacker rusher off the edge and the rush end drops in coverage.

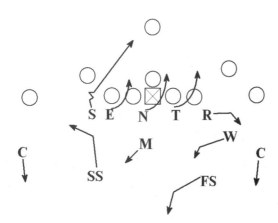

Diagram #18. South

The difference in the North and South calls is the secondary call behind it. If we call North, the rush end is the fourth rusher and the Sam linebacker drops into coverage. The coverage is cover 6, which is quarter-quarter-half coverage. With a South call, the Sam linebacker is the fourth rusher. The rush end drops into the flat. In half coverage, we play cloud coverage to the boundary side. If the rush end drops to the flat, we do not need the corner roll. The strong safety rolls down to take the Sam linebacker coverage and we end up in cover 3.

On the North or South call, the rush end and Sam linebacker have to let the end and tackle know who has containment. On South, the Sam linebacker tells the defensive end, "me-me." That tells the end that the Sam linebacker has containment. On the North call, the Sam linebacker tells the defensive end, "you-you." Obviously, that means the defensive end has containment and the Sam drops into coverage. To the boundary side, the rush end makes the exact opposite calls to the 3 technique tackle.

We can add more criteria for the calls by adding East and West. East means the fourth rusher comes from the strongside of the set. West means the fourth rusher comes from the weakside of the set. It really does not matter. It is the way the coaches package the rush. We could add tight and open as a criterion.

If we want to bring pressure from the field, we run field scrape (Diagram #19). The 5 technique end spikes into the B gap. The shade nose spikes into the boundary A gap. The 3 technique tackle loops across the offensive tackle to the boundary C gap. The Mike linebacker runs through the fieldside C gap and the Sam linebacker blitzes off the edge. The scrape blitz is good to run against the three-man surface.

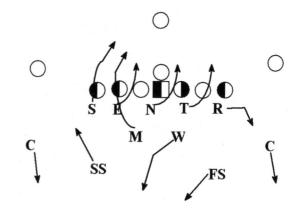

Diagram #19. Field Scrape

In the secondary, the rush end drops into coverage to the boundary side flat and the boundary corner drops into the deep third. The free safety drops to the middle and the strong safety drops down into the strongside flat area. The fieldside corner drops into the deep third.

If we wanted a different pressure, we can run the screw to the fieldside. It is better run to the two-man surface than the three-man. In the double-slot formation, the screw is a good pressure from the field or boundary.

We use the same thought process with the triple set. We are solid in the 6 coverage against the set. If we run a field crash (Diagram #20), we have to keep our numbers straight. To the strongside, the corner takes the number 1 receiver and the strong safety takes the number 2 receiver. The Sam

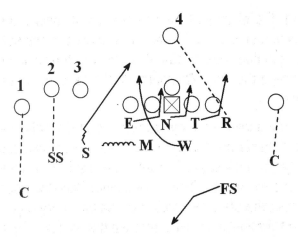

Diagram #20. Crash

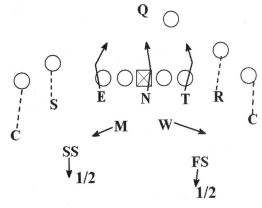

Diagram #21. Cover 20

linebacker has the number 3 receiver, except he is in the blitz scheme.

To the backside, the corner has the number 5 receiver and the rush end has the number 4 receiver. The Mike linebacker is involved in the blitz, and runs through the C gap to the strongside. The Will linebacker has to take the number 3 receiver. The free safety plays the middle of the field.

It makes no sense for the Will to come across the Mike linebacker to get to his pass coverage. The Mike and Will linebackers exchange responsibility. Mike linebacker takes the number 3 receiver and Will linebacker runs the stunt. He knows how to run the stunt because we also run the crash to the boundary side.

The end, nose tackle, and Sam linebacker are spiking their gaps toward the boundary side and the Will linebacker is coming outside to the fieldside.

We can restrict the coverage by using a special call. If we want to play the trips set in a three-man rush, we call field-crash, field-zone, and trips-20 (Diagram #21). If the offense comes out in anything but the trips set, we play field-crash and field-zone. If the offense comes out in the trips set, we play cover 20, which is the three-man rush, six-under, and two-deep.

When we play the cover 20, we cover up everyone eligible for a pass. We like to cover the back in the backfield, but if he is no threat, we put the linebacker in double on good receivers.

The coach can package the defenses so the players do not have to think about it. That is what we are trying to do.

Two years ago we played UConn and the first time they come out in the empty set we ran field-scrape, field-zone and knocked the quarterback on his butt (Diagram #22). For five weeks, we did not see the empty set again.

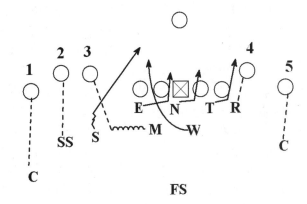

Diagram #22. Empty

In the empty set, we match the coverage. The corners have the number 1 and number 5 receivers. The strong safety has number 2, the rush end has number 4, and the Mike linebacker has number 3. The free safety sits in the middle. The Sam and Will linebackers are on the crash stunt. Our rules tell us to zone pressure against the empty set.

This is a simple package you can use that is easy for your players to understand and play. It is functional and allows you to drill confidence into your players.

PUNT-RETURN AND PUNT-BLOCK SCHEMES

Virginia Tech University

I want to thank Nike for the opportunity to speak here today. Their people treat us great. I have been impressed with the personnel they have and the way they do business. Bill Kellar has headed up the program for us and has been a good friend to high school and college football.

If you have heard me talk before I think you will find some new wrinkles and ideas in the topic. I really believe the quickest way to win a football game is through the kicking game. There is no question in my mind. I coached in high school for a number of years and have watched it for a long time.

If I were coaching in high school, I would wear out the preparation in the kicking game. I watch a lot of tape on high school teams and I see a bunch of shaky long snappers. If you can block kicks, you have an advantage against that type of snapper.

If you find a team that is not settled as to how they protect the punt, you have an advantage. You may think the kicking game is boring. However, I can guarantee it is without a doubt the quickest way to get you beat or win a game for you.

The chart I am going to show you is all about percentages and makes perfect sense to me. If you won any money in the casino last night, you probably understand percentages. If a team takes over on their own 20-yard line, they have a one out of 30 chance of scoring. If they take over on their own 40-yard line, the chance of scoring is one out of eight. However, if they get 10 more yards on the punt return and move the possession up to the 50-yard line, they have a one out of five chance to score.

In the kicking game, we always talk about big plays and momentum gains. There is a lot of yardage involved with the kicking game. If you block a field goal and return it for a touchdown, that is a difference of 10 points. The difference is the three they did not get and the seven you got.

Coaches think we spend a lot of time practicing the kicking game. I do not think that is true at all. What we do with the kicking game is make it important. The most important thing to making the kicking game successful is to have the head coach involved. I worked and played under some excellent kicking-team coaches. I played and coached for Jerry Claiborne, I worked for Bobby Ross and Mike Gottfried, just to mention a few. I have always been around some good kicking coaches.

When I became a head coach, I emphasized that part of the game. I knew how important it was. I always had a coach that headed up our kicking teams. I was always involved with the offense and defense. However, the head coaching duties took me away from that type of planning. When I lost a couple of assistant coaches that were involved with the kicking game, I decided to take over that portion of the game myself. What I found was it helped our overall operation.

When the head coach is actively involved in the kicking game, the players become more inclined to become a part of it. That fact helps with the success of that part of the game.

Having the kicking game as my responsibility is the most efficient way to run our operation. Bud Foster used to have the punt-protection team. He is now our defensive coordinator. Before Bud could work on his defensive plans, he had to get the punt-protection scheme ready. Now I take the kicking game and he can concentrate on the defensive responsibility he has.

I spend hours studying the opponent's punt-blocking assignments. I want to know the way they protect and if there is a weak link in their protection. I look at when and how they snap the ball. The secret is that I spend the time instead of one of my offensive or defensive coaches. I have a new punt rush prepared for each game. It takes time to get that all done.

The first four periods of our practice each day have to do with kicking. The periods are five minutes in length for a total of 20 minutes in all. We start out with a field-goal competition. We have players kicking field goals competing against one another. That is one of the toughest plays in football. Coming off the bench to kick a field goal or catch a punt has a lot of pressure attached to it. The more times you can put these players in pressure situations that count, the better prepared they are to handle the pressure. It is difficult to come off the sideline and kick a field goal to determine the result of the game. It amounts to only one play. Working through the competition in practice helps in preparation for the games.

I time the punters' hang time and the time it takes to get the snap. We practice kicking directional and pooch kicks. Any time you can kick a team inside the 10-yard line is a big play in a football game. If you can start a team inside their 10-yard line, the percentages against them scoring really go up. We also compete with our kickoff men. We want to see which one can kick the ball the deepest and who can keep it in the air the longest.

This happens every day, and I can see all kinds of benefits from that part of the game. One of the points I use in finding players for special-team work is the benefits that can come from it. The last five or six spots on a pro rooster are filled with players who can play on special teams. We tell our players that if they do something well in the college kicking game, they may be helping themselves at the next level. We had one of our former players quoted as saying the reason he made the Washington Redskins was his ability to play special teams.

Those types of statements really help boost your players' attitudes about playing special teams.

You need your best players playing on those teams. You cannot take a substitute and block kicks. It will not happen. It takes a good athlete with speed and height. He has to bend his body and get his arms out. You cannot block kicks with average people. You must get your best people into that part of the game.

Never come before practice or stay after practice to practice kicking. If you do, you punish those players who play on special teams. When you do your kicking drills outside the realm of practice, you reinforce the fact that kicking is not as important as offense or defense.

We stop practice right in the middle and bring everyone to one field. If you came to a practice at Virginia Tech, you see everyone moving around. We do not have players standing around doing nothing. We practice with a fast tempo. All of a sudden we stop that tempo and bring everyone together for a kicking drill.

That immediately tells everyone that this phase of the game is important. If we stop our practice and everyone is looking at what is going on, it has to be important. I think that is the way you must approach it.

We also use our punt-return game as our conditioning period. While everyone else is conditioning, our punt-return team is practicing the returns. They have to do it perfectly for one to count. I promise you, the return team will finish its conditioning before everyone else. The punt-return players are running off the field while the conditioning people are still working. There are advantages to playing on these teams.

On Tuesday, in the middle of practice we practice our punt team against our punt-block team. The players on these teams work extremely hard. If they work hard in this drill, there will be less work for them at the end of practice. Give your players privileges for playing on those teams. The players watching may begin to think they would like to be on one of those teams.

Everyone pays lip service to the importance of the kicking game, but you have to show your players you mean it. Give them the same awards as you do offensive or defensive players. If you have an "offensive player of the game," you need a "special teams player of the game." If you give awards for big hits, make sure you include the special teams play in that area.

When we give offensive and defensive awards, we do it in their meetings. When we give special team awards, we do it in front of the team. There are generally offensive and defensive players on those teams. In addition, it is another chance to praise those players.

When you do your goal charts for your locker room, make sure there are special team goal charts as well. We want to make sure the goals are not too complicated. Sometimes the goals are so complicated they lose emphasis. Our goals have a basic theme of, "Did you get the job done or not?"

We have simple goals. The punt-coverage team strives to allow no more than six yards per return and to down a punt inside the 10-yard-line. The kickoff-coverage team goal is to force the offense to start behind the 20-yard line. The goal for the punt-return team is to average 10 yards on a punt return. On our punt- and kick-block team, we want to block a kick or force a bad kick.

Forcing the bad kick is the particular statistic missed on most occasions. If the punting team gets off a 20-yard punt instead of a 40-yard punt, that amounts to two first downs. That is a lot of yardage when it comes to big plays. If you look at defensive goals, most of the time they have "allow no big plays" as one of their goals. They define big plays as 15-yard runs and 20-yard passes. It is the same thing with the bad kick. It is the hidden yardage in the kicking game that adds up to big gains.

Our goal for our kickoff-return team is to start at the 20-yard line. On extra point and field goals, we want to be 100 percent on the extra points and 67 percent on the field goals. We want no penalties or mental errors in the kicking game. This goal is the one I like the most. We want our punt-return and kickoff-return teams to gain an advantage of 20 yards over their opponent's kickoff- and punt-return teams.

On Monday, we go over game planning in offensive and defensive meetings. The same should hold true for special teams. They should watch films of their play and corrections made. They get a game plan in the kicking game for the upcoming opponent during their meeting. On Friday, we do the same thing, with the teams evaluating their week's practice and looking forward to the game.

We strive to have entirely different personnel on our punt-protection team and our punt-block team. We may have one or two players we need on both, but we try to prevent that from happening. The reason for that is the ability to work against each other at practice. That is a big advantage because we work good on good.

The next day we watch the tape of that competition in the meetings and learn from it. The blocked punt is probably the biggest play in college football as a momentum turner. It generally leads to points on the scoreboard or at least a drastic change in field position.

We have a section in our game preparation called "Pride and Joy." This involves the new punt-block scheme, the return, and the fakes in the kicking game. The "Joy" personnel consists of our punt-block team and the "Pride" personnel is the punt-protection team. Before our pregame meal, we have a 10-minute session with "Pride and Joy." In that session, we go over who is responsible for the fakes in all phases of the kicking game.

I want to go through the way we practice. When we start Monday, we go a shorter period than other days. We go over the scouting report before we get on the field. In Monday's practice I like to get out and start practice fast. It does not matter whether we won or lost, I want the tempo upbeat. We work the offense and defense on plays that are big plays one way or the other.

We run screens, reverses, halfback passes, and big-play type of plays. We get the offense going against the defense for about five plays. From there, we go to a field-goal and field goal—block team for one kick. That builds confidence in the kicker, knowing he can perform under pressure.

We put our punt-protection team with their backs to the camera and work on that scheme for five minutes. We block any special punt-block scheme the opponent might have installed.

We put in our new "Pride and Joy" punt block for the week. Our punt-protection team works against our "Pride and Joy" personnel in some instances. That is what we do on Monday.

On Tuesday, in the middle of practice we stop practice and bring our team together. We have our punt-protection team against our punt-block team. I like to practice this way. The first thing we do is set up a rush scheme. It may be the one I use in the upcoming game or one we have used before.

We do not physically block any kicks during this part of the drill. I give them landmarks to rush through, but no kick blocking. We go through the rush and protection scheme and punt the ball.

The next phase is punt and cover. I like to break up the coverage and concentrate on the coverage in piecemeal segments. If we have a return left, I send the headhunters and anyone assigned to block them. The headhunters are the wide players on the coverage team. On the left return, we double-team the left headhunter and single-block the right headhunter.

We have a punt return man catching the ball, the two headhunters, and the three blockers going in this portion of the drill. It is easier to show the responsibilities and correct the mistakes when you have only a few bodies going in the drill. Doing the drill this way isolates the action and you can see more. We go through the coverage and return three times using the part method.

On Wednesday, we have a specialty period. That period is not so much for your first kickers and catchers, but the reserve and back-up kickers and snappers. We want to give the back-up players time to work on their skills. We have our pooch kickers working with the player who might return those types of kicks. We have punters kicking to the return players.

I want players going down under the punt to make the punt return man make a move after catching the ball. They do not tackle the return man. They simply try to touch him, which gives him the added pressure of the coverage coming down on him. I do not want the return man to catch the ball and throw it back. I want him to concentrate on the catch and make a move as if he were going into a wall. If the return is a side return, I want him catching the punt, taking a hard step up the middle, and breaking outside. He does the opposite thing on a middle return.

In another area of the field, we have kickoff and kickoff-return personnel working in that phase of the game. I want the catchers to simulate game situations when they catch the ball. This is not a lollygag part of practice. We want game situation and intense concentration in each phase of the game.

In another area of the field, we work on punt blocking. I will talk about that part of the game later in detail.

In the middle of practice that day we have a kicking drill. We bring everyone together in the middle of the field and give out the helmet covers for our kicking opponents. We wear maroon and white jerseys in practice. The special teams have people wearing both jerseys on them. Therefore, when we go to a kicking period, we use blue helmet covers to designate the opponents. It takes less time to get them on than a scrimmage vest.

During this period we bring our kick-block and punt-protection teams together and work. During this period, if we can block the punt, we do. This is a live punt-block period. The next thing is field-goal and the field goal–block team. We run them on and off the field in a high-tempo movement. We want it fast.

"Pride and Joy" is our punt-block team. We have running backs and receivers as part of this team. Andre Davis, who is with New England as a wide receiver, was one of our "Pride and Joy" personnel. He blocked two kicks at Boston College on a Thursday night on ESPN. The personnel on this team includes the best players we have available who can block kicks. They are not necessarily defensive personnel.

Our first punt-protection team could be tight ends or defensive ends. We have the best people available for that team. Our first punt-protection team and punt-block team go against each other. We put the blue helmet covers on the "Pride and Joy" personnel.

After that, we practice the onside kick–prevention game. During that period we look and practice against all kinds of different onside kicks. When it comes to this part of the game, we have to get the ball. We practice hard at this phase because the results usually determine the outcome of the game.

We come back with the punt and punt-block teams again. From there, we go to the field-goal and field goal–block teams again. Then we practice a punt safe kick. That is a situation where the defense is not sure the punting team will punt the ball. We keep our defense in the game and put a return man deep to receive the ball around the 10-yard line. We also practice the other side of the situation and kick the ball inside the 10-yard line.

We work on returning the crazy kickoffs. The squib and pooch kicks are the ones most teams use. We do all this kicking within a 10-minute period and do it at a fast tempo. Getting the teams on and off the field is part of the drill. We want them moving when they go on or come off the field. The blocking in the drills is full speed and it is live. However, we do not tackle live. We look up the runner and butt him.

On Thursday, we start with kickoff returns. It is basic and we do the same thing every week. We make sure we get the numbering of the opponent's kick personnel during this period. That is a 10-minute period. The kickoff-coverage team remains very consistent from week to week. However, I have four headhunters covering on the team, which I move around each week. We spend 10 minutes doing that part of the kicking period.

The "Pride and Joy" spends five minutes on a block at this time. We work them against the scout team. The Pride team is next in the progression of kicking. We like to install a fake every week with the punt team. We practice the fake, pooch, and playing our headhunters in a tight formation.

We have to practice that because of the way we protect the kick. We man protect to one side and zone protect to the other, depending on the rush scheme we face. When the headhunters come to the inside, they become part of the protection scheme. They need to know the scheme we use. The headhunter on the zone side blocks zone and the headhunter on the man side blocks man.

In our offensive team period, we practice a couple of field goals and during the defensive team period, we practice a couple of field-goal blocks. The last thing we do is practice kicking the field goal with the clock running down. We must get on the field, set the team, and kick the field goal while the clock is running out. If you do not practice those situations, you cannot execute them when you need them.

Here we use man blocking to the kicking team's right and zone blocking to the left (Diagram #1). The blocking back blocks the number 1 man from the center. The right guard blocks the number 2 rusher, the right tackle blocks the number 3 rusher, and the wingback blocks the number 4 rusher. When we punt the ball, we kick it to the man-blocking side. We kick that way because the blockers make contact with the rushers, knock them off their stride, and release in the coverage.

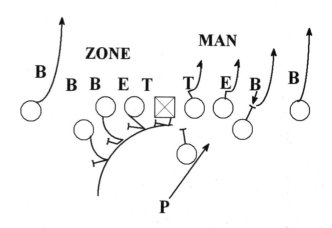

Diagram #1. Punt to Man Side

The zone blocking side gives ground in their scheme. They cannot cover immediately and must drop in their protection. If the punter kicks the ball toward that side, the coverage is not as good. The headhunter to the man side releases outside and the headhunter to the zone side releases inside.

On the overload side we zone block and man block the other side. In theory, if the zone side stays solid, the rushers have to come outside to get to the ball. Since we are kicking away from that rush line, we should get the kick off.

For many years, we were a zone-protection scheme. However, when you zone protect, the coverage has a hard time releasing to cover the kick. In addition, when you zone protect, you need bigger players to match up with the rushers. Consequently, the bigger players do not run as fast as the smaller ones. That gives the good punt return man an advantage. That is why we went to a man-protection side in our scheme.

Our guards and tackles are tight-end and defensive-end type personnel. They are bigger bodies that can get their hands on the defender and get through them. The wingbacks may be back-up linebackers. However, they are the most dependable players you have on the team. The headhunters are fast receiver-types or maybe defensive backs. The personal protector has to be a quarterback-type in a linebacker's body. He has to be a smart player. He makes all the calls, talks, and keeps people under control.

We align with our inside foot forward in the stance. As we step, we shuffle inside. To the zone side, we want to form a wall. The center snaps the ball and takes a shuffle-set back to his zone side. The guard next to him shuffles inside and back on him and sets. The tackle outside the guard takes a couple more shuffle steps back and is deeper than the guard as he sets. The wingback is off the ball in his alignment, but still gives ground to form the wall. They protect with the inside arm and look outside.

They protect the inside with their arm, but they are responsible for the outside gap. They take anyone coming into that gap. To the man blocking side, the technique is the same for all three of the blockers. They take one shuffle step, face up on the defender, make him redirect his charge, and release. They take the best possible release they can get. We would prefer to release outside if we can get that release.

On Friday, this is break-a-sweat day. We check our special teams for the first-line players and back-up players. We bring the Pride team out and pooch the ball into the 10-yard line area with the safe punt scheme. We practice kicking out of the end zone. The personal protector has to move his alignment up to account for the reduced yardage we have to kick the ball. If he tries to align at his regular depth, he gets the ball up his butt.

We practice kicking the ball at three seconds. In the fourth quarter if we are ahead, we want to take time off the clock. We practice snapping the ball with three second left on the play clock. If we have to punt on the last play of the game against an 11-man rush, the punter takes a rocker step and kicks.

We practice taking a safety. We may substitute the quarterback for the punter. We let him take the snap and at the last second step out of the back of the end zone and not take a hit.

On the kickoff return, we practice all the different kinds of kicks. We practice all the quirky things that could happen in a game. We practice how to handle the blocked kick. If we block the kick behind the line of scrimmage, we want to get it to the end zone. We cover kicks after a safety as part of this period. We do not want something to happen in the game that we have not practiced. We have to cover all the fakes that could come in the kicking game.

On our kickoff team, we practice the squib and onside kicks. We practice kicking off after a 15-yard penalty against the other team. We try to kick the ball as high as we can to the one-yard line. We also practice the kickoff after a safety. All this occurs in a 15-minute period.

I want to get into blocking kicks. We have a drill we use to find our punt blockers. If they turn their head or close their eyes, they cannot block a punt. We give them two shots at the ball. If they do either one of those things we send them packing.

Not everyone can block a kick. I look for players with great speed, quickness, and a knack for blocking the ball. The longer and taller they are the better I like them. The quicker the player can go from point A to point B and the further he can reach out at the end makes the difference.

The biggest thing in blocking kicks is the landmark. If a team kicks at nine yards, my landmark is seven and half yards. We are very exact on that distance. The body has to go through the landmark, not on a collision path with the punter. We want our hands to the sides of our bodies to keep the body away from the punter's leg. If the punter is a right-footed kicker, a rusher coming from the left side reaches his hands to the left of his body to stay away from the punter's leg as he comes through the landmark.

Finding the landmark of the opposing punter is my job. That comes from film study. Most of the time it is the same spot every week. I do not like players leaving their feet because they have no control of where they will land. However, if they do leave their feet at the last second and have a good rush line, it is alright with me. What we have to prevent is them leaving their feet and coming down on the punter.

The proper angle for the block is not a straight line. If the protection is zone, the rusher has to clear the outside of the zone and bend in to the landmark. The only time you come on a straight line is when the protection misses an assignment.

If the punt rusher is knocked off his course more than one step, he stops and makes sure the ball is kicked. It only takes one person to block a punt. If the rusher is knocked off his course, I want him out of the way. We only want one player free in the punt block scheme. If you break two players loose, they will try to avoid each other, miss the kick, and probably rough the punter.

We never take a personal protector and push him back. We pull him out of the way. That clears the area for another rusher. If the area through the landmark is clear and the rusher does not have to dodge players, he can block the kick. Every rusher leaves the line of scrimmage thinking he will come free. When he is knocked off his course, he stops and clears the area by getting outside.

By releasing outside, the rusher puts himself in a position to tackle the punter. If the punter realizes the punt will be blocked if he kicks it, he pulls it back and starts to run. He runs into the rusher who was knocked off course. If the punter kicks the ball and it is blocked, we are in position to take it to the end zone.

The punt-block scheme and return scheme should look the same. The punting team should not be able to tell if you are blocking the kick or returning the ball. We want to get as close to the ball as possible. We want our hands on the ball and our heads behind our hands. Keying the ball and getting a jump is critical in blocking the punt. Usually when you miss the block, it is only by inches. If we can figure how to make up the distance, we can get the block.

The rusher cannot wait to see if he is open before he accelerates. He has to come out of his stance as quickly as possible. The last movement is to stretch the hands out. Do not run with the hands out. At the last second, the hands are extended to the foot of the punter. They have to look at the ball to block it.

If the blocked ball crosses the line of scrimmage, get away from it. If it stays behind the line of scrimmage get it to the end zone. If the rushers do not practice what to do after the punt block, they will jump on the ball. We blocked four punts one year and did not score with any of them. It did not make sense to me. When you block a punt, you have the advantage in numbers. There always seems to be four of your players and one or two of theirs. Whichever player is closest to the ball takes his time and picks it up. Everyone else turns and blocks the other color jersey. We rehearse so we do not have two players trying to recover the ball.

In the punt-block drill, we use a snapper and a punter. We take air out of the ball so it does not hurt the rushers' hands. We snap the ball to the back-up punter. He punts the ball at three-quarters speed. We practice punt blocking with all our players. The man on the headhunter is also a rusher. We mark the point at which the punter will launch the ball for that week. In this case, it is eight yards.

The blocker coming off the headhunter comes down the line of scrimmage with his shoulders square. That way you can tell he is onside and he can see the ball, plant his foot, and go to the ball. If he comes at an angle, he may get offside.

We bring the rushers in rapid order, one after the other. They use the techniques for the landmark and block the kick. The next drill we use involves the scout punt team (Diagram #2). We align in our punt-block scheme. I designate the blocking assignments for the scout team line. In each case, I leave one rusher unblocked and he blocks the kick. When the kick is blocked, we react and get the ball into the end zone.

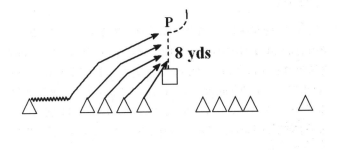

Diagram #2. Punt Block Drill

The punt-rush team does not know who will be unblocked. Everyone comes off the ball as if he will come free. They react to the blocks and play their roles. We do this several times, changing the free rusher every time. We go half line at a time. We do the same thing to the other side.

I want to show you our typical rush formation and talk about the personnel (Diagram #3). We align with 10 men on the line of scrimmage. We have a basic 5-5 alignment on either side of the center. The

number 1, 2, 3, 4, 7, 8, 9, and 10 rushers are defensive-back or running-back types of players. We have two defensive-back types defending the headhunters as they come downfield. The 2 technique players or number 5 and number 6 rushers are defensive ends. We felt we needed bigger players on the inside.

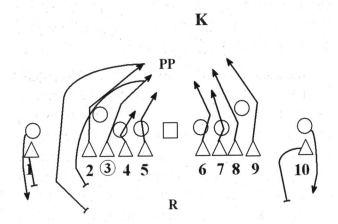

Diagram #3. Punt Block/Return Formation

If the protection is a zone scheme, I want the number 5 rusher to force the offensive guard's block by attacking his outside shoulder. If I can do that, I have three rushers on two blockers to the outside. I want to put my tallest, quickest rusher in the number 3 position coming inside the wingback.

The coaching points for the inside rushers are to come off low and turn their shoulders sideways. If we stay square on the zone blocker, it gives him more surface to block. We want to turn and get small. The number 4 rusher takes off on an outside rush on the tackle and jumps inside. He turns his shoulders and gets small. Once he clears the blocker, he bends to the landmark.

The number 3 rusher fires low and hard upfield until he clears the tackle. At that point, he bends hard inside for the landmark. The number 2 rusher picks a point one step outside the wingback's block. That means one step outside a point where the wingback can get his hands on the rusher. Once he clears the blocker, he bends inside to the landmark. If the rusher gets past his landmark, I want him to stop his rush. All that can happen when a rusher passes his landmark is roughing the kicker. The right side does the same rush with their corresponding players. That is our full rush with a return right.

The return right or left comes out of the full rush. The wall may not be clearly defined, which is not all bad. That prevents the kick-coverage team from totally identifying the return. A cluster of blockers downfield can spring the kick return man.

On the return left, we want a series of double teams (Diagram #4). We want to keep the headhunters from getting downfield instead of simply directing them outside or inside. The number 7 rusher doubles the left headhunter blocker. He may leave the line of scrimmage a little early to get into position. The number 9 rusher comes through from the right to force the kick. If he comes clear, he goes for the landmark to block the kick. However, he has to make sure the blocker is not releasing on a pass to that side.

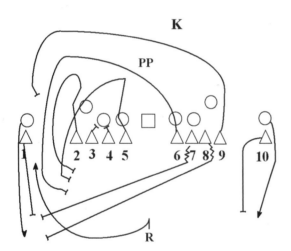

Diagram #4. Left Return

We want to rough up the headhunter and keep him from getting downfield. The only thing you cannot do is let him split the double-team. If he is outside keep him outside. If he is inside, block him inside, but do not let him split that block.

We double-team the left tackle with the number 3 and 4 rushers. They get shoulder to shoulder and block him. If he comes outside, the number 3 rusher takes him and the number 4 rusher circles outside and gets back on him. If he goes inside, the number 4 rusher takes him and number 3

rusher falls back inside and blocks him. The tackle had better not make the play on the return. However, we have to use common sense with the block. If we get down the field and one of the blockers has the tackle blocked, the other blocker can get in the wall and get ready to block someone else.

We want to create a gap between the wingback and the tackle coming down the field. The number 2 rusher makes the wingback stay on him and if he clears, he goes for the block. If he does not clear, he sets the wall. The inside rushers fire into the guards and keep coming upfield. I want them to occupy the personal protector to keep him from going outside if one of the rushers comes clean.

After they do that, they get into the wall. The number 8 rusher comes to the middle of the field and blocks the first threat coming down the middle. He secures the catch of the return man. We want him 25 yards down the field.

If the ball is in the middle of the field, the wall is set at the top of the numbers. If the ball is on the hash mark, the wall sets a couple yards outside the other hash. The wider we can set it the better we are.

We can put a wrinkle into this return by using a reverse (Diagram #5). The blocking is the same as the left return. The difference is the number 8 rusher, instead of blocking the first threat down the middle of the field, becomes the reverse runner. He starts his angle as he would on the return left. The

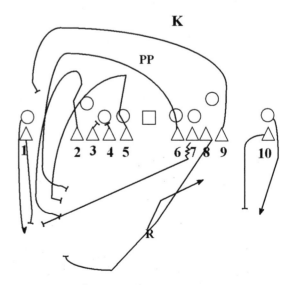

Diagram #5. Reverse Left

kick return man catches the ball and starts right with the ball. He reverses the ball to the number 8 rusher and he returns left.

It keeps the same techniques for the return team and gives misdirection to the play.

Sometimes we cannot predict where the punter will kick the ball. If the ball is coming down the middle, we are fine with the rules for the left return. However, if I cannot tell where the ball is going, I need to double on both sides. I always want to double the headhunter to the side of the return. However, if the ball is on the right hash mark and we have a return left into the wide side of the field, the most dangerous headhunter is the one coming down the right side of the field.

That is the one I want to double because we have space going to the left to make the move on the headhunter coming to that side. We have a chance to run inside or outside of him because of the width of the field. If I cannot predict the position of the kick, I call return left double (Diagram #6). When we do that, the number 4 and number 7 rushers are the double-team players.

Everything is the same except for the double to both sides and the single block on the tackle by the number 3 rusher. When we return the ball to the outside, the return man has to start forward before he breaks outside. The further the return man can take the ball upfield, the better the chance of getting a good side return.

I have made up my mind to reduce the number of schemes we have in the punt return. I want to solidify the personnel on the teams and work on a couple of returns and perfect the techniques on those returns. I am guilty of changing things because they look good on the blackboard. If you do that from week to week, you do not execute as well. The deal is to execute. The secret to a good return is to make the alignments of the rushers look like the block alignment.

We have three basic alignments we use in the punt-block schemes. We do that to keep the kicking team off balance. If they can predict exactly where you will line up, it makes you vulnerable to the fake.

Our punter launches the ball at 10 yards from the line of scrimmage. We align at 13 yards. The snap comes back in 1.7 seconds and the punt comes out in 1.9. We never want the punt coming out over 2.2 seconds. I guess the average time is 2.0 seconds.

Any questions? Fellows, I have enjoyed being with you and I hope you come to Blacksburg to see us. Thank you.

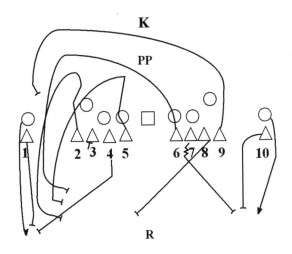

Diagram #6. Return Left Double

OPTION ROUTES IN THE SPREAD PASSING GAME

University of Oregon

Thank you. It is great to be here and have a chance to talk football. When I get the chance to go out and represent the University of Oregon, I get excited.

I was very proud of the way we played this season. In the past, we had not done a good job of focusing and finishing. This year that became our motto. We put emphasis on every thing we did offensively, defensively, and special teams–wise.

We decided to make some changes. We have talked for two years about changing our offense. We decided to change the offense after watching a team on tape against Arizona State. The team was Northwestern. I watched the Arizona State–Northwestern game on tape because we played Arizona State. I knew Northwestern had done a good job in the Big Ten with lesser material than anyone in the league. Watching them move the ball against Arizona State really intrigued me.

This year, we had the fewest sacks allowed in this conference throwing the football. The year before we lead the conference with the most sacks. That really bothered me because the three years before we had been among the leaders in least sacks allowed.

We were number one in pass interceptions, number one in kickoff returns, and number two in turnover margin in the conference. That is the most important statistic. If you win the turnover margin, you will win football games. We were number two in sacks and pass efficiency. We were number three in scoring defense, scoring offense, and pass offense. Statistics do not win games, but it tells you about achievement.

I started to talk about why we went to the spread offense. I had a quarterback who, in my mind, was a great player. He put up good numbers the year before, but we did not win. We had not put him in a situation to be successful. He was 6'2", 218 pounds, and cowboy-tough. He was strong and an accurate passer, but was not comfortable in the pocket.

We ran a pocket-style offense, with play-action passes and a dropback scheme. It did not do him justice. I felt like he would be better in the shotgun set with more space to operate. That was the main justification for going to the offense. We wanted to match our personnel.

What I will talk about today is option routes in the spread passing attack. Even if you do not run this offense, I think you can incorporate elements from what I am going to talk about into your offense. In the past, we ran option routes to our tight ends, but we ran out of room. Now we have spread out the offense and work into open throwing lanes.

I want to show you some advantages and disadvantages to running this offense. Some of these things may seem obvious. This year, we ran the spread/shotgun and 60 to 70 percent of the time we ran four wideouts. Our tight end could line up in a tight or spread position. That kept us from changing personnel to get into the sets. We had the personnel at tight end to either come inside to block or play in space. Defensive coaches like to match personnel packages and this kept them off balance.

If you spread the field, you force the defense to cover the width and depth of the field. That creates more one-on-one situations in the running game and passing game. The offense gets more RAC opportunities. Those initials stand for "run after catch" in the passing game or "run after contact" in the running game.

The spread/shotgun gives the quarterback a chance to see the blitz coming, or the defense must blitz from a distance. If they blitz from a distance, they cannot get to the quarterback. Otherwise, they have to tip their blitz and give the quarterback time to automatic or adjust the blocking scheme.

The defensive secondary has trouble disguising coverage against a spread offense. To get to their positions they have to move early and tip the coverage to the quarterback. That makes it easier for the quarterback to read the coverage and makes it difficult for the secondary to disguise.

In the shotgun set, the quarterback separates from the line of scrimmage. Immediate pressure takes longer to get to him. We do not have to worry about the A and B gaps, because the quarterback has a five-yard cushion. In that amount of time, he can get rid of the ball.

With this type of offense, there are also disadvantages. You lose your lead back in the power-running game. The lack of a power-running game was one thing that concerned our defensive staff. In spring ball and preseason practice, we ran a two-back power-running game for our defense. That helped our defense work on defending the power game, but also let us work on short yardage.

The eyes of the quarterback must be on the shotgun snap as the ball comes back. That means he loses his ability to read the coverage for a split second. When the quarterback is under center, he can concentrate on reading the defense all the time. The bad snap is a possibility with the long snap. That disrupts the running game as well as the passing game.

The offense leaves you with two openside offensive tackles with no help outside of them. That is a mismatch with a speed-rushing defensive end and an offensive tackle. The way we control that is with the option. That puts the defensive end in a two- or three-way bind. He has to respect the fact that the quarterback can run the ball and has threats inside and outside of him.

The defense can always outnumber the offense, which forces the offense to have answers for the blitz. We do it with the option, throwing hot, and using sight adjustments.

For this offense to be effective, the quarterback has to be a viable ballcarrier. That does not mean he has to be a 4.5 running back. All the quarterback has to do is take advantage of a defensive end that takes a wrong step. The bubble screen, to us, is a long handoff.

Let me cover the splits for our receivers in this set. If the ball is in the center of the field, we want to spread the field (Diagram #1). The X-receiver takes a maximum split to the bottom of the numbers on one side of the set. The Z-receiver splits to the bottom of the numbers on the other side. The R-receiver splits the difference between the X-receiver and the offensive tackle. The Y-receiver splits six yards from the offensive tackle.

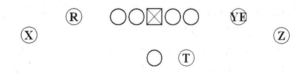

Diagram #1. Splits Double in the Middle

In our formation set, the X- and R-receivers are on the same side of the formation in a double set. The Z- and Y-receivers are to the other side of the formation in a double set.

If we are on the hash marks (Diagram #2), the X-receiver into the boundary side splits to the bottom of the numbers. The R-receiver splits the difference between the X-receiver and the offensive tackle. The Z-receiver splits eight yards outside the openside hash marks. The Y-receiver splits six yards from the offensive tackle.

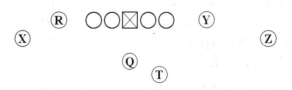

Diagram #2. Splits Double on the Hash

You can choose any splits you want. There are factors to consider when you make your split rules. It depends on the arm strength of the quarterback and the distance the defense will split.

The split rules for the triple set with the ball in the middle of the field (Diagram #3) are as follows. The split of the single receiver is a minimum split four yards from the top of the numbers. To the triple side, the Z-receiver takes a maximum split to the bottom of the numbers. The R-receiver splits four yards outside the wide side hash marks. The Y-receiver splits six yards from the offensive tackle.

Diagram #3. Splits Triple in the Middle

The split rules for the triple set on the hash marks start on the boundary (Diagram #4). The X-receiver's regular split is two yards inside the top of the numbers. To the triple side, the Z-receiver splits to the top of the numbers. The R-receiver splits two yards outside the hash marks. The Y-receiver splits six yards outside the offensive tackle.

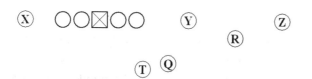

Diagram #4. Splits Triple on the Hash

Our receiver coach would tell you our split rules are simple. He would say spread out, give the R-receiver space, and get the hell out of the way. However, the split rules are simple. Just create room for the option or choice runners to put the defender on an island. Give them room and clear the coverage.

Quarterback timing is important because we go from under the center as well as from the shotgun.

I want to talk about this for a second because it changes. We practice every day taking snaps from under the center. You have to do both. From under the center, the quarterback takes a five-step drop with a hitch step when he reads zone coverage. The hitch gives the quarterback a gather step against a zone defense. There is no hitch step on a fast break against man coverage.

Obviously, the quarterback has to be aware of the object receiver on any particular play. In the shotgun, the quarterback takes a three-step drop and a hitch if he needs to let the receiver separate from any contact.

It is important to teach drops. Drops are like dance steps, the quarterback can practice at home in the mirror. The quarterback should never look at the feet or think about his drop. That has to be an automatic thought process so the eyes can stay on the defense.

An important part to any passing game is protection. We always assume we will get a six-man box. The five offensive linemen and a tailback make up our 600 protection series. The first diagram is our 620 protection against the over 4-3 defense (Diagram #5). In the 600 protection, the offensive linemen take the four down defenders, plus the Will linebacker. The back in the backfield has a double read on the Mike and Sam linebackers. If both linebackers blitz, you must have an answer for the quarterback. It can be a hot receiver or a sight adjustment by a receiver.

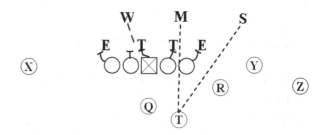

Diagram #5. 620 Protection Against Over 4-3

In the over 4-3, the center and left guard have the shade tackle and Will linebacker. If the defense is an under 4-3, the down four are shifted to the other side. In that case, the center and right guard have the shade tackle and Will linebacker. The tailback double reads and blocks the Mike or Sam linebacker.

In the "3-4 look," we block the same rules. However, there are only three down linemen (Diagram #6). In this case, we consider the Liz, left outside linebacker, as the fourth down linemen. The right guard and center take the noseguard and Will linebacker. The left guard and tackle take the left defensive end and outside linebacker. Nothing changes for the tailback in the scheme.

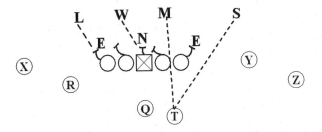

Diagram #6. 620 Against a 3-4 Defense

If the defense runs a split even front, the scheme is the same (Diagram #7). The center sets to the left and keys the Will linebacker. The center, left guard, and tackle have those three defenders. They block them using the techniques for twisting stunts and blitzes.

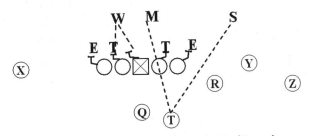

Diagram #7. 620 Against Split (Even)

Against the bear defense (Diagram #8), we block five for five. All the offensive linemen are covered and they block the man on them. The tailback double reads the Mike and Sam linebackers and the quarterback is responsible for the Will linebacker. If the defense brings eight, there is a receiver running in the pattern uncovered.

I do not think that is asking anyone to do something they cannot do. The back is off the ball

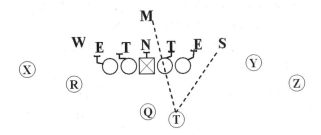

Diagram #8. 620 Against Bear

and takes the first blitz that shows from the inside going out. The quarterback, offensive line, and receivers must be on the same page. If the center steps the wrong way, the back misses an inside read, the receiver misses the hot read, or the quarterback misreads the coverage, you end up with a sack. Everyone has to do his job in the protection scheme.

We have a couple more adjustments I want to talk about in the protection game. This is 620 pro-Ralph (Diagram #9). In this protection, we are gap sliding to the right and passing off stunts.

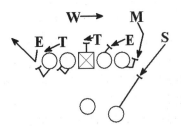

Diagram #9. 620 Pro-Ralph

The other pro protection is 620 pro-out (Diagram #10). In this protection, we use the slide gap blocking to the left. The backside also blocks out. The tailback is responsible for the backside A gap. That allows us to get a full slide protection to the left without the center coming back for the

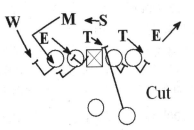

Diagram #10. 620 Pro-Out

slanting noseguard. If the back has to block a lineman coming through that gap, he cuts him.

I want to talk about the R-choice from the two-by-two or double set (Diagram #11). The R-choice route is a play designed to give the R-receiver the option of running a route where he can turn inside or outside at eight to 10 yards against a zone defense. If the defense is man coverage, he stays on the move and runs away from the defender. We build all of the other routes around the R-receiver.

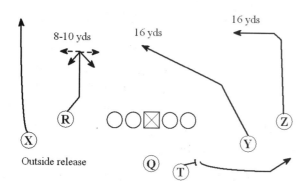

Diagram #11. R-Choice

The R-receiver is the focal point of the route. The quarterback takes his drop either five or three steps, depending on his position under the center or in the shotgun. He reads the object receiver. The tailback goes to his protection scheme and executes a swing pattern if neither linebacker blitzes. The Y-receiver has a close split. He takes the best release he can get and runs a crossing route to a depth of 16 to 18 yards. He is the primary receiver if the coverage squeezes off the choice route.

The X-receiver takes a max split. He outside releases and executes a go route. He looks for the ball in the hole against a cover 2. If the coverage is pressed-man, he has to win that match-up. You must have an X-receiver in this offense that can beat double coverage. The Z-receiver takes a regular split and executes an In route at 16 yards. He is the last resort on this play.

The R-receiver takes a divide split, loses the number 2 defender on the release, and runs a choice route. He runs the pattern at eight to 10 yards and runs away from the defender assigned to cover him.

The quarterback's thought process is to peek at the home run first. If the defense takes away the choice route, the crossing route is the next read. The quarterback has to think deep, choice, cross, and recovery. That means after he reads, he throws the ball away or scrambles. The goal is to get the ball back to the line of scrimmage and not take negative yards.

The next set is a three-by-one set, or triple. We might run the Y-choice with this set (Diagram #12). The Y-choice is just like the R-choice. The Y-receiver is the object receiver to the three-receiver side. However, the quarterback can select a one-on-one route on the other side to the X-receiver. The quarterback bases his choice on the secondary roll.

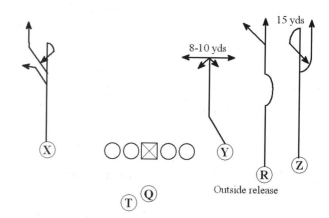

Diagram #12. Triple-Set Y-Choice

The tailback sets away from the triple set. He takes his pass protection read and releases if no one comes. He releases at the outside linebacker and spots up inside or drifts to the flat. We call that a spat route. The Y-receiver runs his option route at eight to 10 yards.

The R-receiver has a plus-two split outside the hash mark. He takes an outside release and executes a hash read. The Z-receiver takes a max split and executes a stem route at 15 yards. On the stem, he plants at 15 yards, turns in to the quarterback, and works back outside. If he reads cover 2, he turns his pattern into a fade.

The X-receiver may become the primary receiver on this play. If we get single coverage, the quarterback throws to him. The X-receiver has to win. Our X-receiver this year was Demetrius Williams. He was a 6'4" and 230-pound wide receiver. He was a special receiver and will be the hardest player to replace next year in our entire offense. The X-receiver has a number of things he can do.

He can run the stem route. If he reads cover 2, he converts to a fade. We may have a signal built in for the receiver as to the pattern we want run. Otherwise, with no signal, he runs a stow route. The stow route is a stop-and-go route. We base the stow pattern on the depth of the corner or the retreat of the corner in his drop. If the receiver can beat the corner deep at 10 to 12 yards, he goes. If the corner gives a big cushion, he stops.

The quarterback's first read in the Y-option is the X-receiver. We base the pattern the receiver runs on game planning. He can run a quick hitch, stow, or out. If the defense doubles the X-receiver in any way, the quarterback looks at the Y-receiver with the R-receiver running an outside hash route. That creates room for the Y-receiver to get open.

If the defense doubles the Y-receiver in a cover 3 look, the quarterback shoots for the hash route by the R-receiver. If the defense plays a quarter scheme, the quarterback looks through the option route to the stow route on the outside.

I want to show you one more option route using the empty set. When we go to the empty set, the R-receiver is to the two-receiver side. The tailback becomes the third receiver to the triple side. He aligns wide with a maximum split. We can get to the empty set by aligning in it, motioning to it, or shifting to it. We do all three of those things.

We call this R-option (Diagram #13). However, since it is run from an empty set, it is slightly different from the R-choice run from the double set. The inside receivers, Y and R, run choice routes at different depths. That gives the quarterback a chance to look at the receivers in the order they come open. The other three receivers run go routes. The quarterback looks for the advantage in match-ups based on the game plan.

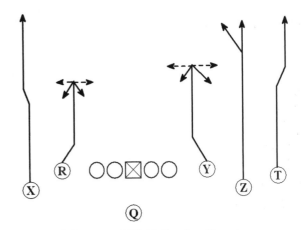

Diagram #13. R-Option Empty

The option route receivers have to handle the bumps they get from the linebackers. They must be able to put their foot in the ground and redirect their pattern. They must be quick enough to run away from a strong safety.

The object of the pass is to clear the coverage with the vertical routes and give the choice routes a chance to operate in space. The quarterback reads from the R-option to the Y-option. He goes to R first because it is the shorter route and comes open more quickly.

The quarterback looks for any match-up he thinks is favorable. If all things are equal, the quarterback looks at the R-receiver and lets him work. If the inside linebacker doubles the R-receiver, he goes to the Y-option on the other side.

It is not rocket science. The spread offense is not a quick passing game. However, it allows the quarterback to make quick decisions so he can get rid of the ball. One of the things we talked about when I hired Gary Crowton was the quarterback holding the ball too long. He stood and waited too long. Part of the reason was getting receivers out from backfield alignments. The quarterbacks love this offense.

In addition to this offense improving our offensive production, it helped our defense. After working against this offense in practice, our secondary and linebackers are more comfortable working in space.

THE ZONE BLITZ PACKAGE

Penn State University

It is a pleasure to be here today. Coach Paterno sends his best to all you coaches. It is always good to come out and represent Penn State University. We had a great year. It could have been better, but it could have been worse.

Since I have been at Penn State, I have coached receivers, backs, defensive linemen, defensive ends, and linebackers for 11 years, and now, defensive backs. The defensive backs complain all the time that the drills we do are linebacker drills. Some of them are, but most of them are good drills.

I do not have all kinds of bags and shields. I do not believe in that. I use cones, footballs, and softballs. If we do not do it in a game, I will not do it in a drill. Do not do a drill just to be doing a drill. Have a purpose for doing the drill.

When we play defense, we do not play many coverages. We play five coverages and the biggest concern in all the secondary play is not to give up the big play. I am not a big statistics coach. I believe in one statistic—the one that records a win or a loss.

The second thing I look for is scoring defense. Did the defense stop the offense from scoring? The third thing is the turnover margin and the fourth thing is loafs by the players. In the last four years, we were one or two in the country in scoring defense.

Our defense is not very complicated. We run to the ball, tackle, and do not give up the big play. In the last two years, in 23 games we have only given up 37 runs over 10 yards.

Let me get into some coaching points on press coverage. The defensive back can encounter a number of problems with press coverage. The first thing is the spread of the feet. If he spreads his feet before the snap of the ball he is in trouble.

The second thing is the level of the hands. We never reach out to contact a receiver. We want to catch him. You cannot lead with the hands. We catch the receiver and steer him the way we want him to go.

As a defensive back, we never want to open the gate. The receiver has to pay the toll. The defensive backs cannot "olé" the receiver and open his hips. The object for the defensive back is to stay square as long as he can. Once the defensive back takes a crossover step, he is in serious trouble. That is the worst position in football. When he crosses his feet, bad things begin to happen.

When the defensive back is ready to fight, I want his hands up. He has to hit the breastplate of the receiver and steer him. Never peek at the quarterback. Every defensive back wants to peek at the quarterback. We are not trying to make an interception is press coverage. We are trying to make the quarterback hold the ball so we can sack him.

We do not want separation in the press coverage. When the receiver starts to take off, the defensive back tries to push him. I do not want that technique. I want to be on his hip, not pushed away from him. The defensive back must feel the receiver. If he accidentally hits him in the family jewels, it will not kill him.

When the defensive back is in position, he does not look back. He looks for indicators as to what the receiver is doing. We look at the hip and hand of the receiver, not back to the quarterback.

The defensive back does battle with the receiver from the line of scrimmage through the first five yards of the route. He applies all the rules of technique in those five yards. He does not spread his feet, slides, stays square, keeps his hands back, and steers the receiver into the sideline. He uses his elbow to hold the receiver back as he tries to release. He gets his hands on his hips and deters the route.

The next stage of the press cover is the chase. That is the stage when the defensive back works on the angles in the route. He watches the receiver's hands, hips, and feet.

The last stage of press coverage is the finish. That is the point where the defensive back prevents the catch and knocks the ball down.

Certain things happen in a pass route. We call it the 5-, 10-, 15-, and 40-yard rule. These are the points at which most patterns have a break point. We eliminate the 20-yard zone because the only thing teams try to ram in on you is the three-step fade route.

Our defensive backs know as soon as the receiver passes 20 yards on an outside release, the pattern is a go route. They put their head down and run as hard as they can to 37 yards from the line of scrimmage. They know the ball is coming down at 37 yards and must fight their butt off to get on top of the receiver and knock the ball down.

Once the receiver gets that deep, there is nothing else the quarterback can do to get the ball to that receiver. You have to teach your defensive backs that fact. The young defensive back wants to look back at the quarterback.

If the receiver takes an inside release, you have to teach the defensive back what reaction he needs. The place a defensive back in press coverage never wants to be is behind the receiver's butt. If that is his position, the receiver has a two-way go. He can break inside or outside. The defensive back wants to be on the inside or outside hip. That gives the receiver only one break.

In press coverage, the defensive back does not know what drop the quarterback takes. His back is to the quarterback and he cannot see. He concentrates on the receiver and fights his butt off.

The defensive back has to see the split of the receiver. He must know if the split is an over or under split. In each of those situations, the receiver

adjusts his split for a reason. If he tightens his split, he probably wants more space to the outside. If he widens his split, he wants to increase the distance between himself and the defender so he can get inside.

The defensive back has to know what type of blitz is coming. If we run a run blitz, the defensive back knows the ball will not likely be forced out quickly. In that case, he plays a "cat technique." That means he is playing cautious man coverage. However, if we run a pass-situation blitz, the defensive back plays a "dog technique." He knows that blitz has a chance to hit home and the ball is coming out.

In the dog technique, he gets all over the receiver and makes it hard for the receiver to get anywhere. He dogs him. When we put any blitz into our scheme, the defensive backs have to be able to draw it up and know what it does.

In our zone-blitz package, we have blitzes for all situations. We have zone blitzes for run and pass. We use the zone blitz to change the tempo of the game.

The offense likes to stay on schedule for the first down. They want second-and-seven and third-and-three in their schedule. If they can do that, they own you. We have to put them behind schedule. We want them in a third-and-seven-plus situation.

By using the zone blitz, it keeps the defense aggressive. Everybody on our team has a zone blitz where they are the blitz runner and the zone dropper. I put a drop in for the defensive tackles, so they get to drop into pass coverage. We want the defense to be aggressive and that is what the zone blitz does.

We do two- and three-deep zone blitzes. You can draw them up in the dirt if you want. Using this scheme gets the defense going so they can gain momentum.

Offenses do not like to see the zone blitz. If gives them problems in their protection scheme. They have to analyze what the defense is doing and slow their tempo. Teams check or automatic when they smell zone blitz. To counter that, we move and bluff with our front. We try to show a zone blitz and move after the offense calls the automatic.

We have a checklist for zone blitzes.

Zone Blitz Checklist

- Be draw- and option-proof
- How quick does the quarterback get rid of the ball?
- How effective is the quarterback under pressure?
- Attack protection rules or weak protectors
- Blitz with your best rushers
- Stay within your system

We can devise a zone blitz for teams that do not run the option. We do that from time to time. I am a big believer in "same as." We may add something, but it is the same as what we always use.

We time every pass the offense throws. We chart the pass, see if it is effective, and see if the blitz will work. We are a big twist team. Most of our zone blitzes are picks. We game plan the stunts we use. We have a bluff package. We come up to the line of scrimmage with our linebacker or secondary players and blitz. When we send five rushers, we make you think we are sending six. When we send six, we want the offense to think we are coming with seven.

When we bring pressure, I want to have a center field player. I do not want to give up the big play. I want the offense to work for everything they get.

In our zone pressure, we want to get a blitz runner on the back right away. We want to see if he can block a linebacker. If he has problems, he will be in for a long night.

We are an over-and-under defense with our front. We designate alignments of our personnel by using bench and field. The bench is the boundary side, or weakside, of the defense. The field is the wide side, or strongside, of the formation.

We play with a 3 technique tackle. We can set anywhere we want according to the formation. In the middle of the field, we can set the 3 technique to the pass set by calling strong. If we want him away from the passing set, we call weak.

We do not have a playbook for our players. We give them a mini-pamphlet they can put in their pocket. If you give your players too much, they will not look at it. The playbook looks good, but the player will not read it if it is too big.

In our front, we play a 3-technique tackle, a shade noseguard, a 5-technique end, and a Will linebacker in a rush end position (Diagram #1). We have a Sam linebacker, aligned on the tight end or strongside. The strongside inside linebacker is our backer linebacker. The openside inside linebacker is the Fritz linebacker. The name comes from a pizza man named Fritz, who used to deliver pizza to the team. That is a true story.

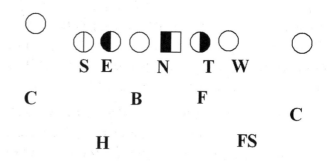

Diagram #1. Base Defense

In the secondary, we play with two corners, a free safety, and a hero back. He is a strong safety. He was named back in the 1950s, when he was a monster back. The name came from the coach who preceded Coach Paterno as head coach. All those names are still part of the defense.

We bring this blitz from the field. We name the blitzes after cities. Joe said you must know national geography to understand our defense. We call the defense based on three choices. Sometimes we base it on the tight end, running back, or game plan.

This first zone blitz is Seattle (Diagram #2). The defensive end aligns in a 5 technique and uses a technique we call a stick. That brings the defensive

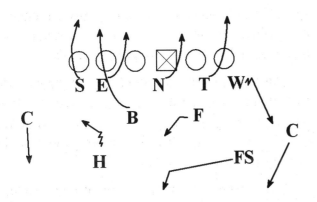

Diagram #2. Seattle

end into the B gap. If they run a stick, the slant is one gap. If we call a long stick, the defensive end goes two gaps. The hero shuffles up and becomes an alley and seam player to the strongside.

When we install the defense in the spring, we stick the end, but in most game situations, we use the long stick. That brings the end into the strongside A gap. The corners play inside technique. They play the post and the streak routes. The out cut is on the defensive coordinator. We do not hold the players responsible for that out cut.

The corner's back foot in his stance is eight-and-a-half yards from the line of scrimmage. They take one step back and hold. They read the three-step move by the quarterback.

The Sam linebacker comes off the edge and is pass and run containment. We have two techniques he can play, which I will talk about later.

To the weakside, the 3-technique tackle and Will linebacker drop or rush depending on the scheme. If the Will linebacker drops into the coverage, the tackle rushes through the offensive tackle outside for containment. We teach both techniques to the Will linebacker and the defensive tackle. That way, the Will linebacker can play the C-gap technique and the tackle can play the hot route, seam, and pump technique in coverage. The Will linebacker could play the tackle's position. He is not good at it, but we could get away with it.

The shade noseguard crosses the center and gets into the weakside A gap. The way we have the diagram drawn, the Will linebacker has the

weakside seam and the Fritz has the hook zone. The free safety has the middle third.

That is how we play the pro set. However, we played two-back offenses 12 percent of the time last year. In our games, we played 25 percent nickel package. We see one-back offenses 52 percent of the time.

Running this blitz into the twin receiver side gets a little ticklish (Diagram #3). If the Sam linebacker comes tight and blows up the play, the ball sometimes gets outside of him. We were pinned inside so many times coming from the openside it was not funny. We have an adjustment we use to keep containment. We let the Sam linebacker seal the C gap and bring the backer outside for containment.

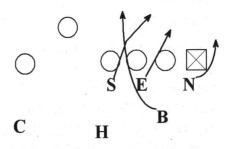

Diagram #3. Seattle Adjustment

In playing the option, we have a number of ways to handle it (Diagram #4). The end and backer have the first threat in the option. The Sam linebacker has the pitch and the hero running the alley takes the quarterback. A change-up brings the Sam

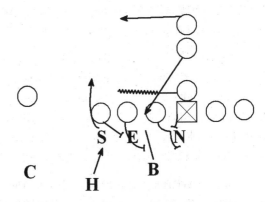

Diagram #4. Responsibility Against the Option

linebacker on the quarterback, with the hero taking the pitch.

When you start to run zone blitzes, give them names that make sense to the players. Every time we line up with a city zone blitz, the name means something. Seattle means "Sam and end" to the players running the stunt. If we call Boston, that means "backer linebacker and Sam linebacker." Buffalo means the backer and Fritz linebackers are running a blitz. If we call Cleveland, the corner is involved in the blitz from the outside.

When you use this type of teaching, the players learn the scheme faster. We use the "same as" method to relate to the blitz we run. If the blitz is to the strongside, it does not matter who runs the blitz. The backside uses the "same as" method. To the backside, the Seattle stunt is the "same as" the Houston stunt.

Houston brings the hero on an inside blitz (Diagram #5). The Sam linebacker is the zone dropper and the hero blitzes the B gap. The defensive end works outside through the C gap. The backer blitzes the A gap. The noseguard cross the center into the weakside A gap and plays the "same as" the Seattle. The 3 technique has the "same as" rule. The Will linebacker comes off into the flat area and the Fritz takes the middle hook zone.

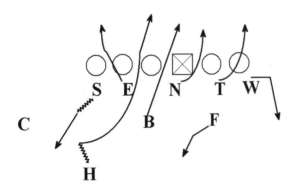

Diagram #5. Houston

If the offense comes out with a twin set to the weakside, that puts your Will linebacker in a bind. We do not expect him to play the wheel route. He is a flat defender and we cannot ask him to run with the wheel deep. We make a "gut" call. That puts the

Fritz linebacker, who is a seam player, on the wheel route. The Will linebacker comes back inside and becomes the nest player. Any time we see two receivers to the weakside, we make the "gut" call.

The Fritz linebacker knows what the Will linebacker can handle and makes the calls to adjust away from a mismatch. If the offense goes to a split backfield, there is a threat of the running back coming out of the backfield on the wheel (Diagram #6). The Fritz gives the gut call and takes the wheel if it comes.

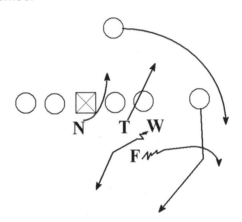

Diagram #6. Gut

We like the hero in what we call a C-7 alignment. He aligns in the C gap seven yards off the line of scrimmage. He has fill responsibilities from that position on flow away from him. If the hero has to leave that alignment, he makes a call to the Sam linebacker. The Sam linebacker has to replace him on flow away.

If we get a double-slot set into the boundary, we get out of the straight defense and play the gut call.

If we want to bring pressure from the outside to the boundary side, we call Cleveland (Diagram #7). The Will linebacker slants inside the offensive tackle into the B gap and the 3 technique tackle slants into the A gap. The noseguard slants into the strongside A gap. The defensive end loops outside in the C gap.

We bring the Cleveland from the boundary side almost all the time. It is too far to come from the fieldside. We can bring the free safety on this blitz

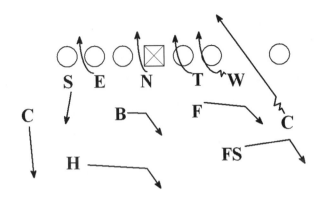

Diagram #7. Cleveland

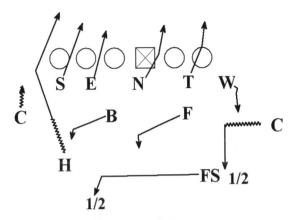

Diagram #8. Harlem

also. The corner gives a "you-me" call to the free safety. The "you" call sends the free safety into the third. The "me" call is the opposite. The safety runs the blitz and the corner stays in the third.

If the quarterback is a right-handed quarterback, the blitz comes from his left. We want to bring the blitz from the short side of the field and quarterback's backside. To eliminate confusion on this stunt, if we have two receivers, the blitz is off. We only run the blitz with one receiver and two backs in the backfield.

In the bowl game against Florida State, they burned us on this blitz. They pinned our Will linebacker and threw a screen pass to the blitz side. The Fritz linebacker had to play slow because he is on the backside and takes the cutback runs. That is the hardest thing to teach your defenders in the zone-blitz game. He could not get out and they scored their touchdown on that play. The linebackers cannot flow quickly. They have to stay at home.

The free safety plays over the top into the outside third and the hero rotates back to the middle third. In this situation, the hero makes the call to the Sam linebacker to let him know he is leaving to cover the middle. The Sam linebacker has to cover for the hero. The Sam and Fritz linebacker become the seam players and the backer linebacker has the hook.

If we call Harlem (Diagram #8), the hero and the Sam linebacker are going on the blitz. The defensive end sticks to the inside B gap. The Sam linebacker

slants through the C gap and the hero comes off the edge. The noseguard crosses the center into the backside A gap and the 3 technique tackle slants outside.

When we send the hero, the problem we have is getting him too close to the line of scrimmage. He aligns at seven yards and cheats to six yards before he comes. He cannot get too close, or the offense sees him and picks him off. When he comes late, he generally comes clean.

When we run this blitz, we play halves in the secondary. The boundary side corner plays half the field to the backside and the free safety plays the strongside half. As the defense moves at the last second to get into position, the boundary side corner gets into a C-9 alignment. That is a position over the C gap, nine yards off the line of scrimmage.

Since the Sam linebacker and hero are both involved in the blitz, we roll the strongside corner into the strong flat. The Will linebacker plays the flat. The Fritz linebacker has the seam to hook on the backside and the back linebacker has hook to curl on the strongside.

The next alignment is Scranton (Diagram #9). This allows us to move our personnel around and create any type of overload we like. On this set, we move the 3 technique into the field. That allows us to get four defenders into the field. We can create overloads to either side of the defense.

The noseguard has to slide over to the weakside (Diagram #10). In passing situations, we take the

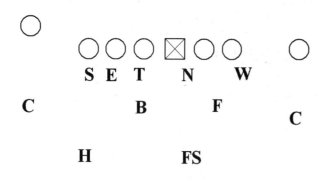

Diagram #9. Scranton

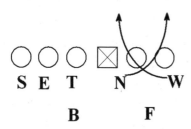

Diagram #10. Weakside Stunt

Will linebacker, spike him to the inside, and bring the nose all the way to the outside for containment.

When we play our nickel package, the nickel is always into the field and the free safety is to the boundary.

If we do not zone blitz, we slant and move the down linemen according to our game planning. We give all our defenders a three-way go. They can move inside, outside, or straight ahead.

I have a coaching point for the outside blitz. If the corner comes down to blitz from the outside and the quarterback goes away from him, he has to "squeeze smart." What that means is he becomes the backside cutback player. He starts on the angle to the quarterback, and if the ball goes away, he stops and shuffles to the inside. He knows there is a cutback lane in the C gap and he has containment on anything coming back.

If he meets a running play coming his way, we do not ask him to sit the corner. He is not that type of player. He goes a thousand miles an hour, blows up the blockers, and bounces the play to the outside. The pursuit runs the ball down. The technique is a "sell-out technique." The corner takes his outside shoulder pad and puts it on the inside thigh pad of the blocker. He tries to drive upfield after he makes contact.

We have a technique we use for our linebackers called "blaze." The linebackers read and flow through the C gap as flow comes their way (Diagram #11). We play this technique when the Sam linebacker is detached from the defense. They have to communicate with the ends on the outside so they will know the linebacker has the containment. In certain sets, we do not come off the edge with our linebackers. If they see the set, they call off the blaze and the ends know they have containment.

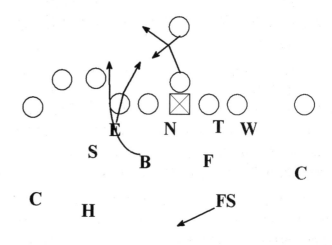

Diagram #11. Blaze

Gentlemen, my time is up. Thank you for your attention. It is nice to be here with a bunch of good football coaches. If we can do anything for you, do not hesitate to call on us.

DEFENDING THE OPTION

University of Kentucky

Thank you very much. Defending the option from the 4-3 defense is my topic. I have been in this business for a long time. Football goes through cycles. A few years ago, the option was the big idea in offensive football.

Nebraska was one of the teams running the option. They had great success with the trap option from the I formation. Their quarterback ran for hundreds of yards, they won national championships, and won 10 or 11 games every year.

We trace the veer option back to Bill Yeoman at the University of Houston. They ran the veer option out of a split-backs set.

There were a lot of high school teams, particularly on the West Coast, that ran the option scheme from a double-wing formation. They had great success with the option because they had misdirection, deception, and could isolate and break down the defense with their option schemes.

In recent years, the passing game has become the main emphasis of offenses across the nation. They spread the field and throw the ball from the shotgun set. The defenses are catching up to the teams that stand back in the pocket and wing the ball every down.

That led to teams using the spread option. That gave the teams in spread shotgun formations with one back a chance to run the ball and be effective.

I consider teams that read defensive linemen in their execution of plays to be option teams. Northwestern started reading the backside defensive end as part of their dart play. Urban Meyer, who coached at Utah and Bowling Green, went one step further and started using one of the wide receivers as the pitch man in the spread option.

He used the shovel pass and the option in combination as an effective option attack. That allowed the spread offenses to set in an obvious passing set and run option plays at the defense.

If the defense was not prepared to play that kind of attack, they could be embarrassed. The option has taken different forms in the past five years. Before you make a plan to defend the option, there are some essential facts you must know. You must know what they are trying to do and which player they prefer to end up with the football.

The old option concept was to have the player keep or deal the ball based on the option read. Most offensive coaches, when they ran the option, wanted a particular player to end up with the ball. Defensive coaches defending the option needed to determine who that particular player was.

In the wishbone triple option, the coaches loaded the option scheme. That means they put a blocker on the defender responsible for the quarterback. They wanted the quarterback to keep the ball, which in essence was a quarterback sweep. If the defense did not understand that concept and tried to defend it as a true option, they had many problems. The other option was to load the scheme and block for the pitch man.

Coaches who ran the option had a conservative streak in them. They got nervous when they had to pitch the ball because the ball could end up on the ground. Most coaches wanted to give the ball on a dive option or have the quarterback keep the ball rather than pitch it. They did not want the negative plays.

The first option we explored was the dive option, or belly option (Diagram #1). That put the quarterback under center taking the snap. That meant the first fake was to the fullback. In most instances, the read is a called play rather than a read option. There was no read by the quarterback. Either he gave the ball to the fullback on the dive play or he faked the ball to the fullback, pulled it, and ran the called option play. On the called option, the quarterback ran the ball or pitched it to the tailback.

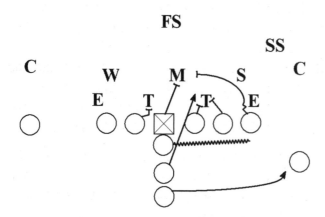

Diagram #1. Dive/Belly Option

The dive, or belly, option is not run as much today as it was 10 years ago. However, it still was an option you had to defend.

The veer option was a read option (Diagram #2). The offense did not block the defender assigned to the dive back. You could run the option from a split-backs or I formation. The linemen blocked down to their inside and left the defender assigned to the dive back unblocked. The quarterback read that defender and pulled the ball or left it with the back, depending on the reaction of the defender. If the defender took the dive back, the quarterback pulled the ball and optioned the next man down the line of scrimmage.

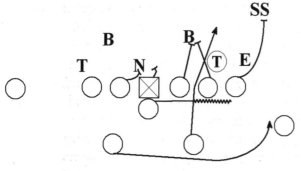

Diagram #2. Veer Option

The end of the option play was the same for the dive and the veer option. If the dive back did not get the ball, the quarterback either pitched the ball to the tailback or ran the ball himself.

The speed option was what I termed a nuisance option (Diagram #3). We used this option at Kentucky. We were not an option team, although the media had fun saying we were. We had a 300-pound quarterback running the speed option. It worked fine because he pitched the ball to a back that could run. All we wanted was the defense to take the quarterback and force the pitch.

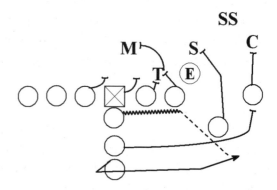

Diagram #3. Speed Option

There was no in-line fake by a back. The quarterback took the ball from the center and sprinted down the line of scrimmage. It worked better to the openside of the formation. The offensive tackle veer blocked to the inside and the quarterback optioned off the defensive end. In principle, it was a delayed sweep. Instead of the quarterback pitching the ball to the running back after the snap, he delayed the pitch until he got to the defensive end.

If the offense did not want the quarterback to keep the ball, this was what the defense did: They forced the quarterback to keep the ball and knocked the crap out of him.

Urban Meyer took the spread option he ran at Utah with him to Florida when he became the head coach there. The difference was he played in the SEC. He ran into a lot of great defensive teams in our league and the option did not work as well. The reason was the quarterback did not want to end up with the ball.

The defense did not want the quarterback pitching the ball to a speedy wide receiver or a tough running back. They took away the dive back and the pitch and let the quarterback run with the ball. He might pick up some yards but he paid for every one of them.

The loaded option could be run from a number of different sets. If it was a two-back set, there was no fake into the line by a back. In this option, the quarterback reversed out or countered one way before running the other way. That left a blocking back in the backfield to load the defender. The blocking back blocked the defender on the quarterback, if the offense wanted him to carry the ball. If they wanted the running back to get the ball, they blocked the support defender covering the pitch.

The loaded option was a problem with teams that had fast-running quarterbacks. I learned how to defend the loaded option a long time age. When I first started coaching, I worked for Tommy Protho at UCLA. We played the University of Texas in Austin. They had a 27-game winning streak in that stadium. They were running the wishbone and ripping up everyone.

Coach Protho devised a scheme to key the path of the near back in the wishbone set. We let the outside linebacker deal with the block of the load blocker. We felt he could play the blocker more easily than the safety or corner. If the near back arced at the force man, the outside linebacker came under the block of the near back, attacked the pitch man, and knocked him down. The safety and corner came inside on the quarterback and made the play.

If the near back tried to load on the outside linebacker, he played him and made the play on the quarterback. That allowed the force defender to attack the pitch man without a blocker.

We were a 17-point underdog and played the hell out of Texas. The only thing we did not do well was cancel the fullback dive. He hurt us running up inside. That was a good scheme, when you knew the offense had the load scheme in their option package.

However, when we played an option team, we needed more than one way to play the option. If you played the load or any other scheme the same way every time, the offense figured out what you were doing. You had to be able to change up the way you played the option.

On some occasions, the defense wanted to read and play a base scheme against the option. At other times, the defense stunted and hit the quarterback in the mouth. When you stunted, it forced a quicker decision by the quarterback. We do not see the loaded option much any more. It reappeared in the Urban Meyer offense at Florida. The defender playing the pitch had to deal with a load blocker.

Another option scheme used today was the counter option (Diagram #4). That option took the quarterback in one direction and countered him back the other way. He faked to the fullback and ran an option to the outside. That allowed the offensive linemen to get better angles on the linebackers and support people.

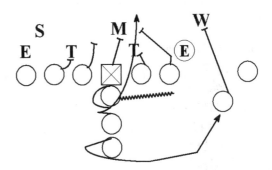

Diagram #4. Counter Option

The option used today by most teams was the spread option from the shotgun set (Diagram #5). You seldom see a team running an option from under the center, except the speed option. The spread-option teams used any number of personnel groupings. They used the quarterback in the shotgun with two backs, one back, one tight end, and no tight ends. The option they ran was a read-type option. The quarterback read the defensive end on the backside of the play. If the defensive end closed down the line, the quarterback pulled the ball and ran out the backside of the formation. If the defensive

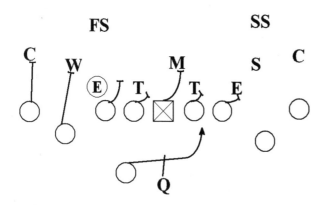

Diagram #5. Spread Option

end hung in the area, the quarterback left the ball in the pocket of the tailback and he ran the play.

The play was a simple read play by the quarterback, but it was hard to handle. However, if the quarterback had a pitch man as part of the option scheme, it was dangerous. If there were two backs in the backfield, the quarterback could read the option to either side. If there was a one-back set, the quarterback read the defensive end on the same side as where the back aligned. The pitch players came from the wide receivers in motion or simply delayed their movement until the quarterback came to them.

Another variation of the option game involved the shovel pass (Diagram #6). Teams used the Utah, or shovel, pass as part of the spread-option scheme. Although the shovel pass was a forward pass, it became an integral part of the option game. Teams incorporated the option and shovel pass in the same play. It became a complicated play and hard to defend. The quarterback took the snap and threatened the run outside. If the end attacked the

quarterback, the quarterback shoveled the ball inside to a back. If the defensive end stayed back on the shovel pass, the quarterback ran the option to the outside. The offense ran the play from one or two backs, with the quarterback in the shotgun set. If the quarterback ran the play from the one-back set, a receiver motioned inside for the shovel or pitch.

The play the offense wanted to complete was the shovel pass. If the back dropped the ball, it was an incomplete pass. Obviously, the defense wanted to cover the shovel and force the option pitch. If the offense dropped the pitch, it was a fumble. Florida ran this play numerous times this year. In the SEC, defensive teams forced the quarterback to keep the ball. The offense, when using motion, had the ability to run the ball to both sides of the formation. The defense could not load up according to the alignment of the back.

There were some defensive principles to obey when defending the option. They were easy to talk about, but hard to execute properly. The first principle was to take the dive back and cancel him from the offense. In the shovel option, the first threat was the shovel pass. The defense had to have a defender responsible for the dive or shovel. The second threat in the option game was the quarterback. The defense had to assign a defender to take the quarterback. In the 4-3 defense, that usually was a linebacker, defensive end, or safety. The third threat in the option game was the pitch.

The goal of an option scheme was to slow the defense and break it into categories. If they found a weakness in any category, they exploited it. If the defense had some part of their scheme that was not sound, the option worked on that weakness.

When the defense gambled with blitzes and many stunts, the responsibilities of playing the option sometimes broke down. However, if the defense sat and read, it took away some of their aggressiveness. That left a fine line between aggressiveness and caution.

One of the most important phases of defending the option was the presence of an alley player. It

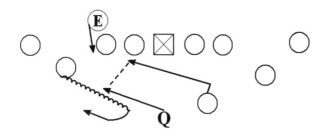

Diagram #6. Shovel Pass

could be a linebacker, but was usually a safety. An alley player was someone who played from the inside out and trailed the ball. If your defender missed the dive back, there was someone filling inside from the right angle that made the tackle.

If the ball was not handed to the dive back, the alley player continued on his inside-out angle to the second threat. He cleaned up on the quarterback, if he escaped. If the offense pitched the ball, the alley player continued inside-out on the pitch player.

The second biggest threat to the defense from the option was the pass. In the old option schemes, the offense ran the running play almost every down. They waited and bided their time for the defense to get impatient in their option responsibilities. When that happened, they went for the home run ball over the top of the defense with the play-action pass. Teams like Oklahoma only threw the ball 10 times a game, but two of them went for touchdowns.

The critical point in defending the option was "defensive discipline." The defense had to read their keys and play their responsibility. Everyone had to play their responsibility first, before they helped in some other phase of the game. If the defender responsible for the dive suddenly jumped on the quarterback, it hurt you defensively. Even if the quarterback was killing the defense, the dive defender had to stay on his responsibility.

The second most important point in defending the option was "tackling." The option isolated and broke down the defense. It stopped the all-out pursuit that came from the normal running game. Tackling became a premium because there were a tremendous amount of one-on-one situations. If the defender missed the tackle, the pursuit was not present to clean up the mistake. A missed tackle against an option team translated into big gains.

The third critical point in defending the option was "pursuit angles." Defenders on the backside of the option must pursue at the proper angle to prevent long runs.

I want to cover some of the schemes we used to defend the option. The first set was an I

formation with no tight end. The basic defense we ran was a 4-3 alignment (Diagram #7). The first thing we considered was the secondary coverage. In the three-deep scheme, there were fewer ways to defend the option to the one-receiver side, but you could play it. On the dive option, there was no read by the quarterback. Therefore, the defensive tackle and end were blocked by the offensive guard and tackle. The Mike linebacker, along with the defensive tackle, took the dive threat in the A gap and B gap. The Sam linebacker and defensive end had responsibility on the quarterback. In the dive option, the defender responsible for the pitch was the strong safety. However, in the dive-option scheme, the offense had a blocker assigned to him. Because the strong safety had trouble getting to the pitch, the Sam linebacker played from the quarterback up to the pitchback.

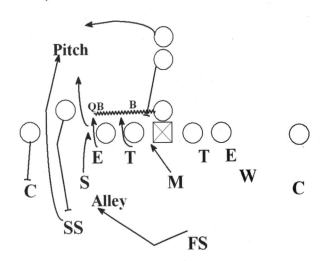

Diagram #7. Dive Option Strong

The free safety flowed from inside the dive to inside the quarterback to inside the pitch. He was the alley defender. The corners played pass most of the time. If we got the hard post pattern from the wide receiver, the free safety had to honor that move and the corner became the secondary pitch defender.

If the offense ran the option to the openside, we had a bigger problem (Diagram #8). They used the wide receiver to run off the corner. The free safety had to be alert to the inside post. The Mike linebacker and defensive tackle played the dive back to the weakside. The defensive end took the quarterback and the Will linebacker ran through for the pitch man. The Sam linebacker filled the backside A gap and looked for the cutback by the dive back.

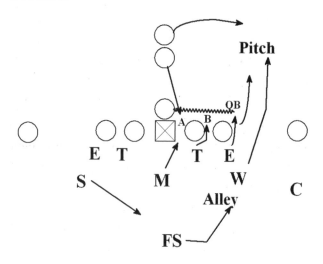

Diagram #8. Dive Option Weak

The veer option presented a different type of threat (Diagram #9). The veer option used split backs in their scheme. The offensive guard and tackle double-teamed the defensive tackle, with the tackle climbing to block the Mike linebacker. The quarterback read the defensive end. If the defensive end came upfield, the quarterback gave the ball to the back. If he stepped down the line, he pulled the ball and ran the option outside. The defense played the option using a base scheme on seven out of 10 plays. In the base scheme, the defensive end took the back and forced the quarterback to pull the ball. The Sam linebacker scraped to the outside and took

the quarterback. The strong safety had to play the pitch man to his side.

The offense blocked with the slotback two different ways. On their base play, he loaded on the strong safety. However, on occasion he cracked inside on the Sam linebacker. The strong safety or the Sam linebacker had to defeat the block of the slotback before they covered their responsibility. The corner played pass and the free safety held off the post route down the middle. Once the corner got over the top and was in control of the pass route, the free safety filled the alley.

If the offense ran the base blocking scheme, the technique of the defender assigned to the quarterback was important. He could slow play the quarterback and string the play out down the line of scrimmage. By slow-playing the quarterback once he pitched the ball, the Sam linebacker ran flat down the line of scrimmage to the ball. When the quarterback pitched the ball, the Sam linebacker turned and pursued. If the linebacker played the quarterback slow, he became an alley player.

The other technique used by the defender playing the quarterback was to attack him hard and fast. By attacking the quarterback, we hoped to cause a bad pitch or fumble. It forced the quarterback to react quickly and could lead to a mistake.

To the weakside of the formation, we encountered another problem (Diagram #10). We played every thing the same except the pitch man.

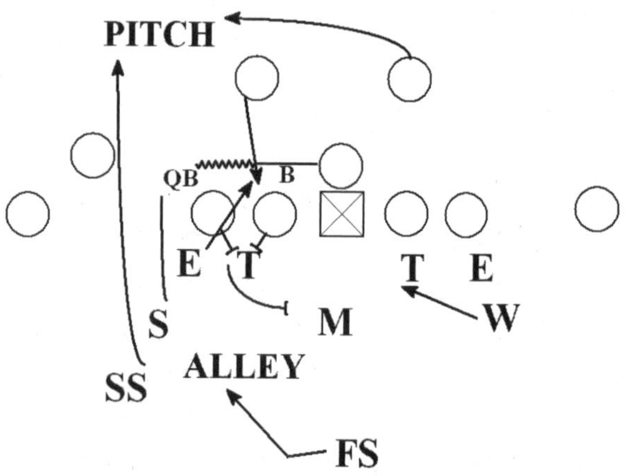

Diagram #9. Veer Option Strong

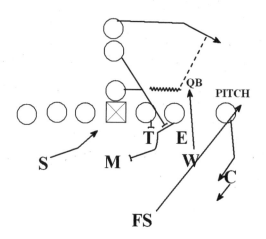

Diagram #10. Veer Option Weak

In a three-deep cover, we had no safety in the flat. The corner played the receiver on the post cut and the free safety ran through the pitch. If the safety took the proper angle, he could play the pitch from that depth.

The best way to play the option was not from a three-deep secondary. If you played some kind of four-deep scheme, the safeties rotated into the flat on flow their way. That gave you a much better option defense to either side of the formation.

The formation we saw most of the time came from the shotgun set. We faced those types of option schemes almost weekly in the Southeastern Conference. If everyone did not do their job, you really had a problem. We were in a position to stunt from either side to bring pressure on the quarterback at the point of attack. Stunting affected the quarterback's decision-making and sped up his reaction time. With the quarterback in the shotgun set, with backs on either side of him, he could run the option either way. For the clinic lecture, I will demonstrate the scheme to the two-receiver side first.

The offense ran the zone or dart play to the left side of the line (Diagram #11). The option depended on the reaction of the right defensive end. If the defensive end stayed home in his area, the quarterback gave the ball to the right halfback, running the zone play left. However, if the defensive end chased the ball down the line of scrimmage, the quarterback pulled the ball and ran the option to the right. The Sam linebacker became the option key for the quarterback. If the linebacker took the quarterback, he pitched the ball and the strong safety had to defeat the block of the slotback to make the tackle.

The Will linebacker and defensive end needed to have a stunt or a call to change their responsibilities. If the defensive end hung to the backside, the Will linebacker had to fill for the cutback of the zone play.

If the offense ran the zone play toward the two-receiver side and the option to the one-receiver side, we played it similarly (Diagram #12). However, we had a bigger problem unless we played a four-deep secondary scheme. The blocking scheme on the Will linebacker amounts to a loaded block. If the Will linebacker filled inside, the tackle tried to block him down. If he hung, the tackle got on him and tried to keep contact with the linebacker. That became a hard technique for the Will linebacker because he had the quarterback on the option toward him.

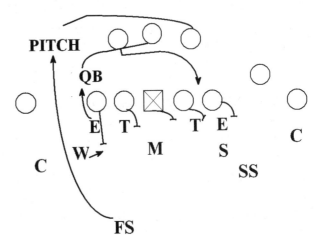

Diagram #12. Spread Option/Two Backs Weak

The Will linebacker had the quarterback on the option his way and the pitch was the free safety's responsibility. That became difficult in the three-deep scheme. A change-up gave the Will linebacker the pitch man and tried to get the Mike linebacker to the quarterback. That was extremely difficult because the Mike linebacker started out playing the zone play to his side (Diagram #13). The best change-up was a change in the secondary. Playing a four-deep or two-deep scheme gave the defense the support needed on the weakside. That

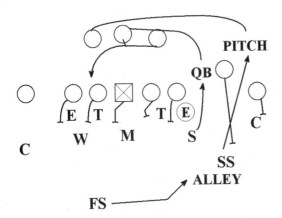

Diagram #11. Spread Option/Two Backs Strong

generally gave the defense corner support with a safety running in the alley to either side.

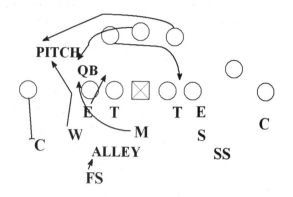

Diagram #13. Spread Option/Cover 2

The next set spreads the defense even more. The offense got into a one-tight-end, one-back, and three-wide-receivers set from the shotgun. Unless they motioned someone into the backfield, the offense had no pitch man. If the offense motioned a wide receiver into the backfield, he was the pitch man and they ran the back on the zone play.

The offense wanted to keep the defense from overplaying the option to the side of the back. They ran the shovel pass away from the alignment of the back (Diagram #14). They used reverse motion by the wide receiver from the side of the shovel pass, or they brought motion by the wide receiver from the side opposite the shovel pass. The quarterback took the snap and started to sprint out into the strongside. The wide receiver came in reverse motion from the strongside and became the pitch

man. The tailback aligned to the left, came under the quarterback behind the line, and looked for the shovel pass from the quarterback.

The quarterback's read was the Sam linebacker aligned outside the tight end. If the Sam linebacker jumped the quarterback, he shoveled the ball to the tailback inside. If the Sam linebacker kept leverage on the tailback, the quarterback ran the speed option, pitching off the strong safety.

What we saw from the shotgun one-back set was shovel option. They could run the play either way with motion. The thing we did not see was the motioned wideout running the zone play. He was always the pitch man on these option plays.

When the offense motioned the wide receiver from the side of the shovel pass, it tightened the corner to the formation and put him in good position to play the pitch. The Sam linebacker cancelled the shovel pass and made the quarterback keep the ball on the option. The Mike linebacker played the quarterback. The corner tightened with the motion and took the pitch. The strong safety became the secondary player on the quarterback and played the quarterback outside to the pitch.

If the motion came from the side opposite the shovel pass, the wide receiver took the corner out of the play by running deep (Diagram #15). In that case, the strong safety became responsible for the pitch man. The Mike linebacker came outside and played the quarterback. The free safety rotated back through the middle to help the corner on the split end.

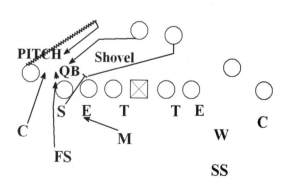

Diagram #14. Shovel Pass/Strong Motion

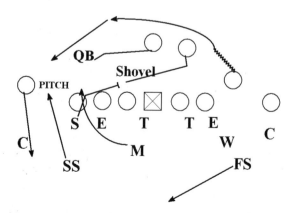

Diagram #15. Shovel Pass/Opposite Motion

At Kentucky, we did some of the same things. People who ran the shotgun and single-running-back sets ran this scheme just as a nuisance to the defense. Teams that did not run the option ran the read play as part of their scheme. They did not read the end totally. They read the end and backside linebacker. If both of them chased down inside, they pulled the ball. Otherwise, they ran the zone play. Those types of teams were not option teams, but in essence they were because they ran a play based on an offensive read of a defender.

One of the toughest sets to defend the option from was the one-back set with two tight ends. Being in a three-deep scheme against this offense presented a few problems. Our adjustments in the 4-3 defense to this set aligned the Sam linebacker on the line of scrimmage to the wide side of the field. We kicked the front down into a 5 technique for the defensive end and a strong 1 technique for the tackle. To the backside, we played a 27 alignment with the tackle and defensive end. We shifted the secondary the other way and widened the Will linebacker. The front looked similar to a 6-1 defense. The Mike linebacker stacked behind the strong 1-technique tackle and the Will linebacker played a 50 technique over the backside offensive tackle.

Most of the conventional option schemes did not work with only one back in the backfield and the quarterback under the center. The option we saw from this set was the speed option (Diagram #16). The quarterback took one step away from the center and ran down the line one way or the other. The single back was the pitch man in the scheme.

Unless you played a four-deep or cover 2 coverage, this scheme was hard to defend. Away from the strong safety, there was no defender on the pitch man. The only defender that could cover the pitch was the free safety. The Mike linebacker worked his way out from the inside, but had to come over blocks to get there.

The only other logical thing we did was roll the coverage into a cloud coverage and put the corner on the pitch. The problem was the wide receiver's block on the corner. The two-deep or four-deep secondary solved all our problems.

We did this at Kentucky with Jarad Lorenzen. Because he was 300 pounds, we did not want him running the ball. Most of the time the defense accommodated us, and we pitched the ball to a running back. It acted as a long-toss sweep. The defense had to go back to the principles of defending the option. They had to know who the offense wanted to carry the ball. If the offense wanted a 300-pound slow-footed quarterback with the ball, then the defense reacted correctly and attacked him. However, if the offense wanted the tailback carrying the ball, the defense covered the pitch and made the quarterback run the ball. That was tremendously important in deciding how to defend the option.

The set we liked was the trips set with two tight ends and one set back (Diagram #17). Most defenses favored the trips side with their secondary. That put almost all the support defenders to the trips side of the formation. We ran the speed option away from the trips and caused

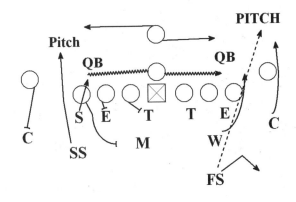

Diagram #16. Speed Option/Two Tights

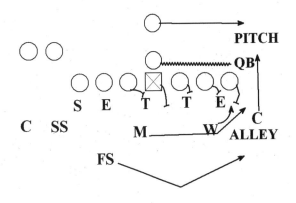

Diagram #17. Trips/Two Tights

people problems. The offensive blocking scheme blocked the 7-technique end and Will linebacker in a combination type of block. The Will linebacker was the defender responsible for the quarterback. He had trouble getting to the quarterback. The corner played the pitch man. This set gave the defense fits.

The stunt that solved our problem was the corner took the quarterback and the Will linebacker fought over the combination block to the outside to take the pitch man. For every solution, there was another problem. You had to be aware of the option pass. The reason this did not present a big problem was any teams running the speed option were not committed to the option. Therefore, their play-action options were not that polished.

The next problem the defense faced was the two-tight-end set from the shotgun. Lump all the problems with the two-tight-end sets and those created by the spread formation and it will give the defense a headache. If they motioned either wideout back into the formation, they could run the shovel and read option.

The big problem was the Will linebacker (Diagram #18). If motion came into the backfield, the Will linebacker knew the read option was the play he had to stop. He was essential, as the cutback defender in the zone played away from him. If he got in a hurry and filled before the ball was seated with the running back, he got pinned inside by the tackle's block. If the quarterback pulled the ball, he was blocked. He had to make sure the ball left before he could pursue. He had the quarterback if he pulled the

ball and ran the option his way. The safeties rolled with the motion and the strong safety played the pitch.

The solution to all these problems was more preparation, coaching, and discipline. We planned what to do. We coached it up in practice and drilled it with reps. Repetition built the confidence to maintain the discipline in covering the option. You had to understand the problem areas, then concentrate on them. If someone broke down, the defense gave up a big play.

The shovel pass, in my opinion, was not a type of play you wanted to run with two tight ends in the game. The shovel pass used with the spread formation was much better than a bunched set. Open spaces made the shovel pass more effective.

The last option I want to talk about is the double-wing option. We did not see much of this set. However, I know high school teams employed this set in their offenses. This was a tough set to defend because it had misdirection and counter plays. It was a balanced set with capabilities of going to either side. It had a variety of offensive schemes that could be run from the set.

I believe cover 2 and 4 were the best coverages to play against option teams. The two-safety system allowed the defense to cover the pitch man to either side. Playing cover 2 in the secondary allowed the defense to get alley runners into almost every running situation. When you play three-deep coverage, the offense could run away from the rotation of the secondary.

The signature play in the double wing was the veer option with a loaded scheme on the outside. The fullback aligned behind the quarterback and ran the dive option into the B gap. The offensive line veer blocked and the quarterback read the defensive end. The wingback to the playside ran three different schemes. He loaded the linebacker responsible for the quarterback or the safety responsible for the pitch. The third option came in the form of an arc block on the corner. If that block occurred, the wide receiver cracked on either the linebacker or the safety. The play designated the

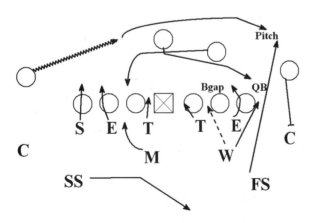

Diagram #18. Two Tights/Shotgun

block of the wingback. If the play called for the quarterback to run the ball, the wingback loaded the linebacker.

The defense to stop the option needed a base scheme and change-ups off that scheme (Diagram #19). Instead of the defensive end closing on the dive back, the linebacker takes the dive and the end can step up on the quarterback.

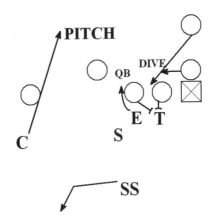

Diagram #20. Change-ups

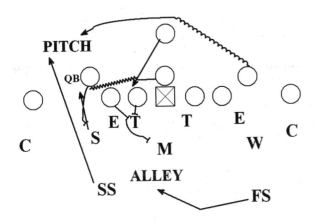

Diagram #19. Double-Wing Option Base

Instead of sending the safety for the pitch, send the linebacker or corner (Diagrams #20 & 21). Let the safety cover the third or crash on the quarterback. If the offense knew how the defense covered, they could find a way to block it. The defense could cause the quarterback to misread his keys by disguised assignments.

The focal point of the defense defending the option had to be the defenders responsible for the quarterback, pitch, and pass. Failure to cover those aspects of the option game means trouble. There are many ways to run the option and many ways to

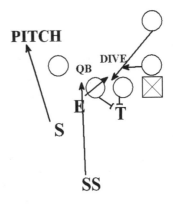

Diagram #21. Change-ups

defend it. But, my first principle was the most important to defending the option. You must cover the dive, quarterback, pitch, and pass, but you must get someone in the alleys to cover up the mistakes. Those were the essential items.

It is a pleasure to be here. Thanks for having me.

DANCE WITH THE ONE WHO BRUNG YA

University of Texas

I am told this is the largest crowd to ever show up for a clinic in Florida. You have had a great group of coaches lecture here this weekend. I appreciate Chuck Rohe having me here today. Chuck and I have been friends for a long time.

It has been a wonderful two months since the national championship game. It has been very interesting. I have been a head coach now for 22 years. I was an assistant coach before I became a head coach. I was lucky to get started as a head coach at such an early age. During my time as a coach, I have been beaten up a lot. There is no one here today that has been scrutinized or criticized more than I have.

I got some good advice from two friends a few years ago. One of them told me this: "Don't ever listen to anyone that you do not really respect that has been successful in your business, or in a business that you respect." If you think about this statement, it makes sense. If you take nothing home today but this one thought, it would be helpful in your career. We are so sensitive in our business that we worry about things we should not be concerned with. I hear about the Internet, the radio, the call-in shows, the TV shows, the writers, the parents, and many others. There are so many things that we worry about that are unimportant. If we can spend our time and energy on things that matter, then we are a lot better off. The kids matter, your coaches matter, the parents matter, and the team matters.

High school coaches raised me. My granddad was a football coach in middle Tennessee for a long time. My dad was a high school coach. They became principals and then superintendents. That is who I am. I was raised wanting to be what you people do every day of your life.

In the championship game, there was 6:32 left and Southern Cal had just scored to go up by two points. It was not as if we had stopped them very often. At that point, you are not really thinking about what you are going to say in your postgame speech. You may have some time on your hands, but that is not what you are thinking about. After the game, the TV host asked me a question. I honestly did not know what the question was. My thought was this: I had waited for 33 years to get up here to say what I want to say, so I did not care what the question was that he asked. I am telling you the truth. Later I had to go back and replay the TV show to find out what he had asked me.

Imagine waiting 33 years, actually 54 years, for someone to ask you, "What did you think about the game?" At that point, I did not care about the game. However, I had some things I wanted to say about the game, regardless of the question anyone asked me. I figured that if I had waited for 33 years I could say what I wanted to say. When you are talking to the media, figure out what you want to say when they ask a question. Say what you want to say, regardless of the question. That is it!

Another point you can learn from this experience is this: When the media ask you a negative question, do not repeat the negative part of the question because then you are answering in the negative. If the media ask me, "Why did your team play so poorly?" I am going to reply, "I am so proud of the effort our guys gave." You do not want to say, "We played poorly because..." You do not want to say, "We did not play as poorly as you think we did." If you give that answer, the media has you and you have lost that battle.

I will never forget when I stood up in the middle of the Rose Bowl with all of the TV audience watching. I did not care what I said at that moment. You want to be in that position and you plan to be in that situation. However, as I said, I had some other things I was concerned about with 6:32 left in the game. I did not have a sheet of paper in my back pocket that said, "If you win... say this. If you lose..." well then they will not care what you say, so you can put that paper back in your pocket.

Coach Darrell Royal said, after you win, brag about the players. After you lose a game, blame yourself, get up, and get out of there. You do not need to get into the specifics. "We are young and we are getting better." They say you are supposed to be good when you are young. If you are bad, you are bad. If they are bad, they are young. And if they are coming back, you can be in for a big disappointment.

I lost my grandfather and my dad before I went to Texas. I went to Texas to coach to honor them. My thoughts were on them at that time. When James Brown asked me the question about the game this was my thought process: "How cool is it that Pete Carroll and the Southern California teams won 34 straight games?" That is hard to do. We must be very careful to keep respect for the people in the game, the people that coach the game, and the kids that play the game. If we lose that respect, we have lost everything. My first comments were, "Congratulations to Pete Carroll and the Southern Cal team. What a great run they have had in college football. The record they made had never been done. The fact that Southern Cal lost tonight does not take away the fact that they won 34 straight games."

The second thing I thought about was about my dad and grandfather. I had to figure they were "watching" and how proud they were. In addition, it gave me a chance to say, "Thanks to high school football." College coaches walk around with our chests stuck out. If it were not for high school football there would not be college football. Many college coaches are getting the credit for winning. We get the players when they are 18 years old. We get them when they are well-coached. We get them when they have won a lot of games. We choose the players we want from the players the high school coaches have. It is all about high school football.

My high school coach is coming to visit us in spring practice. He has been retired for 10 years, but he is going to spend some time with us. I want to give a special thanks to him. I want our players to meet him. I want the players to know the influence he had on my life. So I say to the high school coaches: Don't think for a minute that you do not have a big influence on the players' lives.

A person told me a few years ago that I would win some championships at Texas if I could just outlast them. He told me to put up with the bullcrap long enough and keep plugging and you will win a championship. He did tell me to be smart enough to change things when they needed to be changed. "Don't change because you are covering yourself."

All of you are good at what you do or you would not be here today. There is some reason you got up early enough today for this lecture when some of your friends went home or slept in late. You are here for a reason today.

There is a reason we had a scrimmage yesterday at Texas. I had to run from the field to catch the plane to get here last night. I get excited about talking to high school coaches. Our staff will not be doing any speaking engagements except for high school coaching clinics this year. That is important to us.

There have been some cool things happen in the last two months. The next morning after the championship game, things got interesting. When the President of the United States calls you at 6:00 am, it is something special. I was lying in the bed and the phone rang. My wife answered the phone. The President said, "Sally, is Mack awake?" She looked over to me and said, "Mack, are you awake?" I responded that I was awake because the phone woke me up. "*Who is it?*" Sally answered, "It is the President of the United States!" I said, "Can he call back later?" It was 6:00 am. What did he think he was doing calling me at that time in the morning? I decided to take the call because it was special.

In February, we were invited to the White House. That was the coolest thing in the world. It was so special to see the players we had recruited to the University of Texas walking down the steps of the White House to meet the President of the United States. We were lucky enough to spend one and a half hours with the President. The coaches' wives sat there and cried openly.

The President came up to our players and asked them each a question. "Where are you from? What does you father do? What do you plan on doing after college?" After it was over, Sally and I stayed and ate dinner with the President and First Lady. Out of 120 players who made the trip, the President asked me about four of our players during dinner. He asked me about just four of our players. "Tell me about so and so." Those four kids made an impact on the President.

Most of you remember the movie "Friday Night Lights." In the fall, they are going to do a TV show based on the film. I was asked to be a parent in the TV show. My role was to be a parent talking with the head coach on a Thursday night before the opening game of the season. I can tell you this: I was good in that role. I had 33 years of experience hearing all of the problems from parents. The director came up to me and said, "Coach, here is the script for your role." I replied, "No! Let me give you the script, big boy."

The head coach in the TV show is 28 years old. He did not know anything about football. I really jumped on him hard. "You had my other son play for you and kept him from getting into college football. I have been to practice the last three nights and you and your staff go home after practice. You do not care about the players." I was good. I was as obnoxious as any parent that has ever faced a coach.

After the filming was over, the producer walked over to me and said, "Coach, you need to be more aggressive." He walked away and the guy playing the young coach said, "If parents treat you this way, I would quit. I would not want to be a coach." I assured him it was this way.

Let's get into some football and have some fun. About four years ago, we were in that nine wins, 11 wins, nine wins, 10 wins, 11 wins category. We just could not get over the hump. I called my brother, Watson Brown, who is the head coach at the University of Alabama-Birmingham and talked with him. That year UAB won six games and lost five. I told Watson, "I am so sick of winning nine games." Watson cut me off right there. "Don't you ever talk like that!" I do understand his point. It was a bad call and it was a bad day.

Our staff tried to figure out the teams that were winning national championships in college and *why*! Everyone in this room wants to win a state championship. When you are lucky enough to win a championship, it is the coolest thing. You feel good about yourself, about your players, and all the years you put into the plan to win the championship. It probably will not be your best coaching job. It may not be with your best group of players. It will be a group of kids that that play the best together. That may get confusing at times.

Roy Williams, the basketball coach at North Carolina, called me on game day at the Rose Bowl. He left a voice message. "You really need to win the game because it is really hard to get back to that position again. Your friends will be proud of you like they would anyway. You will enjoy watching your players show their pride. All of the people that you did not know anything about will treat you different. It is really weird."

It is amazing. You will be treated differently because you stopped the other team on a fourth-and-four situation. Neither team knew how to lose. I found out that 19 seconds can be a long time. If Southern Cal had a little more time, they would have beaten us. That is what it all comes down to in the game of football.

Everyone asks me what I told the team before the game. Let me tell you the truth. It was game day and I was sitting in my room by myself. It was a long day before the game. I do not get to watch TV that much, but I had it on to kill time. I was switching from channel to channel. Do you ever watch *Jerry Springer* on TV? I had never watched *Jerry Springer* on TV before. They had five episodes in a row of the TV series. They were the craziest group of people I had ever seen. I will tell you this. If your girlfriend or your wife asks you to go to the program, don't do it. I sat there and watched about three hours of the program and I began to wonder why these fools were going on TV with their problems. My conclusion was these people must not own a TV.

Now, here I was getting ready to play possibly the greatest team to ever play college football. Pete Carroll is a great coach. When you face your team before the game, what do you tell them? I walked into our locker room and I could see they were very nervous. We still were a young team. This is what I figured out about the team.

If the game was important to them, it had to be important for me, because I had spent many years to get to this situation. So the question was what to tell them to get them to relax. I walked into the dressing room and all I said was this. "Have any of you ever watched the program *Jerry Springer*?" The team about died laughing. I told them if they were ever asked to be on the *Jerry Springer* TV show not to do it. "Don't go!" I went on to tell them a few other things before the game.

I have been coaching for 33 years and the only thing I could tell them was to have fun! "What a neat moment for all of the team members. You have worked so hard to get here you have to enjoy the moment. You do not want to get this far and be a noodle. When you go over that hill going into the Rose Bowl there will be a lot of University of Texas fans there. Throw up the "Hook-em Horns" sign to all of the Longhorns and smile. Enjoy that moment! Take that with you for the rest of your life. It is an important time for all of us. When you walk out on the game field, you look up into the hills around the Rose Bowl. Very few people get to play for the national championship. Enjoy this! When the game starts you have fun, but you must work your butt off during the game. But have fun!"

At halftime we were up by a score of 16 to 7. Southern Cal could have been up or we could have been up more. So the question becomes what to tell them at halftime. We told them the score of 16 to 7 was only an illusion. I reminded them that Southern Cal had won 34 straight games and they are going to

come out of their locker room like gangbusters. They are going to play as hard as they can because they like where they are and they do not want to lose what they have accomplished.

I reminded them how cool this feeling was. "Isn't this fun? We are on national TV, it is the last game of the season, and we are fighting a great team for the national championship. Guys, this is the coolest thing in the world."

What do you tell the team after the game? In the dressing room we had University of Texas alumni Lance Armstrong, Matthew McConaughey, the actor, and pitcher Roger Clemens with us. I asked Matthew if this was the same feeling as when you win an Oscar. He replied, "Oh no. This is a lot better." He had been there and knew the feeling. We had touched the hearts of many other people.

This is what I told the team. "This may be the best sports moment for some of you for the rest of your life. However, do not let this be the best moment of your life. When you are 50 years old, I do not want any of you to tell anyone, "The best moment in my life was winning the national championship in 2005-2006." It would be a sad thing if a sporting event would be the best moment for these young men.

I have had guys come up to me in Texas with their wives and children and they tell me an athletic event was the best thing to happen to them in their life. I tell them, "Man, your wife is standing behind you." What is really sad is when the wife steps up and says, "Coach, he is telling the truth." Men, I am having too much fun and I can see I am going to get in trouble if I do not get to the football aspects of this lecture.

We studied the game to see how you win football games. We looked at who had won the national championship since 1980 and why they won. We learned some aspects about the game that had carried over from the past years. Everyone in football used to say, "You win championships with defense." In the modern day of the game, if you do not score a lot of points you are not going to win the big games. The team that scores a lot of points is going to win in modern-day football. You can win by playing defense and by winning the kicking game in most games. But there is going to be a game where you have to score a lot of points to win the game.

We started to open up our offense. We felt we had to throw the ball down the field to get the defense off us. We decided we were going to throw short, throw deep, and we are going to spread the defense out so our offense could be more productive. If that did not work, we were going to the no-huddle offense. We wanted to screw the defense up and get them tired. We decided we were going to be aggressive on offense. We were not going to be stupid and try to throw the ball every play if our offense could not block the defense on the pass rush.

We decided to figure out which players the opponents have that we feel we have a better chance to exploit. We look at their best corner, their best cover man, and their worst cover man. We are going to find their worst defender. We are going to run at their best pass rusher. We must figure out a way to go after him, and then we are going to go after the others. There is always a weak link on the defense. There is always a lazy player on defense. That is true of your team as well. I know the opponents know who our weak link is.

We are going to find the weakest cover man and we are going to wear his butt out. Find the softest defender up front, and when you run the ball, run at that man. Remember the old adage, "We are going to whip their best player." We say: If they have a soft player, don't mess with the best player. Run away from him. Make his coach tell him he likes the way he trails the plays. Don't mess with the best player. We like to think we are smart. Smart means that when that best player gets tired you can run at him. Don't mess with him early in the game. Make him a "chase defender."

Rushing defense was the second point we looked at in our study. You must be able to stop the run on defense. We have two or three points worth considering. We want to win the *turnover battle* first. Next, we want to win the *explosive plays*. An explosive play is a run over 12 yards and a pass over 16 yards. When we win the explosive plays in the game more than our opponents do, we usually win the game.

When we have won both explosive plays and turnovers, we are 100 percent in winning games. We have won every game when we win those two categories. It has nothing to do with stats.

A third point to consider is this. When we have outrushed the opponents we have never lost a game. A lot of this means that at the end of the game, when we are way ahead, we have been able to run the ball and make first downs. Against Ohio State, we beat them and we rushed for 113 yards and they rushed for 112 yards. That stat means we are stopping the opponents rushing the ball and we are able to run the ball against our opponents. Rushing defense means you are able to run the ball more than your opponents are. When the opponents can rush the ball, they beat you down and they discourage your defense. If they can run the ball against us, they are keeping the ball out of our offense's hands.

I do not have the final stats from last season, but at one time we had scored 35 times in four plays or less. We are going to throw the ball down the field. We are going to isolate a good player on a bad player and try to make that work for us. We are going to try to wear them down and keep their defense on the field. Rushing defense and scoring defense are important.

Don't worry about all of the stats. You may have been ahead in every game—and the opponents had to throw the ball at the end of the game all of the time—and that skews your stats.

The other thing we learned came from Greg Robinson when he was our defensive coordinator the year before. He coached at Kansas City before he came to Texas. He did a smart thing with our defense. It really helped us as a team and it helped me as a coach. In the last playoff game, the Kansas City Chiefs lost to Indianapolis. They lost by a score of 49 to 24. On the last play of that game Indianapolis had the ball. It was a fourth-down-and-four situation.

There was no chance for Kansas City to win that game. In our first defensive meeting when he came to Texas he showed that last play from the Kansas City vs. Indianapolis game. It shows every player on the field for Kansas City chasing the ball, even though they had no chance of winning. It was the last play of the year but they were busting their butts on that play. His point was this:

It does not matter if you are a starter or a second-team player, if you are ahead or behind, if it is the first quarter or the last play of the game, you are who you are. Either you *do* chase the ball every play on defense or you *don't* chase it. You cannot be a part-time player. You are either a full-time player or you aren't a full-time player. That makes so much sense to me. Now when our second-team defense is in the game you will see our coaches working with them just as hard as they do on the first play of the game, just because of the message that sends to everyone on the team. I believe that is the reason we kept playing hard when we were down by 12 points. We told our players to keep playing hard. We told them not to look at the clock. If you are a football player, you play hard every play. They are not out there to analyze. If we jump up by 10 points on a team and end up getting beat, we say that is an illusion. If we are a good team, it will come back to you. If the opponents jump up by 10 points, we tell them that is an illusion. That is what football is today. It is different phases of life. You must instill the desire for the team to keep playing hard every play. It will work out for you in the end.

Turnover margin is huge. It just absolutely kills you. We dropped 23 passes that we had a chance to intercept this year. However, we did intercept 10 passes.

You can get into a lot of other stats in determining who wins games. Most teams won more games if they had the best scoring defense in the country. The team with the best scoring offense won 80 percent of the time. All of those stats are the same way as you get into to them.

Coach Royal told me to look for players on the teams that have *it*. When I went to Texas, a young coach came on the field to visit with us. He asked Coach Royal how to become a successful coach. Coach Royal is the type of person that can take something complicated and make it very simple. Coach Royal said, "Well, if you have *it*, you can win. If you do not have *it*, you will not win. If you do not know what *it* is, you do not have a chance of making *it*." The young coach looked at me with a questioning look on his face. I shook my head back and forth and said, "I can't help you with that, Coach." Later the young coach walked away and Coach Royal looked at me and said, "Mack, that young coach does not have *it*."

There are some special players that have *it*. I was listing to Coach Craig Howard of Nease High School. He coached the Player of the Year in Florida in quarterback Tim Tebows. Tim Tebows had it. He is big and tall and fast. He had *it* and he is a leader.

Vince Young had *it*. People talk about how big and strong and fast Vince Young is. All of that is true, but he was not a good quarterback 19 games ago. At some time in between those games, he decided to be a team player and he became a great quarterback. Now he will make about 30 million dollars. About 20 games ago, he completed four passes against Oklahoma. We did not score in that game and that was the first time we did not score in forever. The next week he completed six passes. He completed three to our players and three to Missouri players. I thought he was color-blind. I benched him. I took him out of the game. That was 19 games ago. Most people forgot that fact. I took him out of the game and this is what I told him. "Your career is going to be defined by the way you act in the next half. You need to support the quarterback we are playing when you are not in the game. You must be a team player."

To his credit, he walked over and sat down on the bench. He was a cheerleader for the rest of that game. He started the next week and he played very hard. That was a defining moment for Vince Young. If he had pouted about being benched, he would have quit the team. But he did not pout, because he had *it*.

If there is a player on your team that has *it*, make him the leader of the team. If he does not have *it*, do not let him lead the team. Find the player that has *it*. It may not be the fastest player on the team, or the biggest, or the best. There are enough players on the team that have *it* that you can put together a good team. If you sit around and comment to the coaching staff that you wish one of the players will get better, he probably will not get better. He may at some point, but he is not going to help you win now.

We do not waste any time talking about potential. We practice and we plan on playing those that work hard. I dismissed a player from spring practice the other day because he was late again for practice. I just read some quotes from Coach John Wooden. I use to think being part of the team was a big part of winning. Coach Wooden said, "Being excited about being a part of the team is the answer. Your players must be willing to give up something to be excited about being part of the team."

We have learned so much about teamwork the last two years. Our players may not be as good as you think they are. We have some great players. We have many good players with good character and good hearts. We had 51 players with over a 3.0 average this past year. They go to work every day. We are not flashy. We are going to play to win every game. Find the players that like the game and work with them. If they do not like the process, they will not make good players. Coaches can get into trouble in some of these situations. You do not need to run your mouth and make excuses about the players. The less you say, the less you have to take back. "We did not do a very good job!"

The media wants you to run your mouth so they can run everything you say. If you tell them you have a young team or that you have had many injuries, no one cares about that. "I am the head coach and we did not do a good job of preparing the players for the game. We have to go back to work." That is all you need to say.

Since 1999, we have not lost two games in a row. A lot of that is because we do not spend a lot of time talking about what we did wrong the week before. We want to get rid of all of the excuses. Excuses die. Get rid of them. They are just a cancer to your team. No one wants to hear excuses.

"Dance with the one who brung you!" If you have a real good player, play him. I bet it shocked a lot of you that Vince Young had the ball in his hands on fourth and five yards to go in the fourth quarter. What a shocker! We called a pass play and hoped that Southern Cal had the receivers covered and Vince could scramble with the ball.

This is how you win football games. First, win the turnover battle. Every time you work with the team this spring, you coach turnovers on both sides of the ball, every play, every minute of the day. If a back is carrying the ball low, you should make a big issue out of it. If the ball hits the ground, make the player that caused it go to the ground to get on the ball. If you do not want to do that, have him run a lap or a sprint. The point is to talk about turnovers every day. Pete Carroll and Greg Robinson win games because they force turnovers. They are not as interested in stats as they are in turnovers.

The second point is to figure out how to be explosive on offense. We do not have to block every player on every play. We may only get three yards on a play. Those three yards count for our offense. We run the isolation a lot. We used to think a team could not stop our best play. Now we know if the defense is any good, they can stop our best play. Do not be stubborn about the offense.

We work on situations that come up in a game just as you do. We look at our first-down efficiency and our third-down efficiency. In addition, we look at our red-zone efficiency. We scored points 80 percent of the time when we were in the red zone.

We have kept records on sacks and lost-yardage plays over the last five years. We keep a chart on sacks and scoring. When we are sacked, we have only a 13 percent chance of getting a drive for a score. It is amazing what a sack does to stop our offense. We stress not to be snacked. You have to figure out a system where your quarterback is not sacked a lot. A sack is a huge motivator for the defense. Florida State has done a great job with the sack over the years. They have beaten up on people by making sacks on defense.

I am part of the reason that Coach Bobby Bowden is going into the Hall of Fame. How bad is this? They sent me a letter and asked me to write Coach Bowden a real nice letter on his 25 years of success at Florida State. The reason they asked me to write the letter was because I had been responsible for a large part of his success. He beat us year after year.

As a staff, you must be fair with the players. Fairness is what it takes to win. We chart playing time. We are going to be direct and honest with players and parents. When a parent comes in to see me about not playing their son, I tell them it is not about playing their son. I let them know it is about our team. We keep a file film on each player. We will show the film with the parents and kids. I sit there and watch the film and point out how the player is loafing in practice. I have used this technique three times in eight years. The parents will chew out the players when they see that film. Kids will not tell their parents that they loafed in practice. They will not tell their parents what the problem is because they do not want their parents upset. We tell all of our players we are keeping the film files on them. We want to be direct and to be honest.

Let me touch on our "team game plan." It is an area where I get involved more than anything else. I learned late in my career as a coach that you cannot have an offense by itself and a defense by itself and then try to play together as a team. If the opponents are going to run up and down the field on us, we are not going to kick the ball when we get across the 50-yard line. We are going to run it four downs. If it is a game where the opponents cannot score much on us we will punt the ball to them more. We work this all out together.

In the game against Southern Cal, we knew they were good and they could move the ball on anyone. Early in the first quarter, we had a fourth-and-two at midfield and we went for it and lost two yards. What was important about that situation was that we made a statement to our kids that we needed to score a lot of points to beat them. We did not want them to panic when the other team scored. We wanted them to be aware that we could not stop them from scoring and that we would have to score a lot of points to win.

We chart our kickers on distance and directions. I am sure most of you do the same thing in this area.

On play selection, we have it down to where it is simple. If your kids do not know what your favorite plays are on third and fourth downs, then you are not very good. Our kids can call our plays when it gets down to those situations. If you do not have tendencies, you do not have good players. You need to have someone that the defense has to worry about stopping. Make sure you have your game plans together so your kids know what you are going to do in most of the situations that come up in a game.

The worst thing we do as coaches is that we put too much offense or defense in our system. It is because we have too much time, but we know we cannot practice everything on offense against all the things defenses can do in a game. Then we give the kids a hard time when they screw up in a game.

We may look complicated, but we must stay simple. Use common sense. You must have enough offense to win, but not be so complicated that you cannot execute. Lean on the side of too little rather than too much offense.

We must make sure a kid has done in practice what you are asking him to do when he gets in the game under pressure. If you have not worked with him in practice, it is not going to work in a game under pressure. "We have been over this situation." When did we go over that situation? "Five weeks ago." That does not work.

I get scripts every day of the plays our offense is going to run in practice. I make sure our offense is practicing what is in our game plan. I mark down how many times we run a play and how many people are running the play. Earlier in our career at Texas, we put players in the game that had not practiced the plays we were running in a game. The coaches would tell me we ran those plays in practice this week. But, they did not have that particular player run the play in practice. It is not fair to that player. You must make sure you practice what you are running in a game.

In philosophy, "Be known for something." Do what you do best. We decided a few years ago that the best thing for us to do on offense was to run the zone play. We knew we could throw the ball from that set because we could pass-protect. So we started running the zone play.

We can run the inside zone from every formation we use. When our offensive-line coach and players go to practice, they know they are going to practice the zone play. They know that on fourth down we are going to run the zone play. They know that on first down we are going to run the zone play.

We can run the option out of the set. It is a quick pitch for the quarterback, because we do not want him to be hit on the play. We are going to run a simple draw play for those sets. In addition, we are going to run a counter play, and that is it. You will be shocked to know how simple we are. We have five schemes we use. Our offense is no more complicated than our pass protection. But our running game is going to be consistent. We are going to be good at it and we are not going to make a lot of mistakes in the running game. They are going to run it over and over and over, and we think we are going to outexecute the defense.

We run play-action passes off our best running plays. Vince Young was a real good runner and an average passer. Over the summer, we figured everyone would make a big effort to stop Vince in the running game. We came up with the play-action pass off the zone read play. That is probably the reason we were able to win the national championship. The play-action fake just killed every defense we played. We only gave up sacks because the defense was determined to stop the run first.

You need to figure out the best ways to get ball deep. The reason most players play cornerback in high school is because they cannot catch the football. That is the reason they are playing on defense. We want to find the slowest, shortest,

and weakest player on defense and put our best receiver on him and throw deep. If you throw at him enough, he will get nervous and commit a pass interference penalty, because he is so scared he is going to get beat deep.

You must create explosiveness. Spread the defense out and sling the ball deep. You need to find out what you want to do and then find out a way to do it in the game.

We are going to figure out four plays a game where we feel we have a chance to get a shot at a touchdown off the play. Take a number of TD shots each game. Do not put these plays in the week before the game. Work on them several weeks before you run them in a game. If you are far ahead in a game, do not run those plays. Save those plays for another week.

When things are not going well, the coaches have to figure out how to change the momentum. Have a play that can change the swing of the game. Kids can get emotional when something good happens in that situation.

We must prepare for special situations. We practice these daily game situations as close to full speed as possible and try to take fewer risks.

- First down
- Third down
- Goal line/short yardage
- No huddle
- One minute
- Four minutes

We film these plays and we keep score for our offense and our defense. The best thing we have done in recent years is to concentrate on controlling the ball. If it is third down and we are close to the 50-yard line, we know we have two downs to get a first down. If we cross that 50-yard line, we are going to take our chances on getting the first down.

I do not want to hurt anyone's feelings, but the punters are very different. To ask the placekicker to kick a 35-yard field goal can be difficult at times. You shake his hand on the way out for the kick and he is sweating. You know that is not good. When we played Texas A&M and Oklahoma, I told our kicker that if he missed the field goal against those teams he would have to live in College Station or Norman, Oklahoma the rest of his life. That is when he told me he would make the field goal. You have to have a little fun in this game.

We are going to run our one-minute offense every day. This is the reason we score so much at the end of a half and at the end of the game. It is a part of our regular offense. I do not think you can just throw the ball on Thursday in practice and get the job done.

We are going to run the no-huddle offense that the defense allows us to run. Two years ago, we were behind 35 to 7 with two minutes to go in the first half at home against Oklahoma State. That can really be trouble at Texas because the fans can be tough in those situations.

We went to our one-minute offense and scored. In the second half, we went with the one-minute offense the entire half and we won the game 56 to 35. We did that because we could run the one-minute offense.

We work our best players against each other every day. If you can put your best defenders on your best receiver and so on, then you will see it is easier in the game than it is in practice. When we get to the game, we are going to be fine. We tell our team they will never play a better team on Saturday than what they practiced against every day.

We repeat offensive schemes with multiple plays over and over. We use different formations to run the same plays. In the national championship game, we ran very few formations because, beginning at 10 minutes to go in the second quarter, we stayed in our no-huddle offense the rest of the game.

When we ran the zone play in 1999 along with a lot of other plays, it was not a good play for us. It was not good for us until we really committed to

the zone play and started working on it a lot more than we did before (Diagram #1). When we finally believed in the play, it became a good play.

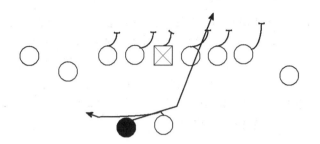

Diagram #1. Inside Zone Play

We run the zone read play. It is a simple option that most of you have run your whole life (Diagram #2). You have seen it recently at a lot of places. Urban Meyer is running the zone read play. Clemson is running it. Tulane is running the play and West Virginia is running the play. It is the simplest play in the world to run if your quarterback can run the ball and get seven yards. We have a bootleg off the zone read play. In addition, we have a play-action play off the zone read.

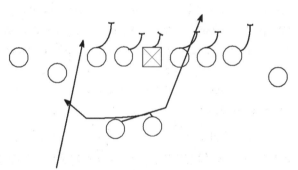

Read Weak end/Give or Keep

Diagram #2. Inside Zone Read

Then we run the Iso play for toughness. We feel we must keep certain plays in our offense that we have to play against. This way, our defense has to see them every day in practice. To me, if your offense is not a reflection of what you are going to face during the coming year, you are not being fair to your defense. We know we are not going to win without a good defense. We may not run a certain play in a game, but we run them in practice against our defense because we know we are going to see those plays during the season and we must be ready to stop certain plays.

We run the lead draw play to the tight-end side and the split-end side. We also run the quarterback draw and the draw pass. We run those with a little different tempo. We are going to run the zone and the draw. Then we are going to run the counter play and the quarterback counter play. Also, we are going to run the counter pass.

We are going to run some type of option with the quarterback where he can pitch the ball (Diagram #3). We do not want him keeping the ball, but we are going to force the defense to look at misdirection plays.

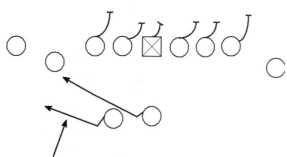

Read Weak end/Pitch or Keep

Diagram #3. Weakside Option

We are going to force the defense to look at the zone play, the iso, the screens, and draws, and make them defend the option plays. That is what we do. That is it on offense. It may sound like it is simple—and it is simple. When we got away from this scheme, we were not very good. We can run the outside zone, but that play is a lot like the outside sweep play.

If you run so many formations that it confuses the quarterback, then you have too many formations. The quarterback must be comfortable with the formations. We are going to build our offense around our quarterback. If he can throw the ball, we will throw it. If he is a great runner, we are going to have him run the ball. It is that simple.

Here are some points we stress with our offensive staff. We use multiple formations with the same personnel. We are not going to hand the ball to a player who fumbles or who does not have a chance to score. We do not throw to a guy that cannot catch it. We put our three best players at quarterback, tailback, and wide receiver. Everyone else is going to be moved over to defense.

Our tailback must be a person that has good ball-security techniques. He must be productive and he must be tough.

Our wide receiver must be able to catch the football. He must be able to get deep on pass routes. He must be able to make YACs: yards after catch.

Our quarterback must be smart. He must be mobile. And he must be an accurate passer.

We use a two-deep chart for every game. We may play our best 15 to 22 players. We play the most productive players, players that are winners who we trust. We must be smart in substituting. We will substitute between the 20-yard lines. We do not sub during the first five minutes of either half. We do not sub in the last five minutes of the half or the last five minutes of the game, depending on the score at that time of the game.

Men, have a great spring and a great season. I appreciate you being here today. Thank you.

Brian Callahan

PASS BLOCKING IN THE OFFENSIVE LINE

University of Akron

In my lecture today, there are some ideas I want to share with you. I want to give you some general information about our protection scheme. I want to talk about the design of our pocket and some individual pass sets. I want to cover the basics for man and zone protections. The last thing is dealing with a dominant pass rusher and twists in the pass rush. The areas of emphasis will be eliminating quarterback pressure, sacks, and interceptions.

To accomplish the goals we have set in the offensive line, there is some theory the line needs to know. They need to know the point to which the quarterback drops and where he launches the ball. They must know if they have help in the blocking scheme and where it is. That fact will directly affect the set of the offensive linemen.

In obvious passing down and in the shotgun set, the offensive linemen must know they can assume a two-point stance. However, since we have become a run-from-the-gun team, we may be in a three-point stance.

The offensive linemen must study the defensive tendencies in rushing the quarterback. They need to know in down and distance situations, the type of stunt, blitz, or secondary pressure to expect from the defense. At our level, we do not have any stationary blitzes. Teams do not align and use straight blitzes against the offense any more. They use line movements, twists, and stunts to pressure the quarterback. Through film study, the linemen need to know the types of pass-rush moves the defenders use in their schemes.

I do not have time to research each defender's individual moves. I assign that to our offensive linemen—to watch film and study their opponents. They must know what they will face in the pass rush.

Each offensive lineman has a responsibility in defending the pocket. The center and both offensive guards are responsible for the depth of the pocket. The offensive tackles and tight ends are responsible for defending the width of the pocket. The offensive tackle defines the width of the pocket by drawing an imaginary line down his outside foot. The offensive tackles and tight ends can also be responsible for the depth of the pocket if the defender takes an inside charge.

The "design of the pocket" is what we refer to as home plate (Diagram #1). From the line of scrimmage, there is a three-yard line of defense, which defines the depth of the guards and center. The imaginary line drawn on the outside foot of the tackles defines the width of the pocket. The tackles maintain that width up to a depth of seven yards. In a five-step drop by the quarterback, his depth is about seven yards. On the seven-step drop, the quarterback is at the depth of nine yards.

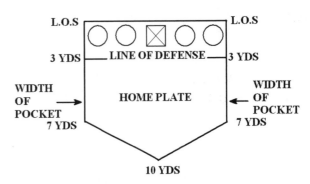

Diagram #1. Design of the Pocket

The three-step drop by the quarterback is from three to five yards in depth. We feel that if the tackle can protect up to the depth of seven yards, he can run the defender past the quarterback on any drop.

The pass set is getting out of the stance and into a position to stop the defender's charge. Pass blocking is like playing defense in basketball. The object is to stay between the defender and the quarterback. The aiming point for an offensive tackle is to get his outside eye on the inside eye of the defender. The aiming point for the center and guards is slightly inside the midline of the defender. They defend the depth and stay more square on the defender. They still have to defend the inside, so they must remain slightly inside with their aiming point. For this alignment, we say the offensive lineman's nose is inside the defender's nose.

I believe one of the most important items in pass-protection technique is pass posture for the lineman. He must maintain his stagger and keep his power foot straight ahead as long as possible. In the alignment of the right guard and tackle, the right foot is staggered. The stagger of the offensive linemen varies with their height and ability. The taller the player, the wider the stagger.

We want the inside foot of the offensive linemen straight ahead. We want their hips as square to the line of scrimmage as possible. We do not want to turn our hips and let the defender counter back to the inside. If the linemen turn too soon before they get to the depth of seven yards, they cannot run the defender past the quarterback.

The linemen bend at the knees and not at the waist. We want them in a power-clean position as in weightlifting. They use short shuffle steps in their retreat from the line of scrimmage. That prevents them from getting outside the center of their gravity. We refer to this technique as skating. We want to punch, redirect, and cancel all inside charges.

We refer to "set and stab" as the hat and hands in the actual set of the offensive lineman. The hat and hands come up from the three-point stance. The stab is the punch with the hands. The coaching points are thumbs up and elbows in close to the body. We want the hands on each number of the opponent's jersey.

We want to strike upward blows with the hands. I want to get a slight upward blow with a partial roll of the hips. We want to sit and separate from the defender. We do not want the defender grabbing the offensive lineman. We want to avoid contact with the defender as much as possible.

In our blocking scheme, we have a "free man" rule. The free man rule applies when the offensive lineman's responsibility drops into coverage or his gap becomes vacated or open. Once they check to see their defender is gone, they look to help someone in the scheme. If there is no help needed, he is to wipe the adjacent defensive lineman's hip or clean up the trash. Cleaning up the trash means to remove some of the defenders and widen the throwing lane of the quarterback.

It is important for the offensive linemen to know where to set. An offensive lineman has two things to take into consideration. He must know the throwing spot for the quarterback. How deep the quarterback sets and his location is the first thing he considers. The second thing the lineman has to consider is the location of the defender. Those two items will determine the rush angle of the defender (Diagram #2). In the diagram, you can see the angle for the defensive end changes with the launch point of the ball. The tackle in the second example has to take two skates to get to the proper depth on the defender.

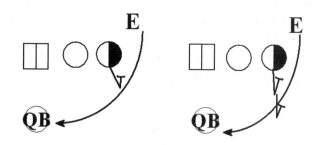

Diagram #2. Angle of Rush

The two biggest mistakes in pass protection are setting in the wrong place and getting outside the center of gravity. Setting in the wrong place is a tackle setting wide on a tight rusher. That gives up the inside to the rusher. Getting outside the center of gravity comes from the offensive lineman taking too big a step in his shuffle. He loses his balance and can be pushed or pulled off balance easily. The key to pass protection is setting in the right place and maintaining great posture. If the blocker keeps great posture and moves his feet, he can win the battle.

The individual pass set on a three-step drop is short (Diagram #3). The quarterback in the three-step drop throws the ball from three to five yards deep. If the defender aligns head-up on the offensive lineman, he short sets to the inside and takes away the inside charge of the defender.

Diagram #3. Head-Up Alignment

The inside power foot is moved about six inches to the inside to secure the inside against the rush that way.

With the outside-eye alignment by the defender, the offensive blocker moves his feet in the set (Diagram #4). However, he does not travel with the foot movement. He picks up the power foot, puts it down in the same spot, and takes on the defender in a short set. With the outside-eye defender, the tackle is already on his aiming point and does not change his alignment. The guard may move slightly inside on his set.

Diagram #4. Outside-Eye Alignment

If the defender aligns on the outside shoulder of the offensive blocker (Diagram #5), he sets short and outside. He makes sure he does not give up an inside gap with his set. If we go back to the two mistakes in the set, this is one of them. If he sets too wide, he gives up the inside gap to a counter move. The set is a step drop and skate back for the tackle.

Diagram #5. Outside-Shoulder Alignment

Offensive tackles face extremely wide alignments by speed rushers. When we encounter these types of alignments, we use a "jump technique" (Diagram #6). The offensive tackle takes a short drop-step and reads the second step of the defensive end. He takes the drop-step because it gives him more time to see which way the defender is going. In addition, it allows the blocker to get on the defender late and keeps the defender's hands down. After he reads the step, he attacks the inside V in the neck of the defender with an aggressive run block. If the defender comes to the inside, the tackle drive blocks him down.

Diagram #6. Wide Defender Alignment

The guard or center also faces a wide technique by the defender. The 3 technique player or shade player in a definite passing situation widens his alignment (Diagram #7). The defenders may widen to a 4i technique on the guard or a 1 technique on the center. If that occurs, the guard and center use the same technique. They may also use the jump technique to cover up the defenders. However, they need to exercise care not to do it every time.

Diagram #7. Center/Guard Wide Alignment

The offensive linemen in that situation set for width and depth. They have to put themselves into a position to get on the defender's number without being turned in his set. They take lateral steps to stay square and not give too much depth. If they drop too deep, they will be in the quarterback's lap.

In the five-step and seven-step drops, the launch point is seven and nine yards, respectively. In our individual pass sets, it does not matter whether it is a five- or seven-step drop. For the interior three offensive linemen, there is no difference among the three-, five-, or seven-step drops. They establish the depth of the pocket on all drops.

They establish the line of defense at three yards and hold. They want to keep the defenders on the line of scrimmage as long as they can. They can use the jump technique if the situation provides for it. However, the center must always set back on the five- or seven-step drop because of the guard's deep alignment. We get our guards off the line of scrimmage in their normal alignment to work our zone-running schemes. If the center does not get back, he opens the twist stunts to get to the hips of the guards.

The offensive tackle's set changes in the five- or seven-step drop. His steps will change. If he faces the head-up defender, he short sets to the inside to take away the inside charge. This set is exactly like the set on a three-step drop. Our tackles never set on a 4i alignment. They pass that off to the guards. The guards have the better angle on the 4i technique.

On the outside-eye alignment on the offensive tackle, we vertical set and "work the line" (Diagram #8). The line is the imaginary line drawn on the outside foot of the tackle seven yards deep. The tackle kicks one step straight back with his outside foot and drags the inside power foot. This allows the offensive tackle to react to the defender's movement inside.

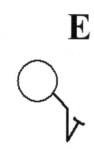

Diagram #8. Work the Line

If there is no inside move, the tackle kicks again down the line. It gives him enough depth so he will not turn before the defensive end passes the quarterback's set point. If he gives too much width as he works the line, he gives up the inside and lets the defender have a two-way go. Giving up too much width allows the defenders to run twist stunts more effectively against the blocker.

The offensive tackle on an outside-shoulder defender vertical sets and works the line (Diagram #9). He sets two steps straight back and repeats that movement as he retreats. Notice the differences between the eye and shoulder alignment in the diagram. In the eye alignment, he sets one step because of the threat of the inside movement.

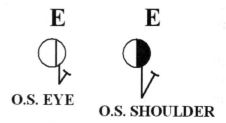

Diagram #9. Three-/Five-Step Outside Shoulder

If the offensive tackle gets the wide alignment, there is no immediate threat to the inside. The tackle works the line with his inside foot. He works for width and depth to one yard outside the original line. Once the tackle gets one yard width, he works that line straight back with his inside foot. He kicks out with width and depth to get his inside foot on the line and works it straight back.

In the offensive line, we have to block twists by the defense. There are two parts to blocking the twist. You have to deal with the penetrator and the looper. The first part of passing the twist between two offensive linemen is dealing with the penetrator (Diagram #10). The offensive guard dealing with the penetrator keeps him on the line of scrimmage. He pounds him with his post foot and gets his hat in the crack of the penetrator going out on the offensive tackle. He stays on the penetrator until he feels and sees the looper. He throws the penetrator outside as he feels inside for the offensive tackle taking him over. When he comes off the penetrator, he sets straight back and looks for a pass rush move by the defender.

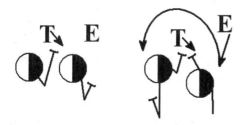

Diagram #10. Passing the Twist Penetrator

If the defender loops on the offensive tackle, he alerts the guard with a "twist" call. He opens his hips for depth and mirrors the looper. If the defenders are on different levels, he stays on the looper and man blocks the twist stunt. If the twist stunt is on the same level, he violently bumps the offensive guard off his block on the penetrator. He passes the looper to the guard. He snatches the penetrator from the guard. We call it ripping the sink off the wall. The tackle grabs the penetrator and pulls him into the block.

We have a man protection scheme. In our man protection, the offensive line has the four down linemen and the Mike linebacker. The running back has either a linebacker or a defensive back. If they bring more than we can block, we throw hot routes or sight-adjust our patterns.

If the defense is a 3-4 type of defense, the offensive line has the three down linemen, the Mike linebacker, and whoever is designated as the extra linebacker. The running backs have assignments on other linebackers and defensive backs.

In our man protection, we use a fan set. The term we use is "Momo," which stands for "man on" and "man outside." The right guard and tackle are responsible for the number 1 and number 2 men on the line of scrimmage. If the right guard is uncovered and the defense covers the right tackle with a man on and a man outside of him, they are number 1 and number 2 on the line of scrimmage.

We do not set wide in that situation. If the defensive end outside the tackle drops into coverage, we have two blockers on one defender. If the tackle kicks out to block the defensive end and the end drops, he has no one to block or we have a double-team on the defender covering the tackle. I do not like that situation. If we do not kick for width, it helps the offensive linemen with the twist pick-up.

This is how we teach the fan set. The offensive tackle sets on the number 1 man on the line of scrimmage, with his eyes on the number 2 defender (Diagram #11). The offensive tackle adjusts to the widest rusher in the rush scheme. He uses a visual key to know the defender he will block. Ninety-nine percent of the time, he blocks the outside rusher.

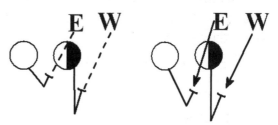

Diagram #11. Tackle on the Fan

On occasion, the guard applies the "use" technique (Diagram #12). That occurs when the defensive end fires into the outside V of the neck of the offensive tackle and drives him inside. The defense rushes a defender outside of the tackle, hoping he comes free. The guard kicks out behind the offensive tackle and takes that rusher. The defense tries to put two defenders in one gap on the offensive tackle.

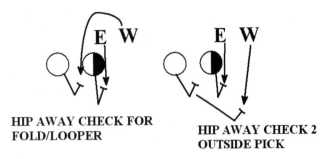

HIP AWAY CHECK FOR FOLD/LOOPER

HIP AWAY CHECK 2 OUTSIDE PICK

Diagram #12. Guard Fan Set

The offensive guard in the fan set sets on an imaginary 4i technique. He keys the hip of the defender over the offensive tackle. If the hip comes his way, he blocks him as shown in Diagram #11.

If the 4i technique's hip goes away from the guard, he has a number of things that can happen. The worst-case, and least-run, situation is two defenders rushing outside the offensive tackle. In that case, he kicks behind the tackle and applies the "use" technique.

The second thing that could occur is the loop stunt coming from the outside. When the hip goes away, the guard sets to the number 1 rusher, checks the number 2 rusher, and reacts. If the number 2 rusher comes on a loop, he sets inside and waits for him. If the number 2 rusher comes straight up the field, he bumps the offensive tackle onto number 2 and he takes number 1.

If the number 1 defender's hip goes away from the offensive guard and the number 2 defender drops into coverage, he checks back inside for an inside-linebacker blitz (Diagram #13).

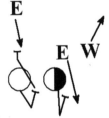

NO #2, CHECK OT, HELP ON INSIDE LB.

Diagram #13. Guard Fan Linebacker

If the inside linebacker is not blitzing, the guard comes back and helps the center on the noseguard or the 1-technique shade.

In our slide or gap protection, we usually have a man slide in the scheme (Diagram #14). The slide starts with the first uncovered offensive lineman to the playside going back. We determine the playside as the side of the running back's block. The protection slides away from the playside and blocks the immediate gap backside. In slide protection, if no threat appears in the gap, we leave the blocker's body in the hole. He long-arms the inside gap. That means the offensive blocker gets his inside hand on the defender in that gap and hold him off.

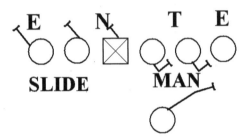

SLIDE   **MAN**

Diagram #14. Slide Protection

If the backside guard has a shade technique to his inside on the center, that is not his responsibility. However, if he is uncovered, he stays in the gap and gets his hand on the shade-technique defender. That is what we refer to as the long-arm technique to the inside. He does not vacate his gap and widen outside. If he widens outside, it creates a large hole in the protection. We want to eliminate that from happening.

If the playside guard is uncovered, he has the playside A gap. When the center slides, he sets to the backside A gap and blocks an imaginary 1 technique to his backside. The backside guard has the B gap and sets to an imaginary 4i technique. The backside tackle uses normal set rules and keys "man on to man outside." If we come up short in the protection scheme, we protect from the inside out and let the furthest man to the outside go. That becomes the hot read or the sight-adjustment read by the quarterback and one of the receivers.

When you put together a pass-protection scheme, you must plan to handle a dominant pass rusher. It must be part of the game plan and preparation handled in practice. Your quarterback must utilize the snap count to keep him off balance and keep him from getting the jump.

To help the tackle, we use the running back to chip on him as he releases from the backfield. We double-team with a tight end or running back. We want to cut him whenever possible. If you cannot protect, move the pocket with a sprint-out or dash play. Have the tight end run his release through him to slow him down on his rush.

If he aligns in the same place, you can devise a plan to deal with him. If he is always to the openside or to the field, we can handle him. If the defense moves him all over the place, it becomes harder to handle and you must be creative.

The first front I want to show is the odd front (Diagram #15). At Akron, we have a directional call in our scheme. The directional call tells the offensive line which way the center will block. In the diagram, we use a left call. The center and left guard are responsible for the nose and backside inside linebacker.

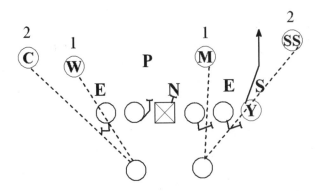

Diagram #15. Man Scheme Vs. Odd Front/Left

The right guard and tackle use the fan scheme to the right. They are responsible for the 5-technique end and the 9-technique Sam linebacker. The back to that side reads for the Mike linebacker or the strong safety. The back to the left double-reads from the Will linebacker to the corner or free safety for his blocking assignment. That is what we call our base "84" protection.

The tight end aligned to the right releases into the pattern. To the left, the guard steps to the A gap,

helps the center with the nose, and keys the backside linebacker for a blitz. The tackle has the defensive end. The quarterback knows the defense will have to blitz the Mike linebacker and strong safety for us to be short on the playside. The back to the playside double-reads the Mike linebacker to the strong safety and blocks one or the other. If both come on the blitz, he blocks the Mike linebacker.

If the defense reduces down on the two-man side, to a 3 technique on the guard and a 5 technique on the tackle, the directional call becomes right (Diagram #16). The center and right guard have the nose and Mike linebacker. The right tackle blocks the 5-technique tackle aligned on him.

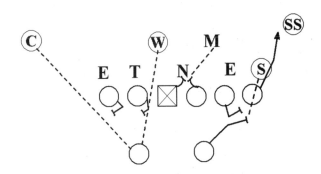

Diagram #16. Man Scheme/Right

The left guard and tackle fan block on the defensive 3 technique and 5 technique. The back to the right double-reads the Sam linebacker to the strong safety. The back to the left double-reads from the Will linebacker to the corner.

If the defense is an eight-man front, with two inside linebackers and two outside linebackers, we make a left call (Diagram #17). The center and left

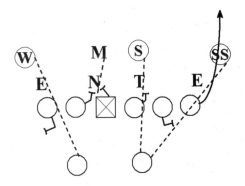

Diagram #17. Eight-Man Front/Left

guard are responsible for the backside shade nose and the backside linebacker. The right guard and tackle fan to the defensive tackle and end to their side.

The back to the right double-reads the Sam linebacker on the inside to the strong safety. The back to the left reads the Will linebacker on the outside to the corner. The tight end releases. The quarterback knows if both the Sam linebacker and the strong safety blitz, he reads hot off the strong safety.

We also use "middle" as a direction call (Diagram #18). In this situation, the scheme is like a left call for the offensive linemen. The 3 technique tackle determines which guard combo blocks with the center. In the diagram, the 3 technique aligns to the right of the offense. The left guard and center are responsible for the shade nose and the Mike linebacker. The left tackle blocks the backside defensive end and the right guard and tackle fan for the 3 technique and 6 technique.

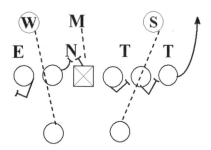

Diagram #18. Middle Call

The backs in the backfield match up on the outside linebackers to the support defenders to their sides. The right back reads the Sam linebacker to the strong safety, while the left back blocks from the Will linebacker to the corner to his side.

We use another scheme if we face a "bear" look on defense. The adjustment call is "big-on-big" (Diagram #19). The strong safety over the tight end, as a rule, does not rush. He has the tight end man-to-man. We tell the right offensive tackle to read from the inside out. He looks at the strong safety, but more than likely will take the defensive end. The back to that side reads from the inside linebacker to

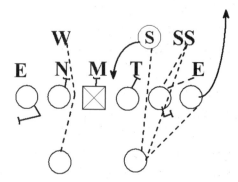

Diagram #19. Bear Front/Big on Big

the outside. The back to the left reads from backside linebacker to the outside.

Coaches that run this defense want to use up the blocks of your center and guards and blitz outside people into those gaps. We block big on big from the inside out.

I want to go back to the Middle call with a coaching point (Diagram #20). With a 3 technique to the playside and a shade noseguard to the backside, we make the Middle call. We coach the center to set in a square set. The left guard sets with the idea of taking over the shade noseguard from the center. We say we have four hands on the shade nose and four eyes on the Mike linebacker.

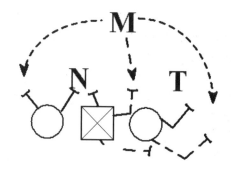

Diagram #20. Middle

If the Mike linebacker drops into coverage, the center is in position to help the right guard on the 3 technique. He does not disengage from the nose once the Mike linebacker drops. He long-arms the noseguard and eyeballs the 3 technique.

If the guard has the 3 technique blocked, he wipes up the block on the nose. If the right guard needs help, he disengages and helps on that block.

The left guard combo blocks with the center. His intent from the beginning of the block was to take over the nose. Therefore, he expects the center to leave him at some point.

If the Mike linebacker blitzes the right A gap, the center calls "backer," releases the nose, and blocks the Mike linebacker. If the Mike linebacker runs through the left B gap, the center bumps the left guard off the block on the nose. The center overtakes the nose and the left guard blocks the Mike linebacker.

The hardest situation to handle is the Mike linebacker blitzing the right B gap. We can handle that in two different ways. We can bring the center out to the right B gap to block him or bump the right guard out. On the blackboard, it does not appear to be sound to bump the right guard off his block on the 3 technique, but in reality, it happens.

You see small things as you scout teams. We coach our players to recognize the hints the defensive front presents each week. We call this adjustment "mountaineer." It comes from a coach at West Virginia, but became one of the Pittsburgh Steelers' best "fire zone" schemes.

The defense aligns in a normal under 4-3 alignment shifted away from the tight end (Diagram #21). The Sam linebacker steps up on the line of scrimmage and aligns on the tight end. The defensive end moves into a 5 technique on the offensive tackle. The nose shades the center to the tight-end side. The stunt brings the Sam and Mike linebacker from the tight side of the formation. The backside 3 technique widens to get outside for containment.

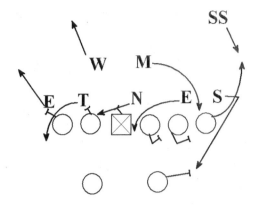

Diagram #21. Mountaineer

The nose comes across the face of the center into the backside A gap. The playside defensive end spikes down from the 5 technique into the playside A gap. The Sam linebacker comes off the edge, with the Mike linebacker blitzing the C gap. The defensive end to the openside of the formation drops into coverage along with the Will linebacker. The strong safety drops down to fill for the blitzing linebackers.

Teams that run this fire zone blitz give the offense some indicators as to what is coming. The first hint is the alignment of the Mike linebacker, who widens to almost a 5-technique stack. The 3 technique is wider than normal and, in some cases, his stance reverses. Instead of having his ball hand on the ground, his outside hand is down to aid his outside movement.

When we see these hints, we have a code word to indicate our protection scheme. In the presnap read, the protection was a middle call. As the Mike linebacker widened, the center realized the Mike linebacker was not his concern and made the appropriate call. The call sent the right guard in a set toward his tackle and they zoned off the stunt.

RUNNING BACK TECHNIQUES AND DRILLS

University of Kentucky

It is a pleasure to be here to represent the University of Kentucky staff and Coach Rich Brooks.

Before I get started, I want to give you one Coach Lombardi quote to start out with. This is one of my favorite quotes: "The challenge for every organization is to build a feeling of oneness, and the dependence on one and another, because the question is usually not how well each person works, but how well they work together."

This quote comes from Vince Lombardi. It is so true. Not just in sports, but in business. This is what is so fun about what we do in working with the young people we work with today. We want our players to work together for a common goal. This is the exciting thing about what we do.

I am going to start with some core fundamentals of what we teach. We always go through this phase in teaching all of our players. These are basic fundamentals, but you can never teach them enough. You lose football games by turning the ball over, by making stupid mistakes, and by getting penalties. By missed assignments. You can lose a football game by making these mistakes.

First we will start with stance. We teach a three-point stance and a two-point stance. The reason we teach the two-point stance is because of the fullback. If the back is in an offset position, or if he is in the I formation, he may use the two-point stance. The feet are shoulder-width apart and slightly staggered. We call it a heel-to-toe relationship. If I am a right-handed player in a right-handed stance, my right toes are even with the heel of my left foot. The weight is on the inside of the foot. The knees are bent, the back is flat, and the head is raised enough to see the feet of the defensive alignment. The down arm drops just below the eyes, inside the foot.

In a two-point stance, the feet and knees are the same as above. The head is raised to see the defensive front and the hands are on the knees.

The second point is ballhandling. First is receiving the handoff. When new players report to us, they make the mistake of keeping their eyes on the quarterback. They must develop a trust with the quarterback. The ball is going to be placed in the belly of the running back. The running back must keep his eyes on the read while receiving a handoff.

We want him to raise the inside arm up and put the outside arm down with the palm up. Then he closes down over the ball. We do not want him to grab for the football. He must secure the ball into the tucked-away position.

Next we talk about ball security. We carry the ball in the outside arm. If I am running to the left side and I get hit from the inside, I have a chance to secure the ball. I have players that come in new to us and tell me they are right-handed and feel better with the ball in the right hand. The first time they run to the left and have the ball in the inside arm, they get hit from the inside and they fumble the football. They have no way to protect the ball. We have to get them used to carrying the ball on the outside arm. That is one reason we lift the inside arm up on a handoff. We do not want them to grab for the football.

We want them to always maintain four points of pressure on the football. The front tip should always be even or up. The ball should be secured into a tuck position. We want the inside of the ball secured by the three fingers from the little finger to the middle finger. The outside of the ball is secured by the thumb and the first finger. The backside part of the football is secured by the biceps. The inside part of the ball is secured by the body. Those are the four points of pressure. Three points of pressure does not get it done.

The other thing I want to talk about is that the front tip of the ball is always up. If the front tip is down, the exposure of the ball is more than 90 degrees and it is harder to hold the ball. If it is less than 90 degrees, the arm is stronger and you can hold the ball much more firmly. We must protect the football.

We do not want to see a lot of air under the arm and the ball. Air is created when you run with the ball and it is away from your body. When I was playing at UCLA, my coach was Terry Donahue, and he always preached ball security and to keep it tucked. That point has stayed with me through the years.

Let's move on to blocking. Blocking can be broken down into three categories. First is the lead block. This block is used on an isolation play. We want to run at the defender and keep the feet shoulder-width apart. I am a better blocker when my feet are shoulder-width apart. This gives me a better base. It is all about base and leverage. By "leverage" we mean you must be underneath the defender.

We want to strike the defender with our hands under his chest. The head should be up and at a level under the defender's chin. We want the elbows inside and the thumbs together. We always strike the defender with the head up.

After striking the defender, we want to sustain our leg drive and roll the hips to create movement. We want to stay square. The best analogy I can think of to rolling the hips is the power cling. If you are power clinging and you have the bar away from the body, you do not have as much power. If you roll the hips into the lift you have more power. The strength comes from rolling the hips. We tell the blocking backs to bring the hips with them when they are making a block.

The other thing on isolation blocking is to stay square. This helps the man carrying the ball in making his cut off the block.

The second type of block is the kick-out block. We use this type of block on a power play off-tackle. The key on the kick-out block is to set an inside-out relationship with the defender. You do not want him to cross your face.

Next, we want to power step off the inside foot, fitting on the inside number of the defender. After striking the defender, sustain the leg drive and roll the hips to create movement. It is the same thing as the isolation block. You must bring the hips when you make the block.

The third type of block is the pass block. We want to go after the defender and set up with an inside position. Why do I say inside positioning? We want to explode upward under the defender's pads, keeping our feet under us. We want to sustain the block, shuffling our feet with a shoulder-width relationship.

The best drill in teaching this block is when we go against our linebackers in our one-on-one drill. We want the contact to be made as far away from the quarterback as possible in making the block.

Let's talk about receiving. The key to receiving is this: Your eyes must look the ball into your hands. We try to train our receivers to be disciplined enough to look the ball into their hands. We want them to catch the ball out in front of the body. After the catch, we want the receiver to bring the ball into his body and tuck it away into his back pocket using four points of pressure.

I use the term "knife up" the field, which means getting as much yardage as possible vertically. We want them to get the first down.

Next, I have some drills on tape that I will show you, but before we go to the video I want to talk about the drills.

The first drill is Bags and Ropes (Diagram #1). This drill is good to help the runners to pick their feet up through traffic. We want them to run

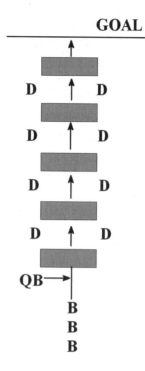

GOAL

Diagram #1. Bags and Ropes

through the bags with high knee action. I will mix the drills up by going over the ropes and then we have them run over the bags. The ropes are more difficult because they trip on the ropes at times. The bags are more forgiving, but the backs can still trip over the bags. We want the backs to go over the ropes or bags by picking up their feet. We want them to establish good balance in the drill. We try to have a gauntlet of players on each side of the bags who are trying to knock the ball out of the runner's arms. They go down one way and they switch the ball to the other arm coming back the other way.

We vary the footwork in the drill. Sometimes we have them jump the bags with both feet or we may have them do a change of direction. We are trying to develop balance and footwork. We want the ballcarrier to get his knees up high. The players on the side of the bags or ropes are trying to knock the ball out of the runner's arms.

We have incorporated this drill into a ball-security drill. Now, while they are running through the bags we want them to carry a football. This forces them to be disciplined while they are concentrating on something else. In the game, they are concentrating on something else and not on

holding on to the ball. We want to make it a habit to have ball security as great as possible.

I will stand off to the side of the drill and I will try to knock the ball out of their arms. This forces them to have good ball security.

Another simple drill is the Cone Drill. This drill is designed to teach the backs how to take the proper steps when cutting off the outside foot. Teaching the players to make the cut off the outside foot is an overextension of "sticking" the outside foot outside of the body. We emphasize a steady "hat level." I want the backs at one continuous level. I do not want them rising up and then lowering their body.

We can vary the distance between the cones. We want them to redirect their body and then to go in another direction. This fundamental is good for all players and not just running backs.

The next drill is the Sideline Run (Diagram #2). This drill forces the ballcarrier to run with leverage and to deliver a blow into the shield-holder (tackler). The high runners will get knocked out of bounds in this drill. We want the ballcarrier to run with leverage. In the drill, the back has to dip and rip through the bag or shield dummy. He has to protect the ball in the outside arm.

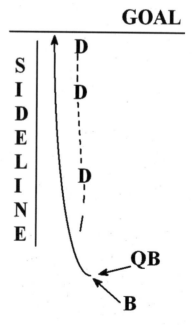

Diagram #2. Sideline Run Drill

The next drill is the Jump Cut Drill. This drill carries over a lot to running the zone play. The back must be able to make a lateral move if he is running downhill on the zone play and a defender is in his path. He has to make the jump cut, get past the defender, and then get back on the running path.

In this drill, I will usually hold the dummy. The back makes his cut and comes downhill on the play. I will throw the bag at his feet and he will cut in the opposite direction of the bag.

The next drill is our One-Versus-Two Pass Protection Drill. This drill forces the blocker to maintain football position and react with a proper upward strike from an inside-out position. We line up two defenders with the blocking shields. I will point to the defender that I want to be the pass rusher. The blocker must have quick feet to set up to take on the pass rusher. The blocker takes on the pass rusher with his inside foot up and then gets back to his original position. Then the other pass rusher may come and the blocker has to be ready to take him on.

The next drill is our Running Back Crossbar Drill. In my first year working with backs, I found the backs were running too high. They did not understand leverage. Our equipment man made us a gadget to help keep the backs low. He made it out of three-quarter-inch PVC pipe with 90-degree edges on it. We set it at 55 inches high. We forced our running backs to run under the PVC pipe. We made them do the isolation block under the pipe. If they were too high they hit their helmets on the pipe. This forces the backs to get down low with their pad level.

We may add a base-board about 10 inches wide. This is used to make sure the backs keep the feet spread as wide as shoulder-width. If the feet are too close together they step on the board and lose their balance.

I am going to show you film of the drills to give you a better idea of what I have been talking about.

You can see one of our old drills that I still use. It is with the Rae Crowther blocking sled. You may have to look on the outskirts of the practice fields to find the blocking sled, but it is still a good teaching tool. I think you can teach "bringing your hips" on the sled.

Next, I want to talk about the inside zone play. I like this play for several reasons. First, it is a simple scheme. For the linemen, they must get great push and they must block the playside gap. There are a lot of various combinations on the blocks, but they must get a great push on the frontside of the play. They must move the defenders. They must use the double-team and get a great push as they come off the ball. It comes down to combination blocks and playside gap blocking.

If you are a lineman on the backside of the play, you are going to scoop block. The line wants to make a wall on the backside to cut off the defenders. If the back does cut it back he will not cut it back into a free defender sitting in position to tackle him.

The inside zone is a "take what the defense gives you" play. The back is going to do one of three things on the play. First, he is going to "cram it." Second, he is going to "cut back." And third, he is going to "bounce it." If you run the play 10 times, he runs the "cram it" six to seven times. It means he is going to do his footwork and "cram it" coming downhill.

Two of the 10 times you run the play he will use the "cutback." When the first down lineman crosses his face he runs the "cutback." He may cut it back to the A gap, or anywhere on the backside.

One out of 10 times you run the play the player will "bounce" the play outside. This does not happen very often, and we do not coach this, but it could happen on the play.

The third reason I like the inside zone is because it is a good play against the zone blitz and the twists. Why is this true? Because it is a zone block play and everyone on the offensive line has a playside gap. They are going to step to the next level and block the defender in that gap, or double-team block on the defender. The offensive lineman has the area and must make the block.

The fourth reason I like the inside zone play is because it easily complements other plays with the play-action pass (Diagram #3). If we are running the wide zone and the safeties are coming downhill and getting into the play, we can run a couple of play-action passes. This is what it would look like on the pass.

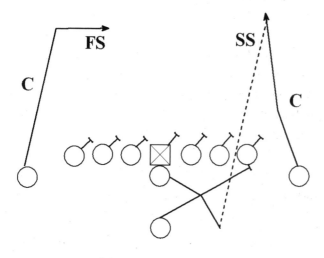

Diagram #3. Play-Action Pass

The other play is to run the naked bootleg on the defense (Diagram #4). If the defense is overpursuing the ball, it is a good play against the defense. The backside end must hit the defensive man and then release on the pass route. The backside end runs the crossing route. You can run the play-action pass on the Inside or outside zone plays.

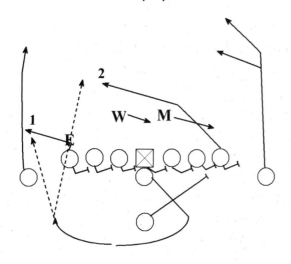

Diagram #4. Naked Bootleg

On any multiple-formation play, you can run it out of the one-back set or the two-back set. We are always going to have a back in front of the tailback or we are going to motion a back to that position. We have different combinations on the frontside.

The deep back takes an open step, a crossover step, and then his aiming point is the outside leg of the playside guard. He wants to be square as he starts downhill. He is reading the first down lineman on the side of the playside guard. If the down lineman is blocked, he continues the play straight ahead. If the hole is not open, he may bend it back to the other side. The up back must block the end on the backside.

You must always have someone that is going to hold off the backside end. If the back does cut the play back, we do not want the defensive end stopping the play.

The last play is the zone option. Now we do not need a back to hold off the backside end. You can be in four wide and the quarterback is the hold-off player against the end. He must "read" the backside end. If the shoulders of the end are square and/or up the field, he gives the ball to the back. If the end turns his shoulders inside, the quarterback pulls the ball and keeps the play. That is a way to keep that backside end accountable.

The thing that gets hurt by the bowl system is the timing on the passing game. The kids get a couple of weeks off before the bowl games and it affects the game. The athletic-type quarterback, such as Young from Texas, has a big advantage because he can run the football as well as pass it. Because he is such a great athlete, he can run the ball with great success. The layoff does not hurt him at all.

GAME PLAN THE THIRD DOWN

University of Pittsburgh

It is good to be back in Pittsburgh. I am going to talk about game planning for third down with the run or pass. I have six points I think are musts when you put your third-down passes together.

Third-Down Musts

- Identify the number of reps for each down and distance
- Use plays that carry over from the base game plan
- Have multiple protections
- Have run/pass balance
- Be prepared with coverage-beater or possession routes
- Kill process to run or pass

The first point is about the number of reps in a situation you get in a game. I think we are all guilty of getting many reps in practice and not checking to see if we are getting them where we need them. It is important to identify the number of reps you will use in each down and distance.

The second point is about carryover from the base offense. The base offense consists of the plays you run on first and second down. Defenses will change on third down if the offense changes their personnel. If the offense puts a different personnel group on the field, some defenses try to match up. If the offense adds a third receiver, the defense puts a nickel back into the game.

If we go to a four-wide scheme, they add the dime back. Every time I open the formation and show less ability to run, the defense puts more cover people on the field. Everything you do in your base package gets the bulk of reps during the course of the week. You should not discount the reps and use those plays on third down.

One of the things I learned from pro football was that the defense does their homework too. If the defense can identify a personnel group locked into a protection, they will make you pay. The defense builds in pressures to make the quarterback throw the ball to the hot receiver. If the situation is third-and-eight and the offense throws hot for a four-yard gain, the defense wins. The offense has to punt the ball and give up possession.

I want to show the defense a bunch of protections so they cannot lock in on one scheme. I want at least two different protections from the same formation.

Having balance in the run and pass is not the only thing to consider. Balance is necessary, but you must have efficiency in both the run and the pass. The tendency you want to avoid is a particular yardage situation throwing you completely out of balance. For instance, you cannot run the ball every time on third-and-one or -two, and then throw it 90 percent of the time when you have to gain four yards for the first. That gives the defense the advantage, because they know what you do.

If you have a great feel for what the defense does, you can call coverage-beaters. If I know the defense is in two-deep coverage on third down, I call the play that beats that coverage. If I do not know and the defense is good at mixing up their coverages, I use progression reads. That means the quarterback is reading the defense and throwing to receivers on a progression read.

The kill package is a great way for a coach to take the thinking out of the quarterback's head. We give the quarterback two plays. If he does not get the look we want on the first play, he kills the play and goes to the second one. We call that in the huddle and audible at the line. It is like a "check with me" call, except we call it a "kill package." When he comes to the line, if the first play is good, he calls the cadence and snaps the ball.

If he does not like the defense, he calls "kill, kill," and runs the second play. The players have to be alert, but they can handle two plays without any problem.

This chart shows you the reps we took in practice on certain situations. The numbers will jump out at you. For instance, on third-and-one, we had 16 snaps for the season. We played 11 games and that is not hard to figure out. We found that 2 percent of our offense is third-and-one. There is no need for us to take five or six plays a week in a third-and-one situation. You do this at the end of the year. You chart the yardage situations and the number of times you were in each situation. The numbers historically do not drastically change from year to year.

You can identify the number of reps you get in a game, so practice accordingly. We are limited on the number of reps we get in practice. Make sure the reps fit what you get in the games.

The next chart shows the practice plan at Pittsburgh. On Monday through Friday, we have a daily breakdown of the number of base plays and the reps we get in each situation. I know in the course of that week, I have 13 reps in third-and-long yardage for the first down. The situation showed that in third-and-seven or more, in the games we had five to six plays. In practice, I am getting about twice as many reps than will happen in the game.

In a third-and-medium situation, the chart showed we had three to four plays a game. We were not very good in that situation. Consequently, we practice at a rate of four-to-one. We practice the play four times for every time the play occurred in the game.

In short yardage and goal line, 15 reps are more than we will need. All coaches worry about short yardage and goal line and we spend time repping that situation. In my opinion, those reps could be spent somewhere else. It is your job as the offensive coordinator or play-caller to decide where you need the reps.

These charts are not difficult to put together if you can operate a spreadsheet on the computer. To do the entire year, it took about 30 minutes.

When we talk about efficiency on third down, the play has to pick up the first down. In a third-and-one situation, we were 12 out 12 running the football. With the number of reps we get in practice, we were comfortable with that part of the game. We had a good package and were solid in what we tried to do.

We were disappointed with the third-and-two or -three yards for the first down. Our efficiency for that down was only 50 percent. That is not good enough to play winning football. The rate should be around 70 percent efficient. That will be a point of emphasis in spring ball, summer camp, and during the season next year. I will put more focus on this situation and make our players aware of the problems.

Our third-and-four to -six yards situation was even worse. Of course, it is harder to pick up those yards. Obviously, the longer the distance, the harder it is to convert with a running play. Most people would say a four-yard run is efficient. However, it is not efficient if you need five to seven yards for the first down. You can see the mistake I am making in this situation. I am throwing the ball too much. I need to run it more in the third–and-medium situation.

If we run the ball and are stuffed, we go right back to throwing it. You have to be patient and have faith in what you are doing. We have to bring some better balance to our run and pass at that down and distance.

The third-and-seven to -10 and 11-plus is a heavy passing down. The runs that you see in this situation are usually Coach Wannstedt saying run the ball. He wants to protect the field position and not risk a turnover. I rarely call a run on third-and-11-plus yardage. If I do not think we can protect the quarterback or the quarterback is making bad decisions, I will run the ball.

Each year we chart all of the down-and-distance situations that occur in our games. From these charts we can see the frequency with which the down and distance occurs in a game. That will be the focus for us in the spring. These things are invaluable aids when making the game plan. Of course, part of the focus in these areas will be what caused the inefficiency. We put a lot of effort into identifying those problems.

I go a step further in the pass game and look at the efficiency of the passes we use in those situations. I do not list every pass we threw, but instead group them into categories. Looking at our charts, I can see we were 75 percent completion on our giant concept. Obviously, the quarterback feels good about that series, the receivers are getting open, and the protection is holding up.

I can go back and see what protection we used and the formation we aligned in to get a visual of what the quarterback likes about this play. The conclusion is this: I need to run more giant series in third-and-medium. It gives me a sense of things that have been good.

Game plan carryovers are important to me, particularly if you have young players. On the first day of practice, we give our quarterbacks a fake game plan. It is exactly like what we give them during the season. We list the runs in red and the passes are in blue. We categorize the plays into base runs, draws, and special runs.

The passes are in blue and placed in categories. We break them down as quicks, dropback, play-action, and verticals. The plays highlighted in green are the plays that showed up in the third-down category. I want carryover from my base game plan to third-down plays as much as I can. I know my quarterback gets many reps in the base game plan. I do not want to create a bunch of new plays for the third-down situation. I want to use the ones we worked on all week in that situation.

You can see I did not do a very good job of that in this game plan. I have 12 passes listed in our third-down situation that are not listed in our base plays.

Am I being fair to the quarterback, receivers, and offensive line? Probably not, because I am asking them to fit 12 new passes in the third-down package that were not in the base package. Most of the reps went into the base package.

If a team is a two-deep team, your base plan should work in the third-down situation because it is the same defense. If we like a play on first and second down, can that play also be successful on third down?

Multiple protections may not be something you want to do at the high school level. I know from my experience with the NFL, if the defense knows what you are doing, they will come after you on third down. They are smart and they will adapt to what you do. I never want to get into the position where the defense knows the protection I am using on any down and distance. In addition, I want to make sure I am not matching up protections with formations. I do not want the defense to know that every time I am in a triple set, I protect a certain way.

Let me discuss this point. If I am in a three-by-one triple formation, I can protect in a different way. In the first diagram (Diagram #1), the first play is a quick. The line is gap protecting with the back blocking on the edge.

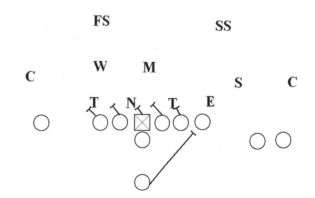

Diagram #1. Gap Protection Back to the Edge

The second example is the six-man turnback protection with the back double-reading two linebackers (Diagram #2). He reads the linebackers and releases if no one comes.

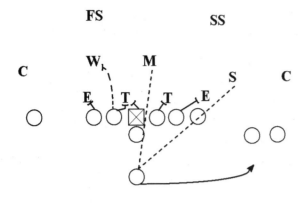

Diagram #2. Six-Man Protection Back Read

The third situation is a seven-man turnback protection with the tight end checking his way out into the pattern (Diagram #3). The back reads the other side for his protection scheme.

The fourth protection is an eight-man protection scheme. We take one of the wide receivers and motion him across the set (Diagram #4). We use reverse motion to bring him back into the position of a tight end and snap the ball. He stays in the backfield and blocks.

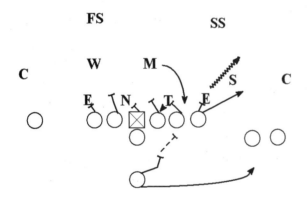

Diagram #3. Seven-Man Protection

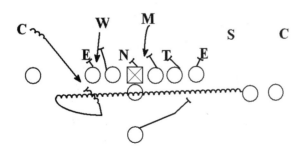

Diagram #4. Eight-Man Protection

I want the defensive coordinator to see the protection from this set and not know how we protect. With the kind of wide receivers in the game of football today, it is dangerous to blitz if you cannot get there.

We strive for balanced in our run/pass ratio. In a third-and-one situation, if you feel good about the line, lead back, and running back, I would run every time. We were good in this area. In third-and-two to -three yards, our balance was good, but our efficiency was not. If we run the ball half the time in that situation, I need to convert more. If I commit to the run, I want to be more efficient.

We want to be about 50 percent efficient in the third-and-four to -six situation. We were not close to that this year. The third-and-seven situation is a bitch. In the third-and-long situation, we are 25 percent, which is as good as anyone else in our league. In pro ball, the goal is 40-percent conversion on third down.

The ideal figure we look for is a high percentage in third-and-short, which we have. In the third-and-two to -three, we want 65 percent. In third-and-four to -six, we look for 50 percent, and in third-and-long, 25 percent is acceptable. If you put all those numbers together, it works out to about 40 percent conversion on third down.

This next agenda is a big coaching point for your quarterback in particular. If you have a strong tendency on the defense, it is my responsibility to call a play that beats that defense. Teams like to play man coverage in third-and-short situations because it allows them to get additional defenders close or into the box. I know the coverage is man, so I call a play that beats man coverage.

We play the percentages in defensive tendencies. If they play two-deep coverage in the third-down situations 80 percent of the time, then that is the type of defense I try to beat. Use the coverage-beaters when you know what the defense will do. Do not guess about the defense and use a coverage-beater.

I give the quarterback a chance to beat the defense by running a pattern that beats two-deep on one side and three-deep on the other. In our terminology, the pattern is "594 Y-shallow" (Diagram #5). If it is three-deep coverage, he goes to the five-route, which is an 18-yard comeback pattern. If the defense is two-deep or quarter coverage, he works the 94 side of the pattern. The inside receiver runs a clear-out pattern. The outside receiver runs a deep In route. The Y-shallow clears the linebacker from the underneath coverage.

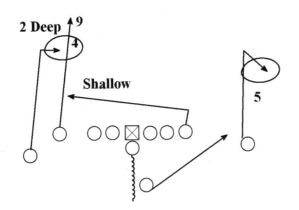

Diagram #5. Coverage-Beater

We like to work the back out in a checkdown to the strongside. That gives us flare control in front of the comeback pattern. The quarterback has a locked-in coverage-beater. All that remains for him is to recognize the coverage and know where to go with the ball. I have to give the quarterback those reps during the week to prepare for the game.

If you are uncertain as to the coverage, use the progression-read scheme. When the defense does a good job of mixing up the coverage, we call a progression read. The quarterback does not have to identify the coverage. All he has to do is progress from one receiver to the other in order. We set it up on one side of the field for him. We take three receivers, flood an area of the field, and let him read one, two, and three.

The last thing I will cover is our "kill package." This allows us to get the look we want from the defense. You have to do your homework when you set up this type of scheme. You must know that when you run a play there is certain criteria you do

not want to run it against. That is the information you have to put in your quarterback's hands.

For example, you tell the quarterback to run this particular play if there are six defenders in the box. If there are seven defenders in the box, the quarterback calls an automatic to get out of the play. The quarterback steps into the huddle and calls "kill." From there, he calls the first play followed by the second play. His huddle call is "kill, fox-right, double-bang" to "fox-right, viper." The first pattern is a three-deep pattern and the second is a two-deep pattern.

The quarterback has to identify the criteria and get out of a bad play into a better one. We can set it up based on a pressure call. He calls "kill" in the huddle and the protection he wants to check. If he reads the pressure, he checks the protection. It is whatever criteria you give them. The linemen get good at listening to the calls. We never give them more than two calls. We adapted the kill package to down and distance, run to run, run to pass, and pass to pass.

The advantage of this scheme is that it allows you to run when you have the numbers advantage in the box. It allows you to pass when the numbers are to your advantage in the secondary. You can get the right route called into the secondary coverage the defense plays. You can get the best protection to match the pressure of the defense.

I want to show you some of the film clips of these adjustments we put into our offense. If you have any question, please ask. I will get you an answer.

The first thing is the short-yardage situation. This is a great formation for us. We bring in two additional tight ends. This is a great formation if you have versatile tight ends. It might be a case where one of your best athletes is the second or third tight end. Put them all on the field and let them play at the same time (Diagram #6). With three tight ends in the game, we can keep any defender from coming off the edge and making a hit on our zone runner. We have a wing set right and the third tight end aligned on the other side. We run the inside zone play and make the first down.

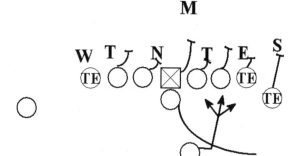

Diagram #6. Three Tight Ends

The next play is a formation we like. We play two tight ends and two wide receivers with one running back (Diagram #7). We run a toss sweep and crack with the wide receiver on the first man inside. This is a good boundary play. The tight end blocks the defensive end. The center and guard reach and the playside tackle pulls for the support. We toss the ball and hit it in the crease outside the end.

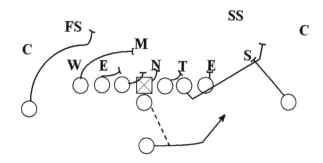

Diagram #7. Short-Yardage Toss

What we try to do is be varied in the looks that we give the defense.

When we played West Virginia, they ran the 3-3-5 alignment on defense. They played three down linemen, three linebacker, and five defensive backs. We knew they were not going to change their scheme in third down. We felt the double-slot formation controlled and isolated their inverted safeties better. If we kept the same personnel in the game on third down, their secondary coverage would not change. We used one of our base passes in a third-and-four situation.

We ran a giant route (Diagram #8). The outside receiver pushes to 14 yards and does a mini-comeback route. The inside receiver pushes vertical to 10 to 12 yards and runs the mini-comeback route. The quarterback runs a play-action fake off the zone play and reads the flat coverage.

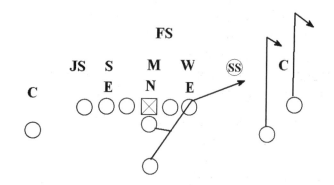

Diagram #8. Giant

This was a good play on first and second down and, as long as we do not change personnel, they will not change their secondary coverage. We got a ton of reps on this play in practice and it became a good third-down play in the game.

Do not be afraid to repeat good plays. If it worked once, come back to it.

The next play is third down and five yards to go for the first down. We were getting our butt kicked in this game against West Virginia. They had a two-touchdown lead and we thought they would be somewhat conservative in their coverage. We called 3-double cloud (Diagram #9). I aligned in a triple formation. They play man coverage with the idea of keeping the ball in front of them. We threw a 3 pattern to the tight end, which is a seam post, and double corner routes.

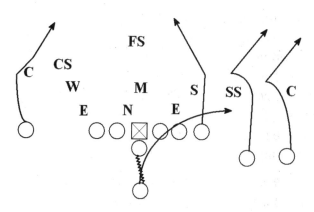

Diagram #9. 3-Double Cloud

We worked this pattern in practice and the quarterback did not have to guess where the tight end would come open. He did not force the ball into the coverage. He laid it up to a spot. He threw the ball to a spot that was 20 yards deep at the near upright of the goalpost, or 20 yards deep between the numbers and the hash mark. It was the receiver's responsibility to get to that spot. He caught the ball at exactly 20 yards deep on the pro hash marks, which is right on the goalpost.

We chose a play against a very passive defense that we knew the quarterback has many reps in practice. He knew where to throw the ball against the look he got. The tight end knew where the ball was going to be thrown. He did not have to look for the ball until he got 15 yards deep. He kept running and tried to get separation. At the last minute, as he got to his landmark, he looked for the ball.

This is an example of the quarterback using his head. The play was a check we put in during the week. It was supposed to control the strong safety and outside linebacker coming from the same side in a 3-4 defensive front. They brought the two defenders, rolled the secondary toward the blitz, and ended up in a two-deep look. If the quarterback saw this look, we had a particular kill we wanted to use.

It was third-and-six from our own four-yard line. If you have ever been in Nebraska's stadium, you cannot hear yourself think. This is one of those situations where I was nervous as hell that we were going to turn the ball over. Coach Wannstedt just wanted to punt the ball and get some better field position. They showed us the look on third down and we had a running play called.

I saw the quarterback going up and down the line of scrimmage checking the play. I put my game plan down and said, "Please let something good come from this." The head coach was screaming "Matt, what's he doing?" I told him, "I'll tell you in a minute, Coach." We snapped the ball, they blitzed, and we picked it up and hit the tight end down the middle against the two-deep.

We worked the same play six or seven times in practice. The only difference was we had an extra tight end instead of the split end in the game. In the

quarterback's mind, that was the same situation and he went to the automatic.

Flexing a tight end out may change the box number for your offense. If the defense takes one defender out of the box to cover the flex, it gives you a better chance to run the ball. Package that adjustment with a kill. If the defense walks the defender out on the tight end, we run the ball. If the defense does not walk the defender out on the flexed tight end, we throw the ball to the tight end.

You can put those packages together for your quarterback. It is not hard and they do not have an array of plays to choose from. It is this run or that pass. You have the flexibility to package it the way you want it to be.

Here is an example of a "kill" in the red zone. The situation is third-and-nine with the score 0-0 in the first quarter. We were unsure what the defense might do. If we have a six-man box, we want to run the ball. If there are seven in the box, we throw the ball. We did not know if they would play quarters or pressure and play cover zero. We had a pattern called for both coverages. When we came to the line, they walked the Will linebacker off and we ran the draw to the tight-end side. We converted on a third-and-nine inside the 12-yard line.

Any time you are not sure what the defense is going to do, opt for protection. If they bring the pressure, you can block it and throw against three-deep. If they do not come, the tight end and backs can check their way out into the pattern. The alternative is to release the receivers and throw hot on the blitz. We like the other scenario.

If we guess wrong, we tell the quarterback to get rid of the ball or get us back to the line of scrimmage. I can live with that decision. What I do not want is the ball forced into coverage or the quarterback taking the sack. That equates to interceptions or negative yardage. If we guess wrong, it does not matter if we make smart decisions. As a play caller, I can live with those decisions. We did not get the first down, but we punted the ball. The defense gets the ball back and we try it again.

Thanks for your attention.

CONCEPTS IN THE PASSING GAME

University of Miami

Thank you. This game has certainly blessed me. I coached high school football in Oklahoma for nine years. I got the opportunity to take a college coaching position at Oklahoma State. I coached Barry Sanders and Thurman Thomas and did some of my best coaching in those years. It was hard to screw those two players up.

From Oklahoma State, I went to Oklahoma and from there to Ohio State. At Ohio State, I coached the secondary. I coached everybody at Ohio State that was any good. From Ohio State, I got a chance to go to the University of Miami.

I played at a small college in Oklahoma and was inducted into the Hall of Fame there. I went in with a guy older than me. At the ceremony, I asked him what I should tell them. He told me, "As old as we are, you can tell them whatever you want. They do not have records that go back that far."

It is a pleasure to be here. I know there is great football up here in the state of Connecticut. Randy Edsal does a tremendous job at the university. We have played them a couple of times and I am sure they will be back on the schedule soon. There are many good players in the Northeast.

Everyone thinks we get all our players from Florida. The best offensive team I had at Miami had eight starters from out of state. The good thing about being at Miami is that we get to see good programs all over the country. We have a wide recruiting base.

It is a privilege to be here. I coached high school football for nine years. I would not trade that for anything. It was one of the best experiences I have had in my life. I am very fortunate to be at the University of Miami. I think it is the best college job

in the country. It is not the easiest job in the country, but it is an awesome opportunity.

I have some things to share with you tonight about the passing game. We try to communicate with our players as much as we can. The things we share with our players, I am going to share with you tonight.

I listened to Bill Walsh lecture and he talked about communication with your players. So many coaches meet with the team and tell them the team rules and important things to know. After they speak with the team that first time, those ideas are not talked about again. Players forget them.

He made a strong point about communicating with your players continuously. He covered the important points repeatedly, in a different way each time. The message and concepts were always the same, but the delivery was different. The messages were the same, but the format was different.

We have a plan to win that we share with our team each year. The key statement is we have to be more physical, tougher, and better fundamentally. We have seven areas of emphasis.

Seven Areas of Emphasis
- Turnover margin
- Big plays (bombs; win the big-play war)
- No missed assignments (no mentals)
- No foolish penalties
- Goal line (must score touchdown inside the 10-yard line)
- Kicking game (always win the kicking game)
- Lost yardage (avoid negative plays)

We work extremely hard on protecting the football. With the way teams coach and play today, securing the football is tremendously important. They punch and grab at the ball on every play. The defense works on scoring on defense. There are more ways to score on defense than there are on offense. We try to protect the ball on offense and create turnovers on defense.

The New England Patriots are a team I like to follow. They do a great job of coaching and the way they conduct themselves is outstanding. The way they win football games is the way to win. The last game they lost, they had five turnovers.

It is important to win the big-play war in a game. We want to make the big play and keep the opponent from making it.

We strive to have no missed assignments in a game. The big problems are mental errors. It is important not to beat yourself. Knowledge is power. A player that knows what to do can play faster than one that does not. That is why a player with less speed can still do the job.

You will have penalties in a game. However, the foolish penalties are the ones you have to avoid. Foolish penalties have to do with the discipline of a team. It goes back to not beating yourself.

Most of the penalties you will find on this list are things that can be taught. The starting snap count and cadence is one of the first things taught on offense. Holding is a technique mistake. Being able to align on the line of scrimmage is a defensive fundamental. Watching movement instead of listening for a snap count is taught from day one. In offensive football, you have to align correctly to start the play.

We go over with our team what we call The Big Seven. They are the seven most-called penalties in college football.

The Big Seven—The Seven Most-Called Penalties

- False start (offense)
- Holding (offense)
- Offsides (defense)
- Delay of game (offense)
- Personal foul (team)
- Illegal formation (offense)
- Pass interference (defense)

Pass interference is one of the toughest calls in football. There is too much judgment that goes into the call for me. However, all the most common penalties are preventable.

Scoring touchdown on the goal line is tremendously important. When you get inside the 10-yard line you must score touchdowns. A few years ago, I watched the Florida and Tennessee game. The game was in Knoxville and I think Peyton Manning was the quarterback at Tennessee. Tennessee was dominating the game. They drove up and down the field, but got field goals instead of touchdowns. They had four field goals and were up 12-0. Florida scored right before the half to make the score 12-7.

Florida came back and won the game 14-12. If the offense gets the ball to the 10-yard line, they need to score touchdowns. At the University of Miami, we have more nonoffensive touchdowns than anyone in the country. You must win the kicking game. Normally, if someone blocks your punt you will lose the game.

In 2001, we played Virginia Tech at Blacksburg. We both had good teams. We were winning the game handily. And they had not pressed us that much in the game. All of a sudden they block one of our punts in the third quarter and return it for a touchdown. From that point on, we were in a war. We had to win the game to give us a chance to play for the national championship. We won the game, but were very lucky to do it.

We played North Carolina this year and were down at halftime. We came out in the third quarter and blocked a punt for a touchdown. Things started to happen for us and we won the game. The game was a close game, but ended with a blowout score. Always win the kicking game if at all possible.

The last thing we try to do is avoid negative plays. We lost two games this past year during the regular season. We lost to Florida State by three points and Georgia Tech by four points. In both of those games, we did not protect our passer. We took negative yardage in both games and had very little chance to win. You are better off taking a penalty than having a negative play. At least if you get a penalty you get to repeat the down.

Another thing we share with our team is the importance of being a better teammate. We work hard at trying to build team unity. The national championship team was the best we have had as far as team unity. They were a very talented team with many all-star performers. We had several players who play in the NFL today. We know that if we have good team unity all the individual honors take care of themselves.

The team matters more than the individual. No one player is more important than the team. You can be the leading receiver or the leading rusher, but if our team does not win, so what! Football is a sport in which you cannot win without a team effort.

I ask my players all the time how many national championships John Elway won while he was at Stanford. They always guess one or two. The correct answer is zero. If fact, they did not go to any bowl games, because they did not win enough games. No one would question the talent or ability of John Elway. However, Stanford, as a team, was not good enough to be a national contender.

Every job is important to the team. If one person fails to do his job properly, then the whole team suffers. There was a pilot named John Bonn who flew missions over Vietnam. He was shot down, parachuted to safety, and was rescued. Several years later he was with his wife and they were enjoying the day together.

A man approached him and asked if he were John Bonn. He told him he was and the man asked if he was shot down over Vietnam. He responded yes again and began to wonder how that fellow knew that. John asked the man how he knew all those things. The man told him he packed his parachute. Everyone's job is important.

That is a simple job, but if it is not done right, John Bonn is not around today. Everybody's job is important from the trainer with the team to the

secretary in the office of the coach. Make sure everyone associated with your program knows how important they are to your operation.

That was the first thing I did when I came to Miami. I wanted to surround our players with the most quality people I could. We are a private school with 8,000 students. Football is very important to the school.

In our program we want to treat everyone with respect. Neither of my parents graduated from high school and both worked all their lives in minimum-wage jobs. I grew up respecting those people that do those types of jobs. When we travel, we fly most of the time. On most of our trips we spend the night in hotels. After the game, we want to leave something behind. We want the people we meet in those experiences to have good thoughts about us.

You must share the victories as well as the defeats. We win as a team; we lose as a team. We stretch together, practice together, meet together, travel together, and we win together as a team. Our team this year was a good defensive football team. We led the nation in pass defense and were third in nation in total defense.

Our offense struggled all year. It was a big juggling act for the coaching staff to keep the team together. You have to learn to share the victories. Bill Parcells said that if you lose the game 49-45, you have to play better offense and score more points. If you lose the game 3-2, you have to play better defense and shut them out.

Losing is painful. I want winning to be fun. If you cannot enjoy winning, what can you enjoy? I want our players to enjoy winning football games.

Players have to accept constructive criticism. Not everything the players do is right. In my opinion, our strength coach is the best in the country. Our players love him because he tells it like it is. They respect the criticism coming from him because he is honest with them. They can accept that from him, because they know he is trying to make them better.

The head coach needs to keep the coaches well informed. By keeping the coaches informed, it gets to the players quickly. We have no problems with players being late to meetings, trips, or practices. If, for some reason, there is an issue out there, they need to touch base with us.

The players must focus on their work ethic and not others. People are always evaluating other people. All you can control is what contribution you are making. We had an All-American tight end that was drafted by the Cleveland Browns. When he was with Miami, his backup was an outstanding tight end. However, he never reached his potential because he was always concerned with what the starter was doing. He needed to concentrate on what he was doing, because he could control that.

The last point about being a better teammate is to allow for differences in lifestyles. That has changed many times since I was a boy. We did not have any earrings, tattoos, or things like that. Kids watch the NBA and the Super Bowl and that is all they see. Is it bad for players to have earrings and tattoos? The society is constantly changing. You have to allow for those differences within your team.

At Miami, we have rich kids and kids that grew up in Liberty City. Players from that area may come to school and have not eaten in two or three days. Roscoe Parrish was a little player that lived in Liberty City. He is now with the Buffalo Bills. When he came in, he did not have all his paperwork finished at the NCAA Clearinghouse for scholarship athletes.

He could practice with us, but we could not house or feed him. I wish someone would explain that rule to me. He weighted 175 pounds when he came to practice. The first day he practiced, he went to 168 pounds. I finally told him to stay home until we got the okay from the Clearinghouse. He commuted from his home every day until we got the okay from the Clearinghouse. He never missed a practice, but he never got a meal, because we could not feed him. That is why I knew he was going to be a good player. It takes all kinds to make up the world.

That is a great deal for football, because it does not matter about a player's background on the football field. Everyone is a part of the team. However, within that team there are some differences and you have to allow for that.

Our passing philosophy at the University of Miami bases our scheme around possession-type passes. Those types of passes are low-risk passes. We want to get the ball in the hands of our playmakers. That was one of the things we did not do at Miami this year.

We want to use the possession-type of pass. However, we take the shot when we get the proper match-up in the secondary. If the defense has a weak player in their secondary, we work to get one of our good receivers matched up on him. When it happens, we take our shot at hitting the big play.

We want to run patterns with basic reads. We give the quarterback three basic reads with an outlet to get rid of the ball if he gets quick pressure. We want to get the ball out of the quarterback's hand quickly. The quarterback must have a time clock in his head that tells him to get rid of the ball. He cannot hold the ball, because the protection cannot block for any measurable time against the personnel on today's defenses.

On each pattern you throw, you need a deep opportunity. We call it an alert. When you get those opportunities in a game, you must take advantage of them. The big play is what all defenses try to prevent. Those are the momentum changers in a close game.

The first down is the most important play on each series of downs. If you can win on first down, that establishes what you can do on second and third downs. If we can gain four or more yards on first down, we are on schedule in that series of downs. It puts the defense at a disadvantage and keeps the run or pass options open. First down is the only down that is unpredictable. You can run or pass the football on that down.

When Butch Davis came to Miami, we were on probation. For four or five years, we were not on the same playing field with Florida State. We looked into why we were having no success against them. We found out that on our first-down play we gained no yards or lost yardage. When we started to win the first-down play, we became more competitive. Until this year, we put together a six-game winning streak against Florida State. It was nothing more than recording positive yardage on first down.

The design of the passing game is for the quarterback. Try to make his reads as simple as you can so he does not make mistakes. If his reads are simple, he throws quickly and has success.

This next point is important and I will cover it in depth as we go through this lecture. Concepts of the play are more important than the play itself. Player assignments do not change. However, formations and personnel groups do. The quarterback may be running the exact same play, but the receiver is someone different. The read was the same, but the receiver changed. That builds consistency and confidence into a quarterback and makes the offense more productive.

At Miami, we do not have a unique system with the types of plays we run in a game. What we stress is the run after the catch of the ball. When we coach the quarterback, we do not have to emphasize the deep downfield throws. That is what he wants to throw. We have to emphasize the check-down and outlet throws. Those patterns are generally what the defense will give up. Those throws are always there for the quarterback.

In our practices, we set the defense to force the quarterback to use the check-down routes. If he dumps the ball to a running back who is a playmaker, a three-yard pass becomes a long-yardage touchdown. It may not be a touchdown, but good things will happen. We want to treat high-percentage passes as runs.

When you run your passing game against air, you must have a 99-percent completion rate. To do that, you must throw passes the receiver can catch and in places where he can catch them. A dropped pass in practice is unacceptable for our receivers. When the quarterback runs his patterns, he must think man coverage first and then adjust to zone coverage.

When we play Florida State, in 70 plays, they may blitz us 65 times. They bring the house when they play us. If we think a team may blitz, we try to handle it by calling no double moves by the receiver, no play-action passes, and no boots, waggles, or naked boots.

We want to eliminate penalties by maintaining a tempo in what we do. We like to maintain a rhythm of cadence. This next point may sound minor, but consider what the defense looks at. Defensive coaches try to keep the defenses disguised as long as possible. They look for tips from the quarterback as to when the snap of the ball is coming.

I know one thing: The ball will not be snapped until the quarterback has his hands under the center. If the quarterback is trying to get the defense to move, he had better have his hands under the center.

When you make a game plan, call what you planned. Do not make things up on the sidelines. Do not do things you have not practiced. High school and college players do not have the ability to adjust greatly to something that deviates from what they practiced. Professional players can do it because of the length of time and experience they have had with the offense.

The left tackle position is important because he protects the quarterback's backside. Most quarterbacks are right-handed and expose their backs to someone coming from the left. Good pass blockers at left tackle are invaluable.

We want to make sure the calls get into the game. Whatever system you use to communicate to the huddle, make sure it is sound. What drives me crazy in practice is to break the huddle and not know the snap count. I hate players headed to the line of scrimmage asking someone the snap count.

We do not check from a pass to another pass unless it is a blitz-beater. The rule we use is never check from a good play to another good play. If it is a bad play, that is another situation. We want rhythm in the offense and as few checks as we can use.

When we find the defense playing off our receivers, we like to run hitches and slants. If the defensive back is off and inside, we use the speed out. That puts the ball in the hands of the playmakers, with a quick and safe throw.

I do not want to say we never use sight adjustments, but they are difficult to teach. When they bring the extra man we cannot block, you have to depend on both the receiver and quarterback seeing it. Sometimes that does not happen and we end up throwing the ball to the defense. We'd rather handle that situation with hot routes.

Before I get to the tape, I want to show you what I call concept passing. We call this pass Texas (Diagram #1). In this formation, we have standard personnel in the game. We have two wide receivers, two backs, and a tight end in the game. The pass is a five-step drop. The formation is a pro set, with the fullback in the king position in the backfield. The tailback is behind the quarterback in his I-back position.

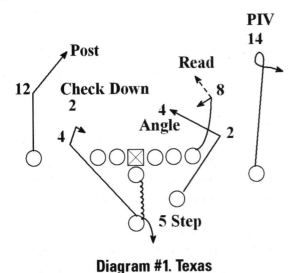

Diagram #1. Texas

The split end runs a post route breaking at 12 yards. We call it an alert route. The tight end runs a read route in the middle of the field. He must be able to read the secondary. If the secondary is in a three-deep scheme, the middle has a closed look because there is a defender in the deep middle third. If the secondary is in a two-deep scheme, the middle has an open look because there is no defender in the deep middle.

If the middle is closed, the tight end runs an eight-yard comeback route. If the middle is open, he runs a post. The flanker runs a pivot at 14-12 yards. He plants his outside foot at 14 yards, pivots, and comes back to the outside at 12 yards.

The fullback either aligns or quick motions to the king position behind the offensive tackle. He runs an angle route outside the tight end. He goes two yards outside and angles inside to a depth of four yards. The tailback runs a four-yards-wide-by-two-yards-deep check-down outside the weakside tackle.

The concept of the pass has an alert, read, pivot, angle, and a checkdown. Any formation in which we align will have this combination of passes.

If we run the play with three wide receivers, the pattern is the same combination (Diagram #2). The wide slot for us may be a tight end because of the personnel we have. From the three-wide formation, we motion the slot into position before we snap the ball. This formation is what we refer to as "20 personnel." That tells us we have two backs and zero tight ends in the game.

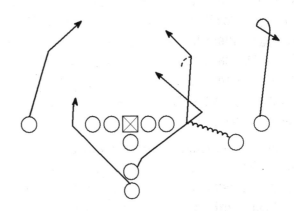

Diagram #2. Texas—Three Wide Receivers

In the one-back set, we align the fullback in the weakside slot (Diagram #3). We motion him to the strongside and run the same combination. In our terminology, this is "11 personnel." That means one back and one tight end.

If you are a two-tight-end team, you can do the same pattern (Diagram #4). We got a great tight end out of New Jersey named Greg Olson. He runs this

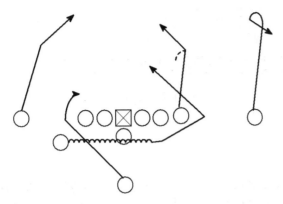

Diagram #3. Texas—Weak Slot One Back

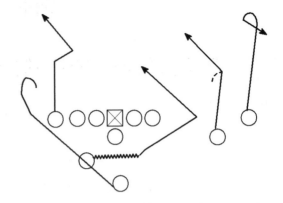

Diagram #5. Texas—Twins

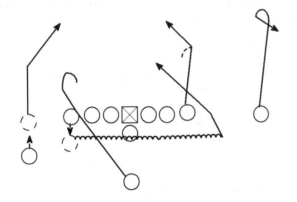

Diagram #4. Texas—Two Tight Ends, One Back

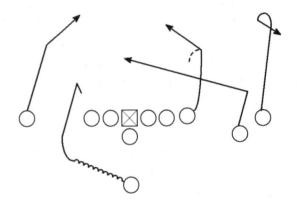

Diagram #6. Texas—Empty

route extremely well. He aligns at the left tight end and shifts into the backfield. He motions across the set and runs the angle route. The split end aligns off the line of scrimmage and shifts on as the tight end moves off the line.

If we run the twins set, the alert route changes because of the tight-end alignment (Diagram #5). He is the outside receiver to the alert side. He cannot run a post because the read route comes down the middle. He runs the post-corner, gets to the outside, and widens the middle of the field. The slot receiver runs the read route to the middle third. The rest of the pattern remains the same.

In this set, we end up in the empty set (Diagram #6). We align with a triple set right, with the tight end and double wide receivers. On the backside, we have the single receiver and motion the tailback to

that side. The outside flanker runs the pivot route and the inside receiver runs the angle route. The tight end runs the read pattern and the split end runs the alert. The tailback goes in motion and runs his check-down.

You can see the flexibility in your formations while keeping the routes the same. We run this concept pass as part of our package. Let me show you the tape of this pattern.

The first thing we see is the angle route. If it is open, take it. The angle in this play is a four-yard catch that ended up being a 17-yard gain. It is a simple throw with a high-percentage rate.

In the alert throw, we read the safety in a two-deep look. If the safety comes off the hash mark, we have the shot inside.

OFFENSIVE LINE DRILLS AND INSIDE ZONE PLAY

Marshall University

Thank you. I have coached at every level of football over the years and the thing that I have been able to do, which I take a little bit of pride in, is develop players, and that is really going to be my talk today. I would like to go over some fundamentals, and then I would like to go through and begin to work on the Inside Zone play, the teaching concepts of it, and how we get it done by developing players.

Quite honestly, we do not have a lot of "made" players. We just do not have a lot of players who show up and come off the ball and reach a 5 technique when we ask them to do it. Okay? We have to work on it in a way that is very similar to what you men have to do. So there are a lot of developmental things in there that I want to talk about.

Men, I recruit in West Virginia, Alabama, Florida, and parts of Pennsylvania, and I have learned some things in each of those areas. For example, in Alabama I learned to talk slowly, and to listen to what the Bear said. Here are a couple of things he said, and I think they have a lot to do with our talk here.

"You can reach a kid with little talent as long as he does not know it." I deal with those guys. I get guys who come in that we recruit, but they cannot do it yet. We cannot let them know that they cannot do it, because a lot of guys, when they show up, they cannot reach a 3 technique or knock someone off the ball.

"We have to drive our players, because you do not know how far they can go until you hook them to a heavy load." As an offensive line coach, I will push my players. This lecture is essentially a video presentation, and as we go through it I will stress that I am constantly pushing my guys to get them to do what you see on tape. Our practice schedule is a grind. We hook our guys up and we work them very hard. We want to make sure that when they play the game, it is the easiest thing they have done that week.

Here are three rules for coaching football. These are, of course, from Bear Bryant:

- Surround yourself with people who cannot live without football.
- Recognize winners; they come in all forms.
- Have a plan for everything.

Men, you know as offensive line coaches, we have to have to plan for everything. We are the guys that no one wants to listen to during the week, but on Friday night or on Saturday they are going to turn to you and say "Hey, Coach! Fix it!" So you need to have a plan for all of that.

One of the things that we do is to practice against all kinds of looks that we have not seen on the tape during the week. We do that just to be ready for those kinds of situations that come up.

We recognize all forms of winners. I am talking about offensive linemen now, and this is a team thing. We recognize our winners—guys who are tough guys. We have some walk-ons, and I love walk-ons because they always give their most— the most they have. I recognize those guys, point them out to the team, and praise them in front of the other players who have scholarships.

When you talk about people who cannot live without football, there are the offensive line coaches right there. You spend your money to come to clinics. You do not go to the beach in the summer.

You are committed to the game. Those are the kind of people you want to be around, and those are the kind of players that you want—the guys who will do anything that you ask. When the gym is open in the summer, and it is time to run, those are the guys who are there, while the guys who are missing are the guys who wear wristbands. We all know about that.

Now, I want to go to the video and show you what we do in practice with our drills. We start with *stance*. To begin with, we are on our insteps. We want a balanced stance and we want to be able to change directions. We have to take all different angles out of our stance, and one thing that helps do all that is to be on our insteps so we can get in a braced position to change direction.

We work on a *posture* technique and I will show you this on film. A posture technique is actually sticking your butt out. When we teach the stance and I tell them to posture, they actually stick their butt out as far as they can, and they move it around to find out where the power is in their butt.

Most young linemen do not know where that is. You tell them to keep their weight back, but it is on their thighs. We generate power from our glutes, from our lower body. It is not the front, and not the thighs, so when we posture, we are able to get the weight back in our stance but still develop that power.

We need to have the ability to *brace*, which is sticking your instep in the ground, with your knee inside. All of you sitting there right now could stick your instep in the ground and your knee inside, and you would know exactly what I am talking about. So we have to develop the ability to brace.

The last thing we need is the ability to *get upright*, which is a pass set. In other words, getting your shoulders up in a position where you still have your insteps in the ground and you can change direction. Those are the main points for an effective stance for our offensive linemen.

We go with a toe-to-instep relationship between our feet with our guards and tackles. This is just how we teach them. We tell them to walk out, move around a little bit, and get your weight on your insteps, and get toe to instep, and balance.

Next, we tell them to get into a *preset*, or two-point position, rest their forearms on top of their thighs, and stick their butts out. That is where we want them to be when we teach them that—two points first. Do not get in a stance first and put your hand down, because all of your weight goes on your hand. They will not have their weight back if you tell them just to put their hand down. It is going to go forward, I promise you.

That is how we teach stance. I will take them on the first day and we will get toe-to-instep and walk them out, shift their weight around, and get into a two-point stance, or preset, before they have their hand down. Now, there are some important things about this.

When they get into this position, we are constantly fighting to have their knees bent and their butt up. That is a difficult thing to do. If you tell your players to bend their knees, their butt goes down. We have to make them stick their butts out to get both of those things to happen. So that is what we are working on there—keep the butt up and keep the knees bent. That is the position we are looking for right there.

So we get into the posture position, stick our butt out, and move until we find that position where our butt is tight and we have power. Once you feel that you have gotten all that power right there, and you have moved it around enough, you can then go ahead and put your hand on the ground, because right there, that is your stance. All you have to do is put your hand on the ground lightly.

Now, I have big guys. Everybody is 300 pounds, but if I did not have big guys, I would do the same thing. I just might put a little more weight on my hand, because I know my guys have to change direction. Everybody has to change direction. The old thing about knock them off the ball, and the Oklahoma drill with the guy lined up head on you, when does that ever happen? When does the guy line up head on you and you knock him off the ball? It just does not happen because everybody is playing gap defense now. So you have to change direction.

My coaching point is not, "Get your butt down." It is, "Pull your hips back." Now you have some power that you can take in any direction. I am not so sure that your hand even has to be on the ground, but the thing that it does is lower your shoulders, lower your blocking surface. There is no need to have all the weight on the hand.

Now, I do this drill where I tell them to get into preset and just reach their hand out forward. If you are in a good position, you can reach your hand straight out, but if you have a lot of weight forward, you cannot reach straight out. I coach them to reach straight out and then put the hand down on the ground. That way, they will have the weight back.

I do not really coach the off hand. The player can put it on the side someplace. I coach the shoulders. The shoulders have to be in a flat plane. If the off hand is up on the thigh, and it makes the shoulders dip away from the off hand, we do not like it. The shoulders should be on a flat plane.

To get players on their insteps, we just tell them to hop. What you will find is, as they hop until they get comfortable, they will end up on their insteps, and their knees will be right under their armpits. That is a perfect position for them to get into a stance. It is very similar to a traffic cone, because it is tapered all the way down, with a nice base, and the player should be balanced. We have all of this in a teaching progression on our instructional tapes, and you can call me if you would like a copy.

Now, let us talk about the center's stance. We teach our centers a parallel stance, so that the feet are toe to toe across the front. Now, when you watch our tape, you may see our center sometimes in a right-handed or left-handed stagger, and it would be on a passing down. He may have it set one way or the other based upon the protection or IDing the Mike linebacker.

We teach him to get in that stance and then go grab the ball. We do not let the center ever take the ball first and then get set. We cannot have the center walk with the football because then he never gets in the right stance and does not know how to handle the ball. We get him in that balanced stance first. Now he can reach. Now his weight is back in his hips. Now he can change direction when he snaps the football.

Now, about *bracing*. This is a very important part of any block. In a brace step, the weight is on the instep and the knee is inside. Imagine a defensive tackle is on my outside shoulder here and I have to block him. I would like to have the instep of my outside foot on the ground with my outside knee underneath my body, and I am going to create torque off of that brace step to go forward. We brace and we punch. We do this with our guys in our board drills. We start with our young guys in camp and we brace with the right foot and punch, brace with the left foot and punch, and keep that knee to the inside.

I really emphasize picking the foot up, and then working off of it at an angle. We do a lot of blocking on angles because that is where the defense lines up—on angles. As we do this, we keep our knees inside and generate torque. The knees are still under the armpits.

We do not lead step a lot. We do not step upfield to block people. We are somewhat of a drop-step team, okay, but do not get scared about that. When we say "drop," what we are doing is changing direction to get on an angle to intersect the defender. When we do that, we are able to come striking off of the ball with our knees inside the framework of our body, so we still have some power and we can generate our torque without locking our hips up.

Let me talk briefly about the *upright* position. The upright position in pass blocking is something that everybody struggles with. I describe upright to my players as your position in a pass set when the ball is snapped. I say that it is like sitting on a bar stool. It should be somewhere in there where you can sit down with your butt on a stool, not like sitting in a chair, and get your shoulders away from the line of scrimmage—the ability to get the shoulders back away from the line of scrimmage and be able to use your hands. We really work hard to get young linemen into this position.

Let me talk about practice. We start with a Gauntlet Drill. We place four agile dummies parallel to each other in a row about two or three yards apart. The players pick their feet up, step over the dummies, and then work back around each one laterally. Finally, they do a shuffle move back to the end. When they get to the end, they switch their stagger foot, get into an upright position, gather, and punch a shield dummy at the second level as if blocking a linebacker. This drill has about as little application as possible with blocking at the snap of the ball, but it has a lot to do with being in on the play later in the down. We get their hands down, their eyes up, and they gather and punch to finish the drill.

We do the gather and punch fairly slowly, because what I think we do not do well these days is gather and punch on the second level. Linebackers are on the move, either laterally or closing up straight ahead, and we need to work on getting our hips down slightly, gathering, punching, and finishing on the block. On some days, I may finish the drill by throwing a ball on the ground, so the blocker has to come off the block and practice recovering the ball.

As soon as we finish this drill, we go to the Square Drill. We motivate our players with this because every pro scout that comes in wants to see them run the square. The players just work around a five-yard square, starting with the bear crawl, then transition to carioca, then backpedal, and finally turn and run the last five yards. We work two squares at once so the players run the drill in both directions. As soon as they finish one square, they get in the opposite line, and they are up and ready to go again.

We do a Demeanor Drill in which we work on just being balanced and maintaining our balance as we move our feet in an upright position, just like the old Wave Drill. We do this from two different stances. We do it from a two-point stance because we run some shotgun runs and we are in a two-point stance. We also do a third-down two-point stance,

and there is a difference. When you are in a shotgun stance, you have to be able to come off of the ball and block run and pass. It is easier to get into more of an upright position. In a third-down stance, everyone knows you are going to throw the ball, so just get in a good position to pass protect. So there are two different drills here.

The Demeanor Drill is just a stay-balanced drill, change direction, work on moving our feet, and then get out of there on command. The one thing I would emphasize is that when I slap that ball with my hand, I want them running through with their eyes downfield, not looking at the ground. We cover the football down the field and our eyes should be up.

It is important for the players to stay on their insteps. They work the drill on their insteps and stay balanced on their insteps so they can change direction in the middle of a down on any play.

The next drill right after that is the Zigzag Drill. This will look very similar, but the difference is that this is a third-down drill, for the obvious throwing down. We change our stance slightly in this drill. We will lean in to the inside, take our forearm and put it on top of our thigh, and have a much bigger stagger. This is a better stance for pass protection. Everybody knows we are throwing the ball, and, if not, it would likely be a draw, and it is a good stance there as well. Otherwise, the drill is run like the Demeanor Drill.

In the Zigzag Drill, we are looking for the players to kick at an angle so they can intersect a defender who is lined up to the outside. When they come inside, the post foot should come straight across.

We coach them in this drill to carry their hands low. We do not want their hands extended, and we do not want them up high, because the defenders will grab them or they will knock them down. We make every player go through the drill twice.

The next drill we go to is the Board Drill. We set up five offensive linemen in normal splits to brace and come off the ball in unison, blocking shields down boards set at an angle. We do this to the right and to the left.

When we do board drills, there are two points of emphasis that we are going to stress: We are going to brace and we are going to punch. As an offensive line coach, you can emphasize certain things in certain drills. You say you want it exactly perfect every time, but if you are coaching five guys, you cannot watch all five guys all the time.

There must be certain things you are looking for, and in the board drills we are looking for a brace. I coach the drill from the side and I want to see that there is going to be a turn, and that we are going to block on the correct angle. I am looking for that foot to turn and I am looking for the brace. I am looking for movement coming down the line of scrimmage, and the other thing I can coach is the punch. We can punch. I know a lot of people do not do that, but we do, and then we finish down the board. We do not usually put our head down the middle, but on this drill we do.

We are also working on the timing from the brace to the punch, hitting on the second step. There are times when I turn around and do not even watch, and all I want to do is hear the punch. If I hear 10 fists hitting the shields at once, I know it is a good drill. If it sounds like a typewriter, all hitting at different times, it is a bad drill.

We also go to a Chute Drill to work on coming off straight ahead with good body angles, punching the shields, and driving to the second level, but we start with a *tight fit progression*. Tight fit is the position we have when we fit ourselves in the block already. We teach it kind of backward. There is a point of contact where you have an outside defender in front of you, you have taken your steps and punched, and now we are going to work the fit we are in. We are going to work the progression from when we are into the block to when we finish the block.

We will start with our tackles on the open-end side, and we will "hang" to make the wide defensive end declare his intention. That is how we start. We are going to block these guys on angles. If we start right at the defensive end, the defensive end may beat us up the field and we have our feet together. That is not what we want.

We use what we call a "hang drive." We slow down the step, just slightly, let the defensive end declare his intention, and then we block him on the angle. We will use the defensive end's momentum against him, and we will maintain our balance.

This drill will be a progression, so we will walk it first and get into the correct fit. The defensive end is going to come upfield and that is where his line of force is. Our tackle will open up, and we will have his line of force go off in a direction that will intersect the defensive end's, with a resulting force line that should be somewhere to the outside. We are going to create some separation, and the coach should get in position to check that angle.

We walk our tackles through this to get them into a fit position with proper balance. This particular situation is exclusive to the offensive tackle against the wide defensive end, but we will tight fit each of our offensive linemen to the particular outside techniques that they will face, and work them through the progression.

Our next point of emphasis for all offensive linemen is the aiming point. Our aim point on the tight fit progression is to take our inside eye to the outside number. The offensive tackle will come off and tight fit on the angle against a wide defensive end, and the offensive guard will tight fit on a 3 technique, both with the inside eye to the outside number.

If we can get to the outside number and get control, then we own the defensive player and the ball should go on outside, but if the defensive player does as he is coached to do—widens and tries to stay in his gap—then the inside opens up. We are using the defensive player's power, his weight, and how he was coached, all against him.

The center's technique may be a little different. He has to work on an outside block where we are trying to gain lateral position on the defender on an outside sweep. In that situation, he will just drop-step, rip his arm through the nose man, and finish up the field with his arm into the defender.

If you use the fit and drive drills, you have to coach the defense as much as the offense, which most of us know already. If you use scout team players, you have to coach them so they will work on the proper angles and give the blockers pressure on those angles.

As the blocker goes through the block and extends his arms, he will use what we call a strong playside hand. He will lock out with his playside arm and continue to move, which will open up the outside gap, or widen it so that we have the inside gap to run in. Again, I will coach from a position where I can check the angle of the block. If I want the angle to be 45 degrees, then I will stand there at 45 degrees and see that he is blocking on that angle.

Here is how we teach *double-teams*. Both blockers will settle step with the foot away from the defender, step upfield, and hit with the top of their pads. I repeat, settle with the foot away, step upfield, and hit with the top of the pads. Now, that is assuming that the defender comes off of the ball. If he just stands there, you could just lead step, get into him, and knock him as far off the ball as you can, but the guys we see are going to come off of the ball.

If you settle with the foot away, which is really just a timing step, and then step upfield and hit with the top of your pads, you will catch the defensive lineman with one foot in the air. Even if you do not catch him with one foot in the air, you will definitely have your pads under his pads, because a lunge off the ball most likely will bring his pads to a horizontal plane.

When we work the Double-Team Drill, we do not necessarily work two guys who ordinarily work together. We may work two centers together, or maybe a center and a tackle, because they are all the same. We use this block on the isolation play, where we isolate the playside linebacker and then we will double-team off to the backside linebacker.

What I am looking for in this drill are the pads: Can I see their number? Do they have a wide base? Since I cannot see everything at once, I like to do this in a half-line situation so I can watch the things I need to watch. What happens on double-teams a lot is that one blocker will be too high, looking for the linebacker, and we lose the power of the block. If one of them is too high I can see his numbers, but if they both block with the top of their pads, I cannot see their numbers. The rest of the contact is with the near forearm. It is not with the elbow, but the top part of the forearm right here.

We do not get much movement on our double-teams. I would like to tell you that we knock them all off the ball, but with a good nose man, if you can stalemate him and get him a couple of steps off the ball, that is pretty good football. With our guard and tackle on a power play, we seem to get more movement because a 3 technique is a two-way player, but with a one-way player such as an A gap player, it is hard because they read that double-team and they can sit in there.

So, we are working to get the double-team moved off the ball, and we say that whoever is coming off comes off at linebacker level, meaning the level where the double-team gets to the linebacker. If the linebacker were to blitz, then that is linebacker level when he gets onto your plane.

We teach the double-team in a fit position. We fit them with the top of their pads in there. We get the defender right over the top. We are going to learn to roll our hips and use our butts to lift the defender. I really emphasize rolling the hips and using their forearms.

If the settle step is too deep, you will turn your shoulders. If the uncovered lineman turns his shoulders, now that becomes a down block, the covered lineman has 600 pounds on him, and he cannot get off the block. We do not want that. We want to work the double-team straight back off of the ball.

Let me go to the tape and look at some applications. We start with the power play (Diagram #1). Look at the guard and tackle taking their settle steps, double-teaming, and coming off to the backside linebacker. The guard is a little high and you can see his numbers, but the tackle is pretty good. He is low enough that we are getting some movement. We tell the ballcarrier on the power play to read the A gap to the pulling guard. If the A gap is closed, then he follows the guard.

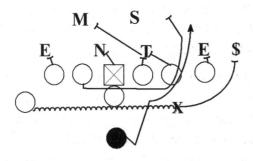

Diagram #1. Power Play

Here is a look at the isolation play (Diagram #2). The opponent here is Virginia Tech, and frankly they are a little better than we are. They are hard guys to move and they are hard guys to block, so there are some real good applications in here. I put this one in here because it is a good example of when guys are better than my guys, or my guys are a little smaller. We are double-teaming the nose man to the Sam linebacker. We do not get a lot of movement because that A-gap player knows where the ball is. If you double-team him, he will sit the A gap. His coach told him to keep the A gap, set the point, and do not get out of the A gap.

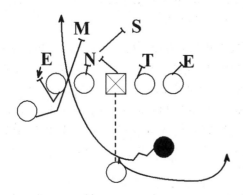

Diagram #2. Isolation Play

We are able to come off at linebacker level, because we had a little leverage on the defender. We do not have a great deal of movement, but we do have them all blocked, except for the safety.

Here is another good look at the isolation play against the same opponent (Diagram #3). We do not get a lot of movement there, but we block the play and the back made the safety miss.

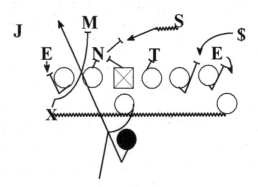

Diagram #3. Isolation Play

Here our center comes off the double-team at linebacker level (Diagram #4). Something else to point out here is the defensive end that is wide. Our left tackle sits on him and then uses his momentum against him. I would bet we do not move this guy a bit, but he cannot make the tackle because we blocked him on his angle. He can make a choice here: He can go inside and let the safety make the tackle, or he can just hang right here or go up the field and we have a run lane.

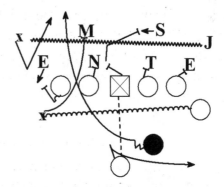

Diagram #4. Isolation Play

Now, let us look at another isolation play. On the double-team we get our two settle steps and we get a little movement. The nose man moves to the outside, so our center should work up to linebacker level (Diagram #5). The defensive end takes himself up the field and we are able to get a running lane, but the center decides to come off early when instead he should keep climbing to linebacker level.

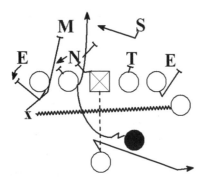

Diagram #5. Isolation Play

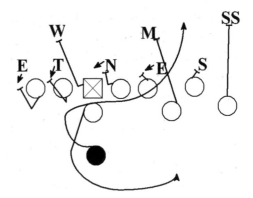

Diagram #7. Inside Zone

Here is the last isolation play I will show you (Diagram #6). We get a very good double-team and the center comes off at linebacker level, but watch the left offensive tackle. We were just talking about blocking the wide defensive end and we said that his tight fit was inside eye to outside number. Our tackle goes a little too far here and the end is able to go inside. What saves him is that he gets his weight on his left instep. This is where instep and bracing really take over. As the defender moves, he is able to push off his left instep, redirect, and take him inside. The ballcarrier adjusts, breaks a tackle and is able to get a couple of yards.

Here, the center, left guard, and left tackle are blocking on angles, and we chop the 3 technique (Diagram #8). We get a little running lane and the back is able to break a tackle and score.

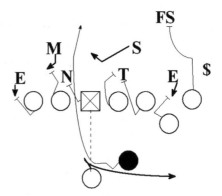

Diagram #8. Inside Zone

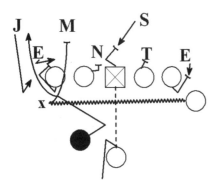

Diagram #6. Isolation Play

We will just talk coaching points on these two zone plays before we actually get to how we teach the inside zone (Diagram #7). These are angle blocks, and our left tackle and left guard are blocking them on those angles. The same with the right guard. Everyone is blocking on angles, we use what the defense does against them, and we get a cutback in there.

I want to go over how we teach the inside zone play and I have several good cut-ups to show you. I want to show you how we teach the double-teams, how we run the play, and what our back's aiming point is.

Here are our coaching points for inside zone. We just did a lead-up on it when we talked about all of our fundamentals. We block on the angle. You saw that in the last applications we just looked at.

A second coaching point for our offensive line is to stay on the course. You take your brace step to wherever your assignment is, and you stay on that course. That is what "course" is. Do not turn back inside. The only thing that would take you off your course is another adjacent offensive lineman shoving you off.

You want to cover the defender. The back runs where he does not see the other color jersey. If you are the home team and your back sees a white jersey sitting right there, he is going to run the other way.

As blockers, we are going to lose ground. Slow down and be on the block when the ball hits the line of scrimmage. Now, I am really reluctant to say "slow down," and it does not sound like it makes sense because we have got to come off the ball. But we need to be in our blocks when the ball hits the line of scrimmage. In other words, if we are blocking a linebacker, we want to be on him when that ballcarrier gets there, rather than get to the linebacker right away and he sheds the block by the time the ballcarrier gets there.

For our next coaching point, we tell our blocker that his course should intersect the defender's line of force. We know that line of force means the angle at which the defender comes off the ball, whether it is a linebacker who fits the B gap, the defensive end who fits the C gap, or the nose man in the A gap.

We do not leave the defensive lineman unless you are shoved or scooped off. We stay on him. Uncovered offensive linemen must get your head in front of defender when scooping your adjacent offensive lineman.

Our running back must read/chase the inside leg of the frontside tackle. This is an angle zone for us. If we are in the shotgun, we have the same aim point for our back. He takes three steps beyond the mesh, one, two, three, then he reads, or chases, the inside leg of his offensive tackle.

Let me get back to the tape. This is our play, and this is a great diagram (Diagram #9). The back is in the shotgun. He is going three steps and reading the inside leg of that tackle. We are going to double-team. We want to get as many double-teams as we can. When the center and guard work together, the tackle is by himself and we have to make a call.

We work to an ID'd linebacker. We have to call the "ID" that we are working to. In this case, we are

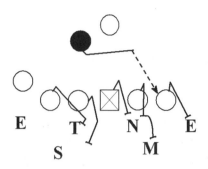

Diagram #9. The Zone Blocking Scheme

working to the Mike, so "Mike" is our ID. On the backside, we are going to zone. The guard zones the A gap and the tackle zones the B gap.

We get a better picture from the end-zone shot. There is the running back's aim point right there. He reads the inside leg of the tackle and he has space there, so he takes that course right there.

The center can read this by himself and he calls for the guard and says he needs some help on this one, so they are going to double-team back into this linebacker. One of the coaching points of this is that if that linebacker is stacked on the defensive lineman, we have to keep our heads out of the block, and adjust on the run.

You can see what the back sees. He takes his steps, and as he pushes on his third step he is either going to go B gap, or if the double-team pushes across the zone, he is going to cut it back.

As you can see on the film, I am going to be upset with the backside guard. He did not take a course to intersect the defender's line of force. The line of force for that Sam linebacker is the A gap. He has it. The guard is there and what does he do? He turns back toward the linebacker's original alignment, because that is what they all want to do.

Had he just stayed on his original course, he would have been on the block when the ballcarrier hit the line of scrimmage.

We will make a "cut" call on the backside and clip the 3 technique if the Sam linebacker "plusses" over too far to the frontside. The guard essentially says for the tackle to cut this guy because "I am not going to touch him."

Here is how we teach the frontside combination (Diagram #10). Covered or uncovered linemen: If covered, use a drive block. You saw that. He just did a tight fit. Our uncovered lineman reads the linebacker and he feels the down lineman, so his eyes are going to stay on his linebacker. Now, I have done it both ways, men. I have had him keep his eyes on that down lineman and he chases it too far. He chases it so far that he lets the linebacker have a two-way go.

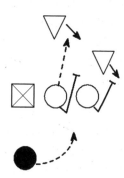

Diagram #10. Frontside Combination

Remember, the ball is going right here at the aim point. I have the uncovered man read the linebacker, and he sticks his near hand out and feels for the down lineman. That is what we want. Of course, there will be two brace steps in there to begin with.

Here is what happens if the down lineman comes inside (Diagram #11). If the defensive lineman comes inside, the uncovered lineman is going to shove the covered lineman off to the linebacker. A

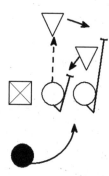

Diagram #11. Defensive Lineman Comes Inside

key point there is the uncovered lineman's hand has to go into the ribs, because there is no pad there. If the hand goes on the shoulder pad, the covered lineman cannot tell who is shoving him. It could be anybody grabbing him, so we put that hand out and shove him in the ribs. As we take the block over, we want that helmet to cross over to the defender as well. We also give them the same aim points as before, which is inside eye on outside number. We say to stay on course and cover the defender. The ballcarrier will read it and find the open space.

Let's look at the combination involving the center and the frontside guard versus the 3 technique and the ID'd linebacker (Diagram #12). We do the same two braces as before, with the center reading the linebacker and feeling the down lineman, coming off on that angle, and shoving with the near hand.

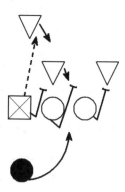

Diagram #12. Center/Guard Combo to ID'd Linebacker

Let me put it all together and look at some tapes on the inside zone play. (Video)

Guys, that is it. I appreciate your attention. If you need anything from me, or if you would like to get these instructional tapes, I hope you would just give me a call or stop over at Marshall University at any time. I would be happy to talk to you about football, or recruiting, and if you have some good players, just let us know. We always need a bunch of them. Thank you.

RUN AND PLAY-ACTION PASS FROM THE SPREAD

University of Toledo

Thank you. I have been at Toledo for five years. In those five years, our offense has been in the top 15 in the country. We use a balanced attack by running and passing from the spread offense.

I will start out talking about our one-back offense and our inside zone plays. I will show it to you from under the center and in the shotgun. In the shotgun, we have a read zone play also.

With the inside zone play, the first thing you have to look at is the philosophy of the play. Your players have to know what the number-one play in your offense is. On what play does the coach hang his hat? What is the featured play in your offense? You have to instill in your players that in a critical situation, they know we will run the inside zone.

We do not huddle. We get off the ground, get back on the line, and attack. We attack defenses and put them on their heels. That is one reason we have been successful. The bottom line is our players know our number-one play is the inside zone.

When we run the Inside Drill, we play seven on nine. We have seven offensive players against nine defensive personnel. In that period, we run 12 plays and 10 of them are inside zone. It does not matter what type of defense they play, we run the inside zone. Your players have to understand that the inside zone is a tough, physical play.

Our linemen align in a two-point stance. If we are on the one-yard line or the 99-yard line, our linemen are in a two-point stance. We practice that every day. The most important thing on the zone play are the steps within the offense. Footwork is critical to this offense. The steps of the running back have to mirror the steps of the linemen.

The footwork of the offensive linemen and the running back has to be exact. If there is no sync in the steps, separation occurs. That cannot happen because when the hole opens, the back has to cut immediately into it. If he has to take one more step to get to his plant foot, he may miss the hole.

To run the inside zone play, the splits in the offensive line have to be exact. The split we look for is 24 inches. That gives you six inches to play with in the split. If the right guard is quicker than the tackle, we probably end up with an 18-inch split, which is almost perfect. The guards and tackles have to work together. They do so many combination blocks, so they must to be on the same page.

The first thing I need to talk about is the combo block. I will draw up a 4-3 defensive front with the quarterback under the center. The first combo block is over the tight end. The first step is a zone bucket step where we lose three to six inches of our depth. The second step is the most important step. The lineman must get his foot back on the ground, pointed to the crotch of the defensive end. The next part of the block is the gap block stage. That is a series of two-step movements on the zone track going down the line of scrimmage and up the field.

The technique is the same for a guard, tackle, or tight end. The blocking rules start with cover or uncovered. The guard is covered and the tackle is uncovered (Diagram #1). The tight end has a 7-technique defensive end aligned on him. That defender is the block of the tackle. His blocking assignment is the Sam linebacker that is off the line of scrimmage and outside. That gives him time to pound the double-team with the tackle on the 7 technique and work toward his outside block. He does not want to leave immediately and leave the tackle on an island.

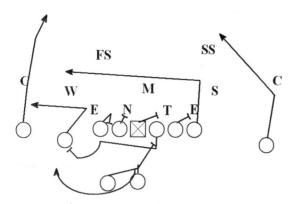

Diagram #1. Tight End/Tackle Double-Team

The tight end steps with the tackle and gets his inside hand on the 7 technique. His eyes are outside on his blocking assignment. The tackle is trying to take the 7 technique over and block him off the ball. We want to displace the line of scrimmage and stay on the double-team as long as we can. If the 7 technique works outside, that is fine. The wider he goes, the better the play.

The guard has a 3-technique tackle aligned on him. He works his zone two-step just like the tackle and tight end. If the 3 technique plays in the B gap, the guard has done his job. He continues to block the 3 technique, looking for movement out and back off the line of scrimmage.

If the 3 technique spikes inside the guard, the offensive guard post blocks him as the center comes on him. The center has the toughest job in America. He has a backside shade nose aligned on him and a possible inside spike from the strongside. However, the first thing he has to do is snap the ball.

If the center has the quarterback under him, he cannot take his six-inch bucket step without screwing up the exchange (Diagram #2). He can in the shotgun, but not with the quarterback under. He has to get his steps as flat as he can toward the guard and keep his arm and hand back on the shade nose to the backside. If he gets no spike from the 3 technique, he stays on the shade nose with the backside guard. His eyes are up on the linebacker. He

plays the same technique as the tight end on the 7 technique.

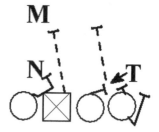

Diagram #2. Guard/Center/Guard

The chief coaching point for the center and tight end is to use one hand on the inside shade. By doing that, he keeps his shoulders square to the line of scrimmage. If he puts both hands on the inside shade, his shoulder turn, and he will never get back outside if the linebacker runs through the gap. The backside guard and tackle use the six-inch bucket step just like the frontside.

If the playside guard is uncovered, the center knows he is by himself on his block (Diagram #3). If the playside tackle has a 4i or inside shoulder on him, his technique is the same as the tight end's technique in the first situation. His blocking assignment is the linebacker off the line of scrimmage. He steps and gets his inside hand on the 4i with the guard coming to take over the block.

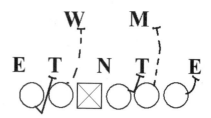

Diagram #3. Zone-Blocking Scheme

The playside guard zone steps anticipating the slant from the 4i. We teach these techniques under the chute. The offensive linemen have to stay low and keep their pad levels down. They make contact under the chute and work the defender out from under the chute before working up for the linebacker. We work hard on all the individual technique before we work outside the chute. We want to build great habits and techniques.

The backside guard and tackle have a double-team block, with the guard as the post and the tackle taking over the block. The guard holds off the defensive tackle with his hand, and eyeballs the linebacker. They work the defensive tackle down the line and up the field toward the guard's block on the linebacker.

On the double-teams, the worst thing that can happen is to have separation between the linemen. They have to be foot-to-foot and hip-to-hip. If they can do that, we have a chance to be successful. The number-one killer of the zone play is penetration.

A coaching point for the slip blocker is to stay on the double-team as long as possible. As long as the linebacker keeps his depth, there is no need to get up to him. Until the linebacker starts to move toward the line of scrimmage, the post man stays on the double.

The aiming point for the offensive linemen on the inside zone play is the outside teat of the defensive lineman. If the guard is covered, he will work by himself or with the center on a combo. If he is uncovered, he will work with the tackle on a combo block. Everyone has the same rules.

The running back aligns at a depth of six-and-a-half yards from the line of scrimmage. I have one running back that is quick as a cat. He aligns seven-and-a-half yards from the line of scrimmage. That distance will fluctuate with the speed of the back. The speed of the back is 85 percent as he starts the play. He wants to be under control.

In his stance, if you draw a line along his toes and extend it to his right, that gives you a guide for the steps in the play. When the back takes an open step, his foot should hit three inches behind the line. His next step is a crossover step that hits three inches in front of the line. His third step goes downhill and is approximately six inches in front of the line. The quarterback drives out from the center at four o'clock. He extends the ball and hands it to the running back with the mesh area at four-and-a-half yards deep.

We want the linebackers to see the ball being extended to the running back because that sets up our play-action pass. All five year I have been at Toledo, we have been in the top 15 in total offense and the top 10 in passing efficiency.

On the fourth step, the running back's inside elbow goes up with his thumb turned down on his sternum. That keeps the elbow up and prevents it from falling down and hitting the ball as it comes into the mesh. The key to the entire element of the handoff is the running back having his shoulders square to the line of scrimmage. The aiming point for the running back is the inside leg of the playside offensive tackle.

If the guard is covered, the running back reads the first down linemen over the guard. I coach the running back up to three yards past the line of scrimmage. After that, you recruit what comes next. The skills after that are natural and instinctive. The only thing I coach is ball security. I have coached this for 17 years and I have three running backs playing in the NFL. Once you get by the linebacker, run to daylight. If there is no daylight, create it.

When the running back gets the ball, he presses the line of scrimmage. If his key works outside, the back comes underneath the guard. If the guard reaches the defensive tackle, but there is still color on the outside of the guard, the back comes underneath. If there is no opposite shirts in the hole, he stays on the inside hip of the tackle and runs into the hole.

Teams that want to stop our zone play use line stunts involving the defensive ends. They twist them inside and slant them down the line. The running back reads the 3 technique. When he sees the 3 technique slant inside, he jumps to the C gap and stays as tight to the tackle's hip as he can. Ninety-six percent of missed tackles by the linebacker are the result of overpursuit. If the line is going one way, the linebackers are going the other.

The running back stays tight on the tackle's hip and gets inside the linebacker scraping outside.

We run the tight zone from the shotgun set (Diagram #4). The blocking for the offensive line does not change. The path of the running back and his reads are different. The play for the running back is entirely different. He is looking from a different angle and is tighter in his path. He still is reading the frontside for his key.

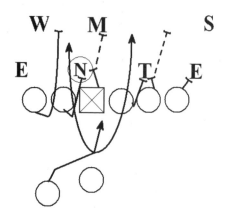

Diagram #4. Tight Zone

The home-run cut is in the backside A gap. The running back has to control his takeoff to give the blocking time to develop. To get the ball all the way back to the A gap, he has to have good hip flexibility. If he is having trouble, I move his alignment back a bit. Be careful not to tip the play with the alignment.

He aims his first step for a spot in front of the toe of the quarterback. He takes the open step, crossover step, and on the third step, he receives the ball from the quarterback. On the third step, the back has to be under control. It is not a flying handoff. On the tight zone, we read the nose or shade on the center, if there is one. If there is no one aligned on the center, we read the man over the guard.

The quarterback can read the backside defensive end and pull the ball, but we did not do that much this past year (Diagram #5). It was a matter of keeping the quarterback from taking too many hits. I think for the year, we ran a designed run for the quarterback about 25 times.

On the read play, the quarterback takes a false step away from the read key. That gives the

quarterback more time to read the defensive end. If the quarterback reads two defenders outside, he gives the ball every time.

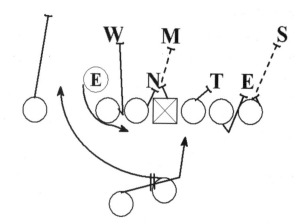

Diagram #5. Quarterback Zone Read

We tell our wideouts to block this play like a sweep play. They do not wait. They attack their blocking assignment right now. They have to assume the quarterback keeps the ball every time. If the quarterback gives the ball to the tailback, and the defensive back runs under him, that is okay.

Most of the time, you run the quarterback away from the tight end (Diagram #6). Against Ball State, we game planned to run the quarterback read to the tight end. We read the defensive end aligned on the tight end. The tight end arc blocks on the support player. The wide receiver to that side goes up on the next level to block.

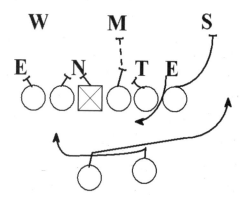

Diagram #6. Quarterback Read Toward the Tight End

There is not a defensive end in America ready to play this scheme. He charges into the C gap and reads the tackle zone scheming away. He expects the tight end to block him, but the tight end takes an outside release. He sees the fake by the tailback and closes to the inside. The quarterback pulls the ball and run to the outside.

Defenses counter the quarterback read by using the "cue" call. They crash the defensive end and give the quarterback a pull read. The linebacker hangs and fills the alley on the quarterback. They never do that to the tight-end side. That is what is so good about the play into the tight end. Usually defenses align their bigger, more physical defensive end on the tight-end side. That is another plus for the play. He is a little slower than, and not as agile as, the other defensive end.

The quarterback, as he makes his ride on the tailback, opens his toe to the side he will run. That allows him to get outside quicker. The tight end on the arc block has to run at the outside shoulder of the force defender. We do not want him to go outside, set inside, and try to block inside. The referee will call him for a hold every time on a move like that.

We design the play to go outside. If the quarterback takes the ball inside, the tight end gets the holding call every time using the wrong technique. If he attacks the outside shoulder, the defender will widen and it is an easier block if the quarterback cut inside.

The next thing I want to get to is the power play we added two years ago. It is a good companion play in the spread offense. It is a hard, physical gap-scheme type of play. You can incorporate this into your spread offense and it works well. You can do some good things with this play using formations to move the defense. We run this from the shotgun formation, which fits with what we do.

This play for the running back is an A-gap, B-gap, or C-gap play (Diagram #7). His toes are seven yards off the line of scrimmage. We snap the ball and he takes a drop set. The drop set is to let the guard pull. He drop steps, open steps, crossover steps, and plants. He comes downhill at that point at the A gap. If the hole is there, he takes it. If there is no hole, he bounces the ball from the B gap to the C gap.

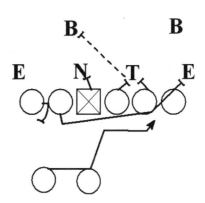

Diagram #7. Power 9 Technique

This is a great gap scheme. It is a great change-up to running the spread zone. It looks like we are running the zone play, but it is the power play. It is a hard downhill play where you can play smashmouth football.

The tight end gives the pulling guard a call as to the defensive alignment on him. If he calls "wide," the pulling guard knows the defender is outside the tight end. His pull will end up in a trap block on the 9-technique defender. The backside tackle steps down into the A gap and turns back. The center blocks back and cuts off for the pulling guard.

The right guard and tackle double on the 3-technique tackle. It is the tackle's block unless the defensive tackle spikes inside. If that happens, the guard washes him down and the tackle goes over the top and seals the backside linebacker. If the tackle is a B-gap player, the guard posts him for the tackle, knowing he has the backside linebacker. They drive the defender and the offensive tackle takes over. The guard comes off for the backside linebacker.

The tight end blocks down on the frontside linebacker and the guard kicks out the 9-technique defender. The running back starts in the A gap and follows the guard outside. He stays tight on the double-team and gets on the backside of the blocks as he goes.

To win championships, you must run the ball and play defense. I was the offensive coordinator at an I-AA school for three years. In all three years, we won the national championship because we ran the ball and played great defense.

In the games played in the NFL last year, the team that won the turnover margin won 82 percent of those games. To win games, you have to hang on to the football. That is not just the running back and quarterback. It is also the wide receivers, tight ends, center, and kick runners.

Our offensive linemen get downfield to block on all passes. If anyone is standing and the whistle has not blown, we get after them. However, we had two tackles recover fumbles downfield last year. That is hustle and extra effort on their part.

If the tight end has a 7-technique defender, he calls "solid" (Diagram #8). The other four linemen block the same as they did on the other play. The guard pulls, and as he passes the center, he looks for daylight. When he finds the daylight, he turns up and blocks any off-colored jersey. If he meets an off-colored jersey on his pull path, he blows it up. It may not be the defender he was supposed to block, but that is his rule. We block the line of scrimmage first, before we move up to the second level.

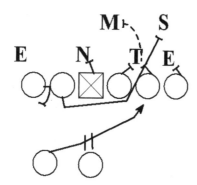

Diagram #8. Power 7 Technique

As the guard pulls, he looks for the playside linebacker. The tight end blocks down on the 7-technique defender. If he gets movement down the line, the guard may go all the way around the horn to get to the linebacker. If the linebacker runs through, he blocks him. If he hangs, he turns up at the first gap and blocks him.

If we get some kind of 50-front look, we get a double-team between the tight end and tackle (Diagram #9). One of them slips to the linebacker. The guard and center double on the noseguard, with

one of them slipping to the backside linebacker. The guard pulls and applies his rules. If the inside linebacker blitzes, the guard blocks him and the back takes the ball into the A gap. If he scrapes, the tight end blocks him. The guard pulls and kicks out on the 9-technique defender.

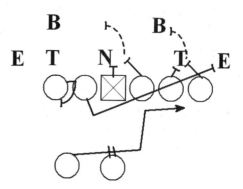

Diagram #9. 50 Front

We can make all kinds of adjustments by using motion (Diagram #10). We can get to the two-back power, except we use a tight end instead of a fullback. We arc the tight end for the support, kick-out with the motion tight end, and turn the guard up inside for the linebacker.

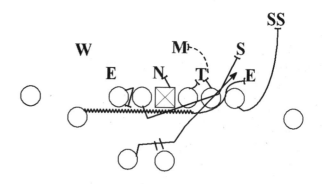

Diagram #10. Two-Back Power

As a running back coach, I have to talk about ball security. I teach five pressure points on the football. I do not cup the end of the ball with the palm of the hand. I split the first and second finger and put the peace sign over the tip of the ball. The palm and remaining fingers are the second and third points. I cover the ball with my forearm as my fourth pressure point. The biceps are the fifth pressure point.

I carry the ball with the tip up. If the ballcarrier lets the tip of the ball go down, he eliminates one pressure point. With the tip up, the ball is secure. I never tell my players to take the ball to the belly.

In your practices every day, you have to teach ball security. We do a drill in practice called the Figure Eight Drill (Diagram #11). I put two dummies on the ground and make the running backs run figure eights around the dummies. I give them two balls to secure. I walk around the dummies with a dummy and punch, pull, and hit them with the dummy. When they run the figure eight around the bag, it makes them think about getting around the bags and takes their minds off the ball.

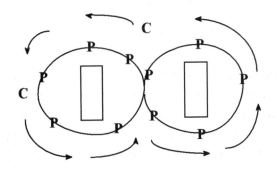

Diagram #11. Figure Eight Drill

We also use a Cone Drill. We make them weave in and out of the cones carrying the ball (Diagram #12). I line a gauntlet of players with dummies on either side of the cones. As the runner weaves through the cones, the dummy-holders hit his arms and ball with the dummies.

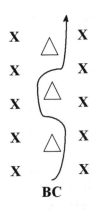

Diagram #12. Cone Drill

When the players do these drills, you must make them think about something other than ball security. If you watch your game films, when the player gets in the open, he has a tendency to rock the ball and not secure it. That is when fumbles occur. When they do not see the defender is when they are vulnerable.

When you do ball-security drills, make the ballcarrier keep running. Do not let him stop and secure the ball. Make him move with the ball, because you never see a player run straight up the field with the ball. Even if he is behind the defense, he has to weave to deter the tackle. In drills, make him slow and accelerate repeatedly, and hit him with dummies.

The last thing I want to do is talk about the play-action pass. I will go through a couple of them and talk about the quarterback action (Diagram #13). The key to play-action passes is the offensive linemen. They have to sell the run. The pad level of the offensive linemen is critical. It has to look like the running play you fake.

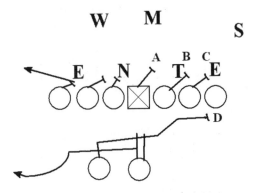

Diagram #13. Play-Action Naked

The running back has to run the inside zone play and sell it to the defense. When we run our zone fake, they have to draw two players with them. If they do not, they get a minus for that play. The running back has to block the D gap outside.

The center has the A gap, the guard has the B gap, and the tackle has the C gap. The running back has the D gap and has protection as his first responsibility. The fake is secondary. If someone is coming off the edge, that is his primary concern.

The first thing the running back has to do in the run fake is keep his eyes up and alert as he does on the zone play. The back does this when there is no blitz threat. The second part of the fake is the burst. The running back changes speed and accelerates for three to four steps and doubles back toward the line. It is not running—it is changing speed.

The burst draws the attention of the linebacker and safety. Teach the back to grab his jersey with his hands because it conceals the fact that he does not have the ball. The defenders cannot see whether he has it or not.

The quarterback extends the ball as the running back comes to the mesh area. He puts the ball in the belly, rides, and pulls the ball, tucking it on his right hip with his left hand. The right hand, now empty, extends as the running back passes the mesh. He takes a brief three-count shuffle of the feet to give the defensive end time to see the fake. The end reacts down to the fake and the quarterback comes out the backside with the ball.

The one, two, three shuffle allows the quarterback to get balanced and under control. He opens his toe and gets around to the outside on the play-action. He bubbles around at a depth of eight to 10 yards from the line of scrimmage. He has to snap his head around quickly to see if the defensive end bit on the play-action fake. If he did not, he has to pull up and start looking for the tight end or the quick-throw receiver.

The tight end runs a zone step to the inside. If the defensive end is a good player, he may have to chip on him before he releases. This year, I always knew the tight end would get open. After he takes his zone steps inside, he releases to the flat. He is alert from the beginning, because the throw may come right away.

As the quarterback comes around the corner, he sees the defensive end coming for him. He gets his toe around toward the line of scrimmage and drifts back slightly. He gets up on his toe and throws the ball. He does not want to continue to attack the perimeter. He has to get his hips around to throw the ball. He takes a half step and gets up on his toe.

If he tries to throw the ball going backward, it will sail on him. His elbow will come forward because he cannot follow through, causing the ball to sail.

He more than likely will take a hit from the defensive end as he tries to throw the ball. That is an occupational hazard for the quarterback. On this play, we like to give the quarterback choices in levels (Diagram #14). In the two-tight-end set, the playside tight end runs the quick-check-out pattern. The backside tight end runs an over pattern. He comes behind the linebacker and gets vertical as he gets to the playside flat area. The third pattern is a deep over pattern coming over the top. That gives the quarterback three levels in his vision.

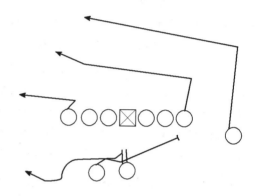

Diagram #14. Over Pattern

We also have the bootleg pass as part of our attack (Diagram #15). We run the bootleg because we can protect the quarterback with a pulling guard. If your quarterback is not a particularly good athlete, he has trouble running the naked. If you pull the guard and protect him, the play-action is a viable part of the passing game. You give up the fake for protection, but you give the quarterback more time to make his decision.

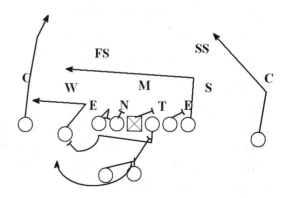

Diagram #15. Bootleg

DEFENSIVE TACKLE PLAY

Auburn University

This was an exciting year at Auburn. Last year at Auburn, we were fortunate to lead the SEC in sacks. My lecture tonight is rushing the passer from the inside. I will talk primarily about defensive tackle play.

We do not have all the answers. If you can get one or two drills from this topic, it should be helpful to you. I appreciate you all coming tonight.

To be a good pass rusher and play good defense, you must have great effort. We strive at Auburn for that one thing. If you did not run to the football at Auburn, you did not play. There was no disgrace if a defensive player was knocked down or blocked.

If you were knocked down, you got up and sprinted to the ball. The first thing we talked about at Auburn was "relentless pursuit." We wanted our players to know what playing hard was. We had signs in all our meeting rooms so our players would see what we thought was important.

We never wanted our players to loaf and described for them what loafing was.

What is a Loaf?

- Changing speeds
- *Not* turning and going to the ball
- Getting passed up by another player
- Lying on the ground—Get up! *Hot stove*
- Turning down a *hit*

If a player slowed or sped up on his way to the ball, that was a loaf. If they did not turn and sprint to the ball every time, that was a loaf. If the player pursuing the football was passed by another player at his position, that was considered a loaf. We referred to lying on the ground as a "hot stove."

They had to get up quickly off the hot stove and pursue the ball. If you turned down a hit, you did not need to be playing defensive football.

We had this on the wall in all of our meeting rooms. We graded the game and every practice session each week on effort. Our players received a plus or minus as a grade in everything they did. We did many pursuit drills and drills that taught effort. Pass rush was nothing but effort.

In a third-and-long situation, we made a huddle call that alerted our players to think "pass rush" first and "run" second. Our call for that alert was "jet." At other times, we used a "bird" call. That call meant we wanted to rush the passer. Our base defense was "stack." If we called "stack-jet," we rushed the passer. That alerted our linemen that it was a passing situation.

We wanted our players to know the down and distance. They changed their stance and crowded the football. We wanted them to be almost offside in their alignment. We changed our stance to a sprinter's stance. When the center put his hand on the ball, our front four made a "ball" call. That alerted everyone on the defense that we were ready to go. The center could not snap the ball unless he had his hand on it.

We had an old football we used in practice that was spray-painted green. We tried to emphasize getting off on the ball. I did not know whether the green ball worked or not, but they thought it did. They concentrated on the green ball more.

We never go on a snap or cadence in our drills or any of our work. We always went on movement. We started every drill we do with movement. We were a ball-key defense. When the ball moved, the defense moved. Do not get lazy in your drills and not use some kind of movement to start each drill you do.

The jet call put our defensive players in a sprinter stance. The base narrowed and the weight went forward on the hands. We took the off hand and cocked it back in our stance. We had a different first step with our run and pass techniques. In run blocking, the first step was a short six-inch step. In the pass rush, the first step was an elongated step. We tried to gain ground in the first step. When the ball moved, the defensive tackle came off low and hard, he threw his off arm, and got upfield as quickly as he could.

Each player had to go through his presnap reads. He read the weight the offensive lineman put on his hand. If he had his weight forward on his hand, we felt it was a running indicator. If the weight was back in his stance, we felt that indicated a pass-block or pull technique. We called that light and heavy.

We watched the line splits of the offensive linemen. If the quarterback was in the shotgun set, we watched the leg kick. Most quarterbacks use a leg kick to tell the center he was ready for him to snap the ball. They had to know what signal the quarterback used. If he used the leg kick, the center usually snapped the ball within one second of the leg kick. We needed to scout the films to see if we could get a jump on the snap. You can teach presnap reads to your players.

Before the snap of the ball, the defensive linemen needed to have a pass-rush move in mind. Every player you have on your team will have a different pass rush. Body styles fit the player's ability to pass rush. A short defensive lineman should not use a swim technique, because it puts him at a disadvantage when he tries to get his arm over. The players with speed will be good speed rushers. Stronger players will be better at bull and power rushes.

We never tried to teach our players five or six different moves, because they could not get good at that many moves. A short, squatty nosetackle did not need to learn how to use a swim technique.

The number-one thing besides effort in the pass rush is to "get off" the ball. Every day we started

practice with a get-off drill. The get-off started the progression we used to defeat the offensive linemen.

The second thing we taught was to attack the blocker. We wanted to close the distance between the defender and the offensive blocker. We wanted to create a new line of scrimmage. The defensive lineman had to close the distance before he could make a defensive move on the offense. We had to get off the ball and attack "half" the offensive lineman. When we talked about half a man, we considered from the armpit of the offensive lineman out as half a man. We never attacked the offense down the middle. If the offensive lineman was in the middle of the defensive player's numbers, he lost that match-up. He wanted to work on the outside of the blocker.

We wanted the defenders coming off low with their pads down. We told our players not to show their numbers to the offense. Some players felt that since the offensive blocker showed a high set, they were supposed to get high. They needed to maintain their pad level with their numbers down on their knees.

During the pass rush, the feet and hands never stopped. If the defender swam with his right arm, his right leg had to work with his arm. If the right arm swam, the right leg had to step through.

The hands and feet never stop. He had to remain active. If the defender stopped his hands and feet and restarted them, it gave the offensive blocker the chance to regroup, reset his feet, and get a new grab on the defender. If the defender could get the offensive blocker's shoulders turned, he could win the battle. If he got the blocker moving side to side in a situation where he was not comfortable in his stance, we could win the war.

Our front was a base 4-3 defense (Diagram #1). The defense was a left jet call. Our left tackle played a 3 technique and the nose aligned right in the 1-technique shade on the center. In the jet scheme, the 3 technique widened to a 4i position on the offensive tackle. The shade nose moved into a G position on the guard. The right and left defensive ends aligned in a 5 technique. However, they widened their techniques and threatened the tackles. We wanted the offensive tackles to be nervous about the speed of the defensive ends.

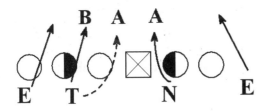

Diagram #1. Base Left Jet

The ends were speed players and had containment on the quarterback. The 3-technique defender was more athletic than the nose. The 3 technique was a "two-way-go" player. That meant that as the guard set, the 3 technique could rush into the B gap or the A gap. The nose rushed through the A gap to the right.

On any pass, we had the opportunity for a "fit" (Diagram #2). The fit was always between the weakside end and nose. In the fit call, the right defensive end had the ability to come underneath the block of the offensive tackle. The nose was the last defender to get any type of pressure. He was not the best athlete in the scheme and was more of a plugger. If he saw the end come under the block of the offensive tackle, he looped to the outside and contained the play. The fit was not a called stunt. It occurred naturally.

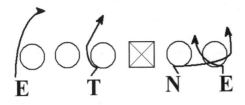

Diagram #2. Fit

The fit was a natural pass rush built into the left jet call. You could teach that on the first day of your practice. We did not call the fit, but it was an understood part of the base pass rush. The fit pressured the offensive tackle because the defensive end had a two-way go on him.

The defensive ends were speed rushers. They rushed using their speed to get up the field. The ends used different moves than the inside tackles. We allowed them to spin and counter back inside if they got even with the quarterback. They could use an in-and-out move and many finesse moves. The defensive ends were the best athletes and more linebacker-types. They had more speed, so we let them do more in the pass-rush games.

The 3 technique was a more athletic player than the nose. We allowed the 3 technique to use a "club and swim," "club and rip," an "in and out," and a bull rush. We taught the nose two options, a "club and rip" and a bull rush. That was all we taught him. We did not want him to swim, spin, and do all the fancy moves. We did not want him pushed out of the A gap. He also had to read the defensive end in the fit move.

We started every practice with the Get Off Drill (Diagram #3). We aligned our defensive line in a defense and gave them a situation. If we called first-and-10, they got into a run stance and got off on the ball.

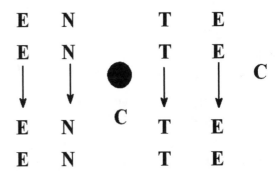

Diagram #3. Get Off Drill

We used the green ball as the get-off key. We did this drill with the ends and tackles and had them go at the same time. We sprinted past a coach, turned them around, and sent them back.

The second time through we called jet. They got into a pass-rush stance, widened their alignment, and got off on the ball. The coach moved the ball and they sprinted up the field for five yards. In this drill, we called cadence and tried to draw them offside before we moved the ball.

The next time through, we ran the fit schemes. We called the fit so we could look at it and make the corrections needed. The end came up and under and the nosed looped to the outside. We practiced all our twist games during this drill also. This drill is quick. It does not take any equipment or space, and we did it as a quick-tempo deal. You worked on get-off, stance, alignment, and effort.

We had a drill we used called Effort Pass Rush (Diagram #4). It was the best drill we did. It is good for conditioning also. It is the same concept as the Get Off Drill as far as alignment. We aligned in our defensive front. There were five offensive blockers in front of them. The center moved the ball and everyone reacted. The offensive blockers, on the snap, tried to grab the defensive linemen. The defensive linemen attacked and made their escape moves.

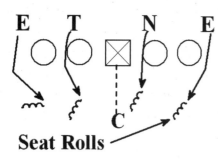

Diagram #4. Effort Pass Rush Part I

The coach stood seven yards deep with a football. The defensive linemen sprinted to the coach at full speed, buzzing their feet. On the signal, they dropped to their stomachs and popped up. They did three seat rolls on the coach's direction and started into the second part of the drill.

The second part of the drill involves a second coach. He stood four yards behind the first coach and dropped two yards as the linemen sprinted toward him (Diagram #5). He had a ball and three options he gave the linemen. He could pass the ball, run a draw, or throw a screen. He showed pass and gave the lineman a direction with the throw. He did not actually the ball, but gave them a direction to run. The defensive linemen redirected in straight lines in the direction of the throw.

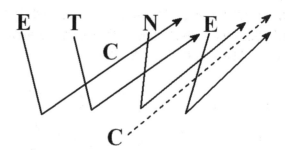

Diagram #5. Effort Pass Rush Part II

The coaching point for the linemen was not to turn their numbers to the quarterback. The linemen sank their hips before they changed direction. They pointed their feet and knees in the direction they had to run.

As they sprinted away from the coach, they made sure not to follow the same-colored jersey. They sprinted back to the line of the first coach.

In every drill, we talked about "three and out." We had to instill in our players everything we did had to be three and out. On first down, we had to be great. On second down, we had to be great. On third down, we had to be excellent.

When our players did the effort drill, they had to do everything perfectly. They planted and redirected at the proper angle. If they did anything wrong, it did not count. If they ran the drill perfectly, we told them, "Good job, and get ready for second down." They had to do three perfect runs to get off the field. If they did not, they started over at first down.

This drill kicked their butts. If one player caused the other three to start over, they were not happy. The second time they ran through the drill, the coach ran a draw. He raised the ball, pulled it down, and called draw. The linemen sank their hips, faced the quarterback, planted their foot and retraced their steps back the way they came. Using those techniques was the way we played the draw. The thing we did not want was a big fishhook instead of a planted foot. Everything in the drill had to be sunken hips and straight lines.

There was no order to the plays. The third time we ran the drill, the players did the same thing at the first coach (Diagram #6). As they sprinted to the second coach the third time, he ran the screen play.

The defensive end sunk his hips, planted, and got into the proper angle to the outside. Each defender had to do the drill perfectly with the proper angle or they started over on first down.

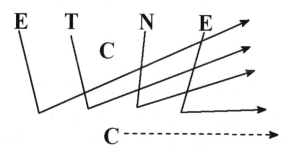

Diagram #6. Effort Pass Rush Part III

We did a team pursuit drill using the same principles. They had to do three perfect exercises to get off the field. We reinforced the three-and-out principles.

We had a coaching point for rushing the passer. If the quarterback threw the ball to the right side, the only defender with his hands up was the left end. The only defender with his hands up was the man coming straight to the quarterback. The other three defenders should be closing with the hands down. We coached them to make the sack and tackle high. If we tackled the quarterback high, he could not throw the ball. If we tackled him around the legs, he could still get the ball off.

The next drill we did was the Close Drill (Diagram #7). We aligned five offensive linemen and two defensive linemen in the drill. We went half line at a time. The offensive tackle and guard were in a two-point stance. The center snapped the ball. The offensive tackle and guard kicked out of their

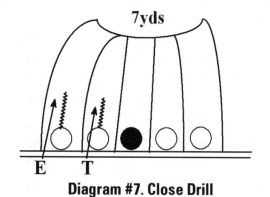

Diagram #7. Close Drill

stance and retreated in a pass set as fast as they could. The defensive tackle and end reacted to the movement of the offensive linemen. They fired off the ball and tried to touch the outside shoulder of the offensive linemen as quickly as they could. What we wanted to teach our defensive linemen was to close the distance on the offensive linemen before making a move.

When we did this drill, we used a grid area designed to help our defensive linemen with their pass-rush lanes.

If the defensive linemen made their moves before they reached the offensive linemen, they would probably be blocked. That was what the offensive linemen wanted the defense to do. If the defender could not touch the offensive lineman, he could not execute an escape.

The next thing we did was to put a defensive lineman in a fitted position on an offensive lineman. The first move we taught was the club. The coaching point was to close at the start of the move. There must be contact before a move was made. When making the move, the pads must be down. The target for the club was the back of the jersey and pads. The club had to be tight and without the arm fully extended.

The defender jabbed with the inside hand, clubbed with the outside hand, and grabbed cloth on the back of the jersey. Offensive linemen tied their jerseys down and greased their arms so the defensive linemen could not grab them. The back of the jersey was the only surface we could grab and hold.

The next technique was to flip the hips past the offensive blocker. The coaching point for flipping the hips was to get the inside hipbone of the defender past the inside hipbone of the blocker. Unless that happened, the pass rush did not happen.

Progression for the Club

- Close
- Outside club and grab cloth
- Pull and flip the inside hip
- Outside hand with outside leg

- Rip with the inside hand
- Step through with the inside leg

When the rip came through, it had to be tight to the body and ripped to the sky on the backside. We felt that once the defender closed the distance between himself and the blocker, there was a one-yard distance in which to make some type of move. We felt that if the end went deeper than seven yards on his charge, he did not help us. The defensive tackle could not go deeper than five yards. When we worked with a quarterback, we tried to get him to step up into the pocket so we could use our counters.

We also taught the swim technique in the Fit Drill. When they did that technique, they had to stay tight coming over the top. We practiced the swim technique in the same way we practiced the rip.

We taught the bull rush to our nose. We used the bull rush when we found a lineman soft setting in his pass block. In the bull rush, we taught the defender to put his eyes right into the V of the neck of the blocker. He shot his hands and took the blocker back as far as he would go. We wanted to push the pocket back into the lap of the quarterback.

Our defensive ends were the speed rushers that collapsed the pocket. The 3 technique had the two-way-go technique and the nose pushed the pocket back. We wanted to build a box around the quarterback.

For every move the defensive linemen had, they needed a counter move. We told our nose that as he pushed the blocker back, when he felt the blocker anchor, he had to use a counter move. The counter we taught the nose was a forward jerk. When the blocker anchored, the nose tackle jerked him forward and down. He completed the counter with a swim move over the top. We told him as long as the blocker was moving back, keep up the push.

We taught an in-and-out move to the 3-technique tackle (Diagram #8). On the out-and-in move, the tackle gave a head fake with the upper body to the outside and kept his feet straight up the

field. He tried to get the blocker to tilt his shoulder and jumped inside. We used a tight club, and ripped across into the opposite gap. The in-and-out was the opposite move.

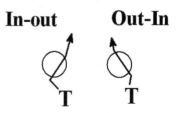

Diagram #8. In and Out

When we ripped across a lineman's body, we kept the arm down and tight. Any time you get the arm too high on a run or pass block, you create a new surface for the offensive blocker to grab. It is the same thing on a slant stunt. The defensive lineman never slants with his arm up in the air.

We restricted the inside linemen as to the pass-rush move they did. We wanted them to get good at performing one or two moves. We wanted them to push the pocket back. The defensive end on the other hand, did a number of different moves. They used speed in their pass rush. They started up the field and came under the blocker if they got the chance. We taught them the spin as their counter. If they got to the point of the shoulder of the offensive blocker, they could turn their rush into a bull rush.

We did not call the natural fit in the huddle. If the nose saw the end come under the offensive tackle, he knew he could get to the outside for containment. This may be a very late move by the nose. Unless there was a twist on, the fit was a live stunt. We told the nose and defensive end from day one, the end had the freedom to come under and he could loop outside.

We called the line stunt between the nose and tackle "tun" (Diagram #9). In the call, the "t" stands for tackle and "n" stands for nose. In the tun stunt, the tackle went first. The 3-technique tackle aligned in his jet alignment and worked two hard steps upfield, keying the center. If he saw the butt of the center, he planted off this outside foot and ripped across the guard's face, attacking the near hip of the center.

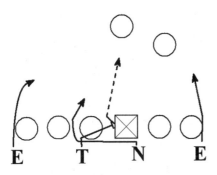

Diagram #9. Tun

He glances off the butt of the center and attacks upfield. If the center turned toward the 3 technique, the tackle went across his face into the weakside A gap. The nose aligned in a shade and pressed the outside number of the center with a low pad level and active feet. He tried to push the center upfield and keep him off the 3 technique. After the 3 technique attacked the center, the nose looped into the opposite B gap, scraping tight.

The ends on this stunt had outside rush and could not come inside until they were at the depth of the quarterback. They must stay outside and could not come under on an inside twist. That put too many pass rushers to the inside. They were ultimately contain players. They could spin back inside as a counter move after they reached the depth of the quarterback.

The opposite of that stunt was the "nut" call (Diagram #10). The speed-rush ends had the same rush rules as for the tun. On the nut, the nose went first and the tackle came second. The nose aligned

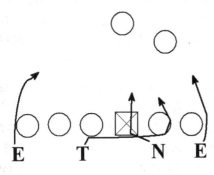

Diagram #10. Nut

in a G alignment on the backside guard. If the center turned away from the nose, he attacked the near hip of the center with his hat and hands, and ricocheted up to the quarterback.

The 3 technique pressed the offensive guard on the snap with great pad level and active feet. He looped to the opposite B gap after the nose penetrated the A gap.

The "read" call (Diagram #11) was similar to a "fit" call, except it was a sideline call. The 3 technique worked a two-way move on the offensive guard. He could rush either the A gap or the B gap on the snap of the ball. The nose aligned in a G alignment on the backside guard. He pressed the outside number of the center and maintained his A-gap rush lane. If the 3 technique took the A gap inside, he looped into the opposite B gap, scraping tight.

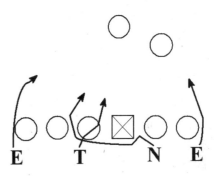

Diagram #11. Read

This was a tun stunt, but the defenders did not have to run the stunt. If the 3 technique took the B-gap rush lane, the nose read the rush of the 3 technique and reacted accordingly. On this stunt, the ends had to stay outside. The read could occur after the tackles attack upfield. If the 3 technique started in the B gap and gained an advantage on the guard, he could come inside into the A gap. The nose read the inside move by the 3 technique and looped across to the opposite B gap. The stunt occurred late in the line charge.

We ran a stunt called "opposite" (Diagram #12). It was an inside stunt, which meant the ends had outside contain and could not come inside until they reached the level of the quarterback. The alignment of the nose was a G alignment on the offensive guard. On the snap of the ball, he crossed the face of the guard and fired into the B gap. The 3 technique aligned in a jet alignment on his guard and crossed the face of the guard into the A gap. They switched gaps as a change-up stunt.

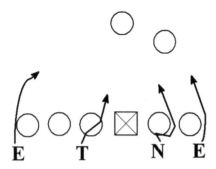

Diagram #12. Opposite

We wanted them to rip across the face of the offensive blockers and not swim.

The "Ted" rush was a tackle and end stunt (Diagram #13). In the diagram, the call was left Ted. We ran the stunt to the left. However, to the backside we could run the fit call. On the Ted, the tackle went first. He aligned in a jet alignment and ripped hard with penetration into the B gap.

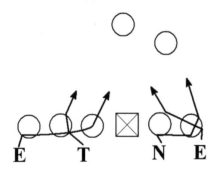

Diagram #13. Ted

Once upfield, he attacked the inside hip of the offensive tackle with his hat and hands. He ricocheted toward the quarterback, keeping the tackle on his inside shoulder. If the offensive tackle blocked down on him, he worked outside of that block for containment. The end in the Ted stunt aligned in a jet alignment. He worked upfield four steps, or to the upfield shoulder of the offensive tackle. He planted off his outside foot and looped

into the A gap. He used a tight scrape as he looped inside. He had a two-way go if the guard or center tried to block him.

The nose and backside end had their normal pass-rush rules. If the end got upfield and came underneath the tackle block, the nose worked outside on the fit stunt.

To the backside, we had an "ex" stunt (Diagram #14). The strongside end had an ultimate-contain rule. That meant he ran no inside moves until he got to the depth of the quarterback. The 3 technique worked an in-and-out move on the offensive guard and rushed through the B gap. The nose aligned in a jet alignment. He pressed the inside number of the guard on the snap of the ball. The defensive end will attack the guard and knock him inside. The nose looped outside for the containment, making sure he used a tight scrape.

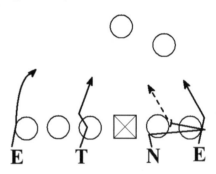

Diagram #14. Ex

The weakside end worked upfield for two steps. He planted his outside foot and slanted inside to attack the outside hip of the offensive guard, picking the guard off the nose. After contacting the outside hip, he ricocheted inside to the quarterback.

If we put the Ted and ex together, we called that stunt "Texas" (Diagram #15). Toward the strongside we ran a Ted call and to the backside we ran an ex call. The rushers coming under on the stunts were

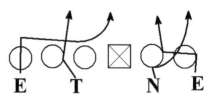

Diagram #15. Texas

responsible for the draw play and the rushers going outside had containment. That was common sense.

In certain situations, we went to special personnel groupings to get pressure on the quarterback. We could go to the three-man front, called the "odd front," and put speed personnel on the field. In that case, we probably would take out the tackles and replace them with a third defensive end or linebacker. If we did it out of the four-man front, we still wanted our four best pass rushers on the field.

In the third-and-long situation, we called "speed." That personnel group was our four best pass rushers. It probably was three defensive ends and a linebacker. We ran all of our games and twists using different personnel. You could do this on the high school level. Your four best pass rushers could be defensive backs in the outside positions.

When we played an odd front, we slanted the defensive linemen almost every time. If we called "odd-slam," we slanted to the strongside of the set. When we slanted, we balanced our feet and got back to parallel in our stance. We took our weight off the hands. On the slant, we stepped laterally in the direction of the call. As we took the lateral step, we dipped and ripped with our outside arm.

We used to take the 45-degree step. When we did that, the offensive blocker caved us in to the inside. When we used the lateral flat step, we could see, use our hands, and not be cut off.

From the odd and speed fronts, we had different personnel on the field. We taught moves for different sets by the offensive blockers. If the offensive blocker gave us an overset, we taught the defenders to go "up and under" in their moves. The defender started up the field into his responsible gap and came under the block of the offensive player.

If the offensive blocker gave a short set, we used a speed rush and ran past him. A short set was the blocker popping into his pass set at the line of scrimmage. The defensive end in a jet alignment ran past the blocker with a speed rush. The defensive

end got an aiming point four yards up the field, beat the blocker to that point, and leaned in to the quarterback.

If the 3-technique tackle got a short set, he used the "quick swim" move. If the center or guard short set on the nose, he used a bull rush. A coaching point we used for our nose involved the shotgun snap. If a team aligned in a shotgun set, we liked the odd front against them. Whichever hand the center used to snap the ball, we aligned the nose to that side in a tilted alignment. The center had a long snap to the quarterback and had trouble getting his hand on the nose aligned to that side. We taught the nose to quick swim the center in the shotgun snap. It was extremely hard for the center to snap the ball and get his hand back up on the defender in that alignment.

When the offensive lineman used a deep set, we taught the up-and-under move. With the offensive linemen using a deep set, the defender had the opportunity to use fakes in his close on the blocker. We faked the outside move and came under on the blocker. If the offense deep sat on the nose, he ran over the blocker. If the offensive blocker was an aggressive-type player, we used the quick swim.

Once the defender defeated the block, he had to finish the rush. Once the defender beat the blocker, he stopped his upfield rush and had to get inside. When he came around the corner on the offensive blocker, he got his toe, knee, and shoulder going in the direction to the quarterback.

The drills that paid the biggest dividends in teaching that skill were the hoops. We ran the single-hoop run and practiced the proper lean to the quarterback. We ran double hoops and used the figure-eight run. We put a stand-up dummy with a Velcro® ball in the drill to practice the strip of the ball from the quarterback. We also put a manager with a hand shield around the hoop. The player ran the hoops and attacked the hand shield with a chop or club.

If the offensive tackle was significantly taller than the defensive end, we used the speed rush. We felt that was the best chance for success. Swim moves did not work well on tall opponents. If we got into him, he probably could lock up the defender. Speed around the corner was the answer to situations like that one.

We taught the spin move when the defender got to the level of the quarterback. As the rusher came upfield on his rush, he had no chance of a sack if he continued upfield. The quarterback, by stepping up into the pocket, moved himself away from the rusher. When the quarterback started up in the pocket, the rusher stopped his rush and sat down. He sank his hips and threw his outside elbow as if he were throwing a shot put. He had to stay tight to the blocker as he made his move.

If the defender did not stay tight in his moves, he allowed the offensive blocker to lock out his arms and created distance between them. That was why the close move was so essential to escape from blockers.

If the offensive blocker got his arms locked out on the defender, he had to chop the arms down. When the defender got too high and allowed the blocker to get into him, he had to have a counter. We taught them to chop down on the arms. The chop occurred in the area behind the elbow. That was the most effective area to break the lock-out. We could chop up or down. If the defender was bull rushing and chopped up on the lock-out, he forced the arms of the blocker up to raise his center of gravity. If the defender got the arms up, he had complete control of the blocker.

The three-step pass game used the cut block to get defensive lineman down. We tried to control the head against the cut-block scheme. We taught our linemen to force the heads of the offensive blockers downward. We pressed down on the heads, gave ground slightly, and jumped into the air. It was hard to get a pass rush when the cut block occurred. If we tried, they probably cut us. We did what we thought was the best thing. We gave ground and tried to knock the ball down with a leap. We drilled those types of situations in practice. The coaching point we used told them not to leave their feet unless the quarterback looked at them.

Our defense had goals we tried to fulfill. We felt that if we could get a sack one out of every 10 passes, that was excellent. When the quarterback tried to pass, we wanted to force a quick or bad throw. Everyone had a rush lane on a jet call. If they could not get to the quarterback, they got their hands up. We treated the batted ball almost like a sack. The big thing we wanted to force was the interception. The last goal was to keep the quarterback contained.

If we played a team with a tremendous scrambling quarterback, we had a call to help us. We called "jet-sink" (Diagram #16). The defensive ends ran their speed containment rush. The 3-technique worked his two-way go to his rush lane. The nose started upfield on the rush, but dropped two yards into the middle of the defense over the quarterback.

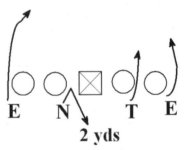

Diagram #16. Jet-Sink

The nose helped on the draw play, middle screen, or the tunnel screen to the inside. He mirrored the quarterback and helped if he ran the ball. It gave the defense another set of hands in the throwing lanes.

Draw blocking was different than pass blocking. We coached our players to recognize those differences. In a pass set, the offensive blockers got their meat hooks up and were ready to grab the defenders. In the draw, the offensive linemen tried to fake the defense. They gave us a high hat, hands, and elbows and they hinged to the outside, opening their shoulders. That was just like opening a gate.

When our players saw those techniques, we told them to sink their hips and retreat. We wanted them to stay in their rush lanes and retrace their steps back the way they came.

We keyed the running back in the shotgun set. If he was even with, or behind, the quarterback, it was probably the draw. If he was set in front of the quarterback, he was there to block.

When we wanted to pressure the quarterback, we made sure we pressured with two people to the side of the blocking back (Diagram #17). Most of the time, the line slides away from the back in their pass-blocking scheme. We brought an end and linebacker from the backside. When we set up in our zone blitzes, we wanted to attack away from the slide and toward the blocking back.

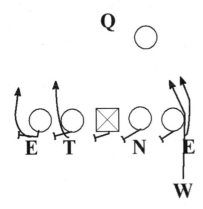

Diagram #17. Backside Blitz

We rushed one defender outside the back and one underneath him. We forced him to do something.

We played the screen the same way we did the draw. The pass mechanics of the quarterback were different in the screen play and a normal pass set. If you studied the film of the quarterback's drop, you could coach your players on the differences. When the quarterback read downfield, he moved with purpose and was ready to throw the ball. In the screen set-up, he drifted back, his shoulders were high, and everything in his mechanics looked different.

We told the defensive end and tackle, when they read the screen set of the quarterback, to stop their rush. If the quarterback drifted to their side, they stopped their rush and retraced their steps. The side away from the quarterback drift continued to rush at full speed.

If everyone stopped rushing, the quarterback had all day to throw the ball and possibly could pick out something else. We told the end and tackle, if they saw the quarterback's back, to keep coming. Playing the screen was the same principle as rushing the passer with your hands up. As long as the quarterback did not face the rusher, he kept coming. If the quarterback faced the rusher, he got his hands up.

We never wanted our players leaving their feet in the pass rush. However, it was a natural thing for the rushers to do. We told them, if the ball was in the air, they could leave their feet. To keep the linemen on the ground was a hard thing to do and we got pump-faked a lot.

On an interception, we wanted everyone to go to the near sideline. The coaching point for interceptions was not to block behind the ball or below the waist.

In closing, remember the number-one thing in pass rushing was effort. If you did not have that, you were not a good pass rusher or a good defensive football player. The thing I hope you got from this lecture was the three-and-out principle for your defense. Everything you do in practice requires three perfect reps before you get off the field. When you conduct practice that way, it gets the defense thinking, "three and out."

THE 3-3 PRESSURE DEFENSE

University of Memphis

Thank you. It is a pleasure to be here representing the University of Memphis. Coach West would rather be here than where he is today. He sends his best to all of you.

Today, I am going to talk about the 3-3 defense and some of the conditioning we do in our program. When we come into fall camp before the opening of the season, we do two things that really help us prepare for the season. We have one workout in the morning practice and one in the evening that is devoted to conditioning.

In the morning practices, we do what I refer to as Packer Day. I have done this since I was at Chattanooga back in the early 70s. It comes from the Green Bay Packers under Vince Lombardi. We take the last 15 minutes of practice and do the Packer Day workout. The first day we do two-and-a-half minutes of up-downs, followed by two-and-a-half minutes of 40s or three sets.

The second day, we increase the time on the up-downs and follow with 40s for the remaining five minutes. We do three sets of those on the second day. We increase the time on the up-downs each day until they reach graduation day, which includes 15 minutes of up-downs. Coach West and all the coaches I have worked for know the last three periods of defensive practice in the morning is Packer Day.

In the afternoon practice we do a conditioning period called Fourth Quarter. That drill takes 20 minutes, or the last four periods of defensive practice. We do our conditioning program and that is part of the understanding I have with the head coach. Those conditioning drills are talked about before I take the job. I feel the conditioning program is vitally important to the success of our defense.

This conditioning program is what allows us to run to the football in the fourth quarter as hard as we do in the first quarter. In the Fourth Quarter Drill, we have four stations. At one station, we run 40-yard sprints. We have a bag station, which acts as a conditioning drill. We run over and in and out of the bags using agility-type drills. We have a push-up and sit-up station. The final station is a cone-run station. This requires changes of direction and shuttle runs in and out of the cones.

We do these workouts during two-a-day practices. Once we finish with early practice, we are finished with Packer Day and Fourth Quarter. During the season, we run 20 40s as our conditioning, plus one 40 for each point we give up in the game.

We practice on Sundays, and Monday is their off day. Our conference has a bunch of teams that score a bunch of points. We have been in some wild games involving lots of scoring. We have run as many as 90 40s on Sunday. You have to be motivated to complete the workout. It takes some time to run 90 40s. We allow them to run in groups of 10, so we can finish before dark. We hope we do not have to run that many too often, but scoring points is the big thing in football these days.

On Tuesday, we run 15 40s. On Wednesday, we run five 40s. We do not run on Thursday or Friday. We do the same thing in our conditioning each week. They know it and I do not have to tell them.

We do run- and pass-pursuit drills during practice. These are two other drills we do only during two-a-day practices. I will show you the drills if I can. The Run Pursuit Drill is somewhat weird (Diagram #1). We align the defense and run a dive-option play to the defensive left. We place two cones 40 yards from the line of scrimmage, with a coach behind each one.

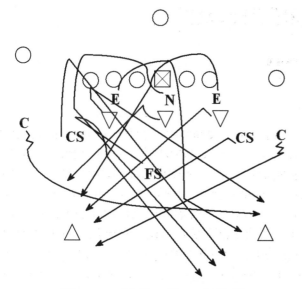

Diagram #1. Run Pursuit Drill

We have one cone on the right hash mark and one on the left hash mark. Defenders on the right side of the defense pursue the football and sprint to the cone on the left. Defenders on the left of the defense pursue the ball and sprint to the right cone. We play a 3-3 defense, with two cat safeties, two corners, and a free safety.

The left defensive end comes off the ball, goes to his responsibility, comes flat behind the line of scrimmage, and turns up between the backside center and guard. From there, he sprints to the cone on the right. The right end does the same thing and sprints to the cone on the left. The noseguard stays flat to the line and sprints to the left cone.

Everyone on the defense goes through his responsibility and pursues the ball. Everyone goes at once and sprints to the opposite cone from their alignment.

I have the whistle and any time within the drill, I can blow the whistle. When that occurs, everyone on the defense stops and does an up-down. I may blow the whistle five or six times during the drill. On each occasion, the defense has to hit the ground and get up. There is no live tackling or blocking in this drill. Everyone goes through their pursuit angles and sprints 40 yards to the opposite cone.

When all the defenders get to the cone, they circle around the coach, chopping their feet. I blow the whistle one more time. They hit the ground, get up, and sprint off the field. They jog back to the position of the ball and prepare to go again. We have three teams run this drill. We can use all our calls and stunts during this drill. If you are interested in seeing this drill, send me a blank tape and I will make you a copy of the drill.

We run the pursuit against the option, but we do not see the option as a full-time offense anymore. The game has changed for the defense. The rules have legalized holding by the offense. With that change, the offenses are throwing the ball all the time.

College football has turned into a pass-first, run-second scheme. The pass now sets up the run. It used to be that all you had to do was stop the run to win the game. Now, you had better have something in your scheme to stop the pass.

The Pass Pursuit Drill (Diagram #2) is similar to the Run Pursuit Drill. We line up in the defense and snap the ball. The quarterback throws the ball to the left and everyone goes through his pass-coverage and rush responsibilities, then sprints to the ball. When they arrive, they chop their feet around the ball. I blow the whistle, they hit the ground and get up, and they sprint off the field. We throw the ball to the left, right, and down the middle deep. In each rep, they go through the defense and pursue the thrown ball. They go three times before they get off the field.

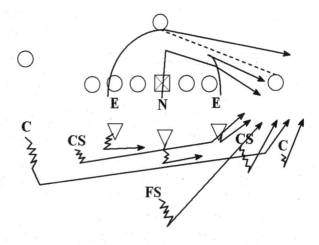

Diagram #2. Pass Pursuit Drill

That is how we run our conditioning drills. The next part of the lecture concerns the defensive scheme and the way we present it to our players. We call the defense "33." This defense evolved from the old 5-3 defense. The 5-3 defense was hard to run against and was very sound. In the old defense, we used the strong safety as one of the linebackers. That way, we did not have to substitute. I still do not like to substitute to run any phases of the defense.

The first time I coached at Memphis, in 1990, we developed this defense. We had to open in the Coliseum against Southern Cal the next season. They sent me to watch their spring game in the Coliseum. That was before the NCAA made scouting in the spring illegal.

I was standing outside the stadium as Southern Cal unloaded the bus to go on the field. They were huge and had some big players. I looked at them and thought to myself, "I don't know what we are going to do." I went into the Coliseum to watch the game and was surprised to see very few people there to watch the game. If there were 1000 people in the stands it would have been a surprise.

I decided I would not watch much of the game. At halftime, I went to the Santa Anita racetrack to watch the horse races. There were 53,000 people at the racetrack betting on the ponies. You could tell where those people's priorities were.

The next year we played Southern Cal with our defensive ends in the alignment played by our cat safeties. We did not let them play man coverage, but they did play the zone coverage. We ended up beating Southern Cal in this defense. They were a hell of a lot better than we were, but we won the game.

It was so effective that I began to run it as a full-time defense. Steve Spurrier changed the face of defensive football in the SEC. He instituted the empty set as part of his offense. He spread five receivers with only the quarterback in the backfield. People did not think he could run that against them.

They made the mistake of not covering all the receivers. Florida quarterbacks got good at hitting the receivers that the defense did not cover. He made the defenses in the SEC change because he did not run the ball—he threw it. Offensive linemen today are so much bigger than they used to be.

I want to keep my players as far from the offensive linemen as I can get them. We have a better chance of dodging those huge offensive linemen after they come off the ball. If we get up on the line of scrimmage, they grab and hold. I guarantee you the offensive linemen will hold you. We played three games last year against teams that threw the ball over 50 times. In those games, the offense did not have one single holding call.

There is no team in America that good. It is unbelievable. We try to keep them away from us unless we can match up with another big player.

The defense is the old 5-3 defense with the end pulled off the line of scrimmage. We added defensive backs into the scheme because of the passing threat.

The makeup of the defense is three down linemen, three linebackers, two cat safeties, two corners, and a free safety (Diagram #3). The down linemen are in head-up positions on the center and two tackles. The linebackers stack behind the down linemen. The cat safeties are three yards outside the tight ends and seven yards deep. The corners are press corners and play within four yards of the

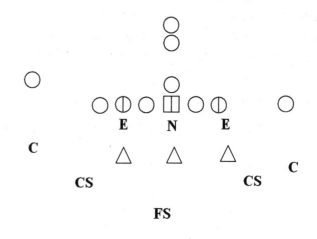

Diagram #3. 33 Defense

line of scrimmage. The free safety aligns somewhere within the middle of the field.

The design of the defense is to defeat the offense with movement, stunts, and numbers. It is not the design of the defense to play a base look and take on offensive blockers. We are a gap-control defense with all the defenders assigned a gap to defend. We defend those gaps on the move.

We do not play anyone straight in this defense. We move the down linemen and linebacker on every play. We have three movements for the down linemen. We can move in a left-and-right direction (Diagram #4). We can move the down linemen to the tight end or to the openside of the formation. We can also pinch the defensive line. Our middle linebacker calls all the directions for the down linemen.

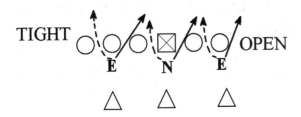

Diagram #4. Tight/Open

He calls the direction of the tight end. The down linemen have to know if they are going toward or away from the tight end. If there are two tight ends in the game, the linebacker makes the call and the linemen apply the defense.

When we run the pinch (Diagram #5), the defensive ends slant inside into the B gaps. The nosetackle uses a stuff technique on the center. On the stuff technique, the nose almost tackles the center to ensure that he does not get off the line of scrimmage.

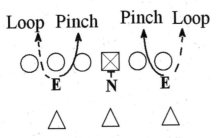

Diagram #5. Pinch/Stuff

If we want to send the defensive end in the opposite direction, we loop him to the outside. On the loop call, the nose stuffs the center as he did on the pinch. We use the loop call in passing situations.

The next part of the defense uses one linebacker blitzing along with front movement. We have a left and right linebacker and a middle linebacker in our scheme. The ram and lion stunt sends the outside linebackers on blitzes. The ram is the right linebacker and the lion is the left linebacker.

On the ram stunt (Diagram #6), the right linebacker runs through the B gap to his side. The defensive ends loop to the outside and the nose slants into the A gap toward the linebacker stunt. If you want to add another wrinkle to the stunt, we can move the nose into a G position on the guard and slant him inside into the A gap.

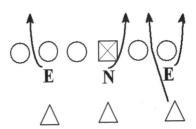

Diagram #6. Ram

The same stunt going the other way is lion (Diagram #7).

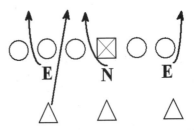

Diagram #7. Lion

The middle-linebacker blitz is "X" (Diagram #8). The direction of the linebacker varies with game planning. However, he runs through one of the A gaps and the nose goes the opposite way. We like to combine the X stunt with a line movement. We run X-pinch or X-loop to get movement in all the down linemen.

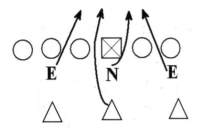

Diagram #8. X-Pinch

To bring the outside linebackers off the edge, we call thunder (Diagram #9) and lightning. Thunder comes from the tight-end side and lightning from the split-end side. The outside linebackers come out of their stack alignment and cheat up to the line of scrimmage at the last minute. They run the bullets charge from the outside coming off the edge. The line movement is away from the tight end.

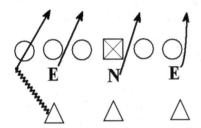

Diagram #9. Thunder

Coming from the openside of the formation is the lightning call (Diagram #10). On this stunt, the defensive-line movement is away from the openside with the linebacker coming off the edge.

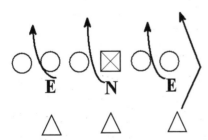

Diagram #10. Lightning

When we teach this in the spring, we go through the progression, from the one-linebacker blitzes to the two-linebacker blitzes. The two-linebacker stunts are go and away. In the go stunt (Diagram #11), the linebackers go toward the tight end. The Mike linebacker runs through the A gap to that side

and the left linebacker runs through the B gap. The defensive ends loop outside and the nose slants into the weakside A gap.

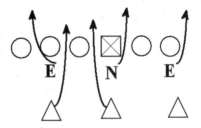

Diagram #11. Go

If we want the linebacker going the other way on the stunt, we call go-switch. That sends the linemen and linebacker into the opposite gaps.

The away stunt (Diagram #12) is the same blitz going away from the tight end.

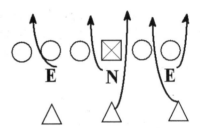

Diagram #12. Away

The backside defensive end on these stunts loops to the outside. We do not have a bunch of big players at Memphis. That is why we move them on every play. If I had a bunch of players that could whip the crap out of the offensive linemen, I would play more base.

The next two-linebacker stunt is spike (Diagram #13). That involves the outside linebackers. We send both of them into the B gaps and loop the defensive ends outside. It is a good stunt, if you have good blitzing linebackers.

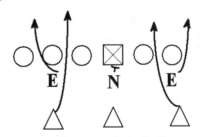

Diagram #13. Spike

In 1992, I was at Ole Miss. We did not move the defensive line as we do now. We had two defensive ends named Norman Hands and Tim Bowens. They both became franchise players in the NFL. This is a little story about Tim Bowens. He did not get eligible and did not practice with our team until the Thursday before we opened with Auburn at Auburn, Alabama. That was the first time he dressed out in football equipment. We started him in that game and told him to tackle anybody that came through his gap. He made more tackles than anyone did in the game.

He was a player extraordinaire. You do not coach players of that caliber. Tim Bowens was as mean as a snake. He would whip your butt in a heartbeat. Norman Hands was entirely different. Norman did not get mean until he got to the pros. You could slap Norman and get away with it. If you did that to Tim, he would kill you. Players like those two will make you a good coach.

The next stunt involving two linebackers is bullets (Diagram #14). This stunt is the thunder and lightning run at the same time. They both cheat outside and come off the edge.

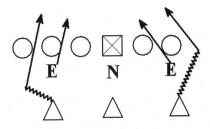

Diagram #14. Bullets

The secondary coverages behind all of these movements can be the same. We can run man-to-man, man/free, or zone.

The progression continues with the three-linebacker blitz. The three-linebacker game is trips (Diagram #15). When we run this scheme, we have

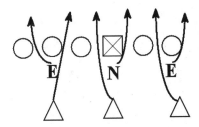

Diagram #15. Trips

to play man coverage. We rush six defenders and the offense has five eligible receivers. We have to cover them all with the five remaining defenders.

When we run the trips, the outside linebackers run through the B gaps and the Mike linebacker runs through the strong A gap. We can combine the line movement with the trips call. We can run trips right or left, which sends the linemen in a direction and the linebacker blitzing the opposite gaps. We can do the same thing with the tight and open calls. The third thing we can do is trips pinch. The middle stack runs their trips stunt and the outside stacks send the ends inside and the linebackers outside.

The last thing we do from the trips package is bullets X (Diagram #16). That puts the outside linebackers on the line of scrimmage coming off the edges with the Mike linebacker running the X stunt inside.

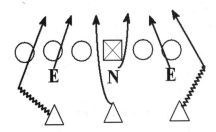

Diagram #16. Bullets X

When we run a six-man blitz, we need to have some peel adjustments. That means that one of the outside blitzers may have to come off his blitz to cover a back coming out of the backfield.

We teach the defense the hawk look (Diagram #17). The hawk look is on the tight-end side of the formation. We move the defensive end from the 4 technique head up on the tackle to a 3 technique on the outside shoulder of the guard. To the split-end

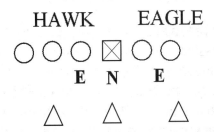

Diagram #17. Hawk/Eagle/Double Eagle

side, we can do the same thing. We call that adjustment eagle. If we want both sides to move we call double eagle.

We like this adjustment because it lets you get a defender into the B gap before they snap the ball. If we have a defensive end that does not pinch very well, we line him up there. Hawk is the adjustment to the tight-end side only. Eagle is to the split-end side and double eagle is the adjustment to both sides.

Of course, you can move the end into a hawk position and move back out on the snap of the ball. We have no problem with line movement, as long as the linebackers know where the linemen are going. You cannot do everything the same way week after week. If you show an adjustment, you can play it one way one week and a totally different way the following week. When you become predictable, it destroys the defense.

The next progression adds a secondary blitz with a one-linebacker stunt. The first stunt is mad thunder (Diagram #18). The stunt comes from the tight-end side of the formation. We run the Thunder stunt with the linebacker coming off the edge. The cat safety to that side cheats up in his alignment. At the last minute, he comes outside of the linebacker off the edge.

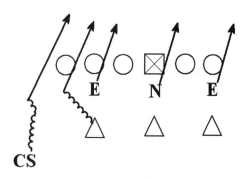

Diagram #18. Mad Thunder

The opposite of that stunt is bad lightning. Bad is to the open or boundary side of the formation.

The hardest thing we find in running this stunt with secondary players is the path they take. Instead of running straight lines to the quarterback, they want to bend their paths. They cannot understand that a straight line is the shortest distance between two points. If they run straight lines, it hits quicker.

The next scheme involves two linebackers and one defensive back. We run mad-thunder-X (Diagram #19). That is a combination stunt that brings the linebacker and cat safety from the tight-end side, with the Mike linebacker coming through the strong A gap. It is the same stunt, adding the middle linebacker to the stunt.

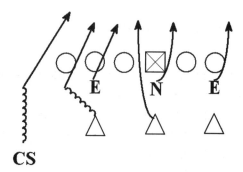

Diagram #19. Mad Thunder X

If we blitz the other outside linebacker, we call mad-thunder-fire (Diagram #20). Instead of an X stunt in the middle, we get a ram stunt to the right side of the defense.

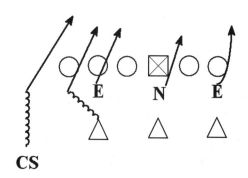

Diagram #20. Mad Thunder Fire

A change-up we added this year that helped us was mad-thunder-bullets (Diagram #21). We brought the backside linebacker from the edge and it helped us tremendously. The defensive end slanted into the B gap and the linebacker came off the edge.

We can run exactly the same stunt from the openside of the formation with the Lightning package. We can run bad-lightning with the X, fire,

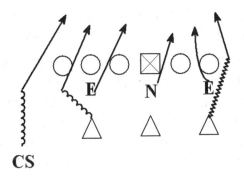

Diagram #21. Mad Thunder Bullets

and bullets combination coming from the split-end side.

If we want to bring seven defenders with the scheme, we call combo. That call brings the thunder, X, and fire stunts all in the same stunt. The problem with that is the number of secondary defenders. When you bring seven, someone in the blitz is responsible for a back in pass coverage.

However, sometimes it does not matter how much you cover and practice a particular point. In the heat of the game, someone misses their assignment and fails to execute. It happened to us in the bowl game this year. We came with an eight-man blitz. We covered the exact play in practice a number of times. We were in dead man coverage. The corners and free safety locked on the three wide receivers. The right linebacker had the tight end.

To the twin-receiver side, the cat safety and left linebacker had coverage on the remaining back. They were both senior players and the coverage went to the player the back tried to block. As it worked, the linebacker charged outside and the safety went inside. Neither of them covered the back and he went straight down the field, wide open for the touchdown. Every time in practice, the defender took the back, but he missed him in the game.

When you involve secondary players in line stunts, the secondary has to move to compensate for the back leaving. We squirm the free safety toward the side of the stunt. The cat safety away from the stunt balances back to the inside of the formation. This is also a time when we can use the

hawk call as a change-up alignment. If you continue to tweak the alignments of the defensive linemen, it makes it hard on the offensive blockers.

One of the strong points of this defense is the ability to confuse the offensive blockers. You need to move the defensive linemen into as many places as you can. The key is to get them to their responsibilities. The hard part with all the freedom is not being in the right place when the offense snaps the ball.

At the end of the season, we found ourselves without many defensive linemen. Let me tell you a little about our season. In the first game, our starting quarterback broke his right leg on the third play of the game. In the third football game, our second quarterback broke his left leg. Our third quarterback was a true freshman that joined the program in January. He became the starting quarterback for a while.

I believe things happen in cycles. We got so many injuries from that point on that it was downright discouraging. It occurred on both sides of the ball. We lost our best defensive lineman in the first game for the year. Our best linebacker played three games and missed the rest of the season. The good news is that both return next year.

These things went on and on during the course of the season. We even had a coach get his knee torn up in practice before the seventh game. He spent the rest of the season in the press box. The following week, the team doctor went down on the sidelines and tore his knee up. The week after that a cheerleader got hurt. They threw her in the air and dropped her.

If that was not enough, one of our best receivers burnt his hands in an apartment fire and was lost for the rest of the year. Of course, after the season, Coach West had triple bypass surgery. I hope that is the end to all the maladies.

We feel that this defense allows you to play with lesser players. You can hide the linebackers in stacks behind a defender. You can get by with a lesser player as a down lineman if you move him.

If we play a team that empties the backfield, we bring a six-man blitz. If they empty and have a tight end as one of their receivers, we bring the defender covering him on the blitz. That assures us that the tight end does not block anyone but the back assigned to him. We do not let the offense use the tight end as their sixth blocker in their scheme.

If you stay in this business long enough, you will see everything. I believe if a team did not have spring training one year and won 10 games the following year, there would be a bunch of people who would cut out spring training. That is how trendy some people are in this game. People follow programs that win. It is the nature of the beast.

I got off track. Let me show you a defense that was good for us. We call this double eagle special (Diagram #22). This is the number-one defense that has been successful since I have been coaching. We go to the double eagle alignment by sliding the defensive ends into 3-technique alignments. The outside linebackers and cat safeties move up to the outside and come off the edges with their mad and bad schemes.

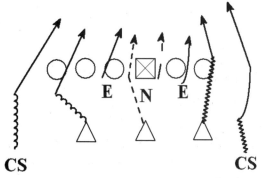
Diagram #22. Double Eagle Special

If you want to bring eight on the rush, we call double eagle special X. That stunt puts the Mike linebacker into the A gap to the strongside and the nose into the A gap to the weakside.

I like to play this defense in short yardage or when we have the offensive backed up in their own territory. You take a chance because you are dead man in the secondary and peeling on back receivers as you go.

We can get into the split (Diagram #23) look from the 3-3 defense. We take the linebacker that can play on the line of scrimmage and align him over the tight end. We overshift the three down linemen to the weakside of the defense. The left defensive end goes to a strong 2-technique alignment and the nose goes to the weak 2-technique alignment on the guards. The right defensive end slides into a wide 5 technique on the offensive tackle.

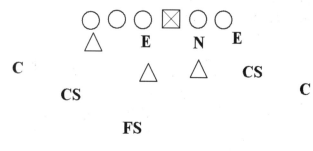
Diagram #23. Split

The remaining linebackers stack behind the 2 techniques. If we do not have a linebacker that can play over a tight end, we slide the line to the tight end. We play the linebacker to the openside of the formation and a defensive end over the tight end.

We can play a split-1 right (Diagram #24). In this diagram, I will show the line overshifted to the tight end and the linebacker to the openside of the set. We align in the split front and slant the down linemen to the right. The left linebacker comes out of the 3 stack and moves to the edge outside the tight end. He comes off the edge and gives the offense an overload to handle from the strongside. The Mike linebacker moves over the center and gives us a one-linebacker look.

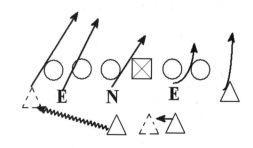
Diagram #24. Split-1 Right

If we call split-1 left, we slant the line to the left. Last year, we substituted a defensive back for one of the blitzing linebackers. We played this defense at Mississippi State a bunch. The defense fit our personnel there.

We have many stunts we can run from the split-1, but the mad and bad stunts are the same stunts from the 3-3 as well as the split-1. One thing we have done is blitz two defenders outside the tight end (Diagram #25). We bring a safety up and blitz him outside the linebacker.

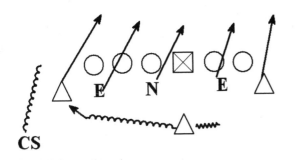

Diagram #25. Split-1 Safety Blitz

This year, because of our injury problems, we ended up playing two down linemen and four linebackers (Diagram #26). They were in 2-technique alignments on the offensive guards. The four linebackers are at linebacker depth in 20-stack. They are aligned in a 60 technique to the tight end and a 50 technique to the split end.

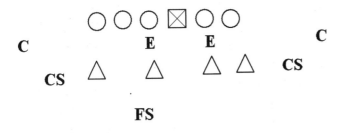

Diagram #26. Two Down Inside

The linebackers started out at linebacker depth, but as the quarterback began to snap the ball, they were on the move to their responsibilities. We really moved from this alignment.

Our wild look is similar to that set. We align in the 3-3 defense, pull the nose off the line of scrimmage, and play him in the middle of the defense. Nothing changes in his stunt package except his position. At the snap of the ball, he is moving down to the line of scrimmage instead of aligning on it.

It is another confusing defense for the offensive linemen. It gives them another chance to block the wrong man and let someone come unblocked. From this alignment, the stunt we like to run is wild go (Diagram #27).

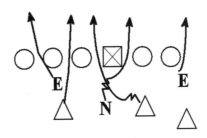

Diagram #27. Wild Go

We played that at New Mexico because of the personnel we had. What this all boils down to is, you do what you have to do. When you get hurt, you cannot cancel the schedule. We played hard all year long with the people we had available. This defense has a lot of flexibility to it. You really have to depend on your secondary to keep you from being blown out. When you blitz for a living, you have to get there. It is too much pressure on the defensive backs to cover good wide receivers when the quarterback has time to get the ball off.

PRINCIPLES FOR A GREAT DEFENSE

Western Kentucky University

Thank you. It is a pleasure for me to be here with you this morning representing Western Kentucky University. I have attended this clinic for the past 10 years and I have heard some great lectures, visited with some old friends, and built some relationships with coaches from high school to the NFL.

We at Western Kentucky appreciate the partnership that we enjoy with the outstanding high school coaches in Kentucky and the surrounding areas.

Before I became the head coach at Western, I was the defensive coordinator and the recruiting coordinator. I have watched the quality of high school football in Kentucky improve dramatically in the past decade, and our school has certainly reaped the benefits of that improvement. When we won the national championship in 2002, 12 of our 22 starters were Kentuckians.

I made the statement when I was hired that the state of Kentucky would be our number-one recruiting objective and we would recruit kids in Kentucky as well as anybody does anywhere. As evidence of that, we have 37 Kentucky players on our current roster, and 10 incoming freshmen, seven of whom have already been invited to play in the Kentucky-Tennessee All Star Game this summer. That is a total of 47 players on the Hilltopper's 2006 roster that played their high school football in the state of Kentucky.

We recognize what you are doing and I can assure you that we are going to continue to be in your schools.

The one thing that I will tell you before I talk about our defense has to do with camps, with recruiting in general, and with a place to send your kids. When it comes time to choose, people are the most important part of that decision. When a kid makes that decision to go to college, he has to look at the staff, the players, and the community, and I feel really good about what is going on at Western in all of those areas, and in the direction that we are moving.

Our president and athletic director are committed to the growth of our university, and to the continued progress of our football program. In this decade alone, there will be $434 million worth of construction being done on our campus, and I tell you that because our team camps are in great dorms with great facilities all centrally located. We have gotten very positive feedback from the guys and coaches who have been in our camps before, so if you are interested in that, please come and check it out.

I also tell you that in regards to our recruiting effort, because $37 million has been committed to the renovation and enlargement of LT Smith Stadium. We will put up another side to the stadium, which will be a two-level, all-football facility that will include a weight room, training room, and players' lounge, with coaches' offices up above. We will then bowl it in with berms at each end zone and make grass seating there. There will be a new video replay board installed, and construction on all of it will begin this summer. It is really going to be something special.

Of course, that brings up the question of Division I-A football for the Hilltoppers. It is certainly a possibility for us. Right now, we are playing I-AA, but Division I-A conferences have requested information from us, and if anybody invites us to come, we have a great president and athletic director who will look at it.

If it makes sense to do it, then we will do it, and if it does not make sense, then we will not. Either way, we will have some of the best facilities in the United States in I-AA, and I would also think that if we were at the I-A level, we would be very competitive at that level as well. That is what is going on at our place and I wanted to share it with you.

Now, let us talk some Western Kentucky defense. I was the defensive coordinator before I became the head coach, and I am back to running the defense now, so the continuity of the past 10 years, along with the success we have had, has enabled us to establish some tradition. That means that there are some things that we do, year in and year out, within our program that our kids buy into. The veterans buy in, and then they sell the young kids coming in. There are three of those things that establish a foundation for our defense.

The most important thing to us, as it is too many people, is *running to the football*. Everybody wants to know what we do in practice to make sure that our guys run to the football. Well, back in 2000, our guys watched a movie starring Eddie Murphy and Martin Lawrence called "Life." There was a jail scene in it with a guard in a tower overlooking a commons area. The prisoners were not allowed to go outside of what was called the "gun line" or they would be summarily shot. Our kids really picked up on the "gun line" thing. So we decided to create a gun line that they have to get into to get to the football. We defined it in practice as a five-yard circle around the point where the ball ends up, and all 11 guys had better be within that fiv- yard circle. You had better get your butt in the gun line.

If they do not, we do not shoot them, of course, but we do grade it off of film. We used to come back the next day in individual period and run them for however many gun lines the entire defense had. Now, we just call them out in practice and we have a guy who charts them. I will call out a player who does not run to the ball and give him a gun line. At the end of practice, we call the defense up and we run "perfect 15s" for every time a guy did not get in the gun line. When you watch us play, you will see that we do run to the football.

That is the first thing we look for as a staff when we watch cut-ups at the end of the season. We mark every single one of them in every single game where a player did not run to the ball. It is very important to us and that is how we have gotten it across. The players have bought into it and we will continue it as long as I am there.

The next thing that is important to us is what we call *grab grass*. We got the idea at this clinic about five years ago when a coach from U of L talked about being in a good football position at the snap of the ball. I went back and looked at us on film and saw that we had not done a good job of coaching that with our defensive players, and had not recognized it during the season.

We met as a staff and realized that we needed to come up with a way to get our guys in a good defensive stance on every play at the snap of the ball. We decided that we would make all of our linebackers and defensive backs go down and touch the ground before every play, and we would call it "grabbing grass." My feeling is that if we cannot as coaches get them in a good stance to start off with, then we are not very good coaches. It has to start with their stance and being in a good football position, and that is what we do to make sure that we get that done.

The third element of our defensive foundation is a thing that we call T-N-T. Everybody talks about *T-N-T*, but I can assure you that *turnovers and tackling* is the first thing we do every day in our individual period. We do some sort of turnover drill as a group, where we have the defensive line, outside backers, inside backers, and defensive backs, and it will be a tip drill one day, and an interception drill, scoop and score, or strip drill the next. After that, we have some form of tackling, and that is the first thing we do at the beginning of our individual drills every single day.

As I said, those are three things that are traditions at our place, on the defensive side of the ball, that we do and will continue to do. They are things that our kids have bought into, and they are foundations of our defensive success. If you want any more information on them, just let me know and I will see that you get it.

Now I want to get to the principles of a great defense. I have to say that these are all things I have gotten from Greg Williams, who coached the defense for the Tennessee Titans, in visiting with him over the years, and from Coach Harbaugh, along with the many things I have learned from him. They have been adjusted a little, but these are things that have been in our book and that we talk about with our players every day.

- Concentration and communication
- Technique
- Effort
- Functional intelligence
- Emotional stability

First, if you look at your film and ask what went wrong on a certain play, I guarantee you it is either *concentration* or *communication*.

Concentrating on the call and getting the call communicated. "I did not hear the call," is a reply by players that drives coaches crazy. It is the player's responsibility to hear the call and that is a part of communication. Players must concentrate and be focused and talk on defense, and make sure everybody is on the same page.

Communication failures occur at all levels of football. Greg Williams told me that the Tennessee Titans missed a call in the Super Bowl that allowed Marshall Faulk to be wide open for a 51-yard touchdown pass. It happens at all levels, and the better we can be at communication, the better chance we have to be great on defense.

When we talk about *technique*, it is stance and first step. It is stance, first step, and being in good football position to read keys and take on blockers.

When we talk about *effort*, that is the gun line. We have already discussed that, but we have to have great effort from every player.

Functional intelligence sounds fancy, but whether or not a kid gets it in the classroom and it makes sense on the board, he has to be able to take it out on the field and function. The strong safety must understand his curl-flat responsibility in cover 3, and the linebacker must understand how his read fits him to a certain gap. I would much rather have 4.8 going in the right direction than 4.5 going in the wrong direction.

You have to have smart guys who know what they are doing. We are constantly evaluating that to make sure we are putting guys on the field that can do the job mentally.

With all of the highs and lows that come with football, our players have to have *emotional stability*. In this day and age, with all the hype and media, and all the talk and the pressure, our players have to understand that they have to play at an even keel. We try to take the adverse situations that players face and turn them into learning lessons, so they can understand that there will be highs and lows throughout a game as there are in life, and coaches as well as players can all get better at keeping our poise.

Now let me put up six things that are important to every defensive football coach and discuss them briefly:

Coaching Habits and Practice Habits to Stress

- Finish plays! "Be good around the ball!"
  - ✓ Turnovers, strips, break-ups, etc.
- Run to the ball! Pursuit! "Get in the gun line."
- Break on all passes! Turn and run!
- Be violent and ballistic with all movements.
- Stress keys! "Believe/trust what you see."
  - ✓ Minimize run/pass conflict.
  - ✓ Play one and react to the other. "You cannot have two masters."
- Coach through your players' eyes.
  - ✓ Develop your players into "coaches on the field."
  - ✓ It is not how much you know, it is how much of what you know that they know.

We had a year in which we got 49 turnovers and the next year we had half of that. We did not change anything. We still did turnovers and tackling at the beginning, and everything was the same. Some of it is that the ball bounces your way, but more than anything else it is just emphasis and talking about *finishing plays* every day. When you see that emphasis being reflected in the way your guys practice, that is when it is getting through. We have to have the habit of always looking to strip the football. There is no magic formula to that. It is simply making sure that your coaches are coaching the heck out of getting to the ball, being active, finishing plays, and trying to get the ball out.

We talked about r*unning to the ball* and getting in the gun line in practice and that is how we handle that.

We want our players to *break on all passes*—to *turn and run*. When we were watching our gun lines on film last week, we saw some guys who were not going full speed when the ball was thrown. I told our staff that if we pulled out our seven-on-seven tape from somewhere in camp or somewhere in practice, we would see where we lost sight of that one.

We tend to think that "just one" may not be all that important, but the heck it is not. I have seen it just this year that we may have lost sight of that one thing a little bit in practice. If the ball goes all the way to one side, then the corner all the way on the other side, if it is zone coverage, had better see that ball thrown, and you better see the same intensity of a break toward that football as you see with the free safety that is close to making a play. That is the guy who will make the touchdown-saving tackle for your team. I think we all may lose sight of that a little at times, but you have to coach it hard in seven-on-seven and any time the ball is thrown.

Defensive players must be *violent and ballistic in all movements*. When we are in individual period, we want to make sure we are not just going through the motions. We are changing directions, it is intense, and we are getting after it. We make sure in all of our change-of-direction drills that we are up on the balls of our feet.

Stress keys and believe/trust what you see. Minimize the run/pass conflict. I tell the story to our defense every year of Blaine Bishop, with whom I played in high school. He was not recruited, went to a Division II school, transferred to Ball State, became a starter there, and was the last guy taken in the draft. He barely made the Tennessee Titans, playing special teams his first year.

All of a sudden, he is starting for the Titans, a four-time Pro Bowl strong safety. He is 5'8" maybe, 195 pounds, and he runs a 4.6. I asked Greg Williams why he was so good. What is he doing that is getting him to the football the way he is getting to the football? Of course he plays hard, he practices hard, and he is great in the weight room, but Greg said the difference was *keys*. He said, "He has trusted me as a coach and he has trusted his keys." When the key says run, he flies to the run, and when it says pass, he flies to the pass.

That is why he is a great player. More than anything else, it is because he got great at reading keys and trusting the coach when he gives him a live key that will tell him what he needs to know.

He also knew his run/pass responsibilities and he knew to play one and react to the other. Every player must understand what he is first in his defense. Is he a run-first defender and pass second, or pass first and run second? You cannot serve two masters.

Linebackers and rolled up safeties play the run first and react to the pass. If you are back there playing the third or the half, then you need to play pass first and react to the run late.

As a defensive coach, you must give them a key, teach them, and make sure they understand the things that key could do on run or pass. Then tell them where they fit, and tell them if they will do that, then they will be in a position to make the play. Stress keys a lot and trust what you see.

With regard to *coach through your players' eyes*, and *develop coaches on the field*, I will say that in the years we have had the best defenses, we have had a linebacker and one of our safeties who could pretty much read my mind. They know in situations what we might see and they pretty well know what I might call. That is when you know that they are really starting to understand, and that you are coaching through them and letting them take ownership in it.

I want to share with you the five principles that we base our blitzing schemes on and discuss each one briefly:

Principles of Great Blitzing Defenses

- Disguise
- Timing
- Collapse the pocket
- Contain the quarterback
- Challenge receivers!

One thing we have tried to do over the years with regard to *disguise* is be four across. In our 50 defense, which I am going to show you here, we line up with a zero nose, two 4s, two outside backers, two 30-alignment inside backers, and we have tried as best we can to just go four across.

We can talk about disguising by showing this and doing that or showing that and doing this, but I think the simplest way to disguise is to show the exact same look every single time.

One of the things that we talk about when we get into the overall philosophies of our defense is that we want to attack and confuse. We want to make all 11 offensive players on the field have to make postsnap decisions. We want them to line up and see the same thing nearly every time, especially the quarterback, and then when the ball is snapped he has to be thinking. We know where we are going, but he has to be thinking about the direction our coverage is going, and whether it is quarters, middle open, or middle closed. So we are going to make sure that our opponent has to make postsnap decisions, and I believe that the easiest way to do that is to show him the same thing every time.

When I think about *timing*, I remember what Blaine Bishop told me was a big key to his success as a blitzer. His position coach with the Titans, Jim Schwartz, prepared a scouting report that included cadence, tips from studying the offensive center,

tips from studying the quarterback's presnap mechanics, and any other tips that would help him time up his blitzes.

On the shotguns, the center may be getting into a rhythm of picking his head up at a certain time prior to the snap, or the quarterback may move his hands in a similar rhythm that might be a key. Any kind of tendency or any little key that Jim Schwartz gave him during the week was studied on film, practiced during the week, and ultimately led to great timing on blitzes.

You have to have team players to be a great blitzing team. When we bring five-man pressure, we have guys whose job in the design of the blitz is to bring inside pressure and *collapse the pocket*. If they do not understand that, and they think that their job is just to get to the quarterback, then we have problems. They may see what they think is an opening to the outside, try to take that opening, and in doing so run into the guy who is assigned to blitz from the outside. When we say collapse the pocket, that sounds simple enough, but the inside rush guys have to trust it, understand their roll in that call, and they have to collapse the pocket. When that means that they have to bull rush and walk that blocker back to the quarterback, then that is what they have to do.

When we study it, we find that it is not always getting hits or getting sacks that causes problems for the quarterback in the passing game, but if we can affect the quarterback's throwing motion and his ability to step through the throw, a lot of times that is just as good as a deflection. That is a "ball disruption," which is a term we got from Dale Lindsey and those guys when we visited their camp last May. It means that we are making the quarterback uncomfortable and unable to follow through in the pocket.

We have to have guys who believe in collapsing the pocket. It is just a case of them accepting their role in that blitz and understanding that if they do what they are supposed to do, we will all do well.

It is the same thing with *containing the quarterback*. We are a 3-4 defense and we have guys coming off of the edge all of the time. If they think that their only job is to get to the quarterback, they may try to go inside when they think that is open to them, and then we may have real problems. The job of the outside rusher is to keep the quarterback inside of him, and if he can get to him by coming outside that is fine, but he has to contain the quarterback. We say to him that if his job is to contain, then contain. Period!

The last of our blitzing principles is to *challenge receivers*. Now, we are not a "man blitz" team, and I do not think you see that very much any more. We probably average eight to 10 times a year when we will send everybody after them and play zero coverage.

Therefore, when we tell our corners to challenge receivers in playing thirds coverage in any type of zone blitz, we are telling them that they are responsible for the three-step drop, the 10- to 12-yard out route, and the 9 route 30 yards downfield. Against the three-step game, they have to make plays. They have to make plays on the 10- to 12-yard out, and they have to make plays when somebody throws a 9 route down the side of the field.

That is what we are talking about when we say to challenge the receivers on the outside. We are certainly playing a lot of three-under, three-deep zone coverage, but offenses are getting pretty good and they are protecting pretty well, and it seems that quarterbacks are getting better every year. That means that our guys have to challenge more, and get away from the notion that in three-deep they only have to run and run and not let anyone get behind them. As our linebackers have to match up on the inside in some of our coverage, our corners have to match up, challenge, and be a little more aggressive on the outside.

Let me go through some of these reminders here quickly, and then I will get to the X's and O's part of it. This is just something that is traditional that we talk to our group about. We try to make sure it is simple, but you cannot be simple enough in this day and age, when they have so many things going on in their minds.

Every Play

- Presnap
  - ✓ Alignment
  - ✓ Stance
  - ✓ Key
  - ✓ Responsibility
- Postsnap
  - ✓ Read-React and execute
  - ✓ Come to your point
  - ✓ Deliver a blow (hands)
  - ✓ Fight pressure/find the ball
  - ✓ Shed the blocker
  - ✓ Pursue and gang tackle
- The Three Nevers
  - ✓ Never get knocked down
  - ✓ Never get knocked off the ball
  - ✓ Never run around the blocker

In the *presnap* phase of every play, there are four points of emphasis: alignment, stance, key, and responsibility. From a defensive back's perspective, lining up requires a vertical alignment and a horizontal alignment, and within the philosophy of disguising with the same look every time, this is absolutely critical. Of course, we want every player in a good stance, with knees bent, hips down, in a good football position, ready to play. The key tells the player where he goes if it is a run and where he goes if it is a pass. It is simple, but that is the way it has to be presented to them.

Now, here are our points of emphasis in the *postsnap* part of every play. At our first team meeting, we put the playbook on the table and we say, "Gentlemen, there is not a single play in this book that is designed to fail. If you believe in it and execute it, it is going to work."

When we talk about read-react and execute, that is what will make it all happen. When we say "come to your point," we are telling each player where he fits in the defense off of his read. A linebacker who fits the B gap versus the isolation play must come to his point and deliver a blow. That is where technique comes into it. He has to have pad under pad, shoot his hands from a good base, and keep his eyes down.

Then he fights pressure and finds the ball in the progression of the play. The thing that we tend to make the biggest mistake on as linebackers and defensive backs is peeking up over the blocker's shoulder when we are supposed to fight pressure and find the ball. To correct that, we coach them to lock out on the blocker and find the ball down here at waist level.

I know that some people like the "swim" technique, but we will not ever teach a defensive player to swim at Western Kentucky. When we talk about shedding the blocker, we want to get in a good football position, and we will slap, dip, rip, and stay down in a good football position.

That is the way we teach our players to get off the block—dip and rip.

Pursue and gang tackle is the last part of the progression. I believe that is the defining characteristic of the defensive tradition of Hilltopper football. It is called "getting in the gun line." It is what we take pride in, and it is what we are known for.

I am also showing you the *three nevers*, but they are included in all the things I have just covered. They are standard rules that all defensive coaches give their players in one form or another, so I will not elaborate any further on them.

Now, I want to get into our 3-4 stuff, into what we are doing, give you a base overview, and then get into some of our zone blitzes. I assure you it is not rocket science, but there are some things we have done off of our base things, including some that we learned at this clinic last year, that have been very good for us.

We are a 3-4 defense. We use a nose man, a right end, and a left end. Our nickel, Mike, and strong safety travel together. Our Will, Joker, and free safety travel together, and our corners are right and left. That is the way we do it.

We line up field and boundary. The nickel, Mike and strong safety go to the field, or to the passing strength. The Will, Joker, and free safety will go opposite.

In our base defense, we are going to line up in our 3-4 and slant to the boundary, or we will stem to it and line up in shades from the field in some kind of "over" defense. We can play some form of three deep with four under, or we can roll the strong corner, or even roll the whole thing and play cover 2 over the top to the field.

If we come back from the weakside instead, we can slant from there, or we can stem from there into what would be an "under" defense. With that, we will play quarters, we will play quarter-quarter-half, and we may play some cover 2.

We can play strong rotation with our corners or weak rotation with our corners. It is all based off which way we are slanting our line. Like I said, we can line up in shades and do it, or we can just slant to it, one way or the other. We can send an outside linebacker and defensive end on what we call a "fill," and we can do some other things within that structure, but that is our base defense, and that is what we do. I might also mention that we play zone coverage about 95 percent of the time.

We have what we call our Okie package. In our Okie package, everybody is up on the line. Those two inside backers are walked up so the quarterback can see the threat, but it will look the same to him every time. All seven guys are in a threatening position showing the possibility of blitz. Any one of them may come, or they may not. At the same time, our secondary aligns four across or in a two shell, not tipping anything off.

What you see here is called South Blue ck Sky Dog (Diagram #1). We can single-call it, but our base way is to double-call it. The double call means that if it is two back or three by one, then we are playing three under and three deep, but if it is a two-by-two formation with one back, then we are playing four under and two deep. We can Zorro it and zone drop them, or we can do what we call a "man under' technique.

Okay, we are running South here, so the nose is the only guy who needs to be told what to do. He

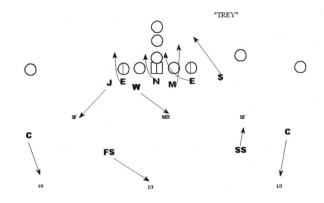

Diagram #1. Okie South Blue ck Sky Dog

has to go to the left. It is two backs here, so we are saying, "Sky Dog! Sky Dog!" We are lining up four across. The nickel is a rush-contain blitzer, the right end is going for the V of the neck of the guard from his 4 technique. If the guard fans out, he will cross his face, and if he blocks down, he is coming right off his butt.

The Mike has to be good at letting that clear and then hitting it hard from there. We can give a call for Mike and Will to line up in their normal alignments so they can hit it from some depth.

We have to count on inside pressure from that right end, the Mike, and the nose, while the left end is blitz-contain on the left.

The three underneath guys cover seam/flat, middle hook, and seam/flat. When we say seam/flat, for the strong safety on a number 2 receiver it is "seeeeam/flat," which is to emphasize that he must hold the seam. He cannot let the number 2 receiver get to 10 yards and then bend in, and be in a hole right down the hash.

If you go back and look where the ball is thrown from this set, you will find that, if the ball is thrown to the field, it will be somewhere from the number 2 receiver back into the middle of the field. The only other place they are throwing it is into the boundary with quick stuff, or the 10- to 12-yard out. So with this defense, we are going to protect where they are throwing the ball.

Our strong safety will sit on the outside shoulder of the number 2 receiver and protect the seam. If number 2 widens, then that is when the strong safety will widen and become the flat player, but he is holding that seam until number 2 takes him somewhere else.

If number 2 goes across right now, the strong safety is not going anywhere. He is holding it right there at about 10 yards and reading the quarterback's intentions. It is zone coverage and he has to see the ball and feel the receivers in zone coverage. If he sees number 2 go across, he will hold it, look for something coming back, and play football.

The middle hook player will drop off of number 3. If he does not know how to find number 3, we coach him to just get over the outside shoulder of the tackle to the field, get his eyes on the quarterback, and play football, because that is where they want to throw it.

There may be times when we want the weak seam/flat player to bale to number 1, or he could get a number 2 out there, but anytime he is unsure, I want him sitting eight to 10 yards on the outside shoulder of the offensive tackle on the weakside, just like the middle hook player is on the strongside. He should also get his eyes on the quarterback and just play football.

As you will see on the film here, if we can get that picture, it is tough, and the quarterback has to take the ball outside, which is a little bit of a more difficult throw.

Middle hook is matching on number 3 and the deepest we are going to carry anything on these inside guys is 15 yards. These guys are classic third-down players reading two-to-one.

If we get a closed backside, we can play what we call "white," which is just a roll-to-the-field cover 2. We will bring the weak corner to half-field coverage over the nub tight end, roll the strong safety up as a curl player, the strong corner up as a flat player, and bale the free safety over into half-field coverage strong. Now, we are playing four-under, two-deep to a single-width formation. I like it because it gives you two fast guys playing zone over their two fast guys, with protection behind them. It also gives you good support against all the bubble-screen and quick stuff out to the strongside of the formation.

We can adjust the blitz with a "fill" call. If we say south fill, then instead of bringing the nickel backer as rush contain, he comes under, and Mike then loops to outside contain. Now, if a back is blocking the nickel, he expects him to contain rush, but this gives him the freedom to come underneath and get inside pressure from there.

Now, before we get to the film I want to show you some of the other Okie blitzes. The coverage principles are the same in all of them, but the fronts will show you some of the different ways we can bring pressure, and I will explain them as we go through the film.

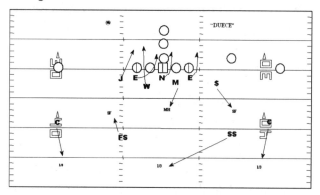

Diagram #2. Okie West Blue ck Sun Dog

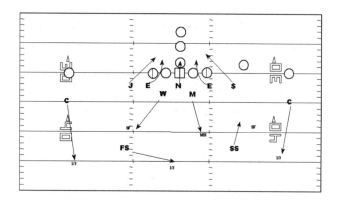

Diagram #3. Okie Southwest Blue ck Sky Dog

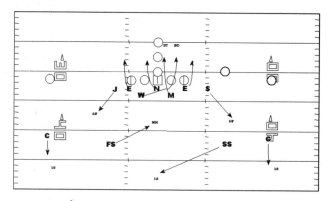

Diagram #4. Okie Jab Blue ck Mars Dog

We have been running the Okie package since 2000 and we have things now that we need to improve on and "tweak," and that is what we are working on right now. We are confident in what we are doing, but we know that, like everybody does, we have to adjust a little each year and realize what people are starting to see from how they line up.

Offensively, we are a two-back team that runs iso and power, but we will also go one-back and throw the ball. We have a senior quarterback named Justin Haddix who, if things keep going well, will have started every game of his career.

We only had nine seniors last year and we are excited about what we have coming back. We are looking forward to the 2006 season, which will open up at Georgia on September 2. After that, we get into the Battle of the Bluegrass with Eastern Kentucky. We then have UT Chattanooga on our schedule, and then we go into the Gateway Conference play. We have a lot of good things going on.

I thank you for listening.

SCREEN PASS AND DRAW PACKAGE

Georgia Tech University

It is good to be here today. The first question we ask ourselves is why we use the screen game. The first thing that coaches talk about is slowing the pass rush. Everyone talked for years and years about that thing. There is nothing wrong with that thinking.

We want to run the screen to get the ball in the hands of our playmakers. The playmakers could be wide receivers or running backs. The screen play can give the quarterback confidence. When I was with Denver, our quarterback was John Elway. If he struggled in the previous game, we started the next game with three or four slip screens. That let him get some completions and gain confidence.

If your quarterback is struggling trying to throw the ball downfield, let him throw a screen or two to get his confidence back. It allows him to get his rhythm and get back in the groove. Throwing the screen allows the quarterback to throw the ball. He does not have to read coverages or dodge the rush.

In your offensive line, you may have smaller but quicker linemen. Use that to your advantage. If you have big, fat, slow linemen, screens may not fit what you want to do. You have to evaluate your offensive line and see what the advantages are for your team.

Formation can create an unbalanced distribution of the defense. If you go to a triple formation or an unbalanced formation, the defense has a tendency to kick to one side. If you can throw a screen back away from that, you have a numbers advantage. If you have a heavy blitzing team, it gives you an advantage in numbers if you can throw the screen.

If the defense is a zone team, is the screen a good play to run? The trendy thing on defense in today's football is the zone blitz. We see it weekly at Georgia Tech.

There are advantages to throwing a screen against zone blitz teams, because normally they will void a zone. Wherever the defense voids a zone, we try to put the screen in that spot.

If the defense wants to blitz linebackers and put defensive linemen in coverage, that is a mismatch in my opinion. I like the idea of a defensive end in space trying to avoid offensive linemen and tackle a running back in the open field.

We saw more zone blitzes this year than we ever have. That is why we threw more screen passes this year than we ever have before.

Screens against man coverage are great as long as you can block the man. If you cannot block the man, you do not need to run them against man defenses.

I am not going to talk about the tunnel screen or the jailbreak screen. Those are screens run by every spread team in the land. That is one of their base plays. You can get that information anywhere.

The slow screen and slip screen are two of the best plays in football right now. We run the flare screen some as part of our regular offense. We use the bubble screen and the play-action screen. We throw the wide receiver screens on occasion, but out personnel are not suited for that type of screen.

In football today, there are probably two schools of thought as to when you throw the screen pass. There is a thought process for coaches over 45 years of age and one for coaches under 45 years of age. If you are over 45 years old, you ran the screen on second or third down, and in long-yardage situations.

In that situation, the defensive linemen abandon their run responsibilities to jet up the field to rush the quarterback. Today you can throw the screen on any down. The defense on every play is on a dead run up the field, even on first down. All the defenses are going for penetration and trying to get the first step across the line of scrimmage. They try to win the line of scrimmage.

Today, there is no such thing as a screen down. You can call the screen on any down, any time, and any situation. One place we call the screen is the red zone. We think we can gain an advantage inside the 10-yard line. At the eight-yard line, the screen becomes a good pass play. It is hard to find pass plays in the red zone because of the bracket coverages. You have to protect the quarterback and you do not have any place to squeeze the ball in to a receiver.

That is why the fade route is so popular in the red zone. The ball is thrown outside in a place away from the defense. By throwing the screen in the red zone, we think we get great returns on our investments.

There are some components of a great screen play. We start with the screenside tackle. The technique played by that tackle is 357. That means he sets at three yards, makes contact at five yards, and pushes to seven yards. If we can get the defender seven yards deep, he cannot recover and get back in the play.

The next technique for the onside tackle is 333. We use this technique on the tunnel and quick-flare screen. On that technique, he sets at three yards, makes contact at three yards, and cuts at three yards.

Timing on a screen play is vital. To get good time, you cannot have any double-teams by any of your linemen. We want no double-teams because of the reactions of the defensive linemen in a double-team. The defensive coaches teach them to grab and hold, maintain their territory, and look around. If everything is a single block, the defenders think they have a chance for the sack and go for the quarterback.

If you single block defensive linemen, they are less inclined to stop their charge and look to see what is happening. Most defensive schemes have a spy built into their pass rush. It could be the slow rusher who cannot pressure the quarterback or the small defender that tackles well. He is the one assigned to play the screen and draw. You must know if a team has a spy and have a plan to block him.

I am going to talk about the aiming point for the linemen in just a minute. The aiming point is the track for linemen on the slow screen play. When the offensive linemen get out on a screen, we do not want them to mirror the defender. We want them to come out and throw on them. We want them on the ground, making the defender do something to get out of the way. If we get the ball in the playmaker's hands we want the linemen out of the way.

The quarterback has to drive hard to set up at five yards. He looks downfield and away from the screen. If he does not make the play look like a dropback pass, the defense will see the screen. He has to sell the set at five yards. After that point, he becomes a football player and does whatever he can to get the ball to the screen receiver. If he cannot move and avoid defenders released by screen blockers, you are in trouble anyway. He has to be an athlete and get the ball off.

The receivers or backs catching the screen must have a feel for the play. We teach the receiver where the defense is, who will block them, and where the ball is going. We cannot teach him everything, and that is where his feel for the screen comes into play. He has to understand the principle of what you are trying to do and where the ball has to go. If he understands the principle, he will have a chance to have a feel for that play.

You have to decide where you want the screen to be caught. That is a conscious decision you have to make. You have to decide whether you want the screen thrown wide or tight.

The other tight end or blocking back has to know what is going on and have their blocking assignment down, so they do not get in the way.

The slow screen is the first thing I want to cover. I will give you the base play and when we get to the tape, I will show you some adjustments we add to it. We like to run this screen to the weakside, although we have run it to the strongside.

If we screen to the left side, the left offensive tackle has a 357 technique (Diagram #1). The five offensive linemen have the four down defenders and the Mike linebacker. That is true every time we run this play. If the defense is in a 3-4 front, the five offensive linemen have the three down defender plus the Mike and Sam linebackers. We fan to the weakside.

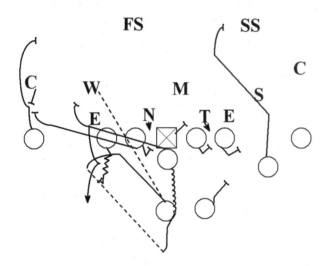

Diagram #1. Slow Screen

We never want to double-team anyone on this play. The center sets away from the backside shade noseguard. The guard invites him into the crease, holds him for two counts, and lets him go. The right guard does the same thing with the 3-technique tackle. He invites him into the B-gap crease, holds for two counts, and lets him go. The running back has the Will linebacker as his pass-protection assignment. If the Will linebacker comes outside, he chips on him. If he runs inside, he lets him go.

The timing comes from the frontside guard. In this case, it is the left guard. The back goes when the frontside guard goes. The rule for the left guard is flat and up. His first rule deals with man-to-man coverage. If either the Will linebacker or the corner

is running hard for the back, he blocks them immediately. He forgets everything else and blocks the defender, aiming for his outside hip.

He goes for the outside hip because the defensive coach taught the curl-flat defender not to let the ball outside of him. If the guard works for the outside, the defender will continue to widen and open the crease inside of him.

If the coverage on that side is a type of zone coverage, the guard runs through the flat and turns up at the numbers. He looks for the corner in cover 2, the safety in some type of invert, or the Will linebacker in cover 3.

The center is the second man in the screen and his rule is out and up. He pulls down the line and turns up in the alley. The backside guard's rule is up and in. Those are the terms we use to describe the blocking assignments for the linemen.

I want to tell you something about the screen. The screen is like the power-O or zone play, in that if you do not work at it, you will not be worth a flip. If you do not commit to it, you will not be any good at it.

Some coaches think I have some bit of magic I can give to them to make them a good screen team. There is only one way to become a good screen team. You have to commit the time to the play so you can execute.

We have a screen period every week as part of our practice. We commit the time in practice to be able to execute in the games.

The outside receiver reads the coverage. If the corner rolls, he outside releases and blocks the half safety coming over the top. If the corner retreats, the receiver runs him as deep as he can and gets square on his outside numbers. If it is bump man coverage, he runs him off.

The tight end or slot receiver in a three-wide-receiver scheme blocks the middle third to the deep half to his side. The outside receiver away from the screen has the corner aligned on him.

The quarterback drops five steps, sets up, and gets the ball to the running back. The running back has to time the play. If the defense clogs the guard up and the center is the first lineman out, the center and guard swap assignments. If that happens, the back must have a clock in his head. That is the feel for the play. He must know when to leave.

We are not a wide screen team. We want the screen thrown in an area two yards outside the offensive tackle. That is about the alignment of a tight end to that side.

When the corner reads the screen, he comes up hard to the outside. If you do not have an athletic lineman, he may not go flat enough to the line of scrimmage. He may get too far upfield and be unable to junction the corner. If the screen is wide, we are dead. However, if it is tight, we have a chance to block the corner, even if the guard took the wrong angle. The tailback catches the ball and turns up in the crease inside the corner.

The slip screen is one of the best plays in football right now. You can run it out of every formation to the strongside or the weakside. It is a tough football play. I will show you the play from a two-back set. The slip screen goes with slide protection. In slide protection, the line slides one way and the back blocks opposite the slide. The slip screen is no more than the back faking his blocking assignment and slipping out into the crease between the down block of the offensive tackle and the defensive end.

In the diagram (Diagram #2), the offensive line blocks a slide-protection scheme to the left. On the right side of the line, the offensive tackle has the B gap, the guard has the A gap, and the center has the backside A gap. The back blocks outside the right tackle. The alignment of the tailback does not matter. He could be in a strong position, behind the quarterback, or to the weakside moving across the set.

The quarterback takes a five-step drop. That is the best depth from which to complete the throw. If he goes three or seven steps, the crease does not open. We do not give the back a particular technique to slip the blocker and get into position.

When I was with the Pittsburgh Steelers in the mid-to-late 90s, that was the first time I ran this

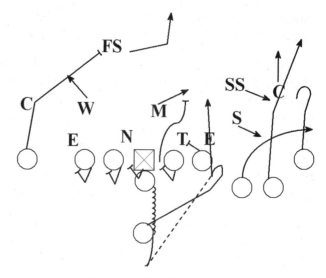

Diagram #2. Slip Screen

play. We had small offensive linemen and the big defensive linemen were giving us problems in our pass protection. We told the back to fake the block and spin inside. He tried the block, but it did not look natural. We told him to get open the best way he could and the play took off. You can use the technique that is effective for you.

We tell the running back to run at the outside shoulder of the defender and try to get him to run upfield. If he goes inside, we tell the back to bump him inside and set up outside in the tight-end area. If the defender runs up the field, there is a natural throwing lane to the inside.

When we run the slip screen, we run a pass route with the receivers. We want the secondary to react to the pass pattern. That way, we can run them into their pass responsibilities. With the triple set to that side, the outside receiver runs a hook, the outside slot runs the flag, and the inside slot runs a flat. We do not change that for the play.

If the tackle has a B-gap defender, he locks on him and blocks him. The defense generally will not have a defender in both the A and B gaps. Therefore, the guard is uncovered and goes upfield. If the defense has a strong shade on the center and a 5-technique defender, the tackle sets inside at a 45-degree angle and checks the B gap. If there is no one in the gap, he is up the field.

The tackle comes upfield, and his rule is to block anyone head up to inside his alignment. He does not chase anyone outside. The defender running to cover the curl or flat will run himself out of the play.

All the offensive linemen do what we call a "pin technique." Once the offensive linemen stop the penetration of the defenders, they work their hips upfield to keep the defender from rolling out of the block. All the defensive linemen are pinned to the line of scrimmage. The defenders outside are in coverage. The lineman coming upfield holds for one count and comes upfield to cut off the backside.

We had one game where we game planned to run the slip screen at the 1-technique noseguard (Diagram #3). The reason we did that was to make sure the tackle got out on the linebacker.

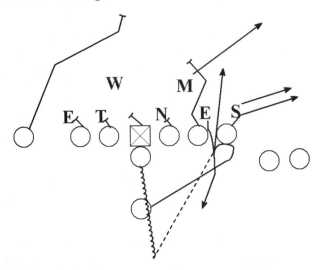

Diagram #3. Slip Against the 1 Technique

The next screen is the bubble screen (Diagram #4). There are three reasons to run the bubble screen. The first reason to run the bubble screen is the alignment is an advantage for the offense. You can also run it on the quick count, get the ball out,

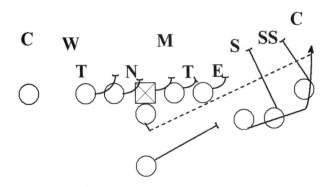

Diagram #4. Bubble Screen

and catch the defense off-balance. The third thing is the offense throws the ball downfield as opposed to laterally or behind the line.

The outside receiver has the MDM, which stands for the "most dangerous man." If he has a soft corner on him and a pressed man inside of him, he blocks inside.

We always run this play to the right. We have a right-handed quarterback. If we had a left-handed quarterback, we would throw it left. The right-handed quarterback has the ball protected against penetration as he steps out to throw right. If the right-handed quarterback tries to throw the ball left, he exposes the ball to the line of scrimmage. In addition, he has to get depth and turn his hips to throw left. That puts the ball traveling tight to the line of scrimmage. The ball can easily be tipped or knocked down.

We found the difference between throwing the ball to the right and left is two yards. We try to throw the ball on the bubble to the right most of the time.

The receiver in the slot opens in his stance and drop steps one yard off his alignment. He turns his shoulders, runs to the sideline, and turns up. He tries to catch the ball one yard behind the line of scrimmage.

If the defense calls a blitz when we run the bubble screen, there is a chance for a big play. Since we call the bubble screen on a quick count, the blitz has no chance to get home and there is one less man in the scheme to block.

On the offensive line, we try to reach a gap-and-a-half to the outside. They try to get on the defenders and stay on the line of scrimmage as much as they can. The playside offensive tackle has the toughest block, particularly if he faces a wide speed rusher. If the rusher is streaking up the field, the tackle gets on him and tries to keep his hands down.

We do not try to cut anyone on this type of situation. We found out that if we tried to cut on the bubble screen, the end saw it coming and looked to knock the ball down. If we got out on him on a reach block, he had a tendency to play run first.

The next screen is the play-action screen. This is the best one we have. You can do it from a number of different formations. This play is from bootleg action with a throw-back screen.

Playing the schedule we play in the ACC, we do not throw many patterns down the field unless we max protect. When you play Miami, Virginia Tech, and Georgia, you do not have the time send out four receivers and throw the ball 18 yards down the field. When we do that, we use this pass. We run the play-action off the counter play and try to get our good receiver on a deep cross or post. On this play, the tight end blocks the defensive end, regardless of where he lines up.

The tackle and guard seal to the inside in the A gap and B gap (Diagram #5). The backside guard pulls for the Sam linebacker. The center blocks the backside A gap. The backside tackle steps into the B gap and pivots back for the backside rush. If anything comes through the B gap, he blocks it. The back makes the fake and blocks the backside.

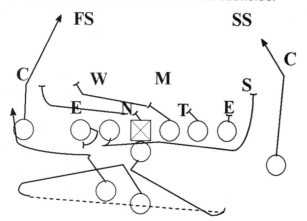

Diagram #5. Play-Action Screen

The quarterback makes the fake and bootlegs the ball to the offensive tackle—tight end gap before he turns back. The center and right guard form the two-man screen to the left. The center is the flat-and-up blocker and the right guard is the out-and-up blocker. There is no out-and-in blocker on this screen. The linemen hold for two counts and get outside for the screen.

The tailback fakes and sets up backside with the offensive tackle. He is responsible for any secondary blitz to that side on the pass play. If the Will linebacker comes on a blitz to his side, he blocks for two counts and lets him go. This screen is a wider screen than the slow screen. The quarterback throws the screen back to the outside.

You can make any kind of adjustments in the formation you want. It can be run with any backfield adjustment. A great way to run this play is unbalanced (Diagram #6). If you go unbalanced to the wide side of the field, with no receiver to the backside, the defense will put a boatload of defenders into the wide side. That allows you the opportunity to run the screen into the boundary.

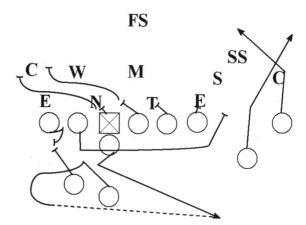

Diagram #6. Play-Action from an Unbalanced Set

I want to go to the film and watch some of the screens. There are good and bad plays on this tape. The first one you will see is almost perfect, but that is the last one like that.

Thank you very much. I appreciate your attention. We would love to have you come and visit at Georgia Tech. I hope you got something from this talk. Just remember, there is no magic in the chalkboard. If you want to run a screen game, you must commit to it and set aside practice time to take care of it. This is a good scheme, but timing is everything. Come see us.

ATTACKING COVERAGES WITH THE DROPBACK PASS

Stanford University

Thank you. I want to talk about some of these coverages, and then I am going to talk about the strengths and weaknesses of them. Then I will show you some plays that we run to defeat them, and the style that we have.

What Are the Coverages We Plan to Attack?

- Cover 0—Man-to-man with a six-, seven, or eight-man rush ratio
- Cover 1—Man-to-man with a five-man rush ratio
- Cover 3—Zone with four-man rush, four underneath and three deep
- Cover 2—Zone with four-man rush, five underneath and two deep
- Cover 4 (Quarters)—Four-man rush, three underneath and three deep

When we refer to cover zero, that is a straight-across man with some form of pressure, either a six-, seven-, or eight-man rush. There are not many teams doing that anymore. Most people are really going crazy in the "fire zone" category.

A lot of people are playing us in cover 1. We had one really good receiver, so they tried to match up, get an extra guy in the box to stop the run game, funnel our guys inside, and not let us throw the ball up for grabs like we did with Larry.

We see a little bit of cover 3, but most of the cover 3 we see is in a "fire-zone," or blitz-zone, concept, as some people call it. In that concept, they will blitz two guys from one side, or they will blitz an outside linebacker and a secondary guy, which makes it hard on any kind of pass offense where you are trying to get guys out.

In order to have a good pass offense, you have to get guys out. I am orientated to a dropback passing game, so that is where I am talking from.

The hard part of being a good pass offense is you have to get guys out, so you free-release backs, or be in a one-back alignment with three wide receivers and a tight end, but you are going to have to have some free releases with six-man protections. That means that somebody is going to have to react hot, or break his route when they come. That is why the fire zones have come in.

Now, they have actually been doing that for a long time, and I think Pete Carroll has really gone bonkers with all the fire zone stuff. The guy at Notre Dame has done the same thing. They are all fire zoning, but Southern Cal blitzed those linebackers and dropped those defensive linemen off against Vince Young in the Rose Bowl, and he scrambled twice to the same side against those defensive linemen in the open field, and that is when he scored those touchdowns. Maybe that might cool them down a little bit.

All right, we see a lot of cover 2, and we really see three kinds of it. We see cover 2 where they will not carry the guy going down the middle, we see cover 2 where they will "man up" the guy going down the middle, and we see cover 2 Tampa, where the middle linebacker is deeper than the guy going down the middle. We are also seeing a little more cover 2 "man under," with a lot of twists underneath so the linemen can make it hard on the quarterback to scramble.

And then cover 4, which is quarters coverage, is a coverage that a lot of people have done to hit the run game. The safeties are keying the tight end into the uncovered linemen and getting involved with the run game.

That is a brief description of some of the coverages we see, so now I want to go through them and talk a little bit about their weaknesses and their strengths.

When you play man-to-man, you are going to open up the post area, so that is one of the things you have to design in your pass offense. One of the things that Bill Walsh always had in his offense was a post pattern. Not on every play, but in a lot of plays where they were working one side of the field, he would have a post in there on the other side. If you ever vacated the middle, whether cover zero, quarter coverage, or any of the things where nobody was deep in the middle, he was going to take it. Paul Hackett also did that at the 49ers with Joe Montana and Jerry Rice, and Joe would even stand in there and take the hit in order to get the ball to Jerry Rice on the post.

You also run the risk of getting picked when you play man coverage, and giving up the easy touchdown.

What you have to do as a defensive coach is learn how to break down the protections that people employ by formation and by down and distance. That is what football has grown to. You have to understand how to defeat protections. If you are going to play blitz coverage, you had better be on, because your defensive backs are not going to be able to stay with them very long. Also, you better be talented at cornerback, because you are putting them on an island.

Of course, there are some obvious advantages in playing man coverage. When you have guys who can run, that is a great way to go. It defines players' responsibilities better than zone because they know who they are going to cover, and it allows them to be a lot more reckless.

Cover zero gives you a chance to possibly bring more rushers than the offense has blockers, which leads to sacks or hurried throws. Then, with inside leverage on the receivers, it is difficult for the offense to beat you inside on the shorter throws.

As I said earlier, we see a lot of cover 1 because we do a great job of throwing what we refer to as the "step and go," which ends up being a fade route. What happens when people play us in cover 1 is they line up outside of us, which really makes it hard for us to get outside and run our little fade game. That

has been a coverage problem for us, and if we go inside we cannot throw the ball up because of the middle safety, so we have to line it. Anyway, this is a coverage that we end up seeing a lot.

Obviously, you have a guy in deep middle, or you can have the free safety read the "tips" and rob the area the offense is attacking, or you can double a receiver who is their best player. Cover 1 also gives you a chance to increase the rush ratio.

Once again, man-to-man makes it easier to define coverage responsibilities. You can also confuse the quarterback, and force him to make more accurate throws and really be on his game. As passing coaches, we always differentiate zone and man coverage, and I think zones are a lot easier, so we are always working to defeat man-to-man. Normally, we like to run away from people playing man coverage. We do not like to hook up against it.

We see a lot of "key blitz" from linebackers in cover 1. If there is a five-man rush and the offensive back blocks, then the linebacker rushes free in the open area, which gives him a straight line to the quarterback. On the other hand, if the back flares, the linebacker runs with him, which takes away the "flare control" from the quarterback and forces him to throw the ball downfield.

The outside leverage on the receivers helps on the outside breaking routes—the quick outs, regular outs, comebacks, and post corners. As I mentioned earlier, it also hurts our fade game, but it does open up the chance to throw the quick inside routes if the quarterback can line the ball. Man coverage of all types can be tough for a quarterback.

Cover 3 is a zone coverage that should be safe with regard to the deep balls—the post patterns and the go patterns. It gives you a balanced underneath coverage, and can create protection problems for offenses that release backs into the pattern, because it leaves five guys blocking four rushers. It is a safe and sound coverage that provides good run support to the wide side of the field.

I think that most of you are familiar with the weaknesses of cover 3. There are certainly big holes underneath, with the possibility of overloading a zone against only four underneath defenders. Four verticals can be a real problem, and the skinny post, which does not seem to be thrown as much any more, might be effective against all the fire zones, especially when they play outside leverage on the wide receivers.

Playing cover 3 puts a lot of pressure on the athletic ability of the underneath cover players. As we all know, it is a very basic coverage and people are usually pretty good at attacking it.

Cover 2 is an excellent short and underneath coverage. At Stanford, we will probably be a big cover 2 team this year, because we are not real fast at cornerback, and it gives us a chance to play with our corners and not get hurt. It can also be a good run-support defense, and it is an excellent contour alignment from which to disguise coverages. Whether it is quarters, cover 2, or cover zero, it all starts off with a little umbrella look.

It forces the quarterback to be an excellent decision-maker and an accurate passer, and it allows the defense to swarm the ball. Because receivers have a more difficult time with releases and getting into those areas, it forces the quarterback to hold the ball and allows the four-man rush more time to get to him.

Now, cover 2 can be vulnerable to three receivers going vertical, so when we get the guy going down the middle, we have to decide how we are going to play the underneath. Are we going to run with him, are we going to play man-to-man on him, or are we going to play "Tampa?" Also, cover 2 requires that we develop two pretty good safeties for back there.

It can be tough trying to defend the tight end in the middle on play-action passes with linebackers biting on the run fake, and we may not always have a linebacker who can run with a fast tight end, whether it is a play-action or not. Cornerbacks may not have to have sprinter speed in this coverage, but they have to be very disciplined in the flat in order to help the two deep safeties. They cannot be biting on the underneath stuff.

Cover 4, which we call "quarters coverage," is excellent coverage for shutting down the run game because it puts nine men in the box. We can also disguise all of our coverages from this contour. It allows us to really pack it in on the short, easy throws in front of the quarterback when the inside receivers stay inside. It also forces the quarterback into more difficult throws to the outside and downfield in order to beat us.

While quarters coverage is strong inside against run and pass, it can leave our cornerbacks on an island, and it can be vulnerable to the double post route or the wheel route. In addition, everyone now runs it to some degree, so familiarity has helped in attacking it.

The secret to successful pass coverage, then, is to do them all, if you are coached well enough and you have those kinds of players.

Offensively now, to attack these coverages that we see, and that is what I really want to talk about, we try to have a couple of different ways to go about it. We will have a progression-read pattern in which, regardless of coverage, the quarterback is going to execute the progression. We might have a couple of different types. It could be a half-field read with the quarterback only working one side, or it could be a full-field read, which means he will read the coverage and go opposite to the way it rolls.

We also have what we call coverage-beaters, which we will call from the sidelines. The head coach or the play caller anticipates that the defense will be in a certain coverage, so he calls a play designed to defeat that certain coverage.

The important part, when you do these things, is that your quarterback needs to understand what you are trying to get done. One of the best things I ever did when I went to work for Coach Majors was I asked him what he expected out of the passing game. In other words, the passing game should not lie dormant until third down and then all of a sudden people say, "All right, let's get a first down!" The run game is really a great way to win, but if you do not have those kinds of people, then you are going to have to throw it, but you do not want to throw it just on third down. So, I was trying to get him to tell me what he believed in, so I could execute what he believed in. If you are a quarterback coach or an offensive coordinator for a head coach, you need to know what he can live with.

I think that is a big part of it. In the same way, the quarterback needs to know what the quarterback coach can live with or the offensive coordinator can live with. There has to be really good communication between each other in order for you to be on the same page. That is what is good about being the head coach, offensive coordinator, play caller, and quarterback coach, because I am all in agreement. The good thing is that I am not trying to throw for yards to get another job. I am trying to do whatever I have to do to win. Ultimately, that is the bottom line.

Now, I want to talk about three styles of patterns that we run against the various coverages. I will list them for you first, and then we will discuss them one at a time.

Examples of Each Style of Pattern Versus Various Coverages

- Progression patterns
  - ✓ X deep over
  - ✓ Y out
  - ✓ All cross
- Full-field reads
  - ✓ Double patterns—out, comeback, go
  - ✓ Hook
- Coverage-beaters
  - ✓ Maximum protection—go pattern
  - ✓ Roll—z quick out

In our progression patterns, our quarterback will read a progression regardless of coverage. I will start with X deep over (Diagram #1). You could say that this is a "dig" route, but it is actually a post-cross route.

It is better, in my opinion, than a dig route and here is why. While I am going vertical and then I go to the post, I get to feel what is dropping out here so I can find the hole.

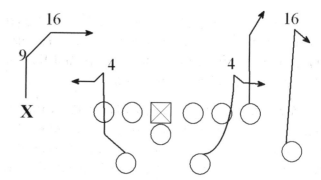

Diagram #1. X Deep Over

When we play against zones, we try to not run, meaning that we do not stay on the run versus zones. We try to find the holes in the zones and settle. That allows a less timed-up quarterback, or one who does not have as good an arm, to be more successful.

We can change the depth of the cuts to fit our personnel, but when you put your left foot in the ground and you start to angle to the post, you should get a good feel for where that linebacker is. When the linebacker drops out toward the route, we are going to come around him and start to "choke," or choke it down. The receiver will actually stop on the deep over when he gets into the hole. If he is in the hole and the quarterback has not thrown it to him, he should stop and start to come back to the quarterback.

Now, on a dig-type of route, that will probably never happen, because it will take too long, but it is the concept I am trying to explain to you that I think is really good. When he is going inside and pushing the top of the coverage, he can get a feel for the drop of the linebacker. If the linebacker drops straight back, which happens a lot on the hash with the wide field to the other side, he may hook it right there and keep it outside.

What we try to do underneath is have our backs get on the outside part of the inside linebacker's hook zones, and hook up at four yards. Whoever are the hook players, we try to have our backs get a yard or two on the outside of those guys and hook up at four yards, so we end up having a little triangle in the middle.

We have three guys on two guys. We are trying to attack the inside, so this becomes a progression pass, where that is one, that is two, and that is three, as you will see on the video. (Video)

You will see on the video that when we play against teams that play quarter coverage, the quarterback will go to the comeback. I think the first one we will see is the comeback against Cal. On this one, our quarterback did not like all the bodies in the middle. It looks like cover 1 with a four-man rush, and they are playing "in and out" on the backs so they get someone free, because our quarterback could run. It looks awfully wadded up in the middle so our quarterback went to the outside. So even on a "dover," which we want to throw inside, we give him the understanding that we want to throw the ball where it is not so crowded.

That takes me back to my first point about a quarterback-friendly offense. Do not put your quarterback in a position to fail. When he fails, you fail. That is not very difficult to understand.

Our tight end is responsible for clearing it out, and our backs are responsible for being four yards outside the hook players. If it is man-to-man, there is no one playing zone, so they will run to their side of the field and clear out.

This is pretty good here. I like this timing. This is not a quarterback lecture, but if you want to study some good stuff, notice that the quarterback has two hands on the ball in the pocket, holds onto the ball and does not pat it, he draws it back, he does not drop it down, and he has a strong arm. Occasionally, quarterbacks have to be able to throw off their back foot when they have no room to step into the throw, and that is what this particular quarterback has to learn to do.

This is also a very good route here on the comeback. He has good feet and he pushes the cornerback, "bursts" at the top, and makes a fine catch. What he should not do is "sit down" on the route. You should never sit down on the route and show your numbers to the cornerback. He should get his shoulder pads over his toes and burst at the top. That is a great coaching point on the comeback route.

Now, that is a very poor job of running with the catch. The first mistake he makes is putting the ball in his inside arm. You always want the ball in the outside arm, so you can use the inside arm to straight-arm the guy or push him away, and you also take the ball farther away from the defense, so he cannot rip it out.

Here is the play again against cover 1. The linebacker is sitting in the middle, so the quarterback does not want to go to the dover, so he goes to the outside guy.

On this next play, the defense is in a zone, in cover 2, and they are running with the tight end. We call that cover 2Y. You can see our receiver start to break down because he gets into the hole. The guy you usually have trouble controlling is the middle linebacker, but he is running with our tight end. That is why this is a great play against cover 2, because now they do not have anybody in the middle.

Normally, when your quarterback's eyes are over here reading this linebacker, the middle linebacker is the guy you have trouble controlling. When you look over here to the dover, he just reads your eyes and he is a hard one to deal with. That is why we try to choke it, but the hole is so big it does not matter. (Film)

Another progression pattern we will run is called Y out (Diagram #2). We will run Y out at 10 yards and put our back in the flat, try to inside-outside the hook defender, and take the curl-flat player out with the back. We will have a hook on the backside.

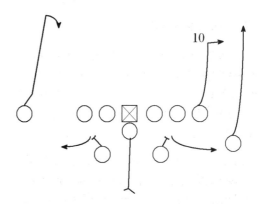

Diagram #2. Y Out

The theory of throwing the ball to the tight ends says that you should throw the ball a lot to tight ends because it is a shorter throw, so even if you are not very good at quarterback you should be able to get something done with the short throws to the tight end. (Film)

This one is a pattern that a lot of people run at our level and in the NFL. Our tight end has to do a better job here of being more physical when they are leaning on him, and he does a poor job of coming out of the break. He is a good football player and a tough guy, but he plays a little high, and he needs to come out of that break, because that guy is kind of playing him man-to-man.

Now, what happened here is that our back had to block, so they picked us up. This would have been a lot tougher if this guy had stayed out here.

We do not like to throw the ball low unless we have to, because we put a lot of emphasis on running with the catch. The other thing the tight end is doing here is running away from that guy. He needs to run straight. By running straight, he will create more room to the next flat defender, and make it easier on the quarterback. (Film)

A third progression pattern that we run is called all cross (Diagram #3). We will be in a three-by-one formation and we will spread these guys out and cross them at different depths. We will do different things with the remaining back. Sometimes we will run him backside, sometimes we will set him there, and sometimes we will just swing him, depending on what we think we need to do to make it happen. (Film)

This is a third-and-five situation here. The first guy has a chance. He is going eight to 10, the second guy is going 12 to 14, and the wide guy is going 14 to 16. We are getting what we call cover zero, or straight-across man coverage, so we are running— running away from guys. There is pretty good movement by the quarterback and we get the first down.

I do not like what the tight end did here, because he let the defensive guy "talk him out of his depth." That is an important coaching point: The inexperienced receiver cannot let the defensive guy talk him out of his depth.

Get your depth. If it is third-and-10 and I have an eight-to-10 yard route, I might go 11, because I have to play the game. I have to get the first down. (Film)

Here is another coaching point for quarterback coaches. The quarterback is moving in the pocket here. We have to be really careful about how much he moves in the pocket. Do not overmove in the pocket. When he moves away from one defender, he puts himself closer to another, so he should only move when he has to.

Now, let us get into the full-field read passes. The first one I want to talk about is the double out route (Diagram #4). We like to get 10 yards vertically and we will roll it over to 12. The tight end has a hook route, but he will take it deep down the middle against cover 2. The backs are out on swing routes to each side, so it is a mirrored pattern.

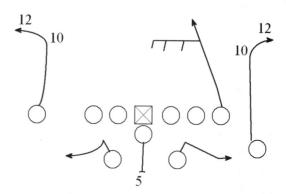

Diagram #4. Double Out

In addition to the double out pattern, we also run double comeback and double go. All are mirrored patterns. Against cover 2, the wide receivers will

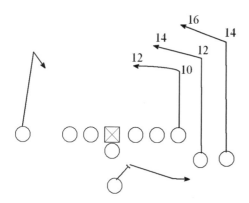

Diagram #3. All Cross

outside release the cloud and go down the pike, so we will have three verticals against cover 2. They are all the same on that. (Film)

All right, so here we go. We are in what we call "strong left," and this is double out. The quarterback reads the strong safety over there to the tight-end side, and for some reason the tight end stayed in. He should not do that. He should be releasing. The quarterback goes away from any kind of rotation, and this is cover 1.

The receiver, quite honestly, runs it a little short. He is not doing what we asked him to do here, but we got it done, although it is a terrible run with the catch. It is not a two-minute drill and we cannot run out of bounds with the ball.

Now, this next play is double go. We made this somewhat famous with Larry Fitzgerald. It gives us the ability to go up versus bump-and-run. This coverage you see is bump-and-run from "off." He is not backing up because we cannot run very fast right now.

On the go, we try to get vertical and give the guy room to fade on the ball and keep it in bounds. We are not going to overthrow a go route. We like to get a big receiver, throw the ball up, and let him make a play.

Okay, this is double comeback. By the way, our fullback here played noseguard for two years and had never carried the ball in college. The tailback was a wide receiver as a true freshman, moved to tailback, and carried the ball twice in the spring game at the end of the game, and had never carried the ball in college. So, we are opening up here with two guys who had never touched the ball in college, and neither had played those positions before.

Anyway, this guy does a nice job here. Nice job by the quarterback and we complete the pass. What we really teach on this is the receiver should shift and head down the field. He is a little too much sideways here, when he should just shift and head down the field. However, once he eventually starts heading down the field he does a good job of getting north and south, makes nine yards, and he finishes the run. I am a really good play caller on second-and-one, but on second-and-10 or -15 I am not so good.

Here is UCLA in a cover 2 defense. This is good. What happened, the corner sunk, the tight end is down the pike, the wide receivers are outside releasing the cloud, the backs are on the outside, and we throw the ball to a wide open guy.

Once again, we are being high percentage. This coverage is what we call cover 2 Tampa, where that middle linebacker really gets deep in the middle.

Our backs have pickup, unless we have six-man protection where we are going to free release a guy. Speaking about protection, if you are going to be a passing team, you had better do a lot of blitz drills— more than anything. That does not have to be zero all of the time, but cover 1 blitzes, fire zones— bring them all.

The quarterback cannot be too prepared for pressure. They do not throw it so well when those guys are coming in their faces. When the pro scouts or the college scouts are watching the tape, they want to see what the quarterback does when they are coming after him. How accurate is he? Will he stand in there and make the throw when guys are coming in his face?

The best play we have is the hook (Diagram #5). It is a very simple play. It is a full-field read play that we throw to one side or the other, based on the rotation. On cover 2, we usually go strong—not always, but usually. Flanker route is at 12, tight end at 14, and the split end is at 12. The backs are swinging. The progression is one, two, three, four, starting away from rotation, and we purposely have our tight end go deeper so he comes open later than our wide receiver.

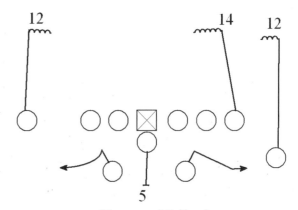

Diagram #5. Hook

It is a good play, amazing really. It has been the most productive play almost every year I have coached, other than when we were running some run-and-shoot patterns. It is the best pass we have. (Film)

This is a big play, but of course any first down is a big play. Once again they are in bump—and-run. Our receiver has to get up inside that guy. He does a nice job of getting vertical, and we are running away from their corners in this game, instead of hooking against their man-to-man coverage.

On this play they rotated up. They went "sky," so our quarterback went away from the rotation—he went weak. Full-field read play and he went weak. There it is.

Here is the play against cover 2, and you will see our quarterback do what we call a "flash." Ever so slightly, he looked to the back. If you watch his left shoulder, it looks like he is going to throw it to the back, and then he comes back and throws it to the wideout. There it is.

Good job by the receiver, getting away from the corner, coming back in the hole, and coming back to the ball. Good job. Always come back to the ball—we use the term "address the ball."

On this next play, you can see our emphasis on yards after catch paying off. This is that fullback who was a noseguard. This is cover 2 and the corner, in our terminology, is sinking. We have two terms, sink and hang. If he hangs, that means we do not throw the ball to the fullback because the corner is not backing up. If he sinks out or cushions deeper, then against cover 2 we throw the ball to the back. Watch our fullback get that guy to overrun and then cut back and get yards after catch.

Finally, let me show you a couple of coverage-beaters. The first one is a maximum protection—go route. Against Arizona State here, this is an eight-man rush. We are going to protect the passer and give our quarterback a chance. The corners are squatting basically, not backing up. They are playing bump-and-run from "off."

Our quarterback gets back, and all he has to do is hold onto the ball. He does not "climb" unless he has to "climb." He has really good protection, which wads them up in the middle, and he just lays it up to the receiver, who makes a great play on the ball. That is all coaching there, men!

Here is another coverage-beater. The quarterback executes a half roll and we run a quick out. We have our best receiver setting them up. This is a key part of the game. We are on the road and it is tied at 14. The quarterback comes out and throws a good ball, the receiver makes a good catch, and we get a key first down.

Men, I appreciate the opportunity to come out here and visit with you, and I appreciate Earl Browning and Nike having me. Thank you.

ATTACKING THE 3-3 DEFENSE

University of Memphis

Thank you. I want to thank Larry and his staff and Nike for inviting me to speak here this evening. When Coach West told me to speak on the 3-3 defense at this clinic, I thought he was kidding me. However, he wanted me to think about the defenses we would face in the fall and the best way to attack them.

It seems we see more eight-man-front defenses than ever before. We played 12 games last year and eight of the 12 teams ran eight-man fronts. I have been studying the 3-3 defense in particular and the eight-man front in general. Three of the teams we play next year run the 3-3 defense and five others run the eight-man front.

This spring we get to go against one of the best defensive coaching minds in the business. Going against Joe Lee Dunn's defense every day will make you a nervous wreck. His defensive scheme is fantastic. It is overly aggressive. Coach West likes that type of football. He likes to be aggressive on the offensive and defensive sides of the ball and put pressure on the opponent with special teams.

Today I want to show you what we look at as we go into our game planning. From there, I will get into the basic scheme of the 3-3 defense. That gives the defensive coaches listening something to evaluate. The last thing is to show you how we attack the 3-3 defense.

When we sit down each week to put the game plan together, we look at six things. We ask ourselves six questions. The first thing we want to know is the base front and structure. We want to identify the defense as it relates to the down linemen. We must know if they have three or four down linemen in their basic scheme. In the identification of the defense, we must know if their coverage is a two- or three-deep scheme.

Understanding the coverage will tell us if they play with a true eight-man front with a three-deep scheme or the 4-3 alignment with a two-deep secondary. We are a no-huddle offense and all our plays are based on whether the defense has one defender or two defenders in the middle of the field.

We feel that if the defense has two safeties in the middle of the field, it is time to run the football. We take what the defense is giving us. You cannot be stubborn and try to throw into a defensive secondary designed to stop the passing game. If the defense has one safety in the middle of the field, the scheme is more conducive to the passing game.

That does not mean we will never run the ball into a three-deep secondary or throw the ball into a two-deep secondary, but we are more inclined to follow the tendencies.

The second thing we consider is the philosophy of the defense in regards to blitzing. We must know if the defense blitzes more often or covers. In Coach Dunn's case, he runs a blitzing defense. He throws everything at your offense except the kitchen sink. That leads to the type of protections you game plan. We do not like to get our quarterback hit. We take pride in not getting our quarterback hit.

The third point we want to know about the defense is the direction of the blitz. We think it is extremely important in your game planning. If you face a blitzing team, it is important to know from where the opponent is blitzing. We must know if the defense sends the majority of its blitzes from the interior or the exterior. We must know if they come in between the tackles or off the edges. We want to know if they blitz from the field or the boundary.

If a team blitzes up the middle the majority of the time, we want to move the pocket and get outside in our set-up. If they come off the edges, we want to stay in the pocket and match our protection to the type of blitz. If the defense brings the blitz from the boundary, we sprint into the field to throw the ball. If the blitz comes from the field, we max protect and try to throw into the boundary.

The fourth point in our game planning is the type of coverage played behind the blitz. The first thing the quarterbacks want to know on Monday is what type of coverages the defense will play. If we play against Coach Dunn, we get three types of coverage. We get cover 3, cover 1, and cover zero.

The fifth point we must consider in game planning is the presence of a dominant player on the defense. When we played Tennessee last year, they had an extremely talented player in Parys Haralson. He came from Madison, Mississippi, and presented a big problem for us. We knew we had to have a special plan to handle him. We found out that he did not like to have a tight end over him. When he was on the openside of the formation, he could not be blocked.

He plays the right defensive end for Tennessee. To help ourselves, we played with a tight end on that side the majority of the time. That presented a problem for him in the pass rush. This type of situation may come up only once or twice a year, but you must deal with it when it occurs.

The last item we consider in our game planning is the defensive philosophy on third down. On third down, are they a blitz team or a coverage team? If the team is a coverage team on third down, do not be stubborn and prepare to run the ball on third down. Do not try to force the ball into areas that are covered. At Memphis, our philosophy is to hit the quarterback on third down. We want to get the ball out of the quarterback's hand as quickly as possible.

The next thing I want to do is show you how we would prepare to play the 3-3 defense that we will face in spring practice. The first thing we do is identify the structure of the defense. At Memphis, we play with three down linemen and three

linebackers on the field. Coach Dunn has two safeties he calls "cat safeties." They are generally flat-zone players. We have one free safety and two corners. The corners are in primary man coverage most of the entire game.

The strength of the 3-3 defense is right down the middle. In this defense, the three best players are the noseguard, Mike linebacker, and free safety.

The 3-3 defense is an eight-man front built to stop the run. Since Coach Dunn came to Memphis, we have ranked nationally in the top 30 in stopping the run. The defense has a tremendous amount of movement. The base alignment of the defense is a three-man stack defense (Diagram #1).

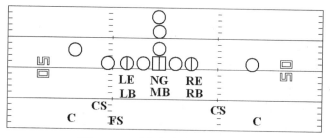

Diagram #1. 3-3 Alignment

The down linemen have a number of different movements. If a "tight" call (Diagram #2) is made, the noseguard and defensive ends slant toward the tight end. If an "open" call is made, they slant the opposite way toward the openside of the formation. By using a "left" or "right" call, we can get the same movement regardless of formation.

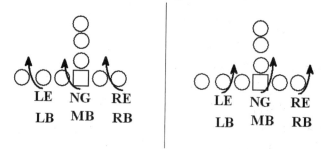

Diagram #2. Line Movement

Another movement we use to free up the linebacker is "pinch" (Diagram #3). In this movement, the right and left ends pinch to the inside B gap, while the noseguard stuffs the center. This movement turns the defense into a double-eagle defense. The last movement to free up linebackers is the "loop." It is the opposite of pinch. The defensive ends loop into the C gaps. We use this movement against teams that like to run inside isolations. That frees up all the linebackers to play inside.

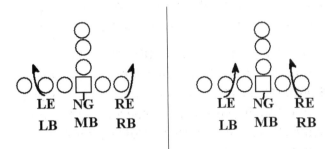

Diagram #3. Pinch and Loop

There are a variety of blitzes called from the 3-3 defense. We start with one-linebacker stunts when we teach our defense. We call our linebackers left, right, and Mike. The first two blitzes we put in are lion and ram (Diagram #4). We run lion to the left and ram to the right. In the lion stunt, the left defensive end slants into the C gap. The noseguard slants into the left A gap. The right defensive end loops into the C gap to his side. The left linebacker runs through the B gap. The ram is the same stunt run to the right.

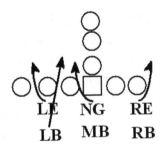

Diagram #4. Lion and Ram

If we want to bring the Mike linebacker as the single blitzer, we call X (Diagram #5). In the stunt, the Mike linebacker runs through the strongside A gap. The noseguard takes the backside A gap. The defensive ends loop into the C gaps to their sides.

If we want to combine the stunt in the one-linebacker package, we can. We can call X-ram. That combines the ram and X stunts.

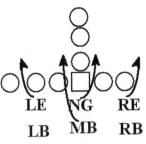

Diagram #5. X Stunt

We call thunder and lightning to get a different look into our one-linebacker scheme. The thunder stunt is a strongside blitz and the lightning is an openside stunt. If the tight end aligns to the left side of the defense, we call thunder left (Diagram #6). The left linebacker moves into the line of scrimmage head up on the tight end. On the snap of the ball, the left linebacker and left end slant away from the tight end into the C gap and B gap. The noseguard and right defensive end loop into the weakside A gap and C gap.

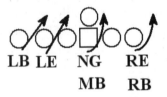

Diagram #6. Thunder

If the tight end aligns to the right, we run right thunder and slant away from the tight end.

On the lightning call, we slant away from the openside of the formation or toward the tight end. If the call is lightning right (Diagram #7), the right linebacker moves outside the defensive end. He aligns on the line of scrimmage and blitzes from the edge. The right defensive end slants into the B gap and the noseguard loops into the strongside A gap. The left defensive end loops into the C gap to the strongside.

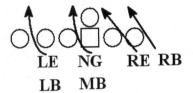

Diagram #7. Lightning

These calls give us the ability to blitz a single linebacker using an interior charge as well as an exterior charge.

The next defensive scheme is the two-linebacker stunts.

When he wants to bring two linebackers, he calls spike or bullets. On spike (Diagram #8), the defensive ends align on the offensive tackles' noses and loop into the C gaps on the snap of the ball. From their stack position, the right and left linebackers run through the B gaps to their side.

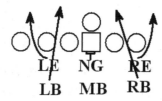

Diagram #8. Spike

If he runs bullets (Diagram #9), the right and left linebackers align on the line of scrimmage in an edge technique and blitz from the outside. The defensive ends, on the snap of the ball, slant into the B gaps.

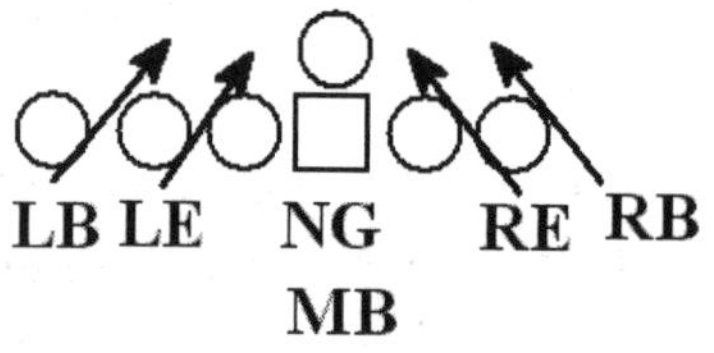

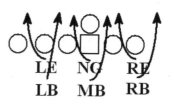

Diagram #9. Bullets

If you watch tape of our defense, you will see that the Mike linebacker is very seldom touched because of our blitz scheme. That is a big deal to free up the Mike linebacker so he can make plays. When we run the Bullets stunt, the Mike linebacker has the ability to fill the lane on either side of the ball against the option.

Coach Dunn, particularly in a third-down situation, has a tendency to bring everyone on the blitz. His philosophy on third down is to outnumber the offense by bringing one more defender than the offense can block.

We have a three-linebacker blitz scheme we usually use in third-down situations. We call the first three-linebacker stunt trips (Diagram #10). In the trips stunt, the defensive ends loop outside and the linebackers come inside. The Mike linebacker and noseguard cover the A gaps, with the noseguard taking the right gap and the Mike linebacker blitzing the left gap.

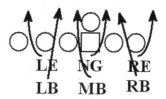

Diagram #10. Trips

We run the trips toward and away from the tight end. If we call tight left trips (Diagram #11), the three down linemen slant toward the tight end and the three linebackers blow the opposite gaps away from the tight end.

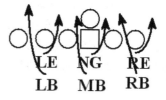

Diagram #11. Tight Left Trips

If we want to run the opposite stunt we call open right trips (Diagram #12) and slant to the openside of the formation. On this call, the down linemen slant to the openside of the formation and the linebackers run through the opposite gaps toward the tight end.

Diagram #12. Open Right Trips

When you think you have the defense figured out, he adds another wrinkle. He involves the cat safeties in the blitz package. That allows us to outnumber the offense from one side or the other. If we think the offense is an outside-zone or sprint-out team, we like to bring pressure from the edges. The cat safeties are the alley players to either side of the defense. The call we use is mad added to a thunder blitz. If we call mad thunder (Diagram #13), we overload and blitz from the tight end's side. The blitz is the thunder blitz with the cat safety coming from the edge outside the tight end.

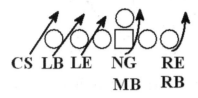

Diagram #13. Mad Thunder

If we want to bring the blitz from the openside of the formation, we call bad lightning (Diagram #14). It is the Lightning stunt run from the openside, bringing the cat safety from the edge.

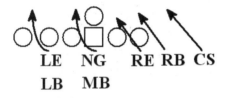

Diagram #14. Bad Lightning

From this scheme, we can bring everyone. We use the special call in certain situations. If we are in a goal-line or short-yardage situation where we must have a stop, we can bring both outside linebackers and cat safeties on the blitz. If we want to involve the Mike linebacker in the blitz, we call special X. On special (Diagram #15), both sides of the defense are pinching inside. The defensive ends slant into the B gaps. The right and left linebackers slant into the C gaps and the cat safeties come off

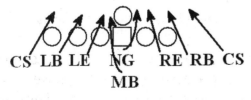

Diagram #15. Special X

the edges. If we add X to the call, the Mike linebacker and noseguard run through the A gaps.

When we bring this blitz, the offense cannot block them all. They have to throw the football quickly or take the sack.

When we run the maximum blitz, we must play cover zero, which is man coverage. However, with the other blitzes we run a varying number of coverages. In our game planning, we must be able to recognize the blitzes and at the same time know the coverages the defense uses. We have three coverages we use. We run 3-zone, which is a three-deep zone. We use cover 5, which is man-to-man coverage. We run cover 5 free, which is the man-to-man coverage with a free safety in the middle.

We like to play the 3-zone when we bring a one-linebacker blitz. When we bring two linebackers, we generally play some type of man-free coverage. When we bring everyone in the special blitz, we use what we call 3-man. That means we play with only three secondary players in locked man coverage.

You can see that as offensive coaches trying to attack the 3-3 defense, we have a number of things to be concerned with. The University of Houston and TCU this past season were 3-3 defenses using attacking pressure.

Coach West has an offensive philosophy to which we adhere. The more complicated the defense, the simpler the offense has to be. When you play a team that uses outside and inside blitzes and constant line movements, you have to reduce what you do. They do not align the same every time, and they continually try to confuse you. He comes in each week and writes on top of our offensive board in big letters, DMSU. Those letters stand for "don't make stuff up." If you use your imagination, there is another term he uses instead of stuff.

We do not put in special plays to counter special defenses. When we come into fall practice, we do not add plays. We work on those types of things in the spring. We do the best job of teaching that package to our players and we do not change during the season. We want to execute what we do better than the defense executes what they play.

We felt the first thing we had to do was stay away from man-blocking schemes in both the run and pass. In our offensive blocking scheme we have become a gap-technique team in both the running game and pass protection. You will see our offensive linemen stepping into gaps rather than at defenders.

When we face our defense during spring practice, we use four protections. Of the four protections we use, two are almost the same package. The quick gap and max protection are about the same scheme. I will take you through these protections quickly.

We call our quick-gap protection 40/50. The offensive front is responsible for the three down linemen and the Mike linebacker. At the snap of the ball, we do not know the defender we have to block until they start to charge. We use the quick-gap protection in our quick-passing game.

When we call 40 or 50 protection, we always help the line and the back has to adjust. If we call 50 protection (Diagram #16), the offensive linemen have the gap to their left side.

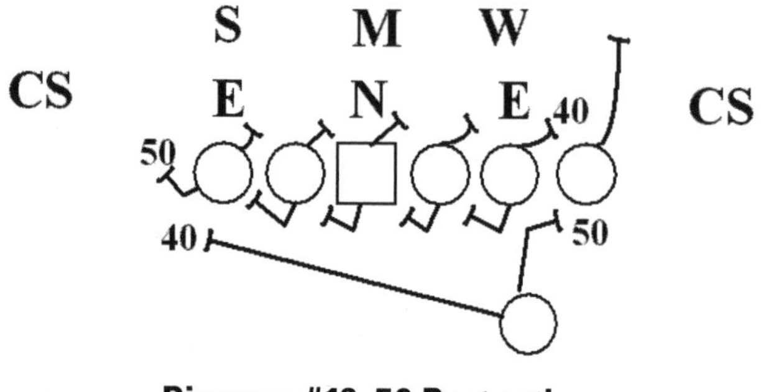

Diagram #16. 50 Protection

If the call is a 40 protection, the offensive line does the exact opposite. The back does not change his alignment in the set. He has to come across the formation, because he is responsible for the left C gap.

If we throw a pattern over 10 yards against our defense, we are in max protection. We call that protection 240/250. The only difference between this protection scheme and the quick-protection scheme is the tight end stays in to block. The protection is 40/50 protection with seven blockers involved in the scheme. The tight end blocks his gap

right or left and the back blocks opposite the call. Toward the tight end, the back blocks the D gap or edge blitz.

The reason we use the 240/250 is to alert the offensive linemen that the pass is a five-step drop and the tight end is in the protection scheme.

To get away from the interior blitzes, we sprint out with the ball. We call our sprint protection 80/90. We are a reach team, which goes with our outside zone play. When we call the 80/90 protection, our offensive linemen reach the gap toward the sprint-out. Everyone in the protection has the playside gap. In an 80 protection (Diagram #17), the back knows he is responsible for the force defender to the right. It could be the linebacker off the edge or the cat safety if he walks up toward the line of scrimmage.

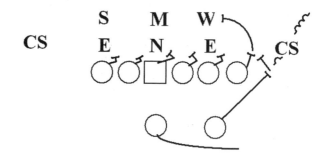

Diagram #17. 80 Protection

The offensive line is responsible for any defender in the box. They step playside and try to reach anybody in their gap. They try to get their helmets to the outside shoulder plate of the defenders and wheel them back inside.

The last protection we use is boot protection. This is also a gap-protection scheme. We call this protection 114/115. The bootleg is set up off the zone play. A bootleg to the right comes off a zone play left. Therefore, we call that protection 115 (Diagram #18). We are faking left, but running the bootleg to the right.

The center is responsible for the left A gap. The left tackle has the left B gap if anyone is coming. If there is no one in the B gap, he wheels to the outside and helps the back blocking the backside C gap after he fakes the zone play.

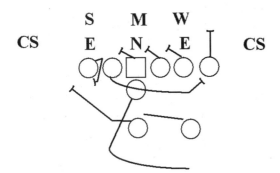

Diagram #18. Boot Protection 114/115

We use the tackle to fill for the pulling guard in the B gap instead of the running back. We are a huge shotgun team and the tackle fill works better than the back fill. The angle for the back to get to the cutoff point is too tight. We make the tackle responsible for the B gap and the back has the C gap.

On the frontside, the right guard and tackle have the A gap and B gap. The left guard pulls to the playside and has the C gap. The majority of the time, the tight end releases into the pattern.

A coaching point I omitted is the responsibility of the offensive linemen in our reach protection scheme. If the linemen reaches to his gap inside and no one comes into that gap, he wheels and blocks backside. In addition, in our scheme we may use the backside slotback to help cut off the backside. We tighten his split or bring him in motion to get him into a position to wheel back and protect from the backside as we sprint away from him.

When we run the football, we stick with the zone- or gap-blocking schemes. The top plays run against the eight-man front or 3-3 defense are the zone play or power play. Central Florida did a great job against us this year and they ran the power play right at us.

Running the unbalanced set helps your offense against a 3-3 defense. Most of the 3-3 defenses we face move or adjust when you go to an unbalanced set. To the weakside in our defense, there is still a cat safety and corner. To the strongside, the cat safety is outside the number 2 receiver and the safety is still in the middle of the field. That presents a problem because it leaves a big hole to

the inside between the cat defender and the outside linebacker. In the 3-3 defense there is no roll to the strength of the unbalanced set. That is the way we attack the Houston 3-3 defense.

If you use a three-by-one formation, it helps you recognize whether the defense is zone or man in the secondary. The thing we have come to realize is the screen play kills a 3-3 defense.

If the defense uses many blitzes, we want to make it tough on them by using the stretch play. That lets us use gap schemes in the run game instead of man schemes. We want to use trips sets to the field and run the ball into it. We call our outside zone play "press" (Diagram #19). The only thing we try to do is reach the next gap and get our heads on the outside shoulder plate. If we can get into that position, our backs will find a crease somewhere.

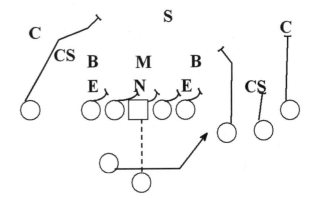

Diagram #19. Outside Zone Press

Another play we like is exactly the same play as far as the blocking is concerned. The only difference is the quarterback carries the ball and we pick up the extra blocker in the running back. We direct snap the ball to the quarterback and he runs the outside zone. It is almost like a toss sweep. We try to outnumber you on the outside. We call the play "clap" (Diagram #20). The line blocking is outside zone.

This next scheme is something that has helped us against eight-man-front teams. We call it "fly." This play allows us to have another run from the shotgun set. It gives us fast flow to the edge. It lets you put your best players in space against the defense. If you call this play, you do not have to

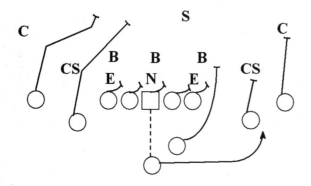

Diagram #20. Clap

check out of it. You can do it from multiple formations and personnel groups. You can use wide receivers as running backs and running backs as wide receivers. The fly allows us to create multiple misdirection plays and allows us to stay within a run scheme we already use.

We ran the ball a ton this year. However, there is only so much DeAngelo Williams can do. Once he got about 30 touches, we limited him. We had to find other ways to run the ball and this was the answer. It will help us next year when he is gone. This is the same play as the clap play, except the wideout carries the ball.

The wide receiver comes in motion toward the quarterback in the shotgun set (Diagram #21). We snap the ball as he reaches the offensive tackle. The wide receiver runs over the toes of the quarterback for the mesh point. The offensive line runs an outside zone-blocking scheme. The lead back and the number 2 receiver reach block the outside linebacker and safety. The number 1 receiver stalk blocks on the corner. The ballcarrier tries to circle the defense and uses his stretch rules and cuts.

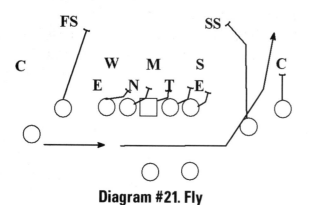

Diagram #21. Fly

The speed of the motion is what makes the play successful. Not just anyone playing in the box can make a play. If you can get the blocks on the alley and force defenders, the play will be huge.

The outside zone, quarterback sweep, and fly are the same play for the offensive line. The difference is that we have three different ballcarriers. It is a great way to attack a multiple-front defense that stems every play.

We call the inside zone play "gut" (Diagram #22). We like to run this play using deep motion and the reverse fake to hold the support defenders. The offensive linemen's job is to take care of the defensive down defenders. Against the 3-3 defense, the right guard and tackle are responsible for the stack on the right tackle. The center and left guard are responsible for the middle stack. The left tackle is responsible for the backside B gap. We want to get four hands on the down linemen with four eyes on the linebackers.

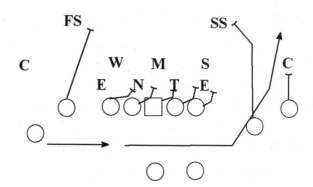

Diagram #22. Gut

That means we want to control the down linemen with a double-team with someone coming off for the linebacker once he declares a side on his fill. By using the reverse fake, it allows the offensive linemen to stay on their double-team longer. The reverse fake keeps the linebacker from running downhill too quickly. The running back runs from A gap strong to A gap weak as his cut zone. He aims for the inside leg of the playside guard.

The reverse fake is only good if you run the reverse play. We use the inside zone to set up the reverse, which has become a great play against the 3-3 defense.

When attacking the 3-3 defense with the pass, you must understand their coverages. The majority of the teams we play run three coverages behind the 3-3 defense. They play cover 3, cover 1, and cover zero.

When we find teams playing cover 3 in the secondary, we must find a way to throw the "vertical" passing game. If the defense puts one safety in the middle, we line up in four-wide-receiver formations and throw four verticals as quickly as we can. We look for and throw flat-curl combinations. Against cover 3, we love the quick hitch patterns.

One of the things I do on game day is watch how the flat-zone defenders are playing. We want to know if they carry verticals deep, collision them, or buzz to the flat. If the defenders buzz to the flat, four verticals will be a successful pattern. If they collision the inside verticals, there is no way they can cover the hitch pattern by the outside receiver. That is an easy throw-and-catch for eight yards, if the quarterback reads the play correctly.

When we face cover 1, we try to work the outside receivers. That eliminates the free safety. In most 3-3 defenses, the cat safeties try to funnel the inside receivers to the safety and that lets us work the outside receivers. We like to run the fade-slant combinations against cover-1 teams.

I want to show you one play before I close. This is a good play against cover 1. We call the play "cowboy" (Diagram #23). It is a naked bootleg coming off fly motion. The quarterback fakes the fly motion and bootlegs to the outside. The running back comes underneath the motion, avoids the defensive end, and gets into the flat. The number 1 receiver to the bootleg side clears out the area. The

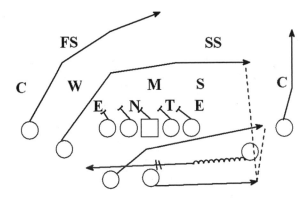

Diagram #23. Cowboy

backside slot receiver runs an over drag route at a depth of 10 yards. The backside split receiver runs into the deep middle between the safeties. The quarterback fakes the fly motion and loses depth after the fake. He looks for the flat pattern first and the drag second. The offensive line is gap protecting away from the bootleg.

What this play does for us is unbelievable. We probably won the Southern Miss game last year off this play. They were in man coverage. We faked the fly and hit DeAnglo in the flat. Their defenders ran into each other and he went 40 yards for the score. We want to run this pattern against the man scheme because of the misdirection. The pass lets you move the pocket and away from the rush. The third thing is the linebacker is trying to cover a back like DeAngelo Williams, all the way across the formation with the responsibility he has.

When we face a team playing cover zero, which is man coverage with no free safety, we work the slot receivers. The best cover men in the secondary are the corners. We attack the safeties because they are the worst cover defenders in the secondary and there is no middle safety. We want to match our best receiver on the defense's worst cover man and take advantage of that situation.

THE TWO-BACK RUNNING GAME

Fresno State University

Thank you very much.

When I talk in front of a group, I want you to know how important it is that you are coaches. I think we have the greatest fraternity in the world. People always say that kids are different now. I do not believe that. They are bigger, faster, and stronger, and face many more challenges than they have ever faced.

I think the problem with our youth today is that the leadership is too soft. That leads into my topic today. My topic is the two-back offense, which is a dinosaur right now. It is a time of revolution in football. I am glad people are going to the spread offense, because that leaves more tight ends and fullbacks out there for me to recruit.

I am in my 34th year in coaching. I came up a little differently from most coaches. I started out as a junior college coach. I lived in my van and worked as a bouncer in a bar. I played rugby and really did not know where I was headed in life.

I was able to find a job as a full-time coach at the University of Utah. I was coaching the offensive line and making $3,000 a year. I thought I was in heaven in 1977. I got married and had children. I thought coaching was a lot of fun. As time went on, I moved around a lot in my early career. I never had a resume. I was able to move to some different colleges and I coached in the NFL.

I was fortunate to come to Fresno State in 1997 as the head football coach. When I got there, we had to make a decision on what type of offense we wanted to run, and the philosophy we were going to use. I knew when I went to Fresno State that we wanted to schedule as many tough opponents as we could. To date, we have played 30 BCS teams and 22 teams ranked in the top 20 at the time we played them. We have won 10 of those games and have built a program that is respectable in college football today.

We built the program because of the offensive and defensive philosophy that we took. I came up in a two-back system and have always been around that kind of system. In our two-back system, we may have a tight end as the lead back.

We needed an offense that could control the tempo of the game. When we decided to play the level of competition we did, we could not run a high-risk offense. We wanted something to control the clock and tempo of the game.

On defense, we do not get the same type of linemen that USC, Miami, or LSU seem to have. Our personnel are smaller and faster. We wanted a hard-playing one-gap team on defense. We wanted to zone blitz, zone pressure, and things of that nature. The third thing we had to do was to put a great deal of emphasis on the special teams.

My philosophy on special teams was that there would be no sacred cows. We have starters playing on our special teams. My starting middle linebacker for seven of the 13 games was the number 4 runner on the kickoff team. That position is a wedge breaker. When I took him off the kickoff team, he was upset about it. That is the kind of attitude I like. That is how we developed our football team.

Today I am going to talk to you about two plays, and I may not get off the first one. I have been to a lot of clinics and I have seen a lot of plays diagrammed. People walk away understanding the play, but never get the details of how to run it.

The first play I want to talk about is the power play (Diagram #1). I was running the power play in high school in 1965. The play has not changed. However, the defense you have to run the play against today is not a 52 monster, cover 3 as it was in those days.

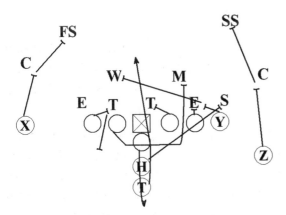

Diagram #1. Power Play

The power play is a simple play. However, it becomes complex in its teaching. The things that you have to understand about a play are the things that are important to make the play successful.

The first thing I want to talk about is the footwork of the running back. The power is an A-gap play. We feel we have to hit the play going downhill. The quarterback has to understand that he cannot block the entrance to the hole. It is almost like a midline dive play. The quarterback makes sure he gives the back a clear entrance to the hole.

The running back is seven yards deep, takes a gap step opposite the hole, and hits downhill to the A gap. A lot of people, when they run the power play, run laterally. I do not believe in that. The blocking schemes and the 3-technique players today almost demand that you run it in the A gap.

It is critical that you keep the line of scrimmage flat. I do not believe that to run the power play you have to knock people off the ball. That is not important in running this play. What is important is to have no run-throughs by the linebackers or penetration by the defensive line. If you can do that, you can execute the play very well.

The fullback and tailback must have an inside-out relationship in their execution. The fullback has to remain inside-out on the Sam linebacker or the C gap defender in the defensive scheme. The tailback has to stay inside-out on his runs in this play. He never turns back inside on the play. As soon as he turns back inside, he runs into pursuit.

The pulling guard has to understand the concept of what to do. He has to understand defensive alignments. If he is covered at the line of scrimmage, there is a good chance there will be a bubble as soon as he passes the center. The exception to that statement is the Bear defense. If there is a bubble past the center, he knows he turns up quicker.

The opposite is true if he is uncovered. If he is uncovered, there is a good chance there will be a 3 technique on the other side of the center. That means he has to take his pull one gap further before he turns up. He has to know that because I want him to turn up as soon as he can. If he has some idea of where he has to turn up, that aids his quickness. I do not want the power held up because the guard is hesitant.

The Z-receiver or flanker is the player who blocks the MDM. MDM stands for the "most dangerous man." All the defensive schemes today try to get the extra man down into run support. They all are dropping the strong safety into the box. It is important to me to have a flanker who is one tough son of a gun.

We do an Okie drill every Tuesday and Wednesday. I like to get the wide receivers involved in that drill. I think the flanker has to be tougher than nails to go into the defense and root out a strong safety. Not every wide receiver by nature is a headhunting player. We try to find that kind of player that will go into the box and block strong safeties and linebackers.

Do not take this the wrong way. We can throw the ball at Fresno State. The last three quarterbacks we had are playing in the NFL. We are a well-rounded offense, but we want to set our personality on running the football.

That does not mean that we run more than we pass. We played Oregon this year and they forced us to pass the football. We passed for 400 yards in that game. We lead with the run, teach the run, and master the run.

In teaching the offensive line, we start with the half line. In the game of football, the defense aligns in three basic fronts. You have cover-cover-backer; backer-cover-backer; or down lineman-down lineman-backer. The first example is pro, the second is Okie, and the third is sink.

The defenses will change with the way they align, but the defensive front can only be one of three fronts. We use what we call "rail" blocking. We block the inside rail, no matter what the defense is. The exception is the Sam linebacker head up on the tight end with the defensive end outside. We swap that block with the tight end going outside to block the defensive end and the fullback on the Sam linebacker.

The rail block in the first situation is the alignment of the defender over the guard (Diagram #2). If the defender is head up or inside the guard, he blocks him. The rail block is now on the tackle.

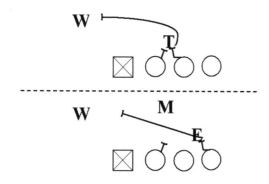

Diagram #2. Rail

The next component of the play is the double-team block. It does not matter whether the double-team is between the tackle and tight end or the tackle and guard. The techniques for coaching that block are the same. The defender can only align in three positions on the offensive lineman.

The defender will be an outside shade, head up, or an inside shade on the offensive lineman. The footwork of the covered lineman is critical. If the defender aligns outside, the offensive lineman steps with his outside foot, throws a flipper, and

has his eyes inside. He comes off the line as hard as he can with the fist in the middle of the defender's sternum.

The second step has to hit the ground as quickly as possible to cover the inside slant of the defender. If we get any kind of inside movement, we hit it on the second step and seal it down the line of scrimmage. We do not allow penetration by that slant. I want the guard's block to look like a scoop block for the zone play the other way. That keeps the defensive tackle confused. He does not know if he should squeeze on the scoop or fight back against the double-team. That is why the running back hits the A gap first. If the defender is fighting the double-team to the outside, we run the play in the A gap.

In the bowl game last year, we played Virginia. We ran the power play 17 times. That in itself is not unusual, but we ran the power play 17 times to the left. We rushed for over 300 yards. We had a good left tackle and guard and ran to the left all day. We ran the power to the left, but we ran the zone cut play to the right. We were successful because the defensive tackle never knew if he was supposed to squeeze on the zone or fight double-team pressure on the power play. The footwork on the two plays has to be exactly the same.

If the defensive tackle moves to head up or inside of the offensive guard, his footwork changes. He steps with his inside foot first. The target is on the inside half of the defender. The offensive guard comes off the ball hard, anticipating an inside movement by the defender. If he does not come off the ball anticipating the inside move, he allows penetration if the defender moves that way.

When the guard comes to the line of scrimmage, he gives the tackle a call. If he is covered, he calls 1, 2, or 3. That gives the offensive tackle a notion of what will happen in the block. The worst thing that can happen to the tackle is a hard movement toward him. If the movement goes the other way, he can adjust to that easily. His first step is a flat step toward the guard. His next step is up on the shoulder of the defender hip-to-hip with the guard. If he steps up the field on the first step, he gets into a bad relationship with the guard. If the defender moves away, he moves to the next level for the next linebacker on his track.

I want the guard stepping off with the proper foot and the tackle taking a flat step inside. The tackle stays as square as he can. He is not worried about driving the defender inside. He wants to prevent penetration. On the zone play, he wants movement up the field on the squeezing defender. If the defender does a good job of squeezing the zone play, the running back can jump to the next wall. However, if the tackle allows penetration, the running back cannot get to the next wall.

If the defender slants out at the tackle, he steps upfield and seals him. If he goes inside, the tackle steps upfield to the next level and seals the next linebacker on his track. I do not want the guard trying to hold the block on power and escaping on the zone. They have to look exactly alike to make the run game effective.

It does not matter where the double-team occurs, because the rules for the power are very simple. The pulling guard has the Mike linebacker. The rail block has the Will linebacker, and the fullback has the Sam linebacker. It does not matter how the defense aligns, that is where we go. The rules are important, but the little details in the scheme are more important.

We teach the double-team a little differently. That does not mean it is the right way. It means that is the way we do it. Our concept ties the zone and power plays together and makes them look alike.

The backside guard pulls for the Mike linebacker. When he gets to the far leg of the center, he has to make a decision. He reads the play like the running back. If the 3 technique is fighting the double-team and moving outside, he turns up in the A gap. If there is a zone blitz scheme, with the defensive end spiking down the line of scrimmage, he has to go wide. He reads the play from A gap to the outside.

His presnap read gives him an idea of the front on the playside. He must anticipate what the defense will do and be prepared to turn up.

It is critical that the backside tackle understands what you want him to do. He runs a backside hinge technique. He steps hard into the B gap and hinges back to the C gap. If there is a bubble in the B gap, he cannot allow a run-through by any linebacker. Otherwise, he steps into the B gap, hinges back, and allows no penetration.

The center has the backside A gap. If there is a tackle in the gap, it is critical that he steps flat. He cannot angle step out of his stance. If takes the flat step, he ends up with a wide base on the second step. He gets his hand up on the inside shoulder of the tackle to take away any cross-face capability. If the center takes a flat step and the tackle is penetrating to the outside, the tackle will pick him up. All he has to do is wall off the backside.

If you listen to a secondary coach talk about coverage, one of the critical points of cover is the help support. Where does the help come from? In the offensive line, that principle is the same. The center has help in the B gap, so he makes sure there is no penetration in the A gap.

The points I just covered are the key points to teaching the play. The base defense played in college football today is some form of the over and under 4-3 front. With those defenses, we see combination fronts. That is where the one side of the front is an over look and the other is an Okie look. We also see the double-Okie look, but that is okay because the double bubble is built for two-back offenses. We see the eagle and double-eagle looks. We do not see many 3-4 defenses, but we like to run against it.

The first front I want to look at is the under 4-3. The defense shifts away from the tight end. The Sam linebacker moves up on the line and plays a 9 technique on the outside shoulder of the tight end. The defensive end drops into a 5 technique on the outside shoulder of the tackle. The tackle slides to a strong shade on the center. To the backside, the defender and end play 3 and 5 techniques.

The Will linebacker aligns in the backside A gap and the Mike linebacker is in the strongside B gap. The first thing the quarterback does when he gets to the line is point out the Mike linebacker. You see a lot of pointing on a pass play and we point on running plays.

The rules for the power play are simple (Diagram #3). The pulling guard has the Mike linebacker, the rail block has the Will linebacker, and the fullback has the Sam linebacker. If the strong safety drops down into the box, the flanker has to root him out of there or we change the play. The backside tackle steps into the B gap, hammers the defender, and hinges back for the defensive end. The backside guard pulls and blocks the Mike linebacker.

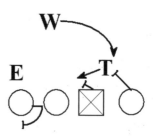

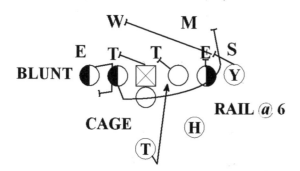

Diagram #3. Power Against Under

The guard should have some idea about the alignment on the other side of the defense. He is covered and guesses the playside guard will be uncovered. That means he could turn up as soon as he passes the center. The center posts the defensive tackle and turns to the A gap to pick up the defender. The center puts his hand on the tackle and he moves to the A gap. If the tackle is looping to the A gap, he takes him.

The playside guard comes down on the defender and single blocks him. The playside tackle and tight end have the rail block to the Will linebacker. The fullback takes a hard inside-out angle at the inside leg of the offensive tackle and kicks out the Sam linebacker.

The defense can run all kinds of stunts (Diagram #4). If there were no 3 techniques to the backside, the center and playside guard could rail the tackle to the Will linebacker or fan to that side. If the tackle went to the backside A gap and the Will linebacker blitzed the strongside A gap, the center goes backside with the tackle and the guard blocks the Will linebacker.

The rail blocker never lets anyone cross his face, but his responsibility runs all the way to the

Diagram #4. Backside Stunt

Will linebacker. If the Mike linebacker moves down into the B gap, we give a gap call, the tackle blocks him, and the tight end blocks the C gap. The running back attacks the A gap and reads inside going out.

I love this play and there are numerous ways to run it. You do not need a fullback. You can use a tight end as the fullback. You can run a one-back and bring motion to block the Sam linebacker. The quarterback on this play can open as he does on the midline veer or reverse out like isolation. You can decide that.

The depth of the running back is seven yards. We try to get the ball to him four yards from the line of scrimmage. I want the back coming hard to the A gap. If I see a back make a double move before he gets to linebacker depth, he does not play long. He cannot make the mistake of getting outside-in on the play.

Against the over defense, the rail block occurs between the playside guard and tackle using the correct techniques (Diagram #5). The tight end blocks the defensive end and the fullback or H back takes the Sam linebacker. In this set, I put the H back in a king position to the tight end. The pulling guard

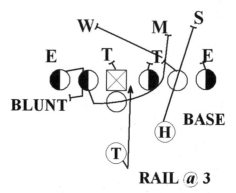

Diagram #5. Power Play Vs. Over

makes a decision to turn up in the A gap or continue into the C gap.

Let me show you some tape of this play. The first clip is against Virginia in the bowl game. The defense starts out in an even look and slides to an Okie look (Diagram #6). When they aligned the defense, we thought the rail would be with the guard and tackle. However, they stemmed the defense and the tackle and tight end blocked the rail. Notice the stunt they ran. They spiked the defensive end into the B gap and scraped the Mike linebacker into the C gap.

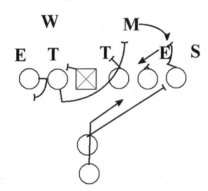

Diagram #6. Spiked 5 Technique

The offensive tackle comes off with his outside foot at the end. The tight end takes a lateral step inside to get hip-to-hip with the tackle. When the end spiked, the tackle washed him to the inside. The tight end started his climb for the Will linebacker, but met the Mike linebacker scraping to the C gap. The tight end lets no defender cross his face and blocks the Mike linebacker. We assign the pulling guard to the Mike linebacker, but he will find someone else.

The split in the offensive line is two to three feet. We do not have a hard rule about splits. I do not want a split too tight.

An important thing to remember is our count system. When the quarterback comes to the line of scrimmage, the man he designates as the Mike linebacker may be a strong safety. If the defense displaces their people in the alignment, we recount them and block our rules.

An example would be a blitz situation, where the Will linebacker went up on the line of scrimmage to blitz from the outside (Diagram #7).

They replaced him in the scheme with the free safety dropping into the box. The free safety becomes the Will linebacker and rail scheme's responsibility.

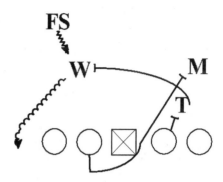

Diagram #7. Rename the Will

We are not necessarily blocking a person, but rather a position. The defense tries to confuse the offense by moving their personnel and stemming the line.

In the BOB, which stands for back on backer, we point out the Mike linebacker. If the defense is an over defense, The Mike is the responsibility of the offensive line. The Will linebacker belongs to the fullback. However, if the offensive formation is a wide slot, the Will linebacker will not be in the box.

The Sam and Mike linebackers move over to the formation side to balance the defense. The Sam linebacker now becomes the Mike linebacker and the Mike linebacker becomes the Will linebacker.

In the running game, I think it is super important to have a simple philosophy for the Mike declaration. It is important to know where the Mike linebacker is in the eight-man front. Defensive teams are using personnel grouping in certain situations. You have to know where the Mike linebacker is in the BOB and the power. The Mike linebacker is the linebacker we designate him to be. That works as long as everyone involved is on the same page.

That is the way you handle protection. Everything in protection boils down to the direction of the slide. When the quarterback reads the defense and he sees an overload to one side or the other, he calls out, "There's a new Mike." The rotation of the secondary, which is a completely different talk, determines the direction of the slide.

The mechanics of the play start with the quarterback. He knows the number of the Mike linebacker and calls "Mike #." When we played USC, we knew their numbers so well we did not do anything but call out numbers. Everyone was on the same page and knew exactly who we designated.

When we run the BOB play, here is the key. It is important to point out the Mike linebacker, because we count him in the blocking scheme.

Let me tell you a short story. When I played the game, I was the center. My rule was to block the zero man. There was no such thing as a combination block in our blocking scheme. I had the zero man, regardless of where he lined up. We played a game where the defense had the defender guard aligned to our strongside, and I could not get to him. I came to the sideline and told the coach it would be easier if the right guard and I changed assignments. If I blocked the number 1 man and the guard blocked the zero man, the play would work. He said, "That is not your rule, you got the zero man." The zero man made many tackles that day.

Here are the coaching points for the BOB play. It is the responsibility of the tailback to move the playside linebacker. The BOB play is a zone play with a lead back (Diagram #8). We could run it without a lead back and call it inside zone. The footwork of the tailback is a lateral lead step followed by a cross step with width. On the third step his shoulders are

square to the line of scrimmage and his aiming point is the inside leg of the offensive tackle.

He takes the play downhill. When he decides to make a vertical cut, it is one vertical cut and go. If the defense on the backside has an Okie look, we have to decide whether to fan block with the center and backside guard or zone block it. The BOB or zone play is not good running into an overhang on the outside.

The fullback has to clear the quarterback and run as hard as he can into the B gap. The playside guard is working to widen the defensive tackle. He puts his outside hand and helmet on the defender's playside number and tries to get him to widen. He is not trying to knock the defender off the line of scrimmage. If the guard continues to press the outside gap, the defender will continue to widen.

The guard continues to press with his outside arm until he starts to lose him. When that happens, he takes his inside arm and throws the defender to the sideline. He has dictated that the ball is going inside of him.

If he can press the defender all the way to the sideline, he does. If he can, it opens a tremendous gap between him and the backside wall. The offensive tackle does the same thing to the defensive end.

The fullback is running for the B gap. When he sees the defensive tackle start to widen, he comes inside the guard and tries to widen the linebacker. The tailback stretches the linebackers as much as he can. As soon as he sees color in the B gap, he cuts the play back into the A gap.

On his cutback, he has to know where the wall is being built. The reason the tailback stretches the Will linebacker is to give the center and guard a chance to build a wall on the backside. If the tailback goes too fast, there is no time to build the wall.

If the guard is covered, the tailback reads the defender over the guard. If the guard is uncovered, he reads the defender over the tackle. On his second-level vision, the tailback cannot cut back early unless he is forced that way. He wants to

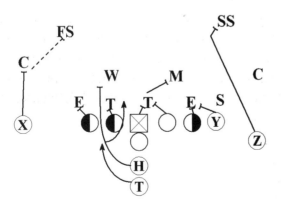

Diagram #8. BOB (Back on Backer)

accelerate through the defense and hug the cutback read area.

The X-receiver blocks the most dangerous man. He blocks the support or the smoke stunt off the edge if possible. The Z-receiver takes a high, hard angle to the safety and convoys the tailback down the field.

The second wall is being built all the way back to the tight end. If the first combo block on the tackle and Mike linebacker stays flat, the ball could come all the way back to the second wall.

If the defense aligns in an over defense, the Mike linebacker is the one in the middle of the defense (Diagram #9). The onside tackle uses the same technique he used on the under front. He uses a high drive block, pressing with his outside hand and trying to get the defensive end to widen.

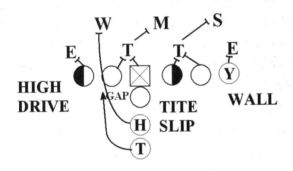

Diagram #9. BOB Vs. Over

The playside guard and center work the combo block on the shade tackle and Mike linebacker. The backside guard and tackle run a tight slip combo on the 3-technique tackle and Sam linebacker. The tight end walls off the 6-technique defensive end. These combo blocks use the techniques for the rail blocks in the power play. Their footwork is exactly like the power play. If you watch good offensive linemen, they have their feet underneath them at all times and their shoulders are square.

The fullback isolates the Will linebacker as he did on the under defense, except he has a clear shot

to the backer. The tailback's footwork is the same as the under defense and he can take the ball all the way back under the second or third wall. The third wall is the tight end's block.

What we try to do on any zone play is to create movement and gap cancellation. The defender on a double-team is taught to fight through the double-team and squeeze on the zone play. They teach him to fight the double-team toward the power play. We run both plays so they look alike.

We can run the same plays from three wide receivers, one tight end, and one back. The secret is the tight end is in the backfield and doing the fullback blocking. You do not have to be in a two-back set to run these plays.

In the spread offense, the running game is almost the same. However, the defense playing against the spread has to play option responsibilities. The secret to running this offense is the scoops and the double-teams have to look the same.

The zone scheme and the power play go hand in hand. The defensive linemen have to play the blocks without seeing what the backfield is doing. I do not think the defensive tackle can tell the difference between the double-team and the rail block when the back goes away.

The tailback tries to stretch the first down lineman past the center and cause the linebacker to widen. If the tailback stretches this play and the defensive lineman jumps inside, the tailback takes the ball outside.

The power play gained an average of 4.3 yards per play. That does not sound like much, but we ran the play 127 times. The BOB play averaged 4.4. Those are our two bread-and-butter plays. We do not always line up in an I formation. We have a ton of way to run those two plays.

LINEBACKER FUNDAMENTALS AND READS

University of Louisville

Thank you for the introduction. For those of you who are visiting from out of town and the local guys as well, I want to welcome you to Louisville. It is always a pleasure to have high school coaches in town visiting, because it gives us an opportunity to share with you some of our thoughts and beliefs, and talk about where we work.

In the interest of time, I am going to move on past our overall team philosophy and get right into some basic principles of linebacker play.

Basic Principles of Linebacker Play

- Stance
- Alignment
- Key
- Responsibility
- Blow delivery
- Read on the move
- Tackle
- Pressure the quarterback

Everything that we do starts with stance. Alignment, key, and responsibility must be taught to our kids with regard to run to, run away, and pass. All of our linebackers must be able to deliver a blow, read on the move, tackle, and pressure the quarterback, and I will talk about those things in detail under the umbrella of what we call our "linebacker must list."

Before we get going each spring, every position coach has to do a must list. This is a list of all the things we feel we need to get done with our position players going into spring ball. Then, after spring ball, we will reevaluate the list and see if we need to adjust it going into fall camp.

Linebacker Must List

- Leadership
  - ✓ By example first
  - ✓ Be vocal (encourage as much as possible)
  - ✓ Be accountable (take the arrow)
- Understand and know offensive football (Talk the way we talk—Diagram the way we diagram)
- Defensive package (Know it all—Be great communicators)
  - ✓ Stance
    - ○ Feet shoulder-width apart
    - ○ Toes pointing straight ahead to slightly inside
    - ○ Weight balanced on the inside balls of your feet
    - ○ Good bend in your knees and hips
    - ○ Pads out over your toes
    - ○ Hands in a ready position
  - ✓ Alignment
  - ✓ Key triangle (Clarifies in false keys)
    - ○ Primary
    - ○ Secondary
  - ✓ Responsibility
    - ○ Run to
    - ○ Run away
    - ○ Pass
- Run game
  - ✓ Proper reaction to run reads (element of the play)
  - ✓ Understand running back angles
  - ✓ Play downhill (press the line of scrimmage)
  - ✓ Pads square (ball is in the box)

- ✓ Cross faces
- ✓ Know where your help is
- Blow delivery and block protection (This is a game of movement, leverage, and striking ability)
- Tackle
- Passing game
  - ✓ Zone
  - ✓ Fire zone
  - ✓ Man (free)
- Pressure the quarterback

I played linebacker in college and I believe it is a position that requires strong leadership. Linebackers are usually some of the more physical players and they are involved in a lot of plays, so I tell my guys that I want leaders who lead by example first. My college coaches told me they would rather see a sermon than to hear one any day. So, I want guys who are on time for meetings, busting their butts in the weight room, and trying to get it done in all of the running and conditioning. It is also vitally important that they get it done in the classroom as well. It is hard to be a leader when you are not doing the big things right, along with all the little things.

Players need to be vocal to be at the linebacker position for us, but in being vocal I want them to always encourage their teammates. When a player screws up on the field, he will hear about it from his coach, so good leaders will pick that guy up. There may be a time when a leader has to call some things out, but for the most part leadership encourages and leadership is positive.

It is also necessary for leaders to be accountable for their own performance—guys who are not afraid to admit it when they make a mistake and then take responsibility for it.

If you can develop young men in your program with these leadership traits, you are well on your way to developing some good players who will play some valuable minutes in helping to build your team and getting you where you need to go.

After recruiting is over, we get an opportunity to meet with our players again. In those meetings, before we discuss anything about our defense, we teach our guys offensive football. They need to understand and know offensive football. They need to understand how personnel groupings are used and how we identify them. We want them to know that "21 personnel" means there are two running backs and one tight end in the game and "11 personnel" means one back and one tight end. All of that is important, because a lot of that will determine how we line up, where we set the front, and what some of the adjustments will be.

They have to know if the formation is a double set, a trips set, trey set, I pro, weak pro, strong pro, and so on. Our guys need to know that information as linebackers, because they are basically coaches on the field and they make a lot of adjustments. I need my guys thinking like I think, talking like I talk, and diagramming like I diagram.

Coach Bobby Petrino is big on this. He believes that communication between coach and player is crucial. He believes that players with questions should speak in the language of our terminology, and that the coach should answer in the same language. That will make the information clear and it should eliminate any confusion.

When you are drawing circles in your position meetings, your players should be drawing what you draw. Our players all get notebooks, and they are required to bring those notebooks to all meetings. There are times when I will ask to see a player's notebook, and I will flip through it to see if they are taking proper notes and writing in it what I am writing on the board.

It is also important to school our players so that they understand the situations of the game. We believe that we have done a good job as a staff of educating our players to game situations and that has been a factor in the success we have had. Our guys not only understand game situations, but they also know how those situations affect the details of their position.

This past year we had one of the best defensive linemen in the country and he understood the details of his position better than anyone else. He was a 6-foot, 258-pound defensive end named Elvis Dumervil, who studied the heck out of film. He understood down-and-distance tendencies, formation and backfield tendencies, and he led the country with 20 sacks.

In one game at Cardinal Stadium last year, we had an opponent that passed 90 percent of the time on second-and-eight or -nine. In the course of the game, we got them into a second-and-eight situation and Elvis got down in his best pass-rush stance. On the snap, the tight end gave him a hard down block, but he still exploded straight up the field. It looked like he was not reacting to the down block as he should have, but instead he sacked the quarterback for a 10-yard loss. Understanding the details of his technique and knowing the tendencies of the offense allowed him to be successful, and to contribute to the overall success of our defense.

After we have educated our guys on offensive football, we start on our defensive package. But before we get into introducing a front or a coverage, we take them back to our basic information and terminology, and we start at the beginning. They will get the same exact spiel every year before we get into our defensive package, because it is an important building block on the way to understanding why we do the things we do.

We expect our linebackers to know the overall package. If the 3 technique lines up in a shade, we expect the linebacker to move him over. If the safety should come down into the box and he has not yet moved, we want the linebacker to move him down. Not only do we teach our linebackers where people should line up in a given defense, we want them to understand what we are trying to get done with that defense. They just have to know it all, so they can become an extension of the coach.

Before we draw circles and introduce fronts, everything starts with the stance for us. We want the feet shoulder-width apart, toes pointing straight ahead to slightly inside, and weight balanced on the inside balls of the feet. The heels

are not off of the ground, so they can push and move in any direction without false stepping. Your players should never have to "move in order to move." If a player false steps in order to move, you need to adjust his stance. A linebacker must move to the football as fast and efficiently as he can and he cannot do it if he is "jump starting."

Of course, we want to see good bend in the knees and hips so that the pads are out over the toes. We want the hands in a ready position and the eyes on the key. Good things will follow from a good stance.

It almost goes without saying that every player must know his alignment on every defensive call, and that our linebackers must know everyone's alignment. Now, based upon the team we are playing and the formations we get, our linebackers may have to adjust their alignments. I tell my linebackers to align in an "ability alignment," where they know that they can handle their run responsibility and their pass responsibility.

The most important thing for a linebacker is vision. We would like to have big, fast, strong guys everywhere, but if we cannot always get guys like that, we will always try to have guys that are smart and that have great vision. Some of them do not come with that great vision, so we have to teach and develop it.

We key offensive line to backfield flow. The offensive line is our primary key and the backfield action is our secondary key. To get that done, we talk about keying their triangle (Diagram #1). In this diagram, we are aligned against an I backfield set. The backer keys over the top of the hat of the guard to the I-back tandem. A young linebacker may see

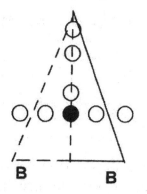

Diagram #1. Key Triangle

only the guard or only the backs, so we teach him to pick a spot right over the guard's hat where he can see him, and he can also see the backs.

The more you teach it and rep it, the more his vision will expand the triangle. He will begin to see that tackle and he can start to see the center, and he will get to where he can see it all.

I believe that vision for linebackers is absolutely critical. What are they looking at? What is their eye progression? You have to teach those things depending upon what you are seeing as a coach as you study your opponent. You have to base your player's eye progression off what it is that you are getting the most. You may design the key from guard to back, from tackle to near back, or whatever it may be that you think is best. You have to figure that out for your players based upon what you are getting.

In this diagram, that would be our Sam linebacker in a 9 technique (Diagram #2). He is keying through the outside pad of the tight end to a near back. We teach the same thing whether our backers are in the box or if they are on the line of scrimmage. Each linebacker has a triangle that he keys, and that triangle will help clarify any false keys.

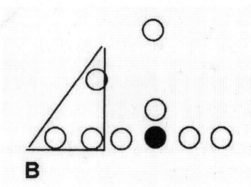

Diagram #2. 9 Technique Triangle

Now, I will break down the keys for you in a little bit, but in talking responsibility, we want our players on every play to know their responsibility on run to them, on run away, and on pass. I am sure that you approach player responsibility the same way.

Within our basic key, which is offensive front to backfield flow, we break the backfield flow down into three categories. First, we talk about "fast flow," which is any play that attacks the perimeter—primarily options and sweeps. If our linebackers can see the running back's ribs, it is an outside running play. If he sees that, he will not keep his pads square. He will take off and run and make a play on the ball.

If we can see the running back's numbers and the ball is in the tackle box, my guys have to play with their pads square and they are in quick shuffles. Again, any time the ball is in the tackle box, we keep our pads square and we shuffle. On any blocking threat to us, we cross faces—we do not come under blocks.

If the ball is outside the box, you get into a crossover run, but immediately when you see that the back is getting ready to choke it down and make a cut, you need to also choke it down, get your pads back square, and react to what he is doing.

Our second flow read is what we call "direct flow," which is basically an iso-lead type of action, with both backs coming downhill at you. When we have a direct flow read at one of our backers, the other backer is in what we call a "stack read." The stack-read backer will shuffle downhill to a stack position and key the tailback. He must be ready to punch the center if he comes off on him, and stay frontside, or if the back cuts back, he has to still be able to punch and rock back to the ball. We expect our linebackers to make plays on the ball.

We want the backer who is taking on the Iso to go "nose it up," and hit it as deep in the backfield as possible. That way, the tailback cannot tell what our fit is. If we take it on with one pad or the other, it becomes an easy cut for the tailback, but if we stuff it, it freezes him a little bit and helps the other guys up front trying to get there.

To me, isos are not one-for-one exchanges. I expect our Mike or our Will linebacker to make plays on the ball when it is directed at them. That is why they play defense—to defeat blocks and make plays.

The last flow read we talk about is "slow flow," which is typically any type of split action in the backfield or a lot of the play-action stuff we see.

I will take you through some of our drill stuff, and it will have some game clips on it. I do not do a lot of drill work. I do not have a million drills. I have a handful that I do, and the ones that I do you will see showing up in game clips. Those are the ones that I do with my players that carry over, and I do not do a lot of extracurricular stuff. (Film)

I want to say some things about blow delivery before we see some of those drills on the tape. In these drills, we want to emphasize the use of eyes, hands, and shoulder pads. We want our linebackers to always play in a good football position with their nose and their pads out over their toes. Then, when we take on a block, we want our eyes underneath the blocker's face mask and our hands to the breastplate with thumbs up and elbows in. We do not always get that, but we want it to be close to that. We do not teach using the flipper.

You always hear about football being a game of movement, leverage, and striking ability. Well, it is hard to defeat a block if the blocker is under our pads and we are standing in an upright position. We cannot defeat him that way, but you will see on the film some 200-pound guys jack some 300-pound guys because they have better pad level and they are striking with their eyes underneath the facemask.

After delivering a blow, we want to find the ball, keep our gapside arm and leg free, disengage, pursue, and make the tackle. It is all about movement, leverage, and striking ability. We will pick these things out in the film. (Film)

We see a lot of cut blocks on our level of play. Again, we try to teach our guys to play cut blocks with their hands and their eyes. We want to target the helmet and shoulder pads, and then with our feet we want to skate with "give and gain." Here is more film of that. (Film)

We teach tackling with our chest and eyes. Our first year here, we missed a ton of tackles. For whatever reason, we had guys dropping their eyes just before tackling and maybe missing the target a little, so we went to saying just go put your face on the guy and tackle him with your chest and eyes.

We want them to shoot their hips and run their feet. After that, our missed tackles improved drastically. Here is some film on that. (Film)

I want to talk about linebacker reads (Diagram #3). During the season, the bulk of my time in regular practice will be spent in key drills on the specific plays that we are going to see that week. That is what we focus on. I have some of those drills on film along with some game clips. (Film)

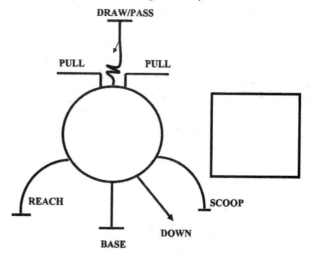

Diagram #3. The Master Plan

Men, I have the linebacker read sheets here that we include in our playbooks. There are about seven run reads for the Mike linebacker, there are four run reads for the Will linebacker, and there are seven run reads for the Sam linebacker. They are all drawn up in the eagle defensive front and they all include our coaching points.

Mike Linebacker Run Reads

Direct (Lead) Coaching Points: Meet the lead

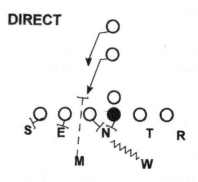

Diagram #4A. Direct (Lead)

blocker on his side of the line of scrimmage. Attack him nose up. Escape to his outside (BIN FIT) and defeat the fullback. This is not a one-for-one exchange. Your fit will change based on safety support. The Will linebacker shuffles to a stack. Read the tailback. If he is frontside, you stay frontside. Be ready to punch the offensive center. If he cuts back, you must rock back.

Fast (Toss) Coaching Points: Shuffle to a stack position. Do not beat the ball outside. Attack the pulling man or the fullback before he gets around the corner and square up.

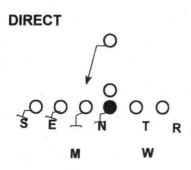

Diagram #4B. Fast (Toss)

Direct (Zone) Coaching Points: Dip and rip to your gap.

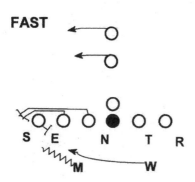

Diagram #4C. Direct (Zone)

Stack (Power) Coaching Points: This is not a lead play. Read the angle of the fullback. Shuffle to a stack set. If it is read force, the Sam linebacker will spill the fullback. Fit outside the Sam linebacker. If it is backer force, fit inside the Sam linebacker.

Fast (Flow Away) Coaching Points: Press the line of scrimmage as soon as possible. Beat the cut-off block by the center.

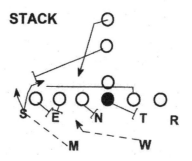

Diagram #4D. Stack (Power)

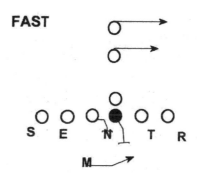

Diagram #5A. Fast (Flow Away)

Slow (Counter) Coaching Points: See the tailback jab step and pick up the pulling lineman. Rocker back to a stack position and locate the ball.

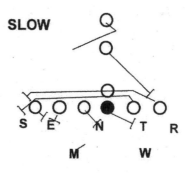

Diagram #5B. Slow (Counter)

Slow (Draw) Coaching Points: Let the quarterback pass the back before you start your drop. Flash your eyes to the tight end to see if he releases on run blocks.

Will Linebacker Run Reads

Direct (Lead) Coaching Points: Meet the lead blocker on his side of the line of scrimmage. Attack him nose up. Escape to his outside (BIN FIT). Defeat the fullback. This is not a one-for-one exchange.

SLOW

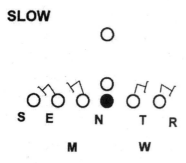

Diagram #5C. Slow (Draw)

Your fit will change based on the safety support. The Mike linebacker shuffles to a stack position. Read the tailback. If he is frontside, you stay frontside. Be ready to punch the offensive center. If he cuts back, you rock back.

Fast (Toss) Coaching Points: Scrape at a downhill angle off the hip of the defensive end. Know if you are scrap and fill, or scrap and force.

DIRECT

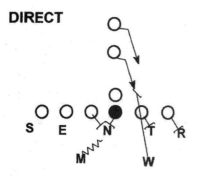

Diagram #6A. Direct (Lead)

FAST

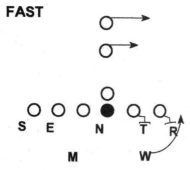

Diagram #6B. Fast (Toss)

Direct (Zone) Coaching Points: Work up and into the A gap. Work to the ball based on the angle of the back.

Slow (Counter) Coaching Points: See the jab step by the tailback and pick up the pulling man. Rocker back to a stack position and locate the ball.

DIRECT

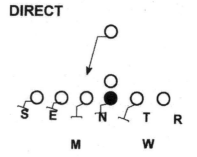

Diagram #6C. Direct (Zone)

SLOW

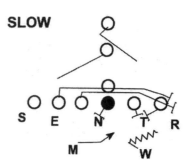

Diagram #6D. Slow (Counter)

Sam Linebacker Run Reads

Reach Coaching Points: Gain leverage on the tight end and squeeze the play. Work the tight end upfield and turn the play inside.

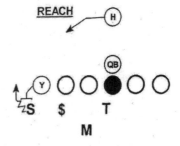

Diagram #7A. Reach

T-Pull Coaching Points: Step down with the tight end. See the tackle quickly. Contact the

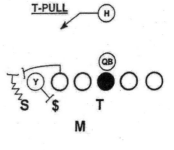

Diagram #7B. T-Pull

offensive tackle just like you would a tight end and play the same. Work him like a tight end on the reach block.

Kick-Out (Counter) Coaching Points: Step down with the tight end. Attack the guard. Be physical at the point of attack. Squeeze or spill the block based on the support call.

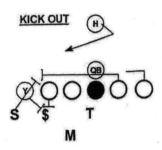

Diagram #7C. Kick-Out (Counter)

Kick-Out (Power) Coaching Points: Step down with the tight end. Attack the fullback nose up and escape inside (spill).

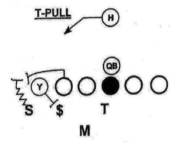

Diagram #7D. Kick-Out (Power)

G-Pull Coaching Points: Step down with the tight end. Use inside shoulder leverage to squeeze the guard. Be physical on the guard and stay square. Be ready for bounce (rails).

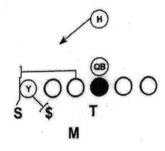

Diagram #8A. G-Pull

Drive Block Coaching Points: Control the blocker with outside leverage. Squeeze the inside area with the blocker's body. Be ready to make the tackle on the bounce out.

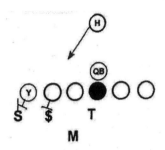

Diagram #8B. Drive Block

Backside Scoop Coaching Points: Work to a slow-fold position. Work the offensive tackle into the B gap. Be able to play the cutback if it breaks all the way back.

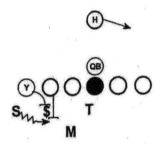

Diagram #8C. Backside Scoop

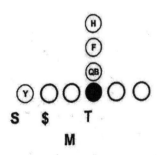

Diagram #8D. I Formation

IN THE PASSING GAME, LESS IS MORE

University of Hawaii

Thank you very much. It is a pleasure to be with you today. I was very fortunate as a young athlete and coach to be with some very intellectual people. They had a unique perception of the game of football. Two coaches influenced me with their ideas on football. That influence led me to become a successful football coach.

Those two coaches were Mouse Davis and Jerry Glanville. The interesting thing is Jerry Glanville now works for me as my defensive coordinator. The third coach that had an effect on my coaching career was Bill Walsh. I have known him for some time. When I tried out with the pros, Bill worked me out. However, it was years later, after he retired, that I got to know him and had a chance to sit down with him and talk football.

He comes to Hawaii every year and we spend seven to 10 days playing golf and talking football. There are reasons that people are successful. It is not magical. You have to look at what those people have done. I brought four things with me today that I think will help you.

I have some people in here today that have heard me harp on these points many times. It comes down to a philosophy and a belief in what you are doing. You have to limit what you are doing so your players can have success. I have coached 20 NFL quarterbacks and a good number at the University of Hawaii.

It is not by coincidence that these players walk into a system where the quarterback can be successful. The success these quarterbacks enjoy is due in part to the way we execute the principles of our systems.

Mouse Davis is probably the most influential person on the system I now run. He was a stubborn coach who had five routes and declared that they were the only five we would run. We were going to work on them every day and adjust them to make them manageable. We did these plays repeatedly until our players could do them with what I call "unconscious confidence."

We could execute those passes under pressure in the heat of battle without having to think about it. The bottom line is in order to beat your opponent, you have to be able to execute your techniques faster than your opponents.

I open every training camp with this quote from Aristotle: "We must manage our behavior to meet our objectors. Excellence is not an act but a habit. We are what we repeatedly do."

I am going to tell you a few stories to confirm the validity of that belief before I get started. When I got my first job in the NFL, it was with Jerry Glanville. Mouse and I were with the Houston Gamblers in the old USFL. We introduced the four-wide-receiver system into the professional football leagues. Our quarterback was Jim Kelly and we had tremendous success with that system.

Jerry was in Houston as defensive coordinator of the Houston Oilers. I played for Jerry in Atlanta for the Falcons. He knew me and hired me with the Oilers. When I got there, he told me we were going to run only five patterns. I thought I was going to get out of this route jamming and expand my horizons.

A good friend just recently passed away, but at that time he worked for Bill Walsh and the 49ers. That was the period when they won their first Super Bowl. We took three routes we ran with the Gamblers, three routes from Bill Walsh, and installed the offense at Houston.

We combined those six passes and went from last in the NFL on offense to first. We made those routes work against every defense we faced. Warren Moon went from being on the trading block to having a Pro Bowl season.

While we were at Houston, we were first or second in the league every year. We went to Detroit and did the same thing. We followed that tenure in Detroit with a venture in Atlanta and had the same success. Nevertheless, through all this, the 49ers were still having tremendous success.

I watched San Francisco and the things that went on there. It seems that every two years they changed offensive coordinators. Two of their offensive coordinators, Mike Holmgren and Mike Shanahan, left for Green Bay and Denver and built successful programs there.

In 1978, I played in the league in Bill Walsh's first season. He went 2-14, that year. In the last game of the year, Atlanta played the 49ers in Atlanta. The 49ers started Joe Montana in his first game. I played for Atlanta and started that game for the Falcons.

I watched the progress of San Francisco from the 2-14 season and saw them grow as a football program. They were the most productive team in the National Football League. The fact that they changed their coordinator every two years did not affect their productivity. They continued to be first or second in the league on offense.

In 1999, when I took the Hawaii job, I got to know Bill Walsh better. We were playing golf one day, and I asked him a question. I told him I had followed his team for 20 years and he continued to win despite all the changes that occurred within his program. It did not seem to matter who the quarterback was, the offense continued to flourish. How was he able to do that?

He told me something that was interesting and confirmed what I am going to tell you today. In his first season, when he installed the West Coast offense, he did it just like I am doing today. In his meeting room, he had an overhead projector and he presented the scheme to his players just as I am doing now. They filmed the presentation of the scheme the way he presented it.

Every coach that comes into their program watches those original tapes of that presentation. They install the offense with the same words and codes. Nothing has changed in that presentation of the program from the first time it was given to the last time. That leant itself to consistency of teaching from the old coach to the new one. We are what we repeatedly do and excellence is not an act, it is a habit.

I tell many stories to my team. One of them is why quarterbacks have success in one aspect of the game, but no success in others. I will give you a good example. My first position at coaching a quarterback was at Hawaii under Dick Tomey. He gave me some freedom in coaching the offense because he was a defensive type of coach. Our philosophies were not alike, but I adjusted to the type of offense he wanted to run.

I had a quarterback by the name of Cherry. The proceeding year he was very unproductive. He had completed only 33 percent of his passes. He had four or five touchdown passes with 15 interceptions. The next season he used my thought process. We simplified the offense and tried to do a few things well.

During that year, we scored 38 touchdowns. Cherry ran or threw for 36 of those touchdowns. He completed 60 percent of his passes and in my opinion was the best player in college football. I left after that season and he went right back to completing 30 percent of his passes.

I am not telling you that to say I am a great coach. I am telling you that this principle of giving your quarterback a few things to do gives him a chance to execute and play at the highest level.

Colin Powell talked about playing the game at the highest level and being the best you could be. He said there are only two things needed to have no limit on performance. He said you need the opportunity and the proper training.

I have added one other item to those two. If you are going to be a leader or coach, and take that step up to the next level, you have to be willing to take a calculated risk. Like other situations, you have to take that calculated risk at the right time.

Our quarterbacks, from the time they hit the field until the time practice is over, are throwing footballs. We have four quarterbacks. Every quarterback is throwing the ball and every receiver is catching the ball doing the same routes. They do it repeatedly in the course of a practice session. That allows them to get better and the routes do not change.

I have expanded our package since my days with Jerry and Mouse, but the philosophy is the same. Although we change the routes somewhat to make them look different to the defense, the read for the quarterback never changes.

A few years ago, we had a situation in the Fresno State game that was interesting. They had us beat. With six or seven minutes left in the game, they were trying to run the clock out by running the football. All they needed to do was pick up another first down and the game would be over. David Carr was the quarterback for Fresno State and we were down by three points.

They decided to throw a play action-pass on third down. Nate Jackson blitzed off the backside and swatted the ball out of David Carr's hand. We recovered the ball, took it in for the score, and won the game.

I watched TV that night and the reporters were interviewing Nate Jackson in the locker room after the game. They asked Nate to tell them about the sack. He said, "It was exactly like I do it in the drills every day." To hear that conformation from your players and believe that will carry on into other areas of their lives is why we coach.

After that fumble recovery, on the winning drive, we had a third-and-17 situation. We could have kicked the field goal from that point, tied the game up, and gone into overtime. I called time-out because I wanted to make one more attempt to score.

We had a great receiver by the name of Ashley Lelie. I called Rolo, our quarterback, and Ashley over to the sidelines. I told them I wanted to run four verticals. I told the quarterback that the ball had to go in the end zone. I told him to look off to the left all the way. I knew the coverage they would play. I told the quarterback to throw the ball to Ashley on a fade-stop pattern where only he could catch it. I told Ashley to protect the ball, turn the body, get one foot down, and win the game.

They went back on the field and did exactly what I told them to do. I cannot tell you how many times Rolovich had thrown that ball exactly that way in practice. He could throw it in his sleep. He has thrown that pass thousands of times in the drills.

People who saw the play thought it was a great throw and a tremendous catch. It happens for a reason. We do not have very many routes. Our receivers have one of six things they do. We can call a play a number of different ways, but one of the things the receiver does is included in those routes. The only thing they have to know is the package.

I tried to come up with a way to use Mouse's and Jerry's plays and continue to stay with the same philosophy. Along with that, I intermingled some patterns I had stolen from Bill Walsh. The one I am going to show you I got from Ted Marchibroda. I watched it repeatedly when he was with Buffalo during the time they went to five Super Bowls. They called the route Levels. We kept the name as part of our package.

I have done this from day one. The only people in our program with a playbook are the coaches. We ask our receivers to identify five things as to the coverage they see. We make our players draw everything up on a play sheet. We have them put their name on the sheet, the play, and the conversions against all coverages.

This package is not one of our read packages. I want to show you the pattern against all different coverages. The only adjustments we make are with the single receiver on the short side of the field. I will show you how we change the pattern with one word. It is the same for the quarterback, but different to the defense and different routes for the receivers.

In our numbering system, odd numbers are to the left and the even numbers are to the right. This is 781 going to the left (Diagram #1). The split of the single receiver is to the bottom of the college numbers. If the corner is off, he runs a five-step speed out. We are in the shotgun set most of the time. If that receiver is open, the quarterback throws the ball to him.

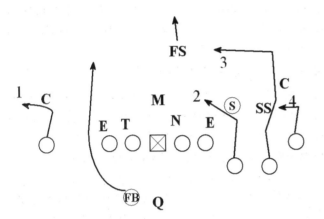

Diagram #1. Levels

The fullback aligns to that side and releases through the outside linebacker and down the seam. I talked to Coach Marchibroda about this pattern. When Jim Kelly threw this pattern, he read the flat coverage to the weakside on a three-deep zone. If the flat defender ran to get under the out, he threw to the fullback up the seam. When we started doing that part of the play, it made the quarterback too slow in getting to the backside progression. We do not look at the fullback, unless it is in the game plan off a certain look in the secondary. If I were teaching the quarterback today, that is not one of his options.

On the backside, the inside slot runs a three-step in pattern. The outside slot runs a 12-yard in pattern and the wide receiver runs a five-yard In pattern. This is not a read pattern for the receivers. They do not settle in the zones. They continue to run across the field.

That is an average play with a read progression. The quarterback reads single receiver, inside slot,

outside slot, and wide receiver. Last year, we threw this pass about 75 times. We completed it probably 80 percent of the time. After looking at the play with all the combinations off the three-receiver side, I do not know why we ran anything else.

It gets back to the original premise that the fewer things you do, the better you are at what you do. If we face a cover 2, the single receiver has a forced outside release. That gives more room to the fullback because the corner is wider.

If the corner roll takes the split end out of the pattern, the quarterback's first read is the linebacker over the inside slot. If he drops, we hit the inside slot immediately. If he hangs on the inside slot, the outside slot will be open behind him. If the strong safety sinks on the outside slot, the wide receiver is open.

When you look at our cut-ups, the fourth option is open every time. This does not look hard to defend, but I watched Jim Kelly throw this for five years. He did not have the other variations we put in.

Another thing that is great about this route is the blitz control that comes from it. If the defense brings seven rushers, you can hit the out if the corner is off. You can hit the inside slot or wide receiver running hot immediately. In every package we have, the quarterback knows where he can go with the ball quickly if he gets pressure. We always have hot reads built into our packages.

The hardest coverage to run this pattern against is 2 man. On that coverage, all the defenders lock on the receivers man-to-man with inside leverage. We keep teams from playing that defense by running the ball. Of the 75 times we ran this play, we saw 2 man twice.

Even if we throw the ball against 2-man coverage, we have the receivers to beat the coverage. We have fast receivers and we work extremely hard on defeating that type of leverage.

Most everything we do in our passing game is words. Over the years, we have evolved to this way of running our plays. Our players learn the routes faster by putting words to them. We have levels, go,

Georgia, Nebraska, choice, streak, switch, and others. One of the terms that is universal on every route is special (Diagram #2). The word "special" means that the two inside receivers exchange routes. If we call 781-special, the inside slot runs the 12-yard in and the outside slot runs the three-step in.

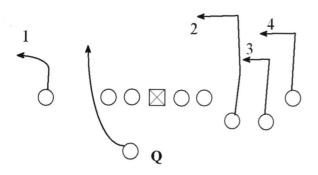

Diagram #2. Levels Special

The read stays the same for the quarterback. It looks different to the defense. Another term we could add to the pattern is "change." This term applies only to the three-man side. If we call 781-change (Diagram #3), the outside receiver runs the 12-yard in, the outside slot runs the five-yard in, and the inside slot runs the three-step in. The quarterback progression stays the same. He reads from the single receiver to the outside receiver on the three-receiver side. It is the same pattern run by different receivers.

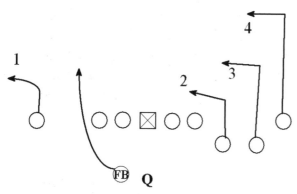

Diagram #3. Levels Change

I think because of what Mouse and Jerry engrained in me in my first 10 years, it allowed me to come up with a system. That system keeps everything the same for the quarterback and allows him to have success.

Colt Brennan was our quarterback this year and led the nation in passing. He had no idea what we were doing. Maybe the last two games, he understood something. I think it is simple, but had it not been for this pattern and a couple of other little things we did, he might have struggled all year.

I kept scaling back the offense, trying to make it simpler. He thought 781 and 781-change were two different plays. After he went over the pattern a million times in practice it finally sunk in. The last three or four games, he was something else. He was not that way in all areas. Next year, I am cutting out more things from the offense. I will not ask him to do as much.

He completed 70 percent of his passes, threw 38 touchdowns, and had 10 interceptions. We watched the tape and he read from one to two, but never could get to three and four. He was a tremendous scrambler and made big plays because he could avoid tacklers, but did not really understand what was going on. When it finally sank in and he got to the third and fourth reads, he started hitting everything.

I had Jimmy Chang for five years. He ran it in high school before he came to Hawaii. It was old hat for him in his senior year.

The next thing I want to show you comes from our read patterns. This is our go pattern (Diagram #4). We run this from a triple formation. We can get into the triple by aligning in it or motioning to it. The outside receivers use maximum splits, which are about five yards from the sidelines. The inside slot is set about three yards outside the offensive tackle.

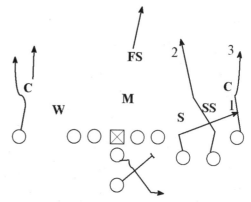

Diagram #4. Go Against Three-Deep

The outside slot is three to five yards outside the inside-slot position. The outside receivers run the go route and clear out the zone.

I will draw this up against three-deep coverage in a 4-3 defense. On the snap of the ball, the outside slot drives at the outside numbers of the strong safety. As the strong safety widens, the slot slips inside the safety into the crease between the safety and linebacker. He looks for the football in that crease. If the Sam linebacker has gotten to the crease, he continues up the seam and looks for the ball past the linebacker.

The inside slot runs a flat pattern, which continues into a flat and up as he drives off the ball toward the Sam linebacker for one step and takes his pattern into the flat at a depth of three to five yards. If he does not get the ball on the flat pattern, he turns the pattern up the sideline.

The quarterback reads the strong safety. If he backs up, the quarterback throws the ball to the flat pattern and we take the five yards the defense wants to give us. If the strong safety widens to the flat, the quarterback looks for the outside slot running the seam. The third read is for the go pattern of the wide receiver.

If the quarterback reads the two-deep zone coverage in the secondary (Diagram #5), the reaction of the receiver changes somewhat. If the defender aligns inside on the outside slot, the slot and quarterback look for the roll of the corner. The outside slot does not widen and drive straight up the field into the seam. The quarterback comes off the safety read and makes a corner read.

If the corner hangs, he throws the flat route. If the corner comes off on the flat, the inside slot takes the pattern up. If the quarterback cannot throw the up because the strong safety has gotten too much width, he hits the seam receiver inside the strong safety.

In the four-deep zone, we read it similar to the three-deep zone (Diagram #6). The quarterback reads the Sam linebacker playing outside of the outside slot. If he backs up, the quarterback throws the flat. If he widens on the flat route, he throws the seam. If the Mike linebacker has jumped inside the seam route, the outside slot takes the pattern on a short post to the inside.

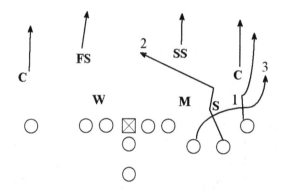

Diagram #6. Go Against Four-Deep

If we read man coverage in the secondary, this becomes a good pattern (Diagram #7). For all you defense coaches out there, we refer to this as a rub. You might call it a pick. The corners may be in a bump position on the outside receiver and a free safety in the middle. If the defense is lock man coverage, the inside and outside slots get a slight rub as they cross their patterns. If the slot defenders are in inside-leverage positions, we probably will get the rub.

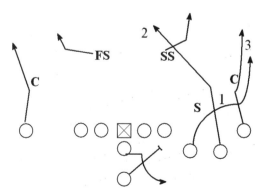

Diagram #5. Go Against Two-Deep

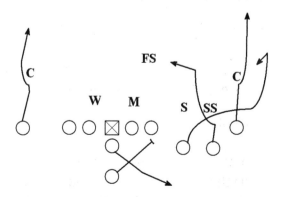

Diagram #7. Go Against Man Coverage

187

If the defenders are inside of the inside slot and outside of the outside slot, they are playing an in-and-out man technique. The defenders are playing zone until the receivers cross. When they cross, the inside defender takes the receiver breaking that way. The outside defender does the same thing to the receiver coming out. If the slot defenders are playing in and out, the receivers will not get the rub.

The quarterback has the same read as in the three-deep zone. He reads the strong safety and his progression is flat, seam, and go. With man coverage, he comes back to the flat and up as his fourth read.

If the strong safety runs to the flat and the Sam linebacker runs flat and chokes off the seam route, the seam receiver breaks off his route and runs into the area under the free safety and behind the linebackers. The flat pattern run by the inside slot becomes an up pattern. If he is open, he keeps running. If there is coverage over the top, he sets down in that area. If it is man coverage, he turns up the sideline and breaks it back.

When the quarterback cannot throw the ball quickly because of the coverage, he shuffles outside slightly. When the receivers see the shuffle by the quarterback, they break their pattern and go to their conversion routes.

This pattern takes a little time to get used to and has to be thrown on air a lot. To start the quarterback in his read progression, we give him one defender to read. The quarterback has to do their routes repeatedly to gain confidence to throw the ball into the seam. The only way he will have the courage to throw the ball in the seam is through repeated reps in practice.

The quarterback has to know when to throw the ball away. Some coaches believe that when the quarterback throws the ball, there are two bad things that can happen. The ball can be intercepted or incomplete. In our philosophy, two good things can happen. The ball can be complete or incomplete.

We do not give our receivers too much to read. They have to identify two- and three-deep, lock man, in-and-out man, and four-deep coverage. The defense can run many different looks, but we think the reads are the same. No matter what else goes on in the defense, they only see what happens in the secondary.

We do this so much that the disguise in the secondary seldom fools us. We are alert to all the moves in the secondary and know where the defenders go.

I think you can see from the film the total picture of this pattern. When we are under the center, these seam passes are 12-yard catches. From the shotgun, the catches are a little further down the field.

To become good in this offense, you have to commit to it and practice it endlessly.

To be perfectly honest with you, I do not talk protections with people. I can give you a general principle we use. If you come to our practices, you will learn the schemes we use. I think our success from pro ball to college is because we do more with pass protection then many people would imagine.

By and large, we have four protections. We run dual, slide, turn-back, and man. We run the protections that everyone else is running. We have the ability to flip the fullback from one side to the other in different schemes. The way we put our protections together helps us get the ball off. We can block any six-man rush scheme. If you bring seven, we throw hot. I am being honest with you when I say I do not know too much about why we do what we do.

The last route is an interesting route. We run a three-step game I think is unique. We run it from the double-slot set and the triple set. The three-step game is a hitch or a fade. We have evolved over the years. We used to let the receiver signal it before the play. We do not signal any more. If the corner is off in his alignment, we throw the hitch. If he is in a bump alignment, we throw the fade-stop.

I think you can implement this into your offense. If you spend the time with this pattern, it is unstoppable. You ask your quarterback on his third step to see the leverage of the defensive back. If the receiver is even or beyond the defensive back, put the ball on top to the corner. Throw the ball high and away to his outside shoulder.

This play is common in the NFL today. I only have five minutes. I am going to show it to you on film and coach it off the tape. My quarterback, Colt Brennan, learned this pattern since he came here. He may be the best fade-stop thrower I have coached.

We throw the ball off the third step in this pass (Diagram #8). He throws the ball high, away, and *behind* the receiver. This is like any other pass in our offense. It is thrown a countless number of times in practice.

The inside receiver in the double set runs the seam route. If the corner is playing off the wide receiver and the defender on the slot runs to the outside to take the hitch away, we throw the seam. Although the fade-stop is a different play, the slot runs his go route assignment.

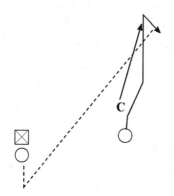

Diagram #8. Fade-Stop

The set is a triple set right with the single receiver to the left. The call is 781 special-X 15 (Diagram #9). To the triple set, we 781 special, which I talked about earlier. To the single-receiver side we run X-15, which is our three-step pass. If the defender is bump-and-run on the single receiver, we throw a fade-stop.

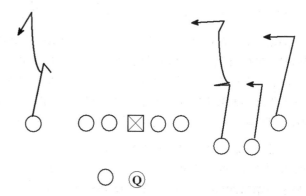

Diagram #9. 781 Special-X 15

If we call 81-15, the inside slot receiver to the triple side has an under pattern. The outside slot has a seam read just like the go pattern. He looks for the safety in the middle. If the safety vacates the middle of the field, he keeps going. If the safety goes over the top to a cover 2, he runs the post to the middle of the field. The quarterback reads the fade-stop route to the weakside to the seam read down the middle.

I have to stop. They are running me out of here. I appreciate your time. Thank you so much.

DEFENDING THE I-FORMATION LEAD PLAY

University of Alabama

We got back from the Cotton Bowl this year and I was sitting at my desk. I was thinking about the things we needed to do for the 2006 season. Each year, Coach Mike Shula gets the staff together for a retreat and he asks the staff to talk about the things we want to accomplish for spring practice and the upcoming football season. He wants to know what we need to work on and what we want to accomplish.

I gave him a list of nine things we wanted to accomplish this spring and in the next football season. Each year, we sit down as a staff and discuss the things we need to work on. We have a new staff member, so we need to spend time with him so we can be on the same page.

Come closer as a staff and as a team. That is very important. Today, with a lot of athletes it is about "me." Those kids want to know, what is in it for me? I am amazed what some parents will do to try to get these kids scholarships. I know the high school coaches are hounded to death with this problem. We still believe that football is a team game. We really make an emphasis that football is a team sport. However, the question is, what can you do to pull the staff together?

How were we going to become a better staff? Several coaches run every day during their lunch period. I played center in college and I always thought a 40-yard dash was "cross country" to me. It makes me hurt just thinking about all of that running. However, I decided that if they wanted to run, I would jog along with them. I was surprised that I did not have a heart attack, so I guess that worked out all right. We did that so we could come together as a staff.

We tried to do things together as a staff. We even went fishing together. One other thing we did as a staff: When one of the staff had a small son that played fall ball, we went to see him play. I think it is important to have the staff on the same page together. We tried to do everything we could to pull the team closer together. We needed to have a plan for that to happen.

We wanted to sell "running to the ball." This is the best thing we do at Alabama. You cannot just talk about it; you cannot just suggest it. You have to demand it on every snap. We said, "It must start with the personnel at the first practice, and it has to go through the same test through the season and to the bowl game." We all must be on the same page with our kids. Our kids make mistakes in practice, the same as your kids make mistakes in practice. Some of our players wanted to get up and debate the mistake instead of chasing the ball after they make a mistake. The ball is still going and the whistle has not sounded. We tell him to chase the ball and we will coach him on the way back to the huddle. We want to sell running to the ball. We want to make sure we run to the ball.

A lot of teams we played talked about how fast our team was. I am not denying that, but we play fast. We try to sell playing fast. We watch a lot of film together. We take about 25 minutes a day when the entire defense is in the room together. We point out when players tend to slow up in chasing a play. We want to sell keeping the same fast pace in getting to the football. That was a big priority for us.

Keep the players focused the whole year. We want to talk about keeping the players focused for the whole year. A lot of teams in high school end up playing 13 to 14 games if you count the playoffs. We play 12 games in a row and go to a bowl game. It is easy to stay focused when the "grass is green," the uniforms are fresh, and everything is new. It is not hard to focus then. If you do not have a plan to stay focused over the long haul, somewhere in the season you are going to rise and fall. We played 10 games where we played as good as we could play. Then we had one bad play in the overtime game against LSU. However, for 10 weeks we had a steady deal going. It was a concerted effort to stay focused.

The only stat we talked about all year was leading the nation in scoring defense. Our offense may have been a little limited at times, but our defense could not do a lot about that fact. Nevertheless, we knew that unless they change the rules of the game of football, if a team does not score, they would have a hard time beating us. We really try to sell this point.

This is simple math by a country boy talking. We have players on our team that cannot relate to big numbers such as 27 or 28. I never talk about those high numbers. This is what we say: one score or one-half of a score. I wish the people that made the rules of football when the game first started would have made the game a lot easier to score. I would like to have seen this. Give one point for a touchdown and one-half of a point for a field goal, because it would have been a lot easier to keep score. We talk to our players about one score because it seems like a lot less than 6 points. This is really true when you get up to 21 points.

One year, we went in at the half and we were behind 21-0. We explained it to the team this way: "We are only three scores behind." The point is this. We do not talk a lot about points. Instead, we talk about scores. We set our goal to lead the nation in scoring defense.

We wanted improved play against the Zone play. I have been in this game so long that I have made every mistake a coach can make. I have made every one of them. My goal now is not to make those mistakes again. I am on the double loop now. "Don't make that same mistake again." The play that hurt us the year before was the zone play.

We went into two-a-days practice and we were determined to work against the zone play. It did not matter what our offense was running, we were going to work on the zone play. Teams may beat us, but they were going to have a hard time beating us with the zone play.

We wanted to become a better blitzing and movement team. This was something we did improve on.

We wanted to be the best third-down team in college football. There are two downs in football that you must be efficient. The outcome of the game depends on these two downs. First is what we call 10 and 10. That is the personnel to each side. The other down is the third down. I cannot remember all of those first downs. I do not worry about all of the first downs. The only first down I am interested in is the first time it is first down.

We want to know what our opponent starts out with on first down. Then we look for what they run on second down. The next is the third down. We want to stop them and get off the field when it is third down. We work on first and third downs. We feel that second down takes care of itself. We really want to do a good job on those two downs. We want to practice, analyze, break down, and sell what the opponents do on third down.

These last points are the reason I am still in coaching at 61 years old.

We want to have a good time every day. Back in 1952, when I was playing, the game was a lot of fun. *It was fun to play football.* Kids played football in the backyard on Sunday evening. Kids played football in the summer. Football was fun to play. I have analyzed it, dissected it, and filmed the game so much that we have really squashed those kids. We are at a point now where I do not know if it is still fun to play football. Every day we go to practice I try to find something to laugh about. We want to try to have a good time every day. If it is funny, we laugh. If it is sad, we cry. We may get on the players hard, but we want to make it fun.

We want to make our players better people. If you have a player that has been with you for four years, he should be a better human being when he goes out the back end. That is what we try to do.

The next thing I want to discuss is how we practice. We are going to talk about defending the I formation later. However, before you can defend the I formation, you must have some kind of system or organizational play, and something you believe in that will get you to the point in practice where you can work on it.

We are a firm believer in circuit training on the practice field. The first thing we do every single day when we come out of special teams is to go out circuit training, which is our tackling practice. In that first period, we are going to work on tackling every day. We tell the players that if lightning strikes about halfway through practice and it starts raining and we have to get off the field, we leave the field with everyone having worked on tackling that day.

Every play ends with three things in football today. It is an incomplete pass, or it is when the men in stripes throw their hands straight up, or it is a tackle. It happens that way on every play. I hope we are going to tackle someone 65 times in a game. So the point is, we are going to work on tackling in the circuit.

One of the reasons we use the circuit system is because I want all of our coaches working with our players. Those young coaches are much better coaches than I am. They are younger, have more enthusiasm, and our players relate to them better. I want those young assistants working in the circuit phase every day.

Circuit training allows our team to work on a specific phase of the game. We played Texas Tech in the Cotton Bowl. Tech has a great passing game. We came up with a "pass skill circuit" for that one game. For one month, we "rode that horse until it was ready to drop." We drilled those kids to death in a Pass Circuit Drill. It allows our team to work on a specific phase of the game. We can get a larger number of reps in a short period of time using the circuit drill.

The one thing that drives us crazy is to look out on a practice field and see 10 players listening, one coach talking, and one player working a little. We do not have enough time to do that. We want to practice where we can get a large number of reps in a short period of time.

Another point about circuit drills is this. It allows every player to get the same reps. The third-team linebacker is being coached by the coaches just as the first-team linebacker is coached. We feel this is much more efficient that putting the players through these drills by only using the first two teams and ignoring the third-string players. We want every kid to be coached in a short period of time and just like everyone else.

We are talking about tackling in this drill. It allows the secondary coach to see how the defensive tackle works. He may learn something from coaching that tackle. We feel our whole team can become better because of using circuit drills.

This is how we break our tackling circuit down. The first thing we are going to teach is how to tackle. There are three things we talk about every day in tackling. We talk about approach, fit, and follow-through (Diagram #1). Most tackles are missed because the person tackling does not do one of those three things.

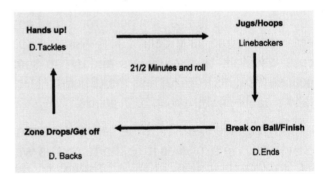

Diagram #1. Pass Skill Circuit

On the approach, the player must take the proper angle. If he misses the tackle, a lot of the time it is because the player takes a bad angle. You must take the proper angle to make a tackle. Then you must come to balance before you make the tackle.

We practice our best offense against our best defense every single day. However, the offense will not let us tackle them. We do not want the players to develop bad habits in this drill. We do not want our players practicing missed tackles. We want them doing the drill correctly, even when we are not tackling live. Even though we are not going to take the offense to the ground, we are going to come to balance, get square, and work on him like a good bird dog on every snap. We are going to work to a breakdown position and shuffle our feet.

The next thing we try to do is step on the toes of the ballcarrier. In the off-season, between 2:00 pm and 4:00 pm, we are going to watch every high school film that is sent to us. We all come together as a defensive staff and look at those films. The biggest mistake I see in high school football is the tackler starts tackling the ballcarrier about a yard and a half before they get to him. We tell our players they must step on the toes of the ballcarrier before they tackle him. You must "get" to him if you are going to tackle him. You must have the knees bent, head up, and then you must come up through the cylinder of the body.

I have heard a lot of coaches talk about getting the head across the bow of the runner. We do not talk much about that. If I am in the middle of the runner, I pick the middle of the cylinder of his body. I want to strike the middle of that cylinder. I must keep my head in front and I must keep my head up. I do now worry about getting the head across the man. We want to strike that cylinder and get a lot of our body mass on his body.

We teach the head in the socket, step on the runner's toes, and fit him up. If you watch film, you will see the teams that tackle the best are those that get a lot of body mass on the ballcarrier. They never swing the hips. If they let their hips fall behind them, all they have left is their arms. We work on getting our hips on his hips. We want to get a lot of our body on him, grab high cloth, and pull, and then follow through with leg drive.

This is how we work on those things I just talked about. The first drill we do is the Peel Off Drill. That group will go to the Shed Tackling Drill. Then we go to the Tackling Sled Drill and then we come over to the Screen Drill.

If you do not get anything from this lecture, I think you will get something out of our Screen Drill. Three years ago, we were the worst team in America in defending the screen pass.

We start with our front linemen. We could not rush the passer a lick. Not a lick! We had a player that had been out on the practice field and he had not even come close to making a tackle. All of a sudden, the offensive back ran past our defender. What was the first thing that entered our defender's mind? "Heck of a move!" Now he was free to rush the quarterback. However, he was caught up in the screen. The quarterback completed the screen pass and the back ran it into our secondary. As a result, I decided we must become better at defending the screen pass.

That year, when I attended the AFCA clinic I must have asked 100 coaches how they played the screen play. Other coaches avoided me like a plague. I would ask those coaches what they did on screens and how they practiced against the screens. After all of the talks with the other coaches, we came up with a drill to work against the screen.

I believe this: "If you can't drill it, you can't teach it." I do not believe that you can just go up to the chalkboard and say, "He goes here, and if they do this, he goes here." I do not think that will get the job done. I believe that you must drill it repeatedly, and by the time they are seniors they may get it. At least you have a chance this way. You have no chance if you one-time it. So we are going to drill the screen play.

We start with a simple drill. Here we go. It is our Peel Off Drill (Diagram #2). We set up three cones.

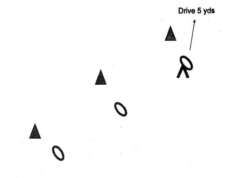

Diagram #2. Peel Off Drill

We put two cutters and a ballcarrier in the drill. The first two men are cutters and the third man has a ball in his arms. When we start out teaching the drill, we put the cones close together. As the season progresses, we spread the cones farther apart. That forces them to travel in space.

The defensive man wants to have great knee bend, keep his eyes on the blockers, and really work on hand placement on the blocks. We want to play with great pad level. We want to keep our pads level with the blocker. It is okay to give ground on the drill. It is okay to come off the blocker. He is trying to stay alive on the drill. In our league, the offense cuts us every snap. I know high schools cannot cut block.

We work on getting our hands on the blocker and trying to get away from him.

This is how we teach it. We tell the defender that the deep man has the football, and the two blockers have "butcher knives." "Who do you want to look at first? Are you going to look at the man that has the football, or are you going to look at the man that has the knife and is trying to cut your heart out?" It just boils down to that situation. They had better look at the blocker if they want to stay alive.

We peel off the first blocker and take on the second man. We peel him off and come to the ballcarrier. We must come to balance, step on his toes, make contact, and drive him back five yards. We are going to play two blocks, make a form tackle, and drive the man five yards.

We go two-and-a-half minutes at each of the circuit stations. There are four stations. In spring practice and in two-a-days, we go for 10 minutes at the circuit. Once the season starts, we start looking at the amount of time we have to work. Late in the season, we may cut the circuit to five minutes. We do stations 1 and 2 on Tuesday, and stations 3 and 4 on Wednesday. So, once a week the players make the circuit. That is the Peel Off Drill.

Next, we go to the Shed Tackle Drill (Diagram #3). All we are going to do here is get into the lockout position. I have the ballcarrier formed up. I have my feet behind me. I have a good power angle

on him. Next, we want to "snatch it" and really be violent when we jerk it. It is the same as the Peel Off Drill. We want to jerk the blockers, come to balance, fit into form, and drive the ballcarrier back five yards.

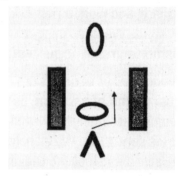

Diagram #3. Shed Tackle Drill

Next, we go to the Tackling Sled Drill (Diagram #4). We use an old-time Crowther-type sled. We are going to tackle it every day. One reason we use the old sled is because the sled has "used up his eligibility." He has played out all of his time. You can hit that old sled, drive it in the ground, and rough it up as much as you want. I have never seen the sled get hurt.

Diagram #4. Tackling Sled Drill

We are going to fit to form, drive the sled, and take it to the ground. We attack the sled, fit to form, and then we are going to drive the sled.

Next, we go to the Screen Drill (Diagram #5). We set up four cones on the drill to simulate the

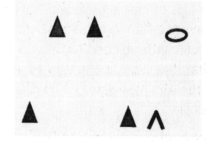

Diagram #5. Screen Drill

offensive-line positions. We have one guy rush the passer. Remember, everyone on the defensive team is going through this drill. We blitz the corners, the safeties, and the linebackers, and we rush the front four. Everyone on the team at some point in time is going to rush the passer.

The outside down lineman rushes the passer. The quarterback drops back and sets up for the screen pass. He throws the ball to one of the receivers or, in this case, one of the cones. Once the defender recognizes a screen pass, he sticks his foot in the ground, turns back toward the line of scrimmage, and pursues to the ball. From this point on, it is not pretty and it is never the same on each play. It depends on the speed of the defender and the angle he has. At the point the rusher recognizes the play is a screen pass he must stick his foot in the ground, come back to where the receiver is, and get on him. We try to find someway to get on that receiver and stay with him to prevent him from receiving the screen pass. We work on this every day. We use those four drills in our circuit-training drills.

I believe this, men. Defensively, your first job is not to come up with a bunch of calls to stop the opponent's offense. Your first job is to solve the puzzle. What does the offense do to try to win the game? If the offensive coaches are worth a dime, they are not out there just calling plays. They usually have some kind of play to win the game. Some offenses try to win the game using different or special formations. Some offenses try to do it with personnel. Some offenses try to win with the power running game. Some offenses try to win the game by throwing the ball to their wideouts. The first thing we want to do is solve that problem. "What are they going to use to try to win the game?"

Once we get that problem solved, it is a lot easier to figure out what we are going to try to do to stop what they are using to try to win the game. I am not sure if this makes sense to you. Let me give you an example.

I like the Peel Off Drill. I looked at Texas Tech on film and I did not see how anything in the tapes showed that the Peel Off Drill would help us win that game. Not one! Their linemen do not cut block and they do not come off the line of scrimmage. They are going to stand up and pass block all of the time. Their plan is to put the ball in the hands of a back or receiver in space and try to make the defense miss on the tackle. Common sense tells us we should come up with something to counteract that tactic by Texas Tech.

When I was young, I went to every clinic I could work into my schedule. I loved clinics. I will tell the young coaches here something that may help you. The best learning situation at a clinic is not necessarily from a speaker. Sometimes the best thing you can do at a clinic is to meet someone in the lobby that has been around the game for a while and pick his brain on the area you need help with. Let me give you an analogy to this.

When I got married, my wife would cut the end off a ham before she cooked it. She would cut the end off the ham, and then wrap that ham in tin foil and put it in a pan and cook it. One day I asked her who taught her to cut the end of the ham off before she cooked it. She replied that her mother taught her to cut the end of the ham before putting it into the pan to cook.

On Thanksgiving, we went up to her mother's house for the holidays and I asked her mother if she could tell me why she cut the end of the ham off before she cooked it. She replied, "My mother taught me to do that." That still did not satisfy me on this question. Then the grandmother came over to visit. I said, "Finally, we are going to settle this third-generation ordeal of why they cut the end of the ham off before they cook the ham." I said, "Grandma, why did you cut the end off the ham before you baked it?" She said, "Because my pan was too little for the ham, so I cut the end of the ham off so I could get it in the pan."

The point I am making is this. Sometimes a coach does a drill and there is no "reason" to use that particular drill. It is done for the sake of doing a drill. There was no reason for us to practice the Peel Off Drill before we played Texas Tech. Done! That drill would not help us in the game against Tech. What we needed was an open-field tackling drill.

The Open-Field Tackling Drill is as old as the game of football (Diagram #6). We have four cones set up in a 10-yard-square box. One defensive player gets on the front edge of a cone and one offensive player gets on the back edge of the line on a cone. This creates the first thing we talked about in tackling, and that is the proper angle. The tackler does not have a choice, because he is lined up in a proper angle. The back is going to run straight down the line until he gets to the next cone.

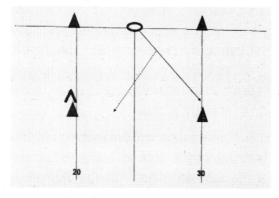

Diagram #6. Open-Field Tackling Drill

Our kids are no different from your kids. We cannot give them a lot of decisions to make in the drill. You cannot tell the defender to run three-and-a-half yards, because he has no clue how far that is. It is very simple if you tell him to put his foot on the white line and go to the next white line in the box.

Once we get to the three-and-a-half yards, the offensive back is going to try to score. The cone represents a pylon in the end zone. If we overrun the back, what is he going to do? He is going to cutback on us. It is a good, natural, open-field tackle situation. We worked on the drill for four weeks before we played Texas Tech. The small players could do the drill without much difficulty. With the big players, it took a little time for them to get adjusted. But, in the Cotton Bowl game, we had very few missed tackles.

Now I am down to the area I was supposed to talk about, and that is "defending the I formation." We are a base defensive football team. You would be disappointed if you came to one of our staff

meetings when we are game planning. We have four fronts we use. We do not try to invent the game every week. We do not sit in our meetings and try to come up with eight "new calls" that would be very good to use on first-down plays. We do not do that at all. We are a base defense. We stay within our base defense.

To run the defense we run, you need two things. First, you must have two cornerbacks that can play man coverage. In addition, you must have two ends that can make a difference in coming off the edges. If you have those two things, then this is a good front to run the base defense. We have had years when the cornerbacks were very good and we have had years when we did not have good cornerbacks and we did not do very well.

We tell those corners something that is really revolutionary. We tell them to take the wide receivers man-to-man and we will see them at halftime. "Check with us at halftime if you need to make any kind of adjustments." This is really hard now, and it takes a lot of meeting time to tell them they have those outside receivers man-to-man. I am not being facetious, because our secondary coach does a great job in working with those two corners. As far as learning their assignment on "jet red," that is what they have on the call.

The two ends must be cocked and they must be ready to come off the edge. I coach the linebackers and I tell them all of the time, "Your best friends are those two defensive ends. They are going to make your life easy or they are going to make it hard." So we make sure the linebackers are very nice to the ends. You can help them in the chow hall by getting their trays and doing things to show respect to those defensive ends.

The ends are cocked, with their butts up, and they are keying the ball. When that ball moves, they are gone. The thing that drives me crazy is for our defense to jump offside on the hard count. We are coming off the ball, but we do not want to jump too quickly. We have to work on the "hard count" all of the time. We run our plays in sets. I tell those GA's this: "Don't ever run a set of cards without two hard counts included." We cannot work Monday through Thursday while going on the first count and then do a good job against the hard count on Saturday. We work on staying onsides on the hard count a great deal of the time. We are keying the ball. When it moves, we are coming hard.

Our aiming point is the V of the neck. We come, bend, and chase. On the split-end side of the formation, we want to cancel the C gap and the B gap on that side of the line of scrimmage. This is where we start every day.

We tell the end on the tight-end side that if the tight end comes out to block on him, we want him to blow the end up. He must shoot his hands into the tight end and prevent him from turning back outside.

We play a 3 technique and a 2 technique inside. We flip-flop them. Why do we flip those two inside men? One year we had a short, squatty body that was very small. He played inside because he could not play a 3 technique. We used that for 10 years before we had total strength at those two positions. Again, it is back to cutting the end of the ham off before cooking it. You have to do what you have to do. We would rather not flip the two inside men. It would allow us to disguise the defense better. I would rather give up on the disguise and have a player that knows what he is doing and can play that technique than flip him around to a position he is not familiar with.

Our four front men are going to get vertical on contact. I hear a lot of coaches talking about getting upfield to get penetration. We do not talk about that very much. We talk about getting off the ball and making contact quickly. "Get up the field and get into that block as quickly as you can." We do not worry with those front four as to where their heads are. I have seen coaches get upset if the 3 technique gets his head on the outside of the man in front of him.

I could care less about where his head is on the play. As long as he is headed north and makes contact with the blocker. We want to do a good job with our front of getting off the ball and getting north on the play.

The next thing our staff does a real good job on is teaching the double-team. I have heard hours of discussions on what it takes to coach the defense to defeat the double-team block. "Get on the bar stool. Do this, do that." The thing that makes the most sense to our players is this analogy.

If you ever lived in a small village, what would you do if a fight broke out? If a couple of thugs tried to take your ball, what would you do? What would you do? It would not be smart to get involved with both of them. You would take on one of those guys and try to whip him. It is not smart to try to whip both of them.

We try to focus on the offensive guard and center, and the tackle if it is a tackle-tight-end combination on one side. We want to whip the post block. We want to work our hips into the play, but hang on to that post player. We do not want to slide off the post block and slide away from the double-team block.

Why do we want to stay with the post blocker? Let me give you a quick analogy. This past year we played four different types of geniuses. We faced an old genius, a young genius, a self-proclaimed genius, and a want-to-be genius. I will let you figure out who they were. They do not want to double-team. What do they want to do? They are going to try to knock the defenders out with one man. They do not want to admit they have to use the double-team block to be successful. All they want to coach is all of the chalk-talk lingo. "Hit him, work on him, and come up to him."

This is what we tell our defenders on the double-team. "Whip the post man, hang on, pray, and when the second blocker comes off, stay in the gap." The reason for this is because we are a gap-control team. What the offense wants to do is to have the second blocker come off the double-team to block our linebacker. They do not want to double-team the down lineman. If they do double him, we have one less blocker we have to worry about. The blockers want to slam the down linemen and climb to the next level.

We tell the defender being double-teamed to whip the post block, hang on, pray, and when the second blocker comes off the double-team, slide into the gap. This sounds simple, but it takes a lot of work. We do not ask our down linemen to do nine things on the double-team. We try to make it simple.

The next thing we talk about is the scoop and the reach blocks. We are not worried about our man staying outside the blocks. If we have five players up front reach blocking, we have the defense moving outside with them and the ballcarrier eventually cuts the play back inside. We want to make contact, hang on, and get north at that point. We want to make the running back make a hard cut on the play. We do not want to run out of the ballpark when the offensive line uses the reach block up front.

I coach the linebackers. I want all of the pressure on me. If something breaks down, it is my fault. What we want to do is to keep the blocker off the linebacker. If our down linemen go east and west, sometimes the linebackers cannot find the ball. We want the down linemen going north, and it will help our linebackers find the ball.

In our base defense against the I formation, we play a shade technique or we will play a 2 technique. It is the same call. We do not have a word that moves the man from the shade technique to the 2 technique. I hate words. We tell our players in our meeting on Sunday if we want him in the shade or the 2 technique. Come Sunday, that is the first thing the down linemen want to know. "Coach, do you want me in the shade technique or the 2 technique?" I may reply something like this. "We are going to use the 2 technique this week." That is all it takes to make that adjustment. We may change during the game at times. They understand this and they can relate to it in a game.

What we are doing is trying to figure out how the blockers are trying to get to our linebackers. The offense is not worried about the down lineman. This is especially true against us. We are not that big inside on defense. That man made a mistake in a game and we wanted to get his attention. In our meeting, we decided to put another player in front of him to make up for the mistake he made. That second player was 6'5" and 300 pounds. We decided to put the big guy in for the smaller player for a day or two in practice. We did not tell them that this was only for a day or two. The big boy thought it was for real. He played with a great deal of pride. He has been at that position for the last two years.

We are going to try to figure out how the offense is going to try to block our linebacker. We are going to cover our best player. We are going to try to make the offense beat us left-handed if we can.

We know we cannot stop everything the offense runs at us. You will never stop every play. We try to pick four running plays and three passes we expect them to use. We have looked at the films and in every game they won, they did it with success on these running plays and the pass plays we have selected to defend. We break this down in our meeting during the week.

We want to figure out how the I-formation team is going to attack us in the middle. We play a shade technique or a 2 technique based on what we figure out about how we think they will attack our middle.

We want to get our strong safety down into the box so we have one more man than they have players to block us with. It is just simple math. We spend a great deal of time working on each side of the formation to get the extra man in the box.

We work on the plays we feel we must stop as many times as we can to win the game. We want as many reps as possible on those plays.

In two-a-day practices, we will walk through the plays in the same manner as we did with Eugene Marve. It is a simple drill where we show them what the offense is doing on each play. For a linebacker, recognition is the whole deal. We want to show them the plays over and over. We want to train his eyes for what to look for and how to pick the play up.

The most important linebacker is the Sam linebacker. He must be dependable, because he has the tight end man-to-man (Diagram #7). That rule never changes. It is the toughest job on the team. If he turns the tight end loose one time, we get burned. This is one reason we want our defensive end on that side to come quick and hard. He cannot pussyfoot around on the snap of the ball. The Sam linebacker must be able to read that tight end on the first two steps. That is when his read starts.

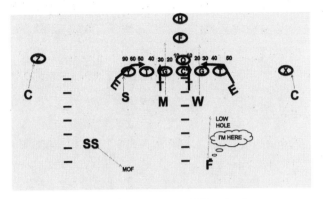

Diagram #7. 21—I Pro Left

The Mike linebacker is responsible for the A gap. He fits it with the Sam and Will linebackers. The Will linebacker has the deep back man-to-man.

I can recall attending several clinics a few years ago when we would sit around and argue if the linebackers should read through the blockers to the backs, or if he should read the offensive guard. For us, it is no argument. We do not feel that you can cover anyone if you do not look at them. It is that simple for us. We want them to get as many reps as they can on the play, so they are confident that they are making the proper reads as quickly as possible.

Now we go to the strongside and get the free safety involved. We want him to come down into the box to give us the advantage. The weakside lead play is the one play we must stop.

The first year I was at Alabama, we were bad. It was a hard year to suffer through until the end of the season. We were not a good football team by any means. I was going home after practice one day and I decided to turn on the radio. It was on a Christian broadcast station. I really did not pay much attention to what they were saying at first. So I hit a button on the radio and picked up a sports talk show.

The discussion was about a coach and how terrible he was as a coach. They brought up a lot of

points and made it plain that the coach in reference was not doing a very good job at all. I got to thinking, "Anyone that bad should be shot." It did not take me long to realize who they were talking about. It was me!

Now, even when we were bad at Alabama, and in the last three years, the weakside lead play has averaged less than one yard against our defense. Our whole deal is based on this point. There is nothing in our defensive scheme where we going to tackle the ballcarrier without going through the lead blocker. First, we do not have anyone that can do that. Second, all we have to do is to make a little mistake and the back is gone on the play.

Our whole theory is this: The offense has a blocker and a ballcarrier. If one man is blocked, we have another man that is going to make the tackle. We are going to have someone on the inside and someone on the outside of the lead block on every play they run. It all boils down to this point. Then it is simple math on the play.

Our whole philosophy is based on the fact that we are going to have a player on the inside and one on the outside of the lead block. We talk about this all of the time when we are in film sessions with the players. "Who was the inside man on the lead block and who was the outside man on the lead block?"

This year we had an experienced team. We had been together for three years. Our players would come off the field to the sideline and they would say, "Coach, I screwed up. I got outside the lead block and we had another man outside the lead block." We had two men outside the lead block and no one on the inside of the lead block. When we get our players to that point, coaching is easy. How many of you have been in this situation?

"John, what happened to you on that last play?" "I was double-teamed on the play." "What happened to you, Joe, on the last play?" "Coach, I got double-teamed on the play." "Mike, what happened to you on the last play?" I tell them this. "No wonder we got beat on the play. They ran that play with 14 players on the field at one time." I have been there before. The point I am making is this. Sometimes those kids do not know what is happening to them. To me, that is another reason for not doing a lot of different things on defense. We can fix what is broken on the sideline. If it is broken, we need to fix it. If the offense had any success on the play, we know we are going to see the play again. We had better get it fixed before they run the play again on us.

We are going to have our three linebackers read off the two down linemen inside. We are always going to have one more man than the offense can block. We always end up with a "free" player.

If we can stop the run, we have a better chance to win than we do if we do not stop the running game. This was even true with Texas Tech. In that game, we did not want the man with the ball to make it a two-dimensional game. It does not matter who we play, it all starts with the theory that we are going to stop the run first. We work on stopping the run over and over. When they get tired, we are going to run it some more, because that is when they start to learn.

The next issue is when we face two tight ends (Diagram #8). Two tight ends do not change it at all. All the fits are the same. We are still going to have an extra player on the play, but it may be to the backside. We have the flexibility to take the play to either side.

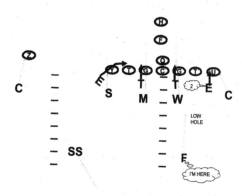

Diagram #8. 22—I Tight Left

When the offensive teams go to the slot formation, we adjust (Diagram #9). When you are a zone team, it is hard to defend the slot. The area in front of the slot man is very soft. We used to tell our linebacker that he could walk outside halfway on the slot man.

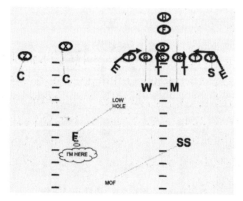

Diagram #9. Slot Formation Adjustments

We would tell the linebacker he could cover the run inside and still cover the pass in the flat. Well, I was as wrong on that as I could be. He can do one or the other, but he cannot do both. You cannot move a man outside and tell him he is right on one play and wrong on the next play. It does not take many mistakes on our part before we are behind. Therefore, we want to have him play one or the other positions, but not both.

I am going to tell you a true story. It happened two Saturdays ago. I talked at a small clinic and I was talking about man defense and rub techniques. This coach came up to me after the lecture and wanted to chat. He was as serious as he could be. He was a good coach. He wanted to know what we did against Texas Tech to shut them down. I told him it was what I had just covered. The fact is, we would rather teach the man over the slot to play one way than to teach him 19 or 20 different calls to use against the slot. Again, we try to do things in a very simple way.

I thank you for listening to me. God bless you.

PLAY-ACTION PASSING GAME

Furman University

I want to start by telling you some things about our school and our football team. Last year we won 11 games and lost three. We lost to Appalachian State in the semifinals of Division I-AA. The year before, we finished 10-4. We lost in the playoffs to the eventual national champions in Division I-AA, James Madison University.

We are a unique blend at Furman. The players that enter Furman University must have 1100 on the SAT or 23 on the ACT. I may not really like this, but those are our standards. We have been fortunate to have won nine games per year since 1978. We have won at least nine games each year and have graduated 99 percent of our football players. We are very proud of that fact. This all started with Coach Art Baker. The next coach was Dick Sheridan. I played quarterback for Coach Sheridan. Jimmy Satterfield took over after that and we won the national championship in 1988. Bobby Johnson took over after Jimmy Satterfield retired. Bobby Johnson took the Vanderbilt head coaching job and I succeed him.

This will be my fifth year as the head coach at Furman. If you look at my resume, it says Furman, Furman, and Furman. I went to Furman in 1982 as a player and played four years. I became a graduate assistant after graduation. I was an assistant coach for 15 years. And as I said, this will be my fifth year as the head coach. I can tell you this: My wife loves the place. We found a home there. I believe in what we are doing at Furman, on and off the field. We are an old-school type of football team. We run the power offense similar to what Pat Hill was talking about earlier. We have gotten a lot more multiple, where we get into different sets.

One thing that really helped us was getting Ingle Martin. Ingle Martin transferred from the University of Florida when Ron Zook was hired and he did not pick Ingle as his starting quarterback. He came to Furman and started two years for us. He did an outstanding job for us in those two years. He has a chance to play at the next level. He had a great week at the combine.

Furman is a private institution. It cost $35,000 a year to go to Furman. As a result, we do not have many walk-ons.

A little about my background. I grew up in a high school coaching family. My dad was a high school coach for 45 years in the state of Georgia. He is in the top 10 in number of wins in the state of Georgia. He won over 250 football games. He is the high school relations director at the University of Georgia. He was hired by Ray Goff and he has been there for 12 years. I guess he and UGA are the safest in the terms of their jobs. He really loves working at Georgia.

My dad is one of the old-school coaches. Bear Bryant put the wishbone offense in at Alabama and dad put in his offense when he was coaching. In the last game he coached, he coached the wishbone offense. When I played quarterback for him, my brother Hal was a wide receiver. We averaged throwing the ball four times per game. My dad literally thought we were wasting a down if we threw a pass. In my senior year, we won the AA state championship in Georgia. We averaged throwing the ball 11 times per game that year. That was because my mother complained about not throwing the ball enough.

My brother, Hal, is the head coach at Calhoun High School in Calhoun, Georgia. They finished 14-1 and lost in the state finals. They have not lost a regular-season game in three years. We are very proud of him.

My brother-in-law is his offensive coordinator. We tell everyone the Lambs are a lot like the Bowden family, except for the decimal point on our paycheck. It is not in the same position for the Lamb family. However, we have a lot of fun coaching.

Today I am going to talk on the play-action passing game. I am going to give you a couple of plays that you can use in your offense, regardless of the formations you use. First, I want to cover our offensive team goals.

Offensive Team Goals

- Win!
- Turnover ratio of +2
- On 55 percent of first-down plays, gain four-plus yards
- 43 percent third-down-conversion rate
- Red-zone touchdown efficiency of at least 75 percent
- Eight explosion plays (runs—12 yards, passes—16 yards)
- Average 4.5 yards per rushing attempt
- Average 7.5 yards per passing attempt
- Complete 60 percent of passes
- Eliminate concentration penalties

Play-Action Passing Game Philosophy

- We feel that it is important to have a plan. We plan to have a play-action pass off each run that we use.
- Our run scheme and our pass protection need to look the same.
- Play-action passes will slow down the pass rush.
- Play-action passes create a better opportunity for one-on-one match-ups.
- Keep the defense guessing!

We spend a lot of time working with the camera in the end zone, running 42 draw and 40 pass. Those two plays had better look the same for our offensive linemen and when our quarterback goes back to set up.

We are an I-formation team. We dropped back to pass last year 145 times. We ran some type of play-action pass 234 times. Most of those dropback passes were with four wideouts, and our spread package that we have. When it is third-and-seven or more, that is going to be our package. If it is third-and-four or -five yards to go, we may be in the I formation, fake the sprint draw, and throw the pass.

If we are successful in running the ball, the defense is going to drop a man down in the box to give us an eight-man look. We must be able to throw the ball effectively to keep the defense honest.

We want to keep the defense guessing and off-balance. We are a run team first. I want to put up a chart to show you our stats for the last four years.

Year	Rush	Pass	Total yards	Record
2002	195.6	218.2	413.8 (2)	8-4 (first round)
2003	221.5	163.0	384.5 (2)	6-5
2004	226.2	228.8	454.9 (2)	10-3 (quarterfinals)
2005	246.8	223.1	469.9 (1)	11-3 (semifinals)

The numbers after the yards indicate where we finished in the Southern Conference in total yards. You can also see that the last two years we were very balanced in the running and passing yards. We try to be balanced. We want the defense to be in question when it is first-and-10 to go. We want to keep those linebackers displaced.

I want to get to the 40 pass protection (Diagram #1). It is our number-one pass protection against a stack defense in a standard 4-3 defense. Our 42 draw play looks the same as the 40 protection.

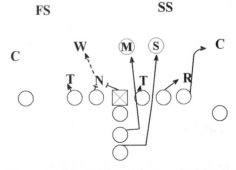

Diagram #1. 40 Protection Vs. Stack

Our tackle on the split-end side is going to set and force the defender to rush upfield. Our center and left guard are going to double-team the nose man and eyeball the Will linebacker. They have the nose man and Will linebacker on 40 pass.

Our fullback takes a slide step to the right toward the center-guard gap and blows the Mike linebacker up. Our tailback takes a slide step and he hits it up in the guard-tackle gap. He is not an isolation tempo runner. It is a draw play. That is why we call the play 42 draw. We want the tempo for 42 draw and 40 pass to be the same. The Mike linebacker does not know which back is coming at him. Our right guard takes the tackle and stays with him upfield. Our right tackle is going to settle and force the outside man upfield. The only difference in 42 draw and 40 pass is with our tight end. On 42 draw, our tight end releases inside so he can get in an inside-out position on the Sam linebacker. Our tailback is responsible for the Sam linebacker on 40 pass. Our number-one play in our offense is 42 draw.

Let me cover the eagle X, or the under defense. We call it eagle X, but most other people call it the under defense (Diagram #2). The tight end is responsible for the same man. When we run 42 draw, the center must make a decision. He must look to the Will linebacker. The splitside tackle and guard force the tackle and nose man to run upfield. The fullback still has the Mike linebacker. If we call 42 draw, the tight end blocks the Sam linebacker. If it is 40 pass, the tight end is going to run his route. Now the tailback is responsible for the Sam linebacker.

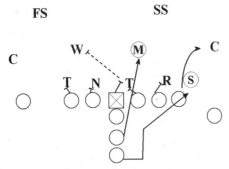

Diagram #2. 40 Protection—Eagle X

Let me talk about the eight-man front (Diagram #3). We can change it up to run the play two ways.

The tight end releases on his route. The fullback has the Sam linebacker and the tailback has the strong safety. The backside guard and tackle fan their men outside. The center and guard work on the nose man and Will linebacker.

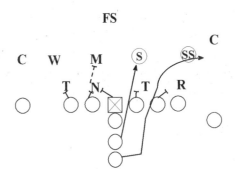

Diagram #3. 40 Protection—Eight-Man Front

We never ask our fullback to block on the backside linebacker. He always blocks the first linebacker to the playside. The tailback is always blocking on the number 2 linebacker on the playside. The way we can change the blocking assignment is to have the center and backside guard eye the Will and Mike linebackers. It is a little different blocking the eight-man front.

The footwork for the quarterback on the draw is similar on the 40 protection and 42 draw. He opens up at 6 o'clock and seeds the ball. He extends the ball so it looks like the draw play. We do the same thing on the pass play. If we are going to throw a speed pass, such as a quick out route, the quarterback never takes his hands off the ball. We call that a skin fake. The quarterback throws the ball on his fifth step. On the deep post route down the field, the quarterback takes a seven-step drop with the fake and throws the ball on his seventh step. It is more a matador thing.

I want to go over the routes. The first play we teach is 40 Pass—383 (Diagram #4). You do not need a strong-armed quarterback to throw the pass that we call our bread and butter. We throw this pass from day one. The quarterback just needs to get a little more air under the ball. Our receivers know their passing assignments as designated by the numbers. The split end runs his 3 route, the tight end runs his 8 route, and the wideout or Z-back run his 3 route.

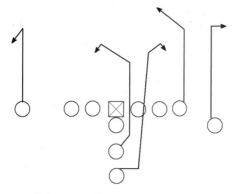

Diagram #4. 40 Pass—383

The routes for the backs are indicated by words. If we want to send a back out on this set, we would call it 383 choice. We start out calling it 383 choice, but as the season goes on the quarterbacks drop the word "choice" because the backs all know what to do on 383.

I want to go over each assignment on the play.

Item	Quarterback	Fullback
Assignment	Draw Fake	Protection Choice route
Drop or depth of route	Quick 5 or flip 3	4 yards
Coaching points	Key frontside corner	

Item	Running back	X-end or split end
Assignment	Fake 40 Protection Choice route	3 Route (break point)
Drop or depth	4 yards	10–12 yards
Coaching points	Key frontside	Convert to 9 vs. cover 2

Item	Y-receiver	Z-receiver
Assignment	8 Route	3 Route (speed)
Drop or depth	8–10 yards	Six-step rollout to 11 yards
Coaching points	Physical middle of field	Convert to 9 vs. cover 2

For the quarterback, you will see that he takes a quick 5 or a flip 3. If the quarterback is going to the left, there is not much faking on the play. The quarterback is going to go one, two, and three and throw the ball. When he gets on his third step, he spins or flips his hips and throws the ball. There is not a hitch involved. If the quarterback is going to his right, it is a quick five steps. He lets the ball go when he hits on that fifth step. Again, there is no hitch involved in this throw.

Most defenses will give up that part of the field. It is a timing route. The coaching point is important. All the quarterback does is to key the frontside corner on the play. The quarterback looks to see if there is a cushion for the receiver to run his route. If the defense is rolled up in cover 2, he will throw the ball deep to the tight end down the middle. If it is a soft corner, we throw the ball outside. This is a frontside throw. We could tag the play by adding the term 40 pass 383 X and throw the ball to the backside.

The Z-receiver is taking six steps and running a speed route. He should catch the ball—in a perfect world—at 11 yards. He takes six steps and rounds off his route. If we face a cover 2, we want the X-end to convert his route to a 9 route.

The tight end runs an 8 route. We want him in the middle of the field. We want him to align on the goal post so he will be in the middle of the field even when we are on one of the two hash marks.

The Z-back runs a break-point 3 route. He drives the defender off 12 yards and breaks off his route to the sideline. If we face cover 2, the Z-back converts to a fade route or to his 9 route.

If the tailback hears the word "choice," he knows that he is going to run that route. It is a four-yards-deep route. He gets over the tackle—tight end block and shows the quarterback his numbers. We do check off a lot to the choice routes. The fullback does the same thing as the tailback, but runs his choice to the backside at four yards deep.

The key for the play is the read by the quarterback. If the corners square up on our wideouts, we have a three-on-two situation, with the tight end and two backs. If the defense switches up on us and ends up in cover 1, which is man-free to us, the quarterback sees the defense in the face of the wide receiver and he must come off the play and throw the fade route to the outside man. It is a one-on-one situation for us on the outside. Our deep passes are built into our passing game. If we run 40 pass 383 a lot in a game, we are going to get a deep ball completed on the play.

The next play is good for us in the red zone. It is the same concept. We call 40 pass—787 choice (Diagram #5). The quarterback runs the draw fake. He takes a "big five drop." It is a standard five-step drop. We teach "big five" and "quick five" on the straight dropback and "big five" and "quick five" on the draw play. It is all the same except the quarterback turns his body differently. On a big five, the quarterback knows he is going to take a hitch step. He must learn with what routes to take the big five steps and the quick five steps. It is the same read for the quarterback.

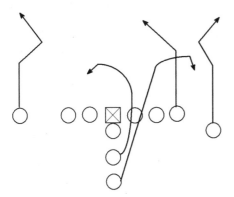

Diagram #5. 40 Pass—787 Choice

If we have a tight split by our Z-back, we try to run the majority of our routes two yards outside the hash marks. The way we call the play would be to call 40 pass 787 tight. That would move our Z-back inside tight next to our tight end. He has to adjust his pattern. Instead of running a 7 route, he would run what we call a step 7 route. The route takes a little longer to develop. We still get a one-on-one on the outside.

When we want to call a deep pass, we call 40 pass—558 choice (Diagram #6). We want to occupy the backside corner and backside safety. The quarterback takes his seven-step drop. If the frontside safety does not bite on the tight end, the quarterback can look for the choice routes underneath, or he can throw the ball to the tight end on the out route.

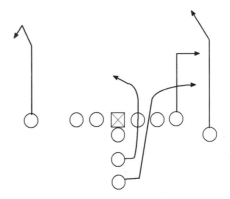

Diagram #6. 40 Pass—558 Choice

We have other passes off those plays. However, those are the three passes we use the most.

We do not meet all day and half of the night at Furman. I was talking to a coach today at lunch and I told him that we do not meet that long even during the season. My dad probably said it best. You can meet so long that some coaches lose confidence in a play and, before you know it, the staff votes to throw out a good football play in your offense. We are lucky at Furman, because we have six assistant coaches that are Furman graduates. Six of the eight coaches are alumni of Furman. We have a great staff and everyone knows what we want and what we are trying to accomplish.

This is as simple as it gets. We call this play naked-chop right-smash. We threw this pass 42 times and we averaged 9.5 plus yards per throw. First, I want to show you how we block on the play.

The offensive line slides down and blocks the back gaps. They are not turning. They are staying square. The fullback cuts the end man on the line of scrimmage (Diagram #7). I know high schools cannot cut defenders. The tailback fakes the run and protects to the backside.

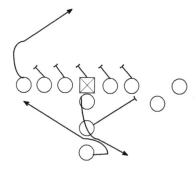

Diagram #7. Naked Chop Protection

You will see on the tape what the tailback does. He goes one, two, and three, crosses over, fakes the handoff, and protects the backside. It is a very little fake. All of the linemen are going in the same direction.

You can run a lot of different combinations on the outside with the two wide receivers. We run naked-chop right-smash. We can run naked-chop right-punch. We can run other pass plays from this set. On the smash, we run the slot receiver deep and he does not cut until his eighth step (Diagram #8). The outside receiver sits down at six yards.

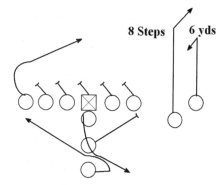

Diagram #8. Naked-Chop Right-Smash

This is a combination of our sprint game. It is the sprint game with counter action for the backs. If we get two men on the outside edge, we tell the fullback he has the most outside defender. We feel we can outrun the inside man.

If we gave the tight end a number to run on the play it would be a 2 route for him. The play would be 271. It would be naked-chop right-271 pass. The tight end knows he has a 2 route every time. The tight end wants to get to a depth of eight to 10 yards.

The inside receiver takes eight steps. We do not want him to cut the route short, because the counter fake gives us a little more time on the play. The outside receiver will go six yards and sometimes he will cut it off at five yards. If the defense is in man coverage, the outside man can run another pattern. It depends on what we want when the defense is in man.

If the defense is in cover 3, the quarterback has to get rid of the ball fast on the out route. We tell the inside receiver, if it is against cover 3 to drive off to eight yards and then to sit down. It is a smash adjustment. What we have is a stop route and a curl route on the outside.

We run the naked-chop right-punch. It is a simple change-up (Diagram #9). We like this play in the red zone. It is the same play action. The outside receivers are changing routes.

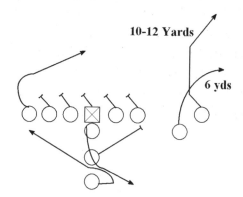

Diagram #9. Naked-Chop Right-Punch

We tell the tight end he is running the 2 route across the field on both the smash and punch. If he sees our inside receiver sit down on the play, he sits. If he does not see the inside receiver sit, he wants to get deep enough and across the field enough so that the quarterback can see him in the area behind the slotside tackle.

If you ask me to draw up the best route we have, this is what I will draw. We are an I-formation football team and we run the belly option. This is the best pass play that we have. I have had defensive coordinators come up to me before the game and say, "Coach Lamb, please run that belly option in the first quarter so we can get it over with." If we had enough guts, we would run the belly option at least one time per quarter. It is very hard play to defend.

First, I want to go over the belly option protection. We call the play our G-pass protection. (Diagram #10). First is the protection against a stack defense.

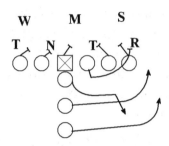

Diagram #10. G-Pass Protection

We pull the guard and he logs on the R defender. However, on the same play against the eagle X defense, we do not pull the guard. The fullback has to pick up the Sam linebacker on the eagle look (Diagram #11). We can make the pitch off the R defender or the Sam linebacker. We run the belly option and the belly option pass.

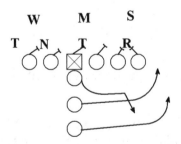

Diagram #11. G-Pass Protection Vs. Eagle X

Our tight end is going to block down in the C gap. He may not block anyone. He may be sitting on air. He delays two counts and then runs his route. He runs the zero route to the backside. We tell the quarterback that the tight end is open 99 percent of the time.

We call the play G-pass—802, or G-pass—208, or G-pass—202 (Diagram #12). We have two or three ways to run the play. We just call G-pass and our linemen know how to protect the play.

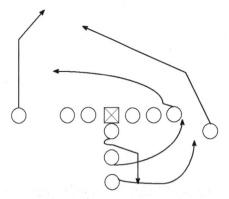

Diagram #12. G-Pass—802

If we get an under defense, we do not pull the guard on the play. Our tight end is going to slam that 5 technique. Then the end can release on his pass route. Our fullback checks the C gap to the D gap on both of these plays. He stays square and checks both gaps. This many not be the best protection in the world, but let me tell you this. If the quarterback gets flushed, we want him to scramble back to the split-end side because the tight end will be wide open.

Our Z-back is split two yards outside the hash mark. We want the split end to run deep and clear everything out on his side of the field. It is a three-level route. Our fullback comes down the line flat and wants to set up in the tackle-end gap, or the C gap and D gap. The tailback comes all the way around and carries out his fake.

You can run this play out of multiple sets. We do not stay in the I formation all of the time. The split end runs his 8 route. The tight end runs the zero route and the Z-back runs his 2 route.

The quarterback reverses as if he is going to come down the line of scrimmage. He wants to get as flat as he does on the option. He runs a quick five steps on the play. Then he looks for the receivers to find the open man. When he gets his depth, we tell him to find the back safety. If the back safety is running like crazy, then the 2 route is wide open. That is the Z-back. We read the defense from the top to the bottom.

Now we will go to the tapes of the plays I just covered. I appreciate your attention.

THE EIGHT-MAN FRONT WITH COVER 2

Colorado State University

Thank you. It is a pleasure to be here. I have not been to Mississippi often and, to be honest with you, my last trip was to Memphis at the Liberty Bowl. Before I start my talk, I want to tell all of you coaches here in Mississippi that Coach Orgeron is a great man and a great coach. We worked together some years back. We had some great teams and thought we were great coaches. We found out our players were pretty darn good.

I know he will do an excellent job at Mississippi and you guys will be proud of him. I heard the end of his speech and heard the enthusiasm and fire that he brings into coaching. I told him he needed to relax and enjoy coaching. He told me that if he lived to be my age, he would do that.

There may be a lot of truth to that. I am at the place in my career where the administration cannot do too much to me. If they want to get my contract and change it around, I may not show up for work. All they can do is fire me and I am ready to quit anyway.

I do not have a coach on my staff that has not been a high school teacher and coach. That means my coaches know how to present things to the players. I have to confess that I do not get in with the team and conduct chalk talks on the board anymore. However, I do chew out the coaches. That is what head coaches do these days. I go into the coaches' meetings, chew their butts out, and walk out and let them straighten things out. An old coach gave me a good piece of advice. When I worked for Jack Elway at Stanford, he gave me the key to handling problems. If an assistant coach came in with a problem, the trick was to put the problem right back on him as he left the room. Let him find the solution, because we cannot figure out everything.

Let me get into the football end of the talk. Our defense at Colorado State is the product of many years of study and association with some good coaches. Most of the defense we run at Colorado State comes from Monte Kiffin. One of Monte's sons was a graduate assistant for us at Colorado State. He is now the defensive coordinator at USC. I tell everyone that he got his start with us, but he was with us only about six months. Monte's younger son played four years for us.

Coach Kiffin spent about one month a year with us talking football and schemes. We learned most of the things we run from his schemes. He is the guru on the 4-3 defense. That is my topic today, along with the incorporation of cover 2 with that defense.

We run cover 2 because it is a good coverage for first down as well as third down. In football today, from high school to college, you cannot set in one coverage and expect to stop people. Today, we have a pass coverage for every down and distance. We also have a coverage for personnel groups we use in the games. Cover 2 for us is the starting point and we expand from there. We play the coverage about 20 percent of the time. The cover 2 shell is the defense we show on each snap. We seldom play the coverage on first down, but we must play it to keep the offense honest.

If the offensive coordinator knows we never roll up in cover 2 on first down, the hitch pattern is the pattern they throw. We cannot let that happen. We must keep the offense guessing as to the coverage we play.

We show the cover 2 shell, because it is a good coverage to roll down into the eight-man front. With two safeties in the game, we get an opportunity to disguise our run support. We play the strong safety down and play man coverage with the free safety in the middle of the field. We drop the free safety down and play another coverage. We can drop the strong or free safety down, shift the linebacker over, and get into the eight-man front.

We call our base defense an over cover 2 (Diagram #1). We tilt the front toward the tight end. To the tight end, we play a defensive end head up on the tight end in a 6 technique. The openside defensive end aligns in a 5 technique on the outside shoulder of the offensive tackle. The defensive tackle is in a 3 technique to the tight-end side and the nose tackle aligns in a backside shade on the center.

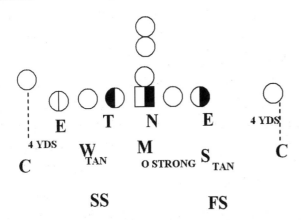

Diagram #1. Over Cover 2

Two years ago, we never played an over cover 2 against an I-formation team. We were afraid of the run and we did not think we could hold up against a strong running team. We play the over cover 2 better today against the run than we ever thought we could.

The 6-technique defensive end is responsible for the C gap to his side. The defensive tackle is responsible for the B gap. The nose tackle has the weakside A gap. The 5-technique defensive end is a C-gap player. They take as much of the football as they can in their alignments. The nose tackle is in a slight tilt. The first thing the down linemen want to do is get off the ball as fast as they can. They align with their inside hand down and the inside foot back. They scream off the ball, reading high hat and low hat.

We have three linebackers. The Sam and Will linebackers align in what we describe as a "tan" alignment. That simply means that they are head up on the offensive tackles. The Mike linebacker aligns in a 0 technique on the center. We call his alignment a strong 0 because he has the strongside A gap.

In the secondary, we align in a cover 2 alignment. The corners are four yards deep with an outside shade forcing the wide receivers to the inside. We call the cover 2 scheme Tampa 2. The name comes from the Tampa Bay Buccaneers. We have run this coverage for the past seven years. From the first day of practice, we tell our corners that the only way we can play cover 2 is for them to get a reroute on the receivers.

The corner aligns at four yards, looking inside at the quarterback. When the offense snaps the ball and he reads pass, his eyes come back to the receiver. He has to get his hands on the receiver for the reroute. After he gets his hands on the receiver, his eyes come back inside to the quarterback. If the receiver wants to go outside, the corner shuffles with him, pivots back inside, and gets ready to play the crossing pattern from the other side. His depth in his drop is around seven yards.

The safeties align at the magic depth of 12 yards. I do not know where that number comes from, but it sounds good. If the ball is in the middle of the field, the safeties align two yards outside the hash marks. On the snap of the ball, the safeties shuffle back, getting width as they go. Their landmark is half-way between the top of the numbers and the hash mark. That puts the safeties about nine yards from the sidelines. They can play the fade by the wide receivers if the corners get the reroute.

The Mike linebacker reads his keys and recognizes pass. He drops to the strongside and takes anything coming down the middle of the field. He is running for depth and playing the middle third. He plays anything down the middle of the football field between the hash marks.

People do not think you can play the middle linebacker in the deep middle of the field. We have played this defense for seven years. The middle linebacker we had this year was 6'4", 240 pounds, and ran 4.8 in the 40-yard dash.

Everyone has a job to do in this coverage. If everyone does what they are supposed to do, we are sound. Everyone thinks that you can dump the ball in the middle after the middle linebacker runs deep. They think the check-down patterns by the offensive backs will net big gains. The Will and Sam linebackers are the seam players who can react back to those patterns. The backs may catch the ball, but they will pay for it. The seam players never get deeper than 12 yards. They react to play-action and never get that deep before the quarterback throws the ball. They have the responsibility for the check-down patterns. They read the quarterback, protect the seams, and drive on the check-down patterns.

We do not play this coverage every play of the game. We use it about 20 percent of the time. However, we disguise the rest of our schemes from the coverage. We look like a cover 2 defense on every play. The reason we have it is to keep the offensive coordinator from throwing the hitch any time he needs six yards. If they do not know when you roll the corners, they cannot throw the hitch at will. We want to take the quick game away from the offense.

Against the wide slot formation, we slide our linebackers to the slot. The Sam linebacker steps out to the slotside in a walk-off position (Diagram #2). He splits the difference between the number 1

and number 2 receivers in the slot. If the ball runs toward him, he is the outside force. His pass coverage is the same as it was in a regular set. The four down linemen's alignment remains the same as the previous defense and their gap responsibilities do not change. The Mike and Will linebacker slide to the slotside and the backside corner slides down to a depth of four yards outside the tight end. This gives us the eight-man front.

The corner has the D gap to the backside on the run. He plays his normal coverage on any pass. The Will linebacker moves into a stack position behind the 3-technique tackle and is responsible for the A gap to his side. The Mike linebacker moves over the guard to the slotside and has the B gap to his side. We cover all gaps in the running game and the secondary coverage does not change.

If the offense runs a slotside isolation-type play (Diagram #3), we fill on the fullback with the Mike linebacker. He attacks the fullback, forcing the ball back inside. The Will linebacker fills over the nose tackle and makes the tackle. If the ball cuts back into the vacated A gap, the strong safety becomes the cutback player and fills the backside A gap.

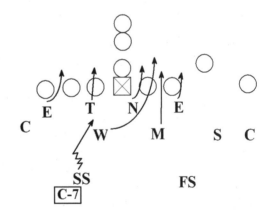

Diagram #3. Isolation to the Slot

It is my job to coach the strong safety. I work with him in the spring and prefall practice on his steps to cover this technique. He keys the quarterback and reacts to play-action by shuffling back for two steps. Once he reads the run, he fills from depth into the A gap. We call his alignment C-7. That means he aligns in the C gap, seven yards deep.

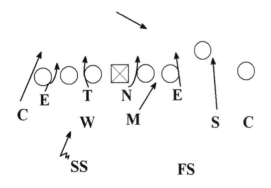

Diagram #2. Cover 2 Vs. Wide Slot

The play the offense tries to take advantage of the C-7 alignment with is a strong flow throwback pass (Diagram #4). The offense shows a strong flow with the two backs in the backfield. They run play-action pass, trying to hit the slot receiver down the middle of the field. They think they can beat the strong safety deep down the middle of the field. Our gap responsibility on the run is sound, because the nose tackle sits in the cutback gap to the backside.

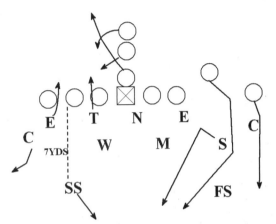

Diagram #4. Strong Flow Throwback

We get both linebackers into the A gap and coverage on all other gaps. The key to stopping the throw back to the slot receiver is the Sam linebacker. He aligns on the slot receiver. When he sees flow away, he gets under the slot receiver and carries him deep. That is his primary pursuit angle. When he recognizes the play-action pass, it becomes his coverage.

The coaching point for the strong safety is to recognize the tight end releasing. He shuffles back and has to realize the corner route run by the tight end is not his coverage. He is responsible for the deep pattern, but he gets help from the corner on an outside pattern by the tight end. We want him nice and deep, and able to play either way on the deep ball.

If the offense flexes or splits the tight end off the formation, we lose a gap on the outside to the strongside. We check to what we call pirate (Diagram #5). On the pirate call, the 6-technique end drops down into a 5 technique on the outside shoulder of the offensive tackle. On the snap of the ball, the defensive end and 3-technique tackle slant

into the B gap and A gap. The check frees the Mike linebacker and he becomes a fast flow player to either side of the defense.

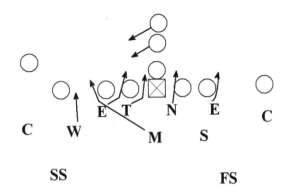

Diagram #5. Pirate

We call the over pirate 2 as a defensive call. However, in certain situations we check to it as an automatic. Everything else in the defense remains the same as far as gap and pass responsibility. This check cuts down on the teaching for the linebackers.

The first two years we ran this defense, we went to pirate automatically. We did not realize it, but it became a tendency of our defense. Teams we played began to bank on us making the pirate adjustment and blocked us pretty well. Now when we play the defense, we only get in the pirate about one out of every four plays. That keeps the offensive line coach guessing.

If the offense aligns in a one-back set with one tight end, the pirate is a good call (Diagram #6). The running strength is toward the tight end. We take

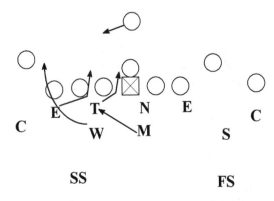

Diagram #6. Pirate Vs. 11 Personnel

the 6-techinique end and slant him all the way to the B gap. The 3-technique tackle slant into the A gap. That allows the Will and Mike linebackers to be extremely aggressive in the C gap. Nothing changes for anyone else in the defense. We have all gaps covered and have a sound scheme in the secondary.

For every good thing, there is a bad thing. I think some guy like Shakespeare said that. The deal with pirate is the pass rush suffers when you run this stunt. So you gain something in the running game, but give up something in the passing game.

If the offense aligns in an ace formation, we still can play the cover 2 scheme (Diagram #7). With two tight ends and two wideouts, we declare a side for the over call. In the diagram, we are over to the left. The 6-technique end and 3-technique tackle align to the left. The shade nose tackle and 5-technique end widen their techniques somewhat. They still have the same gap responsibility. The Sam linebacker moves outside over the second tight end and has D-gap responsibility.

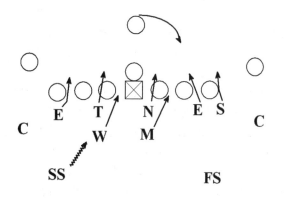

Diagram #7. Cover 2 Vs. Ace

The Mike linebacker cheats slightly to the weakside, because on flow that way he has to fill the B gap. Since the Will linebacker fills the A gap on flow away, we need help in one gap to the backside. The strong safety gives help to the backside on cutback runs that way.

To handle a trips set with a tight end to the trips side, we need to adjust (Diagram #8). The down linemen remain the same in their alignment and gap responsibility. The Will linebacker moves out to the

slot receiver in the twin formation. The Mike linebacker moves into a tan technique over the tackle. The Sam linebacker moves into a stack behind the nose tackle. On flow to the tight end, the Sam linebacker fills the strongside A gap. The Mike linebacker is fitting into the D gap. The Will linebacker is over the slotback and becomes the force player.

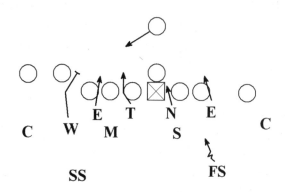

Diagram #8. Cover 2 Vs. Tight End Trips

If flow goes to the openside of the formation, the linebackers fall back into their flow on the ball. The secondary remains the same regarding responsibility. The free safety can give us help on flow toward him.

If the offense runs the trips set with three wide receivers to one side and the tight end to the other, the adjustment is similar (Diagram #9). To the tight-end side, the corner rolls down to four yards outside the tight end. He has the D gap on run his way. The 6-technique end has the C gap and the 3-technique tackle has the B gap.

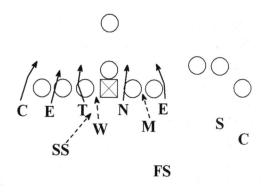

Diagram #9. Cover 2 Vs. Wide Trips

The Will linebacker moves to a 0 technique over the center. He has the A gap on flow toward the tight end and the B gap on flow away from the tight end. The nose tackle is the A-gap player to the openside. The 5-technique end has the C gap on flow to him. The Mike linebacker stacks behind the 5 technique and becomes a D-gap player on flow to him and a B-gap player on flow away from him.

The Sam linebacker aligns on the slot receivers in the trips set and is a seam player. The strong safety moves up to a C-7 position and becomes the cutback player on flow away from him.

The next thing I want to show you is coverage against a split-flow bootleg. In this play, the fullback seeps out into the flat to the side of the bootleg (Diagram #10). The quarterback fakes to the second back going the other direction and comes out on the bootleg. The corner to the bootleg side reroutes his receiver and stays in the flat. He looks for the shallow cross, but in this case he picks up the fullback in the flat and runs with him on the waggle.

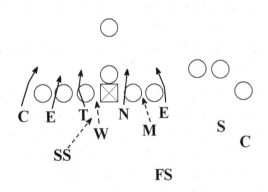

Diagram #10. Cover 2 Vs. Bootleg

The tight end runs a deep crossing pattern across the field. The Will linebacker fills to the line and retreats to his curl. The Sam linebacker drops and has all crosses coming from the other side. The safeties shuffle and get into their halves. The Mike linebacker has to become the secondary contain on the play. We hope the 5-technique end can get out to contain the bootleg, but he may be caught inside. In that case, the Mike linebacker has to contain any breakouts by the quarterback.

From the wide slot, the coverage is almost the same. We align in the C-7 alignment for the strong safety, with the corner up on the line of scrimmage. We still read the bootleg the same way. The corner has to tell the difference between a block and a pass release. He contacts the tight end and gets into his shuffle. When he finds the ball, he settles and looks for the cross coming his way. The corner to the slotside reroutes and stays in the flat. The Sam linebacker is the seam player and looks for the deep cross or the dig pattern down the field. The Mike linebacker is the secondary contain man.

The problem we had was with the Mike linebacker. When we first put this defense in, the Mike linebacker got killed by the tight end deep down the middle of the field. With the play-action fake, the Mike linebacker missed the tight end and it caused some big trouble. The remedy for that mistake was the use of the pirate call. The Mike linebacker's responsibility on the pirate call leads him to the tight end coming up the field.

When teams run the power off-tackle play, we had to work our fits just like the isolation (Diagram #11). The coaching point is with the Sam linebacker. When the offense pulls the backside guard to get him into the off-tackle hole, the Sam linebacker sees the pull. He knows that when the guard pulls there is no cutback lane left on the backside. The nose tackle plays the A gap backside with no one outside him to block down and collapse him. The Sam linebacker fills across the center into the strongside A gap. That allows the Mike linebacker to be aggressive with his fit inside the Will linebacker on the outside.

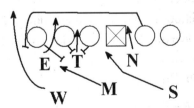

Diagram #11. Cover 2 Vs. Power 0

The end has the C gap and the tackle has the B gap. The Will linebacker fills in the D gap with the Mike linebacker fitting inside him.

The offense from the wide slot formation will work the backside (Diagram #12). They use play-action to get the fullback into the flat and the tight end on the corner route. Our alignment is a C-7 alignment for the strong safety and backside corner. The thing we use to separate the play-action pass and the run is the angle of the fullback. This presents no problem for the corner, because he is in a position to play either play. The problem is with the strong safety. He has to recognize the angle the fullback uses as well as the release of the tight end.

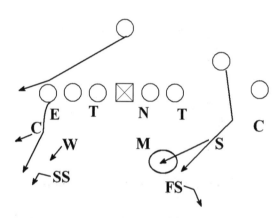

Diagram #12. Fullback Power Angle

The corner sees the angle the fullback uses. He starts by looking for the fullback to kick out the outside force. As the fullback continues to the flat, the corner collisions him, and latches on to his pattern. The angle the fullback takes is not a downhill path like the isolation play. It is what we refer to as a power angle. As soon as the C-7 player sees the power angle of the fullback, he takes his shuffle to the outside. He reads the tight end and gets to the top of the numbers. We tell him the offense will throw to the tight end 12 yards deep and to the outside.

On the backside, the Sam linebacker keys the flow away. He steps into his responsibility and reads the play-action pass. He gets depth down the middle and helps us on the slot receiver trying to get to the deep middle. We do not need him to the

playside, even if it were a running play. We have all the gaps covered and we need him to help the secondary on the throwback pass.

We need another scheme to help us with the over defense. We run the over zone-Y (Diagram #13). We feel good about the over defense, but you need a change-up. The front is the same, but we bring the strong safety down to zone the Y side. If we bring the free safety down, we call the scheme over zone-X. The strong safety comes down to the outside of the tight end in a two-by-four alignment.

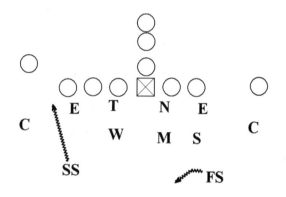

Diagram #13. Over Zone-Y

The alignment of the strong safety is two yards outside and four yards deep from the tight end. The strong safety gives us the eight-man front. We tighten the Will linebacker into a stack behind the 3-technique tackle. With the safety down, the Will linebacker does not have force responsibility to his side.

We roll the free safety back into the middle of the field and play a three-deep with four under coverage. We start out in the cover 2 look and move to the zone-Y at the last second.

On first down, if the offense comes out in a pro I formation, chances are we will be in an eight-man front. The corners align in their normal four-yard alignment on the wide receivers as they would in cover 2. Before the quarterback snaps the ball, they bail out into their deep thirds. The strong safety has the flat area. The Will linebacker works from the hook area into the curl zone. The Mike linebacker works the hook to curl to the weakside and the Sam linebacker works the flat to his side.

If the offense runs the bootleg with the defense in the zone-Y, we play the defense (Diagram #14). The strong safety drops down and buzzes the flat area. If the offense wants to throw the hitch route, they can probably complete it. We hang the strong safety in the flat area and do not widen him outside. The Will linebacker reacts to the run fake and retreats to the hook zone. The Mike linebacker reacts to the run fake, then begins to look for the crossing route. That is the favorite pattern for the bootleg pass.

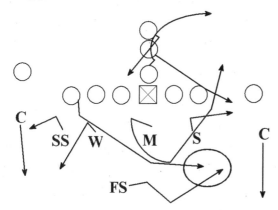

Diagram #14. Over-Y Vs. Bootleg

The Mike linebacker carries the cross and then reacts back as the secondary containment. The Sam linebacker plays the flat area. The free safety keys the quarterback. If he remains square in the pocket, he hangs in the middle third. If the quarterback comes out of the pocket and turns his shoulder toward the sidelines, the safety breaks on the deep cross pattern. We use that technique in all our secondary coverages.

Two years ago, we did a bad job of coaching. We played Boston College. On their first play from scrimmage, they ran the bootleg pass. We coached the safety to key the quarterback's shoulders and drive on the cross. The quarterback ran his bootleg fake, stepped toward the sideline, stepped back, and hit the flanker on a post cut for a touchdown. We did a poor job of relaying the importance of staying in the hole until the quarterback commits to the sidelines.

When the quarterback commits to running to the sidelines, there are only two places to throw the ball. He can throw the ball into the deep third in the direction he is running or, at best, he may be able to hit the cross route. He cannot throw the ball down the middle of the field with any depth. If he tries to throw to the cross route, it is an easy interception for the safety. As long as the quarterback runs, the safety can come out of the hole.

If the offense trades their tight end, we have the answer with the zone-Y. We call the trading of the tight end from one side to the other China (Diagram #15). When the tight end trades to the other side, the defense becomes an under defense. We do not move any of the down linemen. The 6-technique end tightens his alignment to a 5 technique. The Sam linebacker moves up to the line of scrimmage into a 9 technique on the tight end.

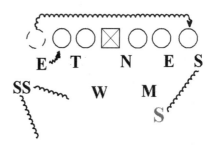

Diagram #15. Zone-Y Vs. China

The Mike linebacker bumps over to the B-gap alignment to the tight end. The Will linebacker bumps over into the A gap. The strong safety drops down into the Tan position behind the 5-technique end.

The zone-Y defense has no problem with a trips set (Diagram #16). If the offense goes into a three-by-one set, we drop the strong safety down and match up on the outside slot receiver in the trips set. The Will linebacker matches up with the inside

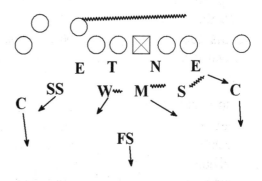

Diagram #16. Zone-Y Vs. Trips

slot receiver. If the inside slot trades to the other side, the linebackers bump over and the Sam linebacker comes to the line and matches up with the traded slot.

Everyone that plays against a three-deep safety tries to run four verticals on the safety. The receivers aligned in the slot should have trouble getting deep if we do our job. The only way to protect the single safety is to beat the hell out of the slot receivers as they try to get up the hash marks.

The run fits are the same when we play the zone-Y defense. Our safety is 10 yards deep before he drops down. He times his move so that he arrives at his position as the quarterback snaps the ball. He is the outside force on running plays his way. The run fits are different for the isolation run at the Mike linebacker (Diagram #17). With the strong safety down, the Mike linebacker attacks the fullback's block using inside leverage. He bounces the ball to the outside and the Will linebacker fits outside of him. The Will linebacker does not worry about it if the ball bounces outside, because the strong safety is out there.

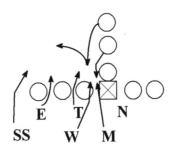

Diagram #17. Run Fit

The off-tackle power play also benefits from the strong safety down, as far as run fits are concerned (Diagram #18). The Will linebacker fits inside the strong safety and the Mike linebacker fits inside the Will linebacker. The Sam linebacker fits in the strongside A gap, because there is no cutback with a pulling guard.

The play we see now is the split belly or split zone play. Two years ago, the big play was the power O. With the strong safety down in the zone-Y, we play single-gap football. That allows the

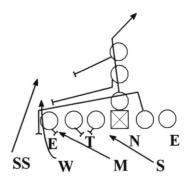

Diagram #18. Power O

linebacker to run through their gaps and put pressure on the split zone play (Diagram # 19). When the linebackers recognize the play, the Will linebacker runs through the strongside A gap. The Mike linebacker runs through the weakside B gap. The defensive ends fill the C gaps. The 3-technique tackle fills the B gap to the strongside and the nose tackle fills the A gap to the weakside. The Sam linebacker and strong safety come off the edges in the D gap. That covers all gaps and gives the zone play nowhere to run.

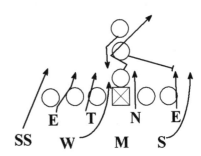

Diagram #19. Split Zone Play

The zone-Y will stop the run because it is an eight-man front. To stop the run, we give up the hitch. If you take something away, you have to give something up. We broke down all our tapes for the year this past week. It is amazing that with the ball on the hash mark, 82 percent of the balls thrown were into the sideline. It is an easy throw and produces yardage. That is why we have to roll up in cover 2. We have to make the quarterback think twice before he throws the hitch or quick pattern to the short side.

People may be catching up to what we do on defense, but I do not care. We play man-to-man coverage in our scheme. When we get to third-and-four or less for the first down, we play man-to-man. The offensive coordinators should listen to this.

My offensive coordinator is the funniest son of a gun in the world. We played San Diego State this year and had a third-and-30 for a first down. On third down, anything over 10 yards meant he ran the draw. The fans boo every time we do it and want to fire me. That is a smart play, but everyone wants to kill him. We had third-and-30 yards to go from our own 15-yard line. We led by three points and the clock was running out. He ran the draw play and gained 31 yards. We ran out the clock and won the game. People in the stands think I call the plays. They boo me and I am not calling that crap.

I know I digress a bit and get off the subject, but that is the way I am. If it is third-and-four or less for the first down, we play man-to-man in the secondary. Third-and-three yards for the first down is a tough call. If the offense has trouble running the ball, I know they will try to throw for the first down. In that situation we are in tough bump-man coverage. It takes courage to throw the fade. If you do not make the catch, you have to punt the ball.

For every rule, there is an exception. I told you that we play man coverage on every third-down-and-four-or-less situation. We play man coverage on every short-yardage play, except the ones we do not. If we think you will run the fade, we fake the bump, bail out, and beat the receiver to the fade route. The call for the bail out is zone-Y box. That tells the corner to pivot and box out the receiver going for the fade. That gives us another way to play the receiver on the outside and not give up the hitch route.

When we add the term black to the zone-Y call, we put the strong safety in man coverage on the tight end (Diagram #20). The alignment is the same as any over defense. The corners are in man coverage and the safety is free in the middle of the field. The defense plays any run to the backside the same as they did on the regular zone-Y scheme.

The defense spills any play run to the strong safety's side. The strong safety does not force the

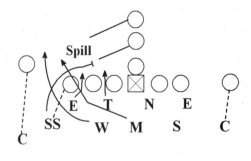

Diagram #20. Over Black

run. He spills everything outside. The Will and Mike linebackers run hard from the inside and play over the top of the strong safety to the outside. The tight end should never catch a pass. He cannot take an inside release, because the 6-technique takes that release away from him. When he releases outside, the strong safety hits him right in the mouth.

If you want techniques, you must talk to my assistant coaches. I know schemes. I do not coach that area of the game anymore. I have a good group of assistants and they had better know what they are doing. I pay them well.

There was a question asked about what type of goal-line defense we play. This past season was the first time in five years that we played a goal-line defense. I think we played eight plays of goal-line defense this season. We played over black as our goal-line defense before last year.

The last thing I want to get to is cover 82. This is the companion scheme to the zone-Y coverage. In this coverage, we roll the free safety down to a depth of four yards. This counters teams that try to run away from the strong safety in the eight-man front. We bring the strong safety into the middle third and roll the free safety down to give us the eight-man front to the openside of the formation.

I know you play good football in the state of Mississippi. I hope you support the program that Ed Orgeron is trying to build. I want to thank you for your attention.

RED ZONE OFFENSE

Louisiana State University

Thank you, gentlemen. It is a pleasure to be here.

As you saw with what went on at LSU this year, we had a challenging season to say the least. We graduated 21 seniors and brought in a new coaching staff. The senior class that graduated this past year was the most successful class in the history of Louisiana State University.

We made a T-shirt for those 21 seniors and put the list of accomplishments on the back of the shirt. On the front of that shirt, we printed Challenge Issued. We issued the underclassmen shirts that said on the front Challenge Accepted. The challenge was to make this program continue to run at a championship level.

When LSU hired me as head coach, they told me they would give me every opportunity to run the finest college football program in the nation. To this day, they have not denied me anything I asked for. They have never said no to me, from facilities to academic support.

Tonight I will talk about the red zone and our approach to it offensively. To be a good football team, you have to execute in the red zone. In the red zone is not the time to do something new. In the red zone, you must do the things that give identity to your offense.

Without success in the red zone, South Carolina would not have been eligible for a bowl game. Arkansas's late run was connected to the red-zone success they had late in the season. Our team enjoyed an 85-percent success rate in the red zone. Our goal was to score every time we entered the red zone. Our success in the red zone spoke to our ability to win games in critical times.

When we get into the red zone, we must avoid negative plays. Red-zone penalties were something the offense could not have. We changed cadence regularly. We changed repeatedly so we knew how to handle a situation when we had cadence change. I could recall two particular turnovers in the red zone during the season. Against Arizona State, our quarterback fumbled the ball in the red zone early in the game, which cost us a chance to go up by 10 points.

We tried to identify the red zone more definitively than other teams. We considered the red zone to be from the 25-yard line to the goal line. Defenses began to attack us differently at the 25-yard line instead of the 20-yard line. We considered the 25-yard line to the 15-yard line to be the "Red Zone." We considered from the 15-yard line to the five-yard line to be the "Tight Zone." In the "Tight Zone," we felt we could still run the ball for first downs. We called the five-yard line to the end zone the "Goal-Line Zone."

When we set up our game plan, we used those zones to define the plays we ran. In our practice, we practiced those zone plays. Early in the week, we practiced tight zone offense, because we encountered a specific coverage from teams. We wanted to throw the routes against that coverage early in the week. We also identified the runs we thought we could rely on to be effective against that type of defense.

We felt that if we got the ball to the five-yard line, we could run it into the end zone. We had great confidence in our goal-line offense. Our execution in our goal-line offense was outstanding.

We practiced tight zone plays on Tuesday. On Wednesday, we practice our red-zone offense. On Thursday, we practiced strong red-zone plays, along with our first-and-10 situations. In the red zone, our run/pass relationship was 61 runs to 40 passes. That imbalance came from the fact that we ran the ball so much more in the tight and goal-line zones.

We had 31 attempts in the red zone. We considered an attempt to be a possession that scored a touchdown or converted a first down in that zone. That was an 84 percent efficiency rate in the red zone. We also scored six touchdowns from the 25-yard line and outside that line.

In the red zone, we ran any formation or personnel grouping we had in the offense. We preferred to run zone plays, gap-scheme plays, and an occasional man-scheme draw play. Anytime we felt the defense wanted to blitz, we ran zone-scheme plays. We used motion and bunch sets to counter man-to-man coverage.

In the red zone, we liked to run the zone play (Diagram #1). On this particular play, we faked the reverse. The action by the motion back brought the defensive end up the field and made the block by the fullback easier. That block created a big seam inside for the tailback.

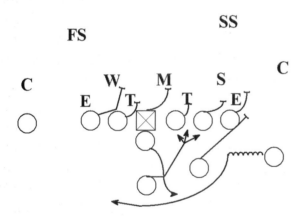

Diagram #1. Zone Play

The reverse was a red-zone play for us. The fake off the reverse was a quality fake. It affected the linebackers and the end and made the dash play more effective.

Another staple play we ran in the red zone was the stretch play (Diagram #2). We ran it toward the tight end. We liked to get the guard around on the outside linebacker and blocked the support with our wide receivers. We used the concept of the zone scheme and built in small adjustments to the plays.

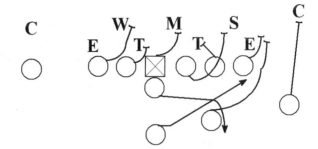

Diagram #2. Stretch

One of the adjustments we built into the play was the stretch play run with a crackback block by the wide receiver on the support (Diagram #3). If we could zone scheme with our offensive line and get a hat on a hat, we thought we could win. We cracked back with the fullback running an arc block on the corner.

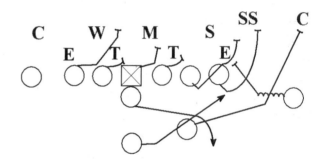

Diagram #3. Stretch Crack

In this defense, they have dropped the strong safety down into the box and got an eight-man front. They still had a high safety in the middle. We cracked on the defensive end and strong safety and zoned up for the Will linebacker. The fullback ran the arc block for the corner and the tailback took the play outside.

Against the eight-man front, we ran a simple off-tackle power (Diagram #4). We motioned the wide receiver inside as we did on the crack. The tight end turned out on the defensive end and the backside guard and fullback turned up inside the block of the end.

From the same action, we threw the power pass (Diagram #5). The offensive line used a zone scheme and blocked away from the play. We could build all types of patterns into the offense, depending on what the defense gave us. On this

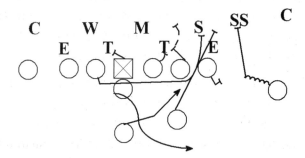

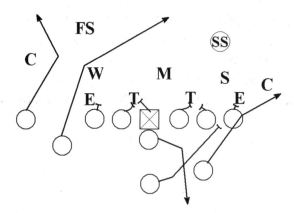

Diagram #4. Power O

free safety sat on the tight end and we ran the slotback behind him for the score. The set was a two-back, tight-end set with a wide slot to the backside.

Diagram #6. Power Pass Throwback

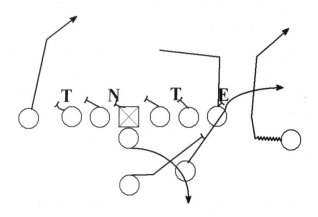

Diagram #5. Power O Pass

particular play, we built the cross route in for the tight end. The tight end collisioned the defensive end and worked his way across the field. The fullback and tailback ran the power fake.

The fullback continued into the flat and the tailback blocked the defensive end. We tried to work the corner pattern of the wide receiver route behind the safety.

Our checks in the red zone had to be sound. We had two veteran quarterbacks that did an excellent job and put us in the right play. The plays you saw on the film were not checks. We felt we needed the ability to aggressively call plays and run them regardless of the defense.

The key to scoring in the red zone was to get a first down in the tight zone. If we could pick up the first down in the tight zone, we would score. The play-action pass was a mainstay in this zone (Diagram #6). On this play, we used the same type action, except we blocked the tight end down. The

If you run this type of offense, change up the patterns of the receivers out of the same look. We had used the Z-receiver to the flag and post. On the flag route, we crossed the tight end. On the post route, we blocked the tight end. On each play, the fullback had been in the flat. This all came off the power-O pass.

An effective play-action for us had been the naked bootleg off the stretch fake (Diagram #7). On this play, the fullback and tailback faked the stretch to the strongside. The split end ran a flag with the tight end running a shallow drag route. The flanker back to the backside ran a deep cross. However, he wanted to catch the ball before he crossed the hash marks. He wanted to stay out of that area, because we had a tight end around the numbers and the split end in the end zone.

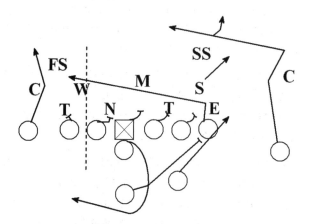

Diagram #7. Naked

The deep cross was a throw our quarterback could make. He knew to throw the ball before the flanker has to set down on the hash marks.

In this area, we ran the bunch set along with the power-O pass (Diagram #8). In our combination pattern, the tight end ran the vertical pass. The flanker ran a sit-down pattern at five yards outside and seven yard deep. The fullback ran the flat route in a rub type of scheme. On this particular play, the quarterback read zero coverage and had to throw the ball in a hurry. The fullback made a great catch on this play.

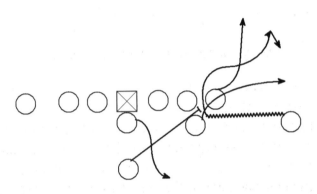

Diagram #8. Bunch Set

The next play you see was what everyone ran in this area. It was a seven-yard slant play. We threw this pattern from a three-step drop, which allowed the quarterback to release the ball quickly. This was an execution type of play. Either you completed the pass or it is incomplete. There was no sack and the intercepted pass seldom happened. It was a high-percentage play for us. This type of play was generally a checked play. The quarterback saw a mismatch or light coverage. The best way to throw the pass was from under center, but our quarterback had large hands and could execute the throw from the shotgun very well.

We also threw the quick five-step skinny post using the same kind of thinking. It allowed the quarterback to get rid of the ball quickly and became a relatively safe throw.

When we got into the tight zone, we were 30/30 with the run and pass. We ran the ball 30 times and passed it 30 times, for a 1:1 ratio. That was what we try to do in this area. We felt that in the

tight zone we could drive for a first down. The comfort was you did not have to score a touchdown in this zone. The run and pass are quality calls as long as you execute. We were 82 percent efficient in the tight zone, with seven touchdowns.

In the tight zone, we routinely went on fourth down. Of course, that depended on the situation and score of the game. We went on fourth down three times during the season. Even if you do not make the first down, you turn the ball over to the opponent deep in his own territory. We have confidence in our defense to hold the opponent and turn the ball back to our offense in good field position.

In the tight zone, we ran more two-tight-end formations. We ran two tight ends, one back, and two wide receivers. We also ran two tight ends, two backs, and one wide receiver. Generally, in a one-wide-receiver set in the tight zone, you got one-on-one coverage. If you had a good wide receiver, that could be a mismatch.

If you had confidence in your passing game, you could throw some simple routes. We threw the slant, comeback, and out. If the defense rolled to our single receiver, it gave us numbers in the running game. When the defense rolled to the single receiver, they still did not keep you from throwing the ball to that receiver. However, when they rolled to the single receiver, they could not cover the run. That meant you could still pass or run the ball.

On this play, we take advantage of the defensive alignment of the Mike linebacker on our fullback. Instead of aligning in his proper position, he aligned over the right guard on the fullback. We stepped the flanker up on the line of scrimmage and slotted the second tight end (Diagram #9). He came in motion to the weakside and blocked the defensive end. We took the fullback to the strongside and countered back with the tailback. Because the Mike linebacker was keying the fullback, he left a nice seam as he vacated to follow the fullback.

The next play we ran twice this year. We ran it once in the first game and once in the bowl game against Miami. We did not run this play any time in

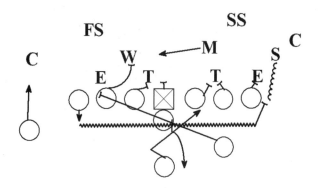

Diagram #9. Counter

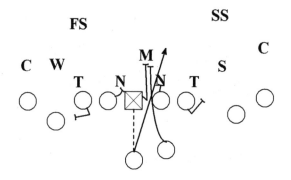

Diagram #11. Quarterback Draw

between those two games. You could not make a living out of this play because it was easy to stop. We faked the fullback over the center and pitched the ball to the tailback running wide (Diagram #10). We got in a set that tells the defense to cover the run. The nature of the play defeated the defensive tackle and linebacker. We did not need to block them because of the speed of the play outside.

In a tight-zone situation, we liked to flood the pattern (Diagram #12). Toward the flanker side, we ran the tight end on a vertical route. The flanker ran a five-yard sit-down route and the fullback ran the flat route. The tailback blocked the first man outside the tackle.

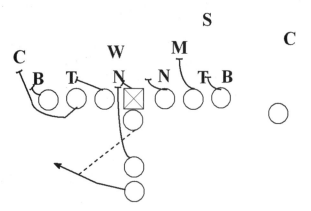

Diagram #10. Quick Pitch

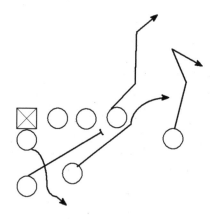

Diagram #12. Flood

If the defensive end and corner keyed and kept themselves square, they could make the play. This was a surprise play to the outside and a great change-up.

We had a large and confident running quarterback. On third down, with three yards to go for the first down or touchdown (Diagram #11), we could run our quarterback. We got into a passing set, which allowed us to get blocking numbers to the inside. We spread the formation and ran the quarterback draw, with the fullback leading up on the Mike linebacker. The blocking put a body on a body and the quarterback with the ball. He was a big body himself.

It was easy to change up the patterns with a tag call. We called the series and tagged a receiver with a different pattern.

This next play on the film shows a pattern for the single receiver. It was probably a check call from the quarterback, who read the safety down in the alley to stop the run. It was a simple choice route for the single receiver. He ran his pattern off the defender. He had the choice of sitting down on the pattern or continuing it upfield.

The power pass away from the two-receiver side was a good play in the red zone (Diagram #13). The tight end read first and ran a flat cut. The backside tight end ran the shallow cross. The flanker ran a deep cross. The read for the

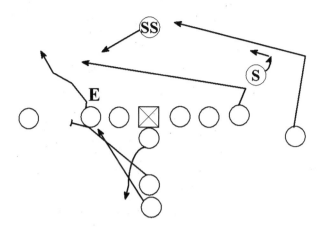

Diagram #13. Power Pass Away

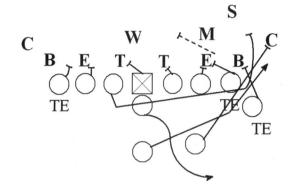

Diagram #14. Goal-Line Power

quarterback was to the tight end first. If he was not open, the quarterback read the safety. The safety is the key. If he came down on the tight end crossing pattern, the quarterback took the mesh route coming across deep. The quarterback had to check for the backside linebacker getting under the flanker before he threw the mesh.

On occasion, we put five receivers on the field. It could be four receivers and a tailback, but the set was the same. We looked for mismatches in the defense with these personnel on the field. In the clip, the safety plays to the three-receiver side with no high safety on that side. That meant the receivers were one-on-one with the defenders.

In the goal-line zone, we were 34 runs and six passes. We scored 18 touchdowns in this zone. In 20 attempts, we had 18 conversions. We were two-for-two on fourth-down plays. We were 90 percent efficient in our goal-line attack. There were two reasons we were successful in the goal-line situation. We called plays that we wanted to run, liked, and could execute. The second reason was we were not afraid to adjust to a new defense. We were not afraid to attack the defense when they aligned in a different scheme than we had anticipated.

In a goal-line situation, we generally started with a power play toward the wing set (Diagram #14). The wing was a tight end. The right tackle and tight end double-teamed on the 5 technique, looking to come off on the backside linebacker. The down block by the tight end should force the 6 technique

to squeeze inside on his technique. That allowed the wing to pin the hip of the 6 technique and drive him inside. The right guard and center blocked back. The backside guard pulled for the playside linebacker and the fullback fired into the hole. The tailback carried the ball and we should get movement even if the defense outnumbered the offense.

We prepared our fullback to play both the fullback and tailback positions. Against Miami, our tailback had an injury late in the game and we used the starting fullback in the goal-line offense as the tailback.

If there was an advantage to running left, that was the way we ran. We looked for match-ups. We wanted our best offensive linemen against the defense's weakest defensive linemen. If you had two tight ends that were decent, the defense had trouble stemming one way or the other.

The defense had seen this play and knew it was coming. We coached our tight ends to get their heads across on the down blocks to prevent penetration from the defensive linemen.

In conjunction with this play, we ran a counter play, counter pass, and a naked bootleg. The counter play was the same blocking scheme away from the fullback (Diagram #15). We got the double down by the tight end with the offensive tackle. The tight end tried to climb to the linebacker. The pulling guard logged or kicked out the defensive end and the back looked for the movement or a crease to score. The quarterback ran the naked fake off the counter.

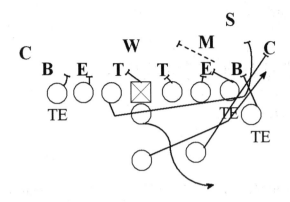

Diagram #15. Goal-Line Counter

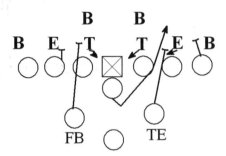

Diagram #16. Inside Slots

We motioned our wing tight end on the goal line. When we came in motion, if the defense bumped over with their linebackers or sent a defender with the motion, we would automatic to the quick pitch. If they did not come over with the motion, we ran the power-O toward the wing.

We were not afraid to change the formation to get a half-yard for the touchdown or first down (Diagram #16). We sat the wing tight end and fullback in the B gaps. They were like slots sitting inside, one yard off the ball. On the snap of the ball, the quarterback ran the sneak wider behind the push of the inside slots. We got great push from the tight end and tackle. In most cases, that was all the movement we needed.

We used this set when teams took the A gaps away. With our goal-line personnel, we had our power passing scheme and a couple of naked bootlegs.

The important thing about goal-line plays is how your players feel about the call. In our goal-line package, our players were extremely confident with all of our calls. That made a big difference in the execution of the play. The comfort our coaches and players had with the goal-line calls gave us an advantage.

THE 4-3 DEFENSE AND FIRE-ZONE CONCEPTS

Notre Dame University

First, I want to give you a rundown on my background. I feel like a true Midwesterner, because I have spent 22 years in the Midwest. I spent seven years at Ball State, and then I went to Notre Dame with Lou Holtz in 1992 and 1993. We won some games during those two years. I was the head coach at the University of Cincinnati from 1994 to 2003. During that time, we became a member of Conference USA. We made our mark in that conference by winning the championship in 2002. Then I went to South Carolina to join Lou Holtz for one year. It was a lot of fun being a defensive coordinator in the SEC. When Lou Holtz retired at South Carolina, our staff split and went in several directions. I was fortunate to have the opportunity to return to Notre Dame as the defensive coordinator.

People have asked me if I knew Charlie Weiss before he was hired as head coach at Notre Dame. I did not know Charlie. After the staff was completed at Notre Dame, Charlie said he hired coaches that had coached at Notre Dame. He wanted to bring back the tradition at Notre Dame. He wanted to bring back coaches that understood Notre Dame. Charlie Weiss is a Notre Dame graduate and he wanted people around him with Notre Dame pedigree. More than half of our staff has a Notre Dame background. It is like a family tree and it is in order. This was big as we all went back to reestablish the "Roar of the Dome."

I am going to talk to you about defense. I will cover the things we tell our football players. This is straight from our playbook. The first thing we start with is our philosophy at Notre Dame.

Anytime you see your defense on the field, the number-one goal must be to take the ball away from the offense. It is not okay to go out on the field to play defense with an attitude of "let's bend but don't break." Send your players on the field to go get the football for your offense. This creates a job among your kids that their job is to take the ball away.

We do not talk about turnovers very much on defense. We use the term "take-away." So our number-one goal is to take the ball away from the offense.

The second goal is to prevent the score. Next, we want to prevent the first down. We want to go three downs and out with our defense. We want to force the kick or punt. At the same time, we want to preserve field position. We do not want to give away field position every time we go out to play defense. We would rather force the offense to try a field goal than to score a touchdown.

The question is how are we going to accomplish the goals in our philosophy? We must have a scheme on defense. Our method of defense is an over-under front. To get this done, we must have a commitment. To be successful, you must have a plan and a philosophy. This is what we try to get across to our players. You must have coaches that believe in what you are doing, and players that believe in what you are doing. You can never second-guess the play. Everyone has to be on the same page on the plan. Whatever you do is the best for your situation.

We must be a complement to the team philosophy. We must realize that we are one of three components that make up the team—the offense, defense, and special teams. Most of the time, as an assistant coach, you work for a head coach. Some head coaches serve as the defensive coordinator for their team. But you must understand how your defensive philosophy complements your head coach or your team philosophy of what you want to get out of the defense.

If your team runs a high-risk offense, what do you do on defense? Is the offense a methodical run-type offense where you try to keep the scores down and win the low-scoring games? The defense will have to complement the type of offense the team employs.

We have a list of things our defense must be good at doing. Fundamentals and techniques must be sound. You can get overwhelmed in the X's and O's portion of the game. I am as guilty as anyone on this fact. If your players are not fundamentally sound, it will not make much difference what you do on defense. You can only trick teams for so long. They need to learn how to take on blockers, split double-team blocks, and tackle. They need to be sound in fundamentals.

We must be disruptive. This is the style of defense you play. We must win the money downs. We became a good defensive team on third down this past year. You must win the first and third downs. If you win the first down, odds are you will be able to win the third down. I am convinced that you must win the first down, because it eventually predicts what teams do on third down. Our philosophy is to not give up more than half of what the offense has to gain for a first down. Look at your defense and determine if you are winning the first down. If you are giving up four-plus yards per game on first down, chances are you are going to struggle on third down. I do not like to use the barometer of four yards. I like to ask this question: Did the offense get half of what they needed on second down to bring up the third down? The second-down ratio is about giving up half the yards for the first down. The third down is a question of whether they are going to make the first down or not. The bottom line is the defense must win the money downs.

Our players must be smart about the game and understand our defense. We do not want missed assignments.

We must stop the big plays. Defense is about percentages and math for the most part. Figure out if your team is winning the big plays. Count the number of big plays given up compared to the number of plays the defense played and you will be able to tell if you are winning the big plays.

We must be good at hitting, tackling, and pursuing the football. We believe pursuit is an attitude. Pursuit has nothing to do with what you thing your talent is. Pursuit is an attitude. It is the ability to run to the ball, and the willingness to do it every day, on every play, with everyone. It is an attitude. It must be something you believe in.

We must deny the run. We are a big believer in stopping the run. We break the run into three categories. Are we any good at stopping the run from the line of scrimmage? I will promise you, to win football games you must stop the run. When you play a good passing team such as BYU or Texas Tech, the good defensive teams try to take half of the game away from the offense. They make the game one-dimensional. Then they go to work to stop the other aspect of the offense. You stop the run first.

When you are on offense and you cannot run the ball, it upsets the coach. It is demoralizing. If you cannot run the ball, the first thing you do is blame it on the players. It is like beating your head against the wall sometimes. The other team may be better than you are on offense. We know we must stop the run at the line of scrimmage.

The second category is this. You must be able to stop the run after the receivers catch the ball. You must be able to stop the run to keep the reception to a minimal gain. Lou Holtz told me 25 years ago, "Teams will not beat you by pitching and catching the ball." He told me that several times. He hired me three times as a graduate assistant, as an assistant, and as the defensive coordinator. He told me that over and over.

When I was the head coach at Cincinnati, we were good at throwing the football. We won some games throwing the ball. But I do not forget what Coach Holtz told me—that you do not beat teams by throwing and catching the football. First, you must not let the offense throw the ball over the heads of the defenders. Second, when they throw the ball in front of the defender, he must come up and knock their jock off. When you do that, you may get a fumble or an interception. If you are playing in the Midwest, it is going to be cold late in the season. You can get some nasty weather late in the season if you are playing in the northern part of the country. There are all kinds of reasons for the offense not to try to win throwing the ball. Teams tend to run the ball more when they face the elements. You must stop the run, because those teams are going to try to run the ball consistently.

The second category is the run with the quarterback ad-libbing and trying to get out of a bad play. Nothing is more demoralizing than to have a quarterback scramble for a first down when it is fourth-and-eight yards to go for the first down. I am not talking about the option game with the quarterback. I am talking about quarterback runs that you do not think of as runs. The quarterback scrambles on the run. What is that? It is a running play. So the bottom line is that we want to stop the run on all three of those categories.

In this day and age, the athleticism of the quarterback is a lot different than it used to be. Look at the BCS bowl games—Texas, Ohio State, Penn State, and West Virginia—and you see those teams could run the ball. All four of those teams had outstanding running quarterbacks. It is a fifth dimension to the game. You must stop an extra area on defense. A team like West Virginia may run a one-back offense, but with the quarterback's ability to run the ball, it really makes it a two-back offense. So the quarterback is a big part of the schemes to stop the run.

We must have unity and we must have the right chemistry. If everyone is on the same page on your team, you have a chance to win. The players are going to believe in what the coaches tell them. We must have trust and we must believe in our system.

The next areas I want to discuss are attitude qualities. These points never change, in my opinion.

We want players in our program and players on our defense that are of great character. I think character is so big in the game today. We are fortunate to have several athletes that fall into this category.

It is important to have players that have high self-esteem. You must believe in yourself as a student-athlete. What is the difference between a low-esteem and a high-esteem player? It is right there. "Do you believe in yourself?" What is your job as a coach with that player? The coach must be able to help each player develop that high esteem. A coach must teach a player more than how to shed a blocker and make a tackle. The question for the coach is, "How do you make that player a better person?"

We want players that love to compete. Defense and improvement is all about competing. We want players that are tough mentally. We want players that play with emotion. We want players that are physical. We want players that love contact. We want players that believe our pursuit must be relentless. It is an attitude problem, but you must have players that are willing to believe in this concept. They must be willing to practice this concept. We want players that care for their teammates. We want players that are committed to excellence in everything they do and players that love Notre Dame.

The selection of personnel will be based on these qualities and the players that can make plays, who can run, who can get off blocks, who can compete, who are tough, the players that can do things the Notre Dame way, and players that fit our system. It is all about being a team.

The fun thing about defense is this. It is 11 against one. There is only one football. All of that crap that teams do on offense is all about how you disguise the defense—or how you employ the defense. The offense wants to make it difficult for our defense to know who has the ball. The offense can run five players out on a pass route and throw the ball to one player. Why are they only going to throw it to one player? Because they only have one football. It is 11 against one in that respect. When you are playing a zone defense, the more eyes you can keep on the quarterback and the football, the more good things can happen.

Another way to spell "defeat" is "no feet." That is a simple phrase we use to describe the defense. I believe you must have good foot quickness on defense. This is especially true for the front seven and really for the front four. We do a lot of moving around on defense. We will come off the ball and butt you in the mouth, but we also do foot movement on defense. You cannot have players that are plow horses, but on the same token, you must coach who you have. It is what you do with them to make them better.

Next, I want to discuss defensive traits. I could give a clinic on each of these points:

- Take-aways
- Pursuit
- Force and support
- Tackle
- Sudden change
- Killer instinct
- Confidence in winning

These things make us tough on defense. How good are we going to be on take-aways? How are we going to instill that philosophy in our kids? We had 24 take-aways this past year. That is not enough. We dropped 12 interceptions. Our goal for take-aways is three per game. That would have allowed us to reach our goal, had we been able to hold on to those dropped balls. It does not matter what alignment you use on defense, you must use some of the defensive traits.

Your players must understand force and support. It is how you eliminate the big run. Everyone on the team has a place where they must be on running schemes. They must know who does what in front of them. The more a player knows about the way the defense plays in front of him, the better and more secure he will play. We must communicate with the other players when we are playing defense.

I believe that everything starts on defense with the take-aways. Why do we send the defense on the field? To get the ball back for our offense. What is our plan to do this?

First, we must compete every day. We do not play a down without our defense trying to get the ball for our offense, in games or in practice. Otherwise, we are just playing for the opportunity of a turnover, which means the offense gives the ball to us. Against the run, if we do not teach our players to strip the ball, how are we going to teach the turnover concept? We are not going to play waiting for the offense to fumble the football. We are going to try to strip them and knock the crap out of the man with the ball to give us the opportunity for the turnover. It has to be an attitude.

You must do the techniques and fundamentals in your drills. You may not be able to do all of these as the season progresses, but in the spring and in early two-a-days you can include these points in practice.

On defense, we practice a turnover or take-away circuit to teach the techniques and fundamentals. We do the drill for about six minutes. We run the drills as 2-2-2. We have linebackers, defensive backs, and our defensive line. We have three groups. I allow the other three coaches to run those drills and I act as the clock operator and oversee the entire circuit. We have three stations. The one coach will stay with the same station and the players rotate to the coaches and each particular drill. I like to do this for several reasons. For one thing, it allows the coaches to coach the other players. All of a sudden, the secondary coach is working with the defensive linemen. Team morale and team chemistry improves in this type of set-up. It is good for the assistant coaches to see the other athletes and not have to coach their same players all of the time.

We are going to do several different things. You can do whatever your imagination comes up with. You need to pick out two or three things you feel your players need to improve on and then work on those things. An example may be the How to Scoop and Score Drill. Players need to know when to scoop and score, and when to fall on the football on a fumble. You need to cover all of the little coaching points about scooping and scoring.

Other drills we use in the circuit are tackling drills. We may use the simple Strip Drill. How do we get the ball out of the hand of the ballcarrier when the ball is in his far arm? We are coming in at a slight angle. We use the punch and try to knock the ball out of the runner's hand as we make the tackle. We do all of the little things it takes for our defense to create the turnover.

Bill Lewis, our secondary coach, came to Notre Dame from the Miami Dolphins. He brought the Eyes Up Drill and we included it in the circuit tackling. You can get your staff together and ask them, what are the drills we can include in the circuit to improve our tackling skills? This is one of the drills Bill said the Dolphins did when he coached at Miami.

The Eyes Up Drill teaches the player to stay with the ball on all tipped balls and on all passes that are in the air and still a live ball. How many times have we seen a ball hit a player in the hands or on the pads and then ricochet up in the air? The same thing happens with the linemen. Sometimes the lineman hits the ball as the quarterback releases it and it ricochets up in the air.

Have you ever been to a baseball practice and a coach is hitting balls off to the side to the outfielders? They call out, "Heads up!" Why don't they say, "Heads down?" Because they do not want their players to be hit in the head.

In the drill, we try to get the players to come out of an awkward position and look upward for the football, as opposed to looking down for the ball. When you are playing the passing game and you get the ricochet, the ball is going to be up in the air or it is going to be on the ground as an incomplete pass.

Our motto is this: "Only good things happen to teams that fly to the football." Take-aways are part of that philosophy.

Let me talk about pursuit. On defense, we discuss pursuit of excellence. Again, only good things happen to teams that fly to the ball. What

does it take to be a good pursuit team? It takes mentally tough players. You are going to have them run to the football almost as if they were robots. To be good on pursuit on defense it has to be what I call "overkill." It must be this way for you to get somewhere, to have the desire, and to create an atmosphere on game day. I do not believe you can turn effort on and off, and conditioning that goes along with this. This is true on mental toughness as well. It cannot be turned off and on. Players want to do these things in the games. They want to be loose, fresh, and ready to fly around the ball in the games. If you have not paid the price during the week in practice to get that done, it is not going to happen in a game. We believe you play the way you practice.

To fly to the ball, you must have great conditioning. As the season goes along, most head coaches will try to back down on conditioning. This is fine with us, because we tell our players that if we play every play in practice full speed we should not have to condition at the end of the day. This means we must run all the way to the ball every play. We try to end each play with an emphasis on pursuit. You can do this in many different ways. Some coaches use Two Whistle Drills.

This is the way we do it. Someone, usually someone on offense—because they do not want their players being hit—will blow the whistle. That whistle does not pertain to our players as far as pursuing to the ball. It may mean we cannot hit the ballcarrier any longer, but it does not stop us from pursuing the football. We want everyone on the team coming to the football. Our team must be willing to practice this way every play. The last man to the ball breaks us down on defense. There does not have to be another whistle. It may be a second coach running to a spot and breaking the defense down. Our players self-police themselves on this. They all run to the ball and the last man there calls out, "Breakdown, ready, break." It is a great conditioning drill.

What do we gain by flying to the ball? I will assure you this: You will cut down on the big plays if your players will run to the ball. On the big plays we gave up this year, they were not about effort or pursuit. It was a couple of pursuit lanes, obviously. Our players run their butts to the ball.

Flying to the ball will break the opponent's will. It creates excitement and gives the defense a chance to make big plays. Also, it provides opportunities for take-aways.

What is important to the defense? It is to play your responsibility on defense first. They must understand force and support. They must choose the proper angle of pursuit. We do not want shadowing of our teammates. What dose this mean? Do not run on the same angle to the ball. Do not shadow another player. We have 11 players we feel can get to the football on pursuit. If we have a player shadow another player, that means we only have 10 players that can get to the ball. We have eliminated one player when that happens.

One reason I like pursuit drills is because they can be used at the start of practice as a tempo-setter. It can serve as a "TTO," or "team take off" concept. It can also be about establishing a mentality of the Perfect Play Drill.

We tell our defense we are going to do the Oskie Pursuit Drill today. It is a dropback interception drill. We are looking for one perfect rush on the play. You have to give them a "bait" to let them know there is a light at the end of the tunnel. If the team does the drill the correct way, they are rewarded and they do not have to come back to repeat the drill.

We believe in tackling fundamentals. I am a big believer that if you cannot tackle on defense you cannot win.

- Foot placement
- Head placement
- Hit on rise—shoot the hips
- Upper club—grab cloth

If the corners are not good at jamming the wideouts, it is because they are not doing the techniques from the waist down. If you have players that are always putting their head behind tackles, it is not because of lack of effort. It is

because they are not bringing the feet up. We lead with the feet in everything we do. Foot placement is very important in tackling. We lead with the near foot, explode, and hit on the rise. We must step toward our target to get that done. We do not want to lead with our head. If you lead with the top of your head, obviously it is a penalty. I believe you can change directions much better with a base under you than you can when you are top-heavy.

Let me get into some diagrams so you can see what we really do on defense. We are in an over front (Diagram #1). If we are talking about a pro set, you are going to have a lot of different coverages you can play. When we call our basic quarters coverage, we are going to try to man press the corners. We are going to play what we call switch coverage. We play a man coverage on our base over front.

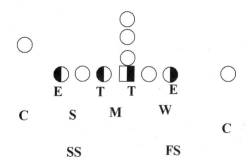

Diagram #1. Over Front—Quarters Man Coverage

On our over-strength alignment, we line up a little differently up front (Diagram #2). We can play it different ways.

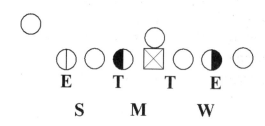

Diagram #2. Over-Strength

If we call under-weak, we adjust with our front line and backers (Diagram #3). You must game plan this from the scouting report each week.

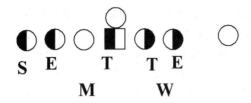

S   E   T   T   E

M   W

Diagram #3. Under-Weak

We play a lot of over defense at Notre Dame. What do we mean by under and over defense? Over to us means the down linemen have over shifted to the tight-end side. In the under package, the down linemen slide away from the tight end or strength most of the time.

I want to talk about the techniques on the over defense first. The Sam linebacker is on the tight-end side and is in a 9 technique. He is an outside-foot player. He keys the head and keeps the man in front of him.

The 5 technique is what we call a hard player. Everything we do on the 5 technique has another term to define it more to that player. Is it a 5 hard or a 5 Q technique? That gets into option football and it gets into the split zone runs that we see today, like WVU runs. We like to tag the techniques so our players will know how we want them to play against certain blocks. The option, and the run-and-gun offense changes our techniques in how we play them.

If we have six men in the box, we do not think the zone runs can really hurt us. There are all kinds of thing the offense can do today. It is not just a zone option one-back play anymore, is it? They can run many different plays other than the zone play. They can take the quarterback and let him follow the pulling tackle and run an isolation play (Diagram #4). The question is, how does the linebacker play?

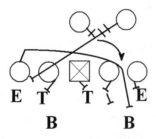

E T   T   E

B   B

Diagram #4. Quarterback Isolation Play

If the hole opens, the linebacker attacks. He must make sure who he is spilling the ball to or who the contain man is.

When we start adding stunts and movements to our calls, if we tell our end he is in a 5 technique and the movement occurs, it makes his technique change. It may be a loop or just a change mentally.

Let me turn the tape on so you can see the stunts we use. First is the over front. We will go fast over these stunts. Here are our strongside stunts. All we are showing are the stunts and how you would adjust your basic coverage. (Film)

- Slip: 2 man
- Sack: 3 man
- Skirt: 2 man
- Slice: 3 man loop away

Some of the plays on the film are part of the philosophy I am going to talk about next. I want to talk about our fire zone concept. It is our overload to one side to get the offense to throw into the zone pressure. We like to bring five or six defenders as much as we can. If you are a 4-3 defense and a four-man rush team and you plan on bringing an extra man on defense, you either void a zone and compensate for it and just play man coverage on that player, or give up a flat or an outside edge and play zone defense on the other side.

You may want to go zone coverage on one side of the formation and go man coverage on the other side. You use this when a linebacker, strong safety, or corner has become involved. You will see when we get into the corner fire games. I will show you those things. In addition, I will get into some true fire zones. We do void zones such as the corner fires, and we do half zone and half man coverage. When you get into your true fire-zone concepts, most teams play a three-deep fire concept.

What does fire zone mean? You are trying to create an illusion between three or four players off one edge or off one side of the formation to give the quarterback the illusion that his hot reads, or blitz reads, are coming. If you bring four defenders from one side, the quarterback cannot help but throw the hot route. He throws hot into a zone player. That is called a fire zone. It is an overloaded package. You are overloading the front on the defense. The idea is to give the quarterback pressure where he thinks the unblocked defender is coming, so he throws hot to a receiver into zone coverage. In our rules, we are concerned with who drops where, and to who it would be. It is, "I am hot at 1, 2, or 3."

The first thing I want to talk about in this concept is the fact that we like to bring corner fires. There will be a lot of movements in our package (Diagram #5). You saw a lot of them in the film a few minutes ago. This is the corner fire game.

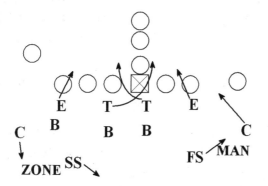

Diagram #5. Zone on One Side—Man on Backside

When we bring corner fire defenders, we are really bringing five players. We bring the four down linemen and we bring an extra player. It can be one of the backers or secondary players (Diagram #6). Here we bring a linebacker and play man on the splitside and zone on the strongside.

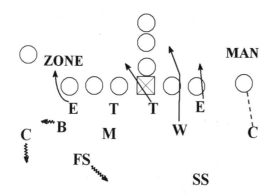

Diagram #6. Corner Fire—Rushing a Fifth Man

This is how we play a twins look. It is the same thing over and over. We keep our corners on the

outside receivers where we have speed on speed. It is just a different linebacker stunt inside. Instead of the looping front, it is the T-T games up inside (Diagram #7). We go man on the strongside and zone on the twins side. This is pressure where we are playing half man and half zone coverages.

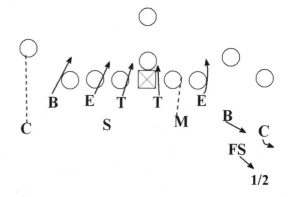

Diagram #7. Half Man and Half Zone Vs. Twins

If we are expecting a run, you will see us run the fire zone much more out of a secured front. It is always a give-and-take game. If you are an odd front, or an under front team that is going to use fire zone and do what we call stick techniques and rip techniques with the backside players, you are going to be better against the running game to the weakside because you are secured. The shade player must get across that backside A gap. Then it becomes a loop to the backside. The run is funneled back to the inside as part of the blitz.

Some teams, when they play fire zone 3, bring the safety down on the inside receiver. There is a host of ways you attack this set. Some teams will bring that safety down and play true cover 3, which means they are going to play the safety outside the number 2 receiver to the inside. If the inside man runs a flat route, the defense is in good shape.

But we say "hot on 2." This means we would prefer to come down on the inside man and play inside-out (Diagram #8). We want to keep the quarterback on the three-step drop. If the quarterback is running a three-step drop, the ball is thrown on the three-step drop and the quarterback looks like he has read our defense as hot and he is coming with double slant routes. On most of the routes today, the receivers are working toward the football.

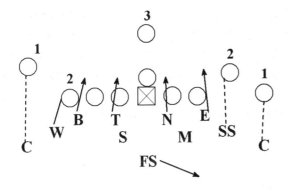

Diagram #8. Hot of 2

If you play outside of the number 2 receiver, you must have a player that is covering the third man and is aware of number 2 as he pushes to get to the area he is to cover. That is hard to do. Any time we have width by the number 2 receiver, and I did not say tight end, the safety coming down can play inside-out on the man. I am talking about a wider receiver than the tight end.

The reason this is important is that we do not want the inside man to catch the ball. The second reason we want to play inside-out on the inside man is this. It is difficult when you are playing three deep and three under schemes, because you cannot take care of all five receivers equally. You have to let someone go on offense. We prefer to let the hot on 1 to the field go. We want to be able to take care of the number 1 receiver and at least be able to drop to the number 2 receiver.

The number 2 receiver on the weakside can be a concern, and the number 1 receiver on the weakside can be a concern. But we would rather be able to drop off the number 1 receiver and work to the number 2 receiver. So what have we done here? The blitz should always take care of the running back. We can take care of four receivers in this set.

What do you have to be aware of in this situation? You have to be aware of the little nudge blitz and the slip screen pass. If the offense screens to the number 3 receiver, you had better have a defender accounting for him. If you do that, you have no one that can take the hot to the number 1 receiver. We teach our players that the blitz will take care of the number 3 receiver.

The corners have the number 1 receivers. The strong safety has the number 2 man to the slotside. The Will has the number 2 man to the tight-end side. We want to bring extra people to rush the passer on the coverages.

In the time I have left, I want to show the tape of the stunts and coverages.

In closing, I want to say thanks for having me here to talk with you. I like talking football and people in this area like to talk football. I know coaches here believe in making their teams better.

Again, take what you believe in and work with it. I am not here to tell you what to do. Take some of the things we talked about on fundamentals and techniques, and some of the philosophy I talked about, and see if you can apply it to your program. That is what I want you to take away from this lecture. It is not necessarily what you do, but it is more important how and why you do things. It is how to get your players to believe in what you are teaching them. Best of luck in the fall.

THE DEFENSIVE FRONT IN THE 4-3 DEFENSE

University of Mississippi

It is a pleasure to be with you guys today.

The things I will talk about today are things that I learned at the University of Miami under Butch Davis and at USC under Pete Carroll. I studied under Monte Kiffin and Rod Marinelli at Tampa Bay.

If you want to play the 4-3 defense, you must have great defensive linemen and a great defensive line coach. To coach the defensive line, the coach has to be high-energy. The coach has to keep himself in good shape and demand that the players go hard. I believe the practices should be harder than the games.

I want defensive linemen to be on the edge and turn it on for Saturday's game. You cannot expect players of that caliber to be model citizens every day. When you recruit them, you have to know that. You have to control them during the week and turn them loose on Saturday. I believe the defensive line is the most technical position in football. The coach has to be ready and have the proper mindset to coach that position.

When my players walk into the meeting room, I want to have a sign to indicate what I want from them. The first sign is a time bomb with a caption that says "Tick, tick, tick!" That illustrates the mindset of the defensive linemen. They are ticking time bombs, and when the ball moves they explode off the line. The second sign says, "What did you do today to get to the quarterback?"

Sacks that cause fumbles are the best plays in football for a defensive lineman. I want defensive linemen to rush the passer. We tackle running backs on the way to the football. If we have a chance to get a sack or the football, we take the football every time. Everything in the thought process of a defensive lineman is to get to the quarterback.

A defensive lineman must have a good attitude toward work. He has to have constant and never-ending improvement daily. They must have relentless hustle to the football. We tell our defensive line that they lead the team. When you see a player who 6'2", 300 pounds, and 4.8 in the 40, he leads the team. He needs to lead the team in practice with second effort.

We are a one-gap defense and want to pound the run. We have to create an atmosphere where the offense becomes one-dimensional. We cannot let the offense run the football. For the defensive line, penetration kills. We want to attack and create a new line of scrimmage at least one yard deep in the backfield. We must squeeze the gap, get upfield pressure, and redirect to the football.

We have a defensive philosophy we post on the board for all to see.

- Mental preparation—concentrate and prepare
- Fundamentally sound
- Be a physical defense—flying tackling
- Hustle
- Quickness
- Consistency
- Be disciplined—take pride in doing the other things
- Trust your coaches
- Accountability
- Team unity

We have a defensive line board in our locker room. We put things on the board that are important to all defensive-line play. This is our stuff. We take pride in our stuff. If defensive linemen want to be great in college and later in the NFL, they have to take pride in their stuff. I take pride in teaching it to them. On our board, you will find the following things:

- Run movement
- Stick and hit
- Mental toughness
- Point of attack
- Detail
- Shoulders square
- Fight

I will show you all these things today in the lecture.

As a defensive lineman, you have to be accountable for our one-on-one rush. That means that if the defensive lineman gets in a one-on-one situation, the defensive lineman has to win. A win for the defensive lineman is a sack or caused fumble. The defensive lineman has to be accountable for that win.

In a situation where the defense rushes four and the offense blocks with five blockers, we have to win that situation. With five offensive blockers, the offense can double only one man. There are three one-on-one contests going on in the play that we have to win.

When we practice at Ole Miss, we preach one-on-one wins. We match up one-on-one with the wide receiver and defensive back, o-line versus d-line, and linebacker versus running back. We film those match-ups and score them. We preach 70 percent one-on-one wins. The coaches grade the films and put the results on the bulletin board the next day. The players have to win 70 percent of these match-ups.

Defensive linemen must develop their one-on-one rush techniques. One of my favorite things to do is ask the defensive linemen who their favorite pass rusher is. Whomever the defensive lineman tells me, I get a training tape of that player and show it to the lineman. They watch their idol and the moves he uses.

Because I had connections with the Tampa Bay Buccaneers, they allowed me to use some of their drill tape on players like Warren Sapp. I brought that tape back to Oxford and filmed our players doing the same drills. I spliced the tapes together with the Bucs going first and the Rebels following them in each drill. Our players got to watch and compare the skill and talent level exhibited in the drill tape.

The next thing we emphasize is "credit card alignment." We align as close to the football as the referee will let us. We want our fingertips on the back of the football. We are so tight to the football that only a credit card passes between the football and the defender's hands. We want the hands in front of the eyes. The hand is always behind the ball.

As we line up, we want to be onside. We want to use the positive thought of being onside, instead of not aligning offside. I am the defensive coordinator and the first thing I do is demand that they are onside. Any time we have a scout team going against the d-line, the cadence is never snapped on the first sound. We want the defensive line to learn to go on movement and not on sound. We use the hard count to train our players to ignore the cadence and react to movement.

It is hot in Mississippi. The hotter it gets, the better I like to practice in it. The heat is our friend. You cannot let your players get tired. We must condition in the heat and push the fatigue away. We rotate defensive linemen to keep them from getting tired. A tired player makes mistakes.

When the center puts his hand on the ball, the e-line has to be ready to play. I do not want our players waiting for the quarterback to get under the center. If the ball is ready, we are ready.

I want our players to have a hair trigger. I want them like a coiled snake. On movement, we attack. We watch a lot of tape on offensive linemen. We find that an offensive lineman in a two-point stance moves his outside knee before he moves any other part of his body. We try to use that to our advantage. When the defensive lineman sees the knee move, he is off as quickly as possible. We look for presnap reads in the offensive linemen's stance. We can identify heavy and light stances. We communicate the stance up and down the line. We give rocket and train calls when we see trap alignments.

The d-line must have cotton in their ears. They move on movement and not sound. We want to be a part of the football. When the ball moves, we move. The get-off is like the time bomb. We only have three seconds to get to the quarterback. That is not a lot of time.

I break down the film and I do it early. I want our defensive linemen to have the film in the summer of the offensive linemen they will play against during the season. They study the player, his set, and the pass-protection scheme. I make them give me a pass-rush plan during the summer. When it comes down to the game and the first third-down play, the defender knows how the offensive lineman sets. We do not wait for halftime or the fourth quarter to figure out what type of set we are getting.

We do our research in the summer and write a pass-rush plan according to which guard, tackle, or center is playing. In the pass rush, the defensive lineman has to keep coming in his rush. He wants to lean in on the quarterback when he gets close in the pocket. As the defender attacks the quarterback, he reduces the shoulder, turns the toe to the quarterback, and stays low.

When the defensive lineman rushes the quarterback, he wants to stay on the level with the quarterback. He never rushes behind the quarterback. If we rush behind the quarterback, he can step up in the pocket and throw. We never want the quarterback to be able to step up in the pocket.

Unless we are blitzing, I do not worry about the containment of the quarterback. In fact, I would rather have the quarterback running with the ball. If we play a great scrambling quarterback, we do some special things to keep him in the pocket. Otherwise, I want the quarterback out of the pocket so we can chase him down. The quarterback does not want to run the ball, but that is what we want him to do.

The pressure starts with the race rush. We believe in beating the offensive lineman with speed. On the outside rush, we want to get wide and up the field as quickly as possible. We must force the offensive tackle to turn his hips and shoulders to the sideline. Once we beat the offensive lineman with speed, that opens many other ways to beat him.

We are not a bull-rush team. We believe that only you can block you. We have to believe that no one can block us one-on-one. We must have that attitude. "Only you can block you" means that the defender did not get off the ball. He did not study film that week. The defender had no pass-rush plan. He had improper alignment and did not use his hands. He was not relentless and was not ready to go. The failure to win in the one-on-one situation has to be put on the defender himself. Every rusher has to have a presnap plan.

When the defender rushes the quarterback, he wants to be a moving target. Pass rushing is like trying to score in a one-on-one basketball game. If the defender can get around the blocker without making contact, that is the quickest way to the quarterback.

Learning pass-rush moves is like wearing a new pair of shoes. When the players try a new pass rush, it seems awkward at first. They do not want to do them. Nevertheless, they do it, they try it, and they do it at full speed.

One of the most important aspects of the pass rush is the hands play. I played d-line at Northwestern State and my best pass-rush move was the swim technique. I grabbed cloth and swam over the top. I went to Penn State as a coach and one of the first games we played was Miami. The swim technique was the move I taught my d-linemen. Miami tied their jerseys down and our defensive linemen could not get a hold on the jersey. I did not have an answer for my players when they told me they could not grab cloth. That was the last time that happened to me. We now grab wrists, elbows, and arms.

One of the most important things the defensive linemen can do is increase their hand speed daily. We film our individual drills. If we practice it, we film it. When we film the drills, we watch the film. We watch our film directly after practice, starting with the individual drill film. The defensive line has to watch 45 minutes of film and they must watch the individual drills. If they watch the drill tape, they will get better.

When the defender rushes the quarterback, he has to know what he is going to do before he does it. He has to have a plan. They have to find out what they are. They have to know what they can do. Your four down linemen are probably all different in what they can do. One player may be a spin defender, while the other one is a bull rusher. One player may be rip man and the other is an over player. We do not know, but we have to find out what they do best.

I tell my players that they must have one signature move they can use. They do not need to know four or five moves. When it is third down and we need a sack, he needs to know exactly what move he is going to use and one counter off that move.

When they get to camp, they need to show up ready to work. They need to be on top of the details. If it moves, you go. When it is time to go to school, we go to school. We make our players go to class and study hall. There is time for that area of study life. However, when they walk into the indoor practice facility, it is time to go to work and they are going to get it.

It is critical that we teach first-down sacks. If we get the offense in a second-and-17 situation, we have a shot. We should never be surprised by a high hat from the offensive lineman. We want to be ready to rush on any down or situation. To us, every down is a rush down. Offensive linemen on first down are not ready for a great pass rush. They want you to rush in the middle and work outside. We do not do that.

We work natural games (Diagram #1) in the defensive line. If the 3 technique rips the offensive guard and gets upfield, the defensive end uses that

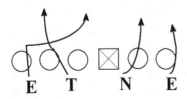

Diagram #1. Natural Twist

move to his advantage. He stops his upfield rush and comes under the 3 technique's charge. We did not call the game, but it occurred naturally as part of their rush.

If the defensive end came off the ball and worked a spin move inside off the offensive tackle, the 3 technique can use that move also. As the 3 technique sees the defensive end gain an advantage inside with the spin, he jabs and comes outside in a natural move. The natural moves are hard for the offense to block. We tell our defensive line that they are spinning coming off the bus.

We have a race concept that we apply to the pass rush. The defensive line has to understand when we are in the nickel package. When we go to the nickel package with a go call, the defensive line steps up and increases their speed. They change their stance. They get their feet closer together and elevate their tails. We are cranking it off the ball. I let the defensive line call their games.

The defensive lineman must identify pass sets. He has to know if the offensive lineman kicks wide, soft sets, or over sets. In each one of those sets, the defensive lineman has to know what to do. It is just like boxing. You have to counter all the moves the offensive lineman uses and "get it."

The d-line has to know how deep the quarterback sets. Most quarterbacks drop seven steps to set up. Every team usually has a three-step scheme in their plan. However, it could be a sprint-out team. If the defense can understand the pass-protection scheme on third down, it will be a long day for the offense.

The defensive line cannot let the offense run the screen and the draw. You have to get some keys to the screen and draw. On the screen, the tackle to the side of the screen will invite the defensive end to rush and cut him. That is one key. The defender that will see the screen first is the nose tackle.

We coach our nose tackle to stay in the vice, which is the double-team by the center and guard. When the guard leaves to get into the screen, the nose sees it before anyone. He gets in the guard's hip pocket and gets into the screen. Our defensive linemen are responsible for the screen. They can do it if they react.

We teach our defensive linemen what the draw set looks like. If the offensive lineman keeps his inside foot on the ground and opens up, the defense does not rush anymore because that is the draw. We coach offensive linemen to stay square to the line of scrimmage as long as they can. They never want to turn their shoulders to the sideline. When they do it without any pressure from the rush, that is the draw set.

There is no way a back should ever block a defensive lineman. It happens sometimes, but it should never happen. There is no way a tight end should block a defensive lineman. In high school, when a back came to cut a defensive lineman, the coaches taught us to get the hands on the blocker and run our feet away from him. What we teach now is to accelerate and run around the attempted cut block. If the defender tries to get low, he is overextended and gets cut.

The same thing is true about the three-step drop. The offensive lineman drops two steps and opens quickly. When that happens, the defender needs to get his hands up.

When we practice the one-on-one pass rush, I want the best on the best. After we work one-on-one, we work two-on-two. We have to work out our natural games in the pass rush, and this presents the best opportunity. The last thing we do is full-line rush, working on pass-rush games. We film all these drills and watch them after practice.

When we condition, we work our pass-rush games. Instead of running 40s, work your pass-rush games. They work on something they like and get conditioning at the same time.

The next thing I want to talk about is getting the right players. That is the key to playing defensive line. In our defense (Diagram #2), we have an end, tackle, nose, and Leo. We flip-flop personnel with the end and tackle playing to the tight end, and the nose and Leo playing the openside. The reason we

flip-flop is to allow the end to always play a 6 technique. The tackle plays a 3 technique. The nose plays a 1 technique away from the strength and the Leo plays a 5 technique.

E   T   N   E

Diagram #2. Defense Alignment

The Leo plays a 5 technique. He aligns on the outside shoulder of the offensive tackle and plays to the openside of the formation. He is a linebacker type of player. He plays with his outside foot back and does not have to play the double-team. He is in the 245-pound range. The defensive end is in a 6 technique, head up with the tight end. He is the big end and plays at 280 pounds.

The player that must make plays is the 3 technique tackle. He plays on the outside shoulder of the offensive guard. He is the best defensive lineman. He has to destroy and wreak havoc in the offense. He is the taller of the two tackles. We had a nose tackle at Southern Cal who was 5'11" and weighed 285 pounds. His name was Mike Patterson and he was a stud. He had quick hips.

The things I look for when I evaluate defensive linemen are feet, hands, and hips. I like leverage linemen. I love short, big men that can move. When Mike was a senior in high school, he weighed about 245 pounds. He had great get-off and was extremely quick. His senior year in high school he got a little heavy. When Coach Carroll came to Southern Cal, it was late in the recruiting season. I coached the d-line at the time. He asked me if we had any linemen signed and I told him about Mike Patterson. Coach Carroll went to see him play and he weighed 324 pounds and just stunk up the place with his play.

Coach Carroll came back to me and told me he could not play for Southern Cal. I told him I would take care of it. I started running him in the mornings in the stadium. Coach Carroll did not think he could play, but under all that fat was a hell of a football player. He got down to 285 pounds and made All American.

The players are out there, but they do not necessarily come in with an "S" on their chests. We take chances on players. They do not necessarily end up the way they come in.

We have a teaching progression. We teach stance, alignment, and assignment. That is the knowledge part of our progression. Before the snap of the ball, we know our alignment and assignment. The next thing in the progression is the get-off. That is the most important thing we do in the start. The next thing is hand placement. After the hands, we have to get separation and we have to escape.

The next part of the progression is technique. We have to practice techniques every day. I believe in drills. I believe in doing them right and I believe in doing the same drills every day. We do the same drill every day so that we can play fast and get better. That is their tool Box.

In the first game, they may play against a guard that they can beat all day long with one move. Nevertheless, eventually they will play against a player in the SEC that is bigger, more physical, and better then they are. When that happens, they have to be fundamentally sound to win. To be a good football player in the SEC, the players must be able to pursue and tackle and have effort and pride.

When the defensive line watches the film, they consider those things. They look at their stance, alignment, assignment, get-off, hand placement, separation, escape, pursuit, and tackle. That is how I train the defensive line. We all respond in the same language. That is how we communicate. You have to get you defensive linemen to talk. By the time they are juniors, they can teach what you have talked about for two years.

When I ask a question, I want everyone in the room to know the answer. I do not let them answer the question until I call on someone. That way, I work on everyone in the room. I want them to know and I want them to speak. They have to know what is going on.

Let me get to some of our fundamentals. We are in a three-point stance with our inside foot back, and the inside hand down to the football. I want the weight on the balls of the feet. The width of our stance is slightly wider than the shoulders. If the player is shorter, his stance is wider. The taller player stance will be narrower. I want everyone to look the same. I want the weight on the inside balls of the feet, with the cleats screwed into the grass. I want the weight on the upfield foot.

The down hand goes in front of the eyes. The shoulders are square to the line of scrimmage. I want the neck bulled, looking through the brow of the eyes. We see the ball out of the corner of our inside eye. We look at the gapside V of the neck of the offensive blocker. The weight is on the fingertips, with his butt slightly higher than the shoulder pads. When they take the six-inch power step, the back is flat. In a game when they get tired, the first thing they do is rise up out of the stance.

If you get one thing from me today, it is this next point. In our alignment, we get as wide as we can. The 3 technique's hand is on the outside foot of the offensive guard. The nose tackle's inside hand is on the ear pad of the center. The end is head up on the tight end with his inside foot back. The Leo is in a 5 technique with his outside foot back. The players on the left of the ball are in a right-handed stance and the players on the right side of the ball are in a left-handed stance.

I let the Leo keep his outside foot back. If the offensive tackle releases inside, the Leo closes. If he gets a high hat, he rushes the passer. He gets up the field and plays football. We play one-gap football.

If the 3 technique gets a reach block, he has to make the play. The same thing is true of the nose tackle. If he gets a reach block, he has to make the play. If those two things do not happen, we do not have a defense. The same thing is true with the Leo. If the offensive tackle reaches our Leo end, we cannot play.

The most important thing the defensive line can do is get off the ball. When I was at Miami, we went to the Dallas Cowboys to get some drills to improve our get-off. They were doing the Tennis Ball Drill. It is a tremendous drill. The coach stands three yards in front of two defensive linemen. He puts the player on the left in a right-handed stance and the player on the right in a left-handed stance. He extends his arms at shoulder height with a tennis ball in each hand. The coach drops the balls and the players must get-off and catch the ball on the first bounce.

We filmed the drill and found that our linemen did not move until the ball was about one-third of the way to the ground. Everyone in our program does this drill now. We have improved our get-off to the point where our linemen move before the ball is out of the hand of the coach.

When the center snaps the ball, the nose tackle has to be into him before he takes his second step. If the center takes his second step, we are not getting off the ball.

When you play with 300-pound linemen, you have to get them in shape. We have to play hard in the fourth quarter to get a sack and win the game. The defensive linemen must know how to rush the passer when they are tired. They must learn to be physical when they are tired. They have to learn to be disciplined when they are tired. The biggest thing about our program is to learn how to compete. I am talking about competing from the time we wake up until the time we go to bed.

We have to find out about our players and if they will compete. After we condition, we go to this drill. We tell them it is a 12-play drive. We are on the turf and it is about 100 degrees, hot and humid. That is the way it will be when we play LSU and Alabama. We give them three reps at three yards, three reps at four yards, three reps at five yards, and three reps at six yards.

I set two cones five yards behind me. After the linemen catch the ball on the first bounce, they burst through the cone. The burst through the cones is like getting a sack. I give them 25 seconds of rest between each rep, just as if it was a play. Of the two defensive linemen, if either of them drops a ball, they have to start all over. You start to find out about your players. When you get down to the six-

yard distance, you begin to hear the competition coming out in them.

On the hand placement, the big thing is to get the hands from the ground up. We would like to hit the breastplate, but the big thing is to get the hands up. We want the elbows in and the thumbs up. The helmet has to stay to the gapside V of the neck. We never look up for the football. We always trust the eyes in front of us. With the eyes closed, we can tell from the pressure of the offensive player what is happening. If the offensive blocker is trying to get to the defender's outside, the defender is pushing with his outside hand, and pulling with the inside hand.

This allows him to turn the shoulder of the offensive blocker to the point where the defender can rip across with his inside arm. We want to make sure separation occurs up the field. The sooner the defender can escape the block, the more effectively he plays.

The next thing in the progression is pursuit. Pursuit is nothing but effort. We have pursuit drills we work. However, all I want is hell-bent for election from my players. We work proper angles in the drill, but it is nothing more than wanting to get to the ball.

We practice tackling every day. We have a saying. We say, "Hat across the rack, five whole steps." We practice inside run every Tuesday and Wednesday at full speed.

In the 4-3 scheme and one-gap football, the defensive linemen have to make plays. I never talk to any of my defensive linemen about looking for the ball. The man trying to block him will tell him where the ball is going.

We grade our players. I grade my players on effectiveness. If you grade two players who play 60 plays with a plus-and-minus grading system, it does not tell you much. Player A in that type of grading had a percentage score of 83 percent. Player B played 60 plays and graded out at 63 percent. That does not tell me anything. When we grade, we have what we call an activity ratio. The minimum ratio is 1:6. That means once in six plays the defender has to make something happen. It could be a tackle, tackle for loss, sack, fumble recovery, or interception.

We give our players an activity ratio and points for plays. This is an incentive program. We post the results on the bulletin board. We have a point winner for each game and one for the season.

Player A played 60 plays and graded out at 83 percent. That is almost perfect. However, he had two tackles, one assist, one sack, and one fumble recovery. He made five plays out of 60 plays. That is an activity ratio of 1:12. Player B graded at 63 percent. He made five tackles, three assists, two sacks, one fumble recovery, and one big hit. In 60 plays, player B had 12 points. That is an activity ratio of 1:5. I will play player B and work on his technique. That is how we grade our players.

We give them five points for a sack, two points for a tackle, and one point for an assist. They receive three points for a caused fumble and eight points for a touchdown. Our players know the point schedule and work for those points.

The defensive linemen must recognize blocking schemes and individual blocks. This explains to them what is happening around them. There are playside blocks and backside blocks. Playside blocks mean the ball is coming to my side. Backside blocks mean the ball is going away from me. The defensive linemen have to be able to tell what type of block it is.

There are two types of blocks in the blocking scheme. There is a single block and a combo block. If the block is a playside single block, the defensive lineman has to make the play.

We subdivide single blocks into types of movement. The first one we deal with is the high hat. That is a pass block and the defender has to rush the passer. The next block they learn to play is the base, or drive, block. The next two blocks are similar, but not the same. The reach block is a direct step by the offensive lineman toward the outside number of the defender. On the over block, the blocker takes a different angle. The angle is down the line and not at the defender. The defender takes

on the reach block and comes under the over block. If the offensive lineman flies out of his stance down the line, the defender comes under the block and gets down the line.

The next segment of blocks is the combo blocks. They all start out as double-team blocks with two offensive blockers.

Let me digress for a moment. I forgot to talk about the power step. We used to teach the six-inch power step with the inside foot. If the offensive blocker tried to reach the defender, that step was fine and the defensive lineman was in good shape. However, if the offensive lineman went inside, the six-inch power step had to redirect to get the defender to squeeze. That meant we read the inside move before we reacted to the movement. We had to step and redirect the foot to get movement inside.

We have a wide alignment with a slight tilt in the 3 technique and 1 technique. We are taking the same six-inch power step. We replace the down hand with the first step. It works fine with an attempted reach block. The difference is the down block by the offensive blocker. If the blocker goes inside, there is no redirection of the feet. We continue to move down the line and squeeze the play. It allows us to close more quickly to the inside.

We do not take care of the linebackers anymore. The linebackers have to learn to play hats and heads. The defensive linemen play hats and cracks.

I am going to use this story as an example. Being the Cajun that I am, if I am on Bourbon Street at 4 o'clock in the morning and I have two big ol' boys coming to get me, I had better know what to do. If I try to whip them both, I will get hurt. I better beat the big one first to have a chance. That is the same way with the double-team. The defender has to get under the offensive blocker on which he aligns. The defender has to treat all combination blocks as a single block. He has to defeat the block of the guard and get his butt into the crack of the tackle doubling down on him. I have to drop the shoulder, push and pull, and split the double-team block.

We play the power scoop the same way. On the power scoop, one of the blockers has to come off the block for the linebacker. When the defender splits a double-team block and one of the blockers comes off for the linebacker, the defender is free to make the tackle. He never lets the base blocker get control of him.

Our linebackers key the backs. They do not key linemen. When they get a read, they are smoking toward the line of scrimmage. If it is a play-action pass, I may get a five-man rush because the linebacker is so committed to his gap. Our linebackers come so fast and hard, the power scoop does not have too much time to develop.

On the playside, when we get a base block from the offensive blocker, we want to stay vertical (Diagram #3). We stay vertical and get up the field. I want great get-off, but I do not want him flat to the line of scrimmage. I want the 3 technique and the 6 technique to get up the field so that they create a path for the linebackers. The linebackers are flying. The extra player in this whole deal is the nose tackle. He has his inside foot back and it becomes a natural path for him to come right down the line of scrimmage and clean up any cutback all the way to the sideline.

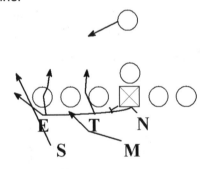

Diagram #3. Vertical Charge

If the 3-technique and 6-technique defenders stay on the line of scrimmage, there is no place for the nose tackle to fit. The linebackers are flying to the gaps and the nose tackle is overlapping the entire scheme.

When you talk about getting vertical and up the field, the first question is about the trap. There are two kinds of traps. There is the veer trap, which is

the guard going inside to block. There is the influence trap, where he pulls outside.

When the 3-technique defender gets the veer release by the offensive guard, he should think trap (Diagram #4). The most important player in this scheme is the nose tackle. If the center blocks back on the nose tackle, the tackle has to knock the center back and get his feet on the line of scrimmage. If he does not do that, we are trapped. That forces the pulling guard back and out of his trap path. That gives the 3-technique defender a little air to come down the line and meet the trap block. He wants to come underneath the trap block, spill it, and come upfield. He wants to keep his inside arm and leg free. After he spills the trap blocker, he squares his shoulders and tries to get upfield and make the tackle.

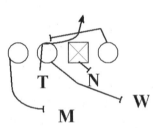

Diagram #4. Veer Trap

In the presnap read, the Mike linebacker sees the wide split by the veer guard and the tight split by the pulling guard. He reads heavy stance in the veer guard and light stance by the pulling guard. The Mike linebacker keys the back and sees the hole. He looks at the hole and wants to know if it is cloudy or clear. If we have spilled the trapper, the hole is cloudy. In that case, the linebacker fills the B gap.

The next type of trap is the influence trap (Diagram #5). On the influence trap, the guard will pass set or pull. If the guard pulls, the 3 technique thinks it is a tug block. A tug block is the offensive tackle blocking down on the 3 technique and the guard pulling around him. If there is no pressure from the offensive tackle, he knows it is an influence trap. He looks inside and squeezes, keeping his outside leg and arm free, and plays the B gap. The Mike linebacker reads the hole as clear. He beats the block of the offensive tackle and fills the A gap.

The nose tackle plays the same technique on the center's back block.

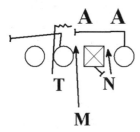

Diagram #5. Influence Trap

To the backside on first down, we play the run. If the Leo gets an inside block by the tackle, he is screaming down the line of scrimmage. If we get a scoop block, we go flat down the line. We never play across the block. We play in our gap backside.

The next part of the lecture is beautiful stuff. In breaking down the protection, we read formations. We know the personnel grouping, how they protect on third down, and we work it. I always have a protection report on each team that we play. The first formation has the tight end to the left of the formation. It is a six-man protection with the back replacing the tight end and the center blocking away from him. We make a rock call (Diagram #6). That means the center is blocking right. We have identified the three-man side as right and the two-man side as left.

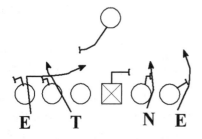

Diagram #6. Rock

The nose tackle and the Leo are to the right and their pass rush has to stay outside. If we get a rock call, the nose tackle moves into a 3 technique so he can get wide. If they come inside, the center is waiting for them. To the left, the 3-technique tackle and 6-technique end can work their natural moves and use inside pass rushes.

If the center blocks to the left, the call is lion (Diagram #7). On this movement, the defenders playing to the left stay outside with their rush lanes, and the right side works their natural games.

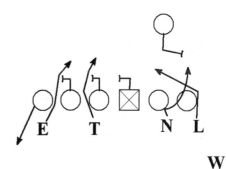

Diagram #7. Lion

We try to defeat the two-man side in the pass-protection scheme. That does not mean the outside rushers do not try to sack the quarterback. It simply means that they avoid the center by staying outside in their rush.

We have defensive games we call. The first call is Tex (Diagram #8). The tackle is the penetrator and the end is the freezer. The penetrater goes first and the freezer comes underneath. The defensive end has to sell his race rush to the outside. If he rushes inside at the start, the game will not work. He charges off the line of scrimmage with his shoulders square and gets eye-to-eye with the offensive tackle.

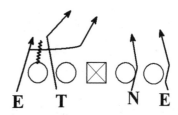

Diagram #8. Tex

The defensive tackle rips across the offensive guard and pins the hips of the offensive tackle. The defensive end comes inside underneath the defensive tackle. If the offensive guard comes off the defensive tackle to pick up the defensive end, the 3 technique pins the hips of the tackle, transfers toward the quarterback, and makes the tackle.

There is no way the offensive tackle can switch onto the 3 technique and make the block. If you run this game toward the center, it is not as good, because the center can help on the inside move.

The inside game is the Tom game (Diagram #9). The 3 technique is the pentetrator and runs into the center. He pins the hip of the center. The nose tackle is the looper and comes around, giving us a two-on-one situation with the offensive guard. When the 3 technique fires inside, the offensive guard has to turn his shoulders to get on him. The nose tackle uses that to pull him around as he loops outside.

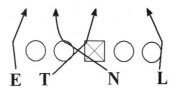

Diagram #9. Tom

I want to show you my drill tape from Southern Cal. It takes all four defensive linemen working together to get a sack. If you want a copy of this drill tape, send me a blank tape and I will send you a copy.

The last line game I want to show you is the ex game (Diagram #10). We use this when we find two offensive blockers on two different levels. That occurs when the offensive tackle retreats hard backward. This stunt is a physical game. The defensive end takes one step upfield. The nose tackle gets in a 3 technique or a 2i technique on the offensive guard. The nose tackle comes off and

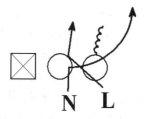

Diagram #10. Ex

gets eye-to-eye with the offensive guard. As soon as he gets in that position, the defensive end comes hard from the outside and blasts the offensive guard with a blindside blow to the head. After he drills the guard, he transfers his direction through the gap to the quarterback.

The nose tackle comes outside and we are two-on-one with the offensive tackle. The offensive guard looks at his tackle and asks him why he let the defensive end do that to him.

After we have done that a couple of times, the guard starts to watch for the defensive end coming inside on him. Remember this fact. An offensive tackle will not change directions three times (Diagram #11). The defensive end takes a step to the outside, he comes in toward the offensive guard, and back outside for his pass rush. The offensive tackle will lose him on that move. The nose tackle makes his move into the offensive guard. He fakes his move outside. The offensive guard thinks the defensive end is coming down, and looks outside to take him on. The nose tackle comes under the offensive guard and goes to the quarterback.

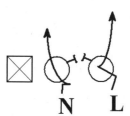

Diagram #11. Sucker Stunt

That leaves the offensive guard and the tackle facing each other, and the defensive end and nose tackle sacking the quarterback. I have seen it happen just that way. That is when you know you have perfected the move. When you can do all of these things, it sets up the one-on-one pass rush. Thank you very much.

THE NO-HUDDLE SPREAD OFFENSE

University of Missouri

Today I want to talk with you about our philosophy. It is not so much our philosophy, but it is what we believe in and how we practice. I will go over the different things we do and I will get into what we do with the spread offense.

We are a no-huddle offense. We changed a couple of years ago. We did not huddle one time last year.

I want to talk to you about why we went to this offense and some of the concepts of why we went to this offense. I could spend 30 minutes just talking about our zone play. I am not going to do that. I am going to give you some concepts on why and how we run the zone play.

I have been the head coach at the University of Missouri for five years. The first couple of years we struggled. We have been to two bowl games in the last three years. We have gone 20-16 in the last three years. Has it been easy? No! It has been very difficult.

I played at Kent State University. I was a captain with Jack Lambert. Jack and I played for Coach Don James at Kent State.

I was an assistant coach at Bowling Green State University before I rejoined Don James at the University of Washington as an assistant. We went to 11 bowl games in 12 years.

To say the least, I am a Don James disciple. Without question, our program is based on that same philosophy. The program was taken from Kent State and then to Washington and then back to Toledo. We took the same program to Missouri.

The first thing I want to cover with you is the University of Missouri practice and teaching philosophy. Our goal is to outpractice our opponents. We do this in the following ways:

- Practice harder
- Practice smarter
- Practice with game-day intensity

We have a walk-through before practice that lasts 15 minutes. Then we go practice. Every drill we do is with game-day intensity. We get after it. That is what we believe in. We want our practices tough so once we get into the games it is easier.

In addition to practicing hard, we want to practice smart. When we go into a drill, our players know what the drill is about and the speed with which we are going to approach the drill. The players know if we are going into the drill in "thud," or if we are going to back off on the drill. They are going to know the speed with which we are going into the drill, so we do not get anyone hurt in the drill.

I want my coaches to teach their players that they are the best position coaches in the league. If they do not believe it, we are not going to win. We must sell the players on this concept. We have to be organized and look like experts in front of the players. If we can do that, the players are going to play at a higher level.

We must be great teachers. I tell the coaches this: "What you see on the video is what you coach." You are a teacher and your evaluation is measured by your players' performance. Professors can have students that make A, B, C, D, and F grades. We must have all A's and B's. We must keep things simple. We do not want to overcoach. We want to find the best way to teach. We must teach fundamentals. Our goal is for each player to master the fundamentals at his position.

We know what must be taught. Staff growth is important. We must improve our schemes. We strive for our players to improve daily. We have a philosophy that players must master the fundamentals at their positions.

We must utilize teaching aids. We change up procedures for our meetings. We must use different techniques in our teaching methods. We know what must be taught. We must use the different methods to teach what we want the players to learn. We have video breakdowns. We must find a way to use them. We make boards and use diagrams to illustrate the points we want to cover. The accuracy of diagrams is critical. We know that 75 percent of learning is visual. How you draw up a play is important, because the way you draw up a play is the way they are going to run the play.

We must find ways to be positive. We do not want our enthusiasm just to be cheerleading. We want everything explained to our athletes. We criticize performance. We do not want the players to take the criticism personally. We want to find things to be positive about. We know that 99 percent of our communication and motivation should be positive. If this is not true, then we need to change the way we communicate with them. We want our coaches to be positive most of the time when dealing with the players.

We must be consistent. All players must be team players and abide by the team covenant. We must be consistent in our player interaction. We must praise and criticize—all players. Players will notice any inconsistency in your player interaction. We must coach toughness, coach toughness, coach toughness. We must coach 100 percent effort on every play—every play, every day. We must play hard. Players must be on time for every scheduled meeting or practice. They must pay attention to detail. We demand players to compete in everything they do.

We want hard workers on the field and in coaching. Coach every play! Coach every play! Coach every play! Coach every play! Don't stand in one spot. Hands in pockets, arms folded is not permitted in our program. Get to where the action is. If the coach stands around, so will the players. We do not want a coach to give a clinic on the field. That is why we meet and have walk-throughs. Coaches will run drills to drill just like the players do. Players must run on the field, never walk. Players don't lie on the ground. Demand enthusiasm, intensity, and make sure the players know their assignments.

Control the hitting! Tag offense. Play ball. Live off. Thud. The best coaches in the country take their players' performance personally. Missouri coaches take their players' performance personally!

Why did we go to the spread offense? First of all, it went against the ideas I was brought up with in football. After the last game in 2004, I went down to Texas Tech to visit. They have a great offense. Because of their offense, they have gone to six or seven bowl games in a roll. I watched the offense change over the years. Urban Meyer at the University of Florida was running the spread offense and they were scoring a lot of points each game.

We decided to use the spread offense for the 2005 season. Our goal for this past season was to score 35 points per game. We knew that we had to have a system that would allow us to accomplish this goal. Before last year, we ran some one-back and two-tight-end offenses. We ran the zone, the counter play, and the naked bootleg play. I felt that we needed to attack and score more points. This is how we evolved to the changes we made on offense. I spent a lot of time talking to other coaches about the system.

The reason we ran this offense was because of the following:

- More attacking
- Point potential
- Offense average of 35 points per game
- No huddle
- Equalizer: spreads people
- Presents problems for defense

- Splits
- No backs
- Option
- Vertical and horizontal stretch

I talked to a lot of other coaching staffs before we added the no-huddle. The advice most people gave me about the no-huddle was this. "If you are going to run the no-huddle, then run the no-huddle. Do it with every play you run." So in the spring we put in the no-huddle with every play we put into our offense. We all knew the signals for the offense and we used the no-huddle on every single play.

We like the no-huddle because we can get great tempo with this offense. We ran more plays than anyone in the country last year. We want to get first downs with our offense. The big thing about the no-huddle is that it allows you to control the tempo of the game. Also, it allows you to slow your tempo down to enable you to see what the defense is doing, so you can take advantage of your offense based on what the defense is doing.

We like to split our linemen to give us running lanes. Defenses do not like teams that split the linemen. They do not like teams that run from the one-back. They do not like teams that run the option.

One of the things we want to do is get the defense playing on their heels. When teams play on their heels we feel we are more effective in using the running game.

We believe you can run the ball 50 percent of the time and pass the ball 50 percent of the time from this formation. We have noticed an expansion of the running game from the no-huddle offense. Now the no-huddle offense has become more complex.

We can go from no backs to one back. We line up with no backs and then motion someone in the backfield into the one-back look. You can motion in and out of this offense, which makes it more complex.

The one thing about this offense is this. If you spread people out, you must force the defense to cover them. If they do not cover the wideouts,

throw them the football. Also, you must throw a lot of hitch routes in this offense. If the defense does not cover the wideouts, we want to get the ball to the open man. What does this do? It spreads the defense out all over the field.

We have two rules on the no-huddle. If a receiver is open, make the throw to the open man. If the hitch route is open, make sure you throw the open receiver the ball.

When we game plan, we want to give three basic concepts. First is our 2 X 2 concept (Diagram #1). We could motion one of the other backs and change the formation. We are going to set our game plan where we have the opportunity to run the 2 X 2 formation.

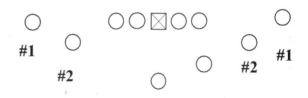

Diagram #1. 2 X 2 Formation—Deuce

We can call this formation six different ways to get our tailback outside. You could just do it one way, but we have several ways to get into this formation. We can get our personnel in the positions we want them in by using different calls.

The next thing we are going to do is look at our 3 X 1 formation. We have the plan where we can go to our 3 X 1 look (Diagram #2). We may motion out of this formation and go to a 2 X 2 look. We are going to use this to give a different look to the defense. It is our trips look. The defense would prefer for us to stay balanced, with two men on each side in a 2 X 2 formation.

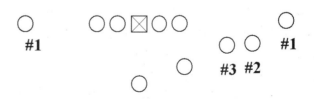

Diagram #2. 3 X 1 Formation—Trips

The next look we have is our 3 X 2 formation (Diagram #3). We can line up in four or five different ways to get into this formation. We can get into the bunch formations and move our receivers out in different ways. That is our diamond formation.

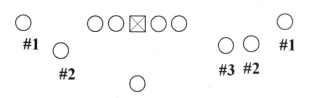

Diagram #3. 3 X 2 Formation —Diamond

The base running plays we can use from these formations include the following: inside zone, speed option, shovel, toe, dive, and the trap plays. We can run the outside veer, which I do not have listed here. We can run the inside veer as well. I really believe in this offense. Obviously, if you have a quarterback that can run and pass as well, the offense is awesome. I think the best way to run the offense is to get the defense playing off their heels. This makes it possible to have large running lanes.

We take the large splits to spread the defense out. On the inside zone play, we do not block the end man on the nose tackle's side unless the defense has five defenders on the line (Diagram #4). Our quarterback opens to the tailback, extends the football, and reads the end man on the line of scrimmage. Against the five-man line, he hands the ball off to the running back. The tailback reads the first down lineman beyond the center. Then he wants to bend, bang, and bounce.

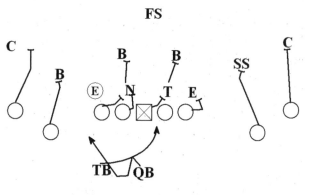

Diagram #4. Inside Zone

If the defensive end cannot make the tackle on the play, we want to hand the ball off (Diagram #5). We want the wide splits, because it helps us on this play.

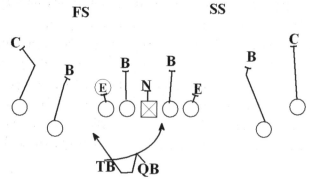

Diagram #5. Vs. 30

We tell the tailback to go two yards, and then bang, bounce, and bend. The tailback takes two steps beyond the quarterback and then he is going to bang it upfield, or he is going to bounce it back inside. We would prefer to press it and bounce it outside.

Against the 30 defense, the read is different. Now we are blocking the end man outside of our center. You will be able to see our splits in the film.

Next is our speed option. This is our 3 X 1 formation (Diagram #6). Basically, we use the drive technique with the tackle. We use that as a game call. If the defensive tackle comes down inside, it becomes a straight man block for us. It becomes a quarterback keep play. The quarterback catches the snap, recognizes the pitch key, and attacks his outside shoulder. He makes the pitch off the center gap defender. He must be ready for a quick pitch. We do not know who is going to be the C-gap defender. Also, we must be ready for the quick pitch.

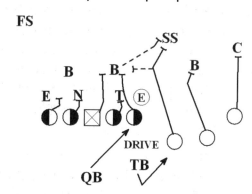

Diagram #6. Speed Option

One thing that helps us in this offense is the fact that the quarterback can see what is coming on defense. It really is not a complex play.

The next play is the shovel play (Diagram #7). We pull the backside guard around on the play. Everyone else blocks back on the play. We want the tailback to get a relationship of six yards deep on the pitch phase. The tailback comes over in a six-yard phase underneath the quarterback. You must work on this pitch relationship. We want him six yards deep and one yard in front of the quarterback.

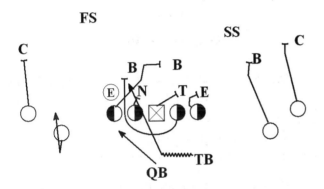

Diagram #7. Shovel Play

We want the quarterback to force the defensive end to move when he comes down the line. If the end just sits there, we are in trouble. If the end sits there, he can take both the quarterback and pitch man on the play. We want to force the end to get a little wider and move one way or the other. If the defensive end comes upfield and outside, we want the quarterback to pitch the ball underneath.

If the defensive end comes upfield toward the quarterback, we want him to shovel the ball underneath to the tailback underneath. The quarterback is five yards deep. He takes the snap and gets width. He pitches off the end man on the line of scrimmage. If he takes the pitch to the tailback away, he keeps the ball. If he squeezes the play inside, the quarterback keeps the ball and runs the option in the alley. You can make the play as complex as you want, and you can also make it simple.

Our trap play is from our 2 X 2 formation. The quarterback steps at the playside leg of the center and reads the pulling guard (Diagram #8). We trap the 3 technique. We do this in our tempo drill.

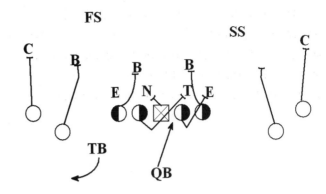

Diagram #8. Trap

I want to talk about our base passes. We want to run our spread-offense passing concepts. Our specific plan is this. We want to spread the field and attack the open zones. The general idea is this: We want to spread the full-field concepts—a group of routes intended to spread the entire field and create open zones. It does not matter if it is our dropback passing game or a running play.

Next is our half-field concepts. They are a group of routes intended to fill open holes on one side of the field. There are always paired with another half-field concept to allow flexibility against different defensive looks. You can run one game plan on one side of the line of scrimmage and another concept on the other side of the line. You can move the play from one concept to the other concept.

Basically, we have two three-step-drop protections. One is the no-back, and it is from man protection, and the other is the concept of turn protection. These are the only two protections we use in our dropback passing game. We cut a lot in the passing game. These are the two concepts we use.

I will show you a couple of plays from our two formations (Diagram #9). Next is our quick game protections—350-351.

- Playside tackle: Covered, block man on. Uncovered, block man outside.
- Playside guard: Covered, block man on. Uncovered, make fan call.
- Center: Covered, block man on, and listen for fan call, then turn back and protect the gap backside.
- Backside guard: Covered, block man on, and

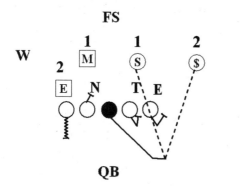

Diagram #9. Quick Game Protections—350-351

listen for fox call. Uncovered, turn back and protect the gap backside.

- Backside tackle: Turn in protection, block outside. Set to the widest defender.

Next is our quick game protection. It involves our 360-361 protections (Diagram #10).

FS

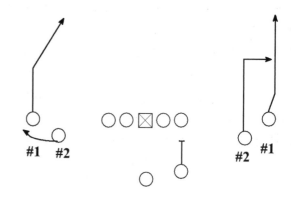

Diagram #10. Quick Game Protections—360-361

- Playside tackle: Set aggressively, get hands down. Covered, block man on. Uncovered, block man outside.
- Playside guard: Set aggressively, get hands down. Covered, block man on. Uncovered, make fan call.
- Center: Set aggressively, get hands down. Covered, block man on. Listen for fan call. Turn back and protect gap backside
- Backside guard: Set aggressively, get hands down.
- Backside Tackle: Set aggressively, get hands down. Turn in protection and block outside. Set to the widest defender.
- Tailback: Read playside A gap out.

I want to move along on these next plays. First is the 2 X 2 quick pass. It is our deuce right 360 gold-tan (Diagram #11).

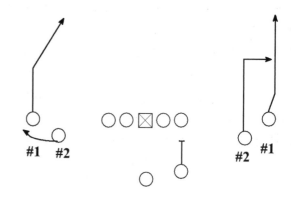

Diagram #11. 2 X 2—Deuce Right 360 Gold-Tan

- Quarterback: Catch and throw. Safety zone, go to tan side (slant/bubble). Two safeties, go to gold side (vertical/speed out). Versus man, take best-located defender: 1-vert, 2-slant, 3-speedout.
- Tailback: Protection, double read the first two linebackers to the playside.
- 1B: Vertical release to six yards. Slant route.
- 2B: Drop-step release, stay flat and parallel to the line of scrimmage until the ball leads you to the LOS.
- 2F: Slight outside release, breaking at six yards from the line of scrimmage.
- 1F: Protection release through the far shoulder of the defender. The landmark is the outside edge of the numbers.

Our next look is the 3 X 1 quick routes. It is trips right 360 spacing-black (Diagram #12).

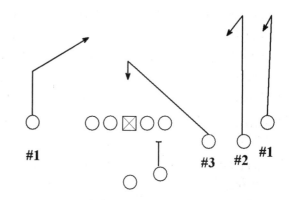

Diagram #12. 3 X 1 Trips Right 360 Spacing-Black

- Quarterback: Catch and throw progression, and slant to the spot to extended hitch. Always look for the slant to give spacing time to develop.

- Tailback: Protection, double read on the first two linebackers to the playside.

- 1B: Vertical release to six yards. Slant route.

- 3F: Come inside flat to four yards over the ball.

- 2B: Run a six-yard hitch route with two yards of width (6x2) from the original alignment.

- 1F: Run a six-yard hitch route with two yards of width (6x2) from the original alignment. We must convert vs. press or hard corner.

On the 3 X 2 quick, we call diamond right 351 sit-gold (Diagram #13).

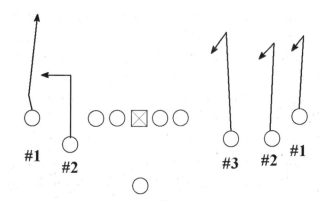

Diagram #13. 3 X 2—Diamond Right 351 Sit-Gold

- Quarterback: Catch and throw. Hitch rule. One safety zone, take sit side (outside in). Two safeties, take gold side (vertical to speed out). If the defense is in man coverage, take the best-positioned defender: 1-vert, 2-speed out, and 3-hitch vs. soft coverage.

- 1B: Protection release through the far shoulder of the defender. The landmark is the outside edge of the numbers.

- 2B: Slight outside release breaking at six yards from the line of scrimmage.

- 3F: Run a six-yard hitch route with vertical push.

- 2F: Run a six-yard hitch route with two yards of width (6x2) from the original alignment.

- 1F: Run a six-yard hitch route with two yards of width (6x2) from the original alignment. We must convert vs. press or hard corner.

Here are our dropback protections—50-51 (Diagram #14).

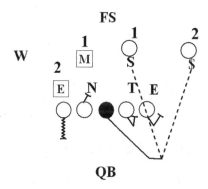

Diagram #14. Dropback Protections—50-51

- Playside tackle: Covered, block man on, be aware of outside linebacker coming underneath for SIFT.

- Playside guard: Covered, block man on. Uncovered, Molly unless fan call is made.

- Center: Needs to identify the five most dangerous defenders. He makes a Mike call against four-down fronts.

- Backside guard: Covered, block man on. Listen for our fan call from center.

- Backside tackle: Covered, block man on.

Our next protection is our dropback protection—60-61 (Diagram #15).

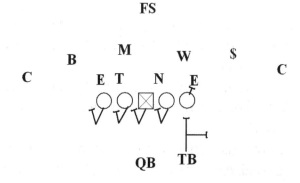

Diagram #15. Dropback Protections (60/61)

- Playside tackle: Covered, block man on. Uncovered, block man outside.

- Playside guard: Covered, block man on. Uncovered, make fan call.

- Center: If covered, block man on. Listen for fan call, turn back, and protect gap backside.
- Backside guard: Covered, block man on. Listen for fan call. Uncovered, turn back and protect gap backside.
- Backside tackle: Turn in, protection block outside. Set to the widest defender.
- Tailback: Read playside A gap out.

Next is our 2 X 2 dropback. It is our deuce right 60 choice (Diagram #16).

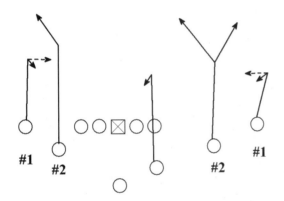

Diagram #16. 2 X 2 Dropback—Deuce Right 60 Choice

- Quarterback: Step drop (one big, two little). Hitch rule—Progression: Hitch-choice-dump. Versus two safeties, chance of post. Versus one safety, only a corner. Versus no safety, think post.
- Tailback: Protection: first or second linebacker playside. Route: No blitz, dump five yards over the ball.
- 1B: Run a six-yard hitch route with two yards of width (6x2) from the original alignment. Run a delay vs. press man coverage.
- 2B: Protection release, vertical push to 10 to12 yards and run a corner route with an aiming point of 25 yards on sideline. Must get open vs. man.
- 2F: Vertical push to 10 yards, make a decision to break to corner or post by doing the opposite of the near safety. Break route at 12 yards.
- 1F: Run a six-yard hitch route with 2 yards of width (6x2) from the original alignment. Run a delay vs. press man coverage.

Our next look is the 3 X 1 dropback. Here is our trips right 60 cross (Diagram #17).

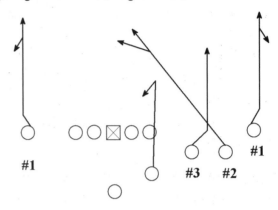

Diagram #17. 3 X 1—Trips Right 60 Cross

We were more successful running the crossing routes than we were on the other plays. We are in a 4 vertical and we are going to push it deep. If it is against a two-deep secondary, we are going to throw the ball off the backside safety. If the safety crosses outside, we want to hit the number 2 receiver in the hole in the middle. If the linebacker gets deep, we throw the dump to the tailback.

- Quarterback: Three-step drop (one big, two little). Against two safeties, read boundary. If the safety gets width, think crosser to the tailback (feel linebackers depth). If the safety sits, go outside to vertical (BND #1) Go to the dropout to the tailback on the dump. Against one-safety zone, read the single safety. If he picks a side, he looks off and drives into the other inside vertical. (Be aware of the corner and linebacker depth.) Against one safety man, he works against the best-positioned defender for us. Against one boundary he goes to the press route. Against man coverage he goes to the two crosser on the man route. His third option is to go to the tailback shooting away from the linebacker.
- Tailback: Protection: first two linebackers playside. Route: five-yard dump route.
- 1B: Vertical release (best release) to 12 yards. If you are hip-to-hip with the corner or past him, continue with the route. Go to the outside edge of the numbers. If the corner is deeper than you

are, then convert to dropout at 15 yards.

- 3F: Width release behind F2 and get to a landmark of plus-two outside the hash. Stay fixed and use best release.
- 2F: Release inside to eight yards on alignment of F3 stick to 20 yards. Run the seam route on the backside hash at plus-two.
- 1F: Vertical release (best release) to 12 yards. If you are hip-to-hip with the corner or past him, continue with the go route on the outside edge of the defender's numbers. If the corner is deeper than you are, then convert to dropout at 15 yards.

Our last play is our 3 X 2 dropback. This is our diamond right 51 smash (Diagram #18).

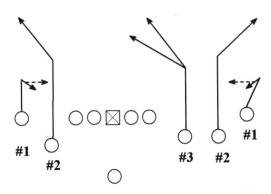

Diagram #18. Dropback—Diamond Right 51 Smash

- Quarterback: Three-step drop (one big, two little). Hitch rule: Read from the boundary—hitch-corner-safety seam. Against a bail corner, throw the hitch on the third step. Against a hard corner, take your eyes to the corner and see where the coverage is coming from: under (corner bounceback)—come back to hitch; on top (safety)—get back to safety seam. Against man: corner route needs to beat the defender.
- 1B: Run a six-yard hitch route with two yards of width (6x2) from the original alignment. Run a delay vs. press man coverage.
- 2B: Protection release: vertical push to 10 to 12 yards and run a corner route with an aiming point

of 25 yards on the sideline. Must get open vs. man coverage.

- 3F: Push vertical for eight to 10 yards. Run a seam post to the backside hash vs. two safeties.
- 2F: Protection release: vertical push to 10 to 12 yards. Run a corner route with an aiming point of 25 yards on the sideline. Must get open vs. man coverage.
- 1F: Run a six-yard hitch route with two yards of width (6x2) from the original alignment. Run a delayed route against press man coverage.

I want to show the film clips of these plays so you can see them in a game.

We do run play-action passes from these formations. We run the wheel route on top to keep the defense honest. Also, we run the sprint-out route with these sets. We move the quarterback around. It helps the quarterback and the offensive line.

I really appreciate your attention. I played for Don James in college. My position coaches in college and my high school coach from Akron, Ohio, were the most influential coaches in my career. We live in a world today where the kids do not have a whole lot of direction. In November of this past year, the one-parent homes surpassed the two-parent homes.

When I was growing up with my 15 buddies, there was not one of them that did not have both parents at home. Life is different now. What do the athletes do today? They turn to their coaches as role models. Our kids turn to me. You have great impact on these kids. I want the kids to say, "My coach is a man of integrity, and he is a coach that cares about us. He is a good person. If I can follow the life he does. I will be a good person as well."

Later in life, they are going to evaluate you as a role model. Coaches have great influence over people. This is true because you are a coach. You must take the responsibility. Help the young kids. Thanks for your attention and may God bless you.

SIX-MAN PASS PROTECTION AND THE TUNNEL SCREEN

Central Michigan University

It is a privilege to speak at the Nike Coach of the Year Clinic. I am proud to represent Coach Brian Kelly and the Chippewa football program.

Today, I am going to talk about two parts of our offense. The first topic is our six-man dropback protection and the second topic is the tunnel screen. Both have been very important to our success.

The offense is a fast-paced, high-tempo type of offense. We communicate everything in the offense to the quarterback, tight end, and receivers from the sideline. The quarterback goes to the line and calls that play for the offensive linemen. We believe in the spread offense and we won a couple of national championships at Grand Valley State using it.

Let me get into our six-man dropback protection. This protection is a man-gap protection with the offensive line and running back. It is a three-by-three protection, but it has the ability to pick up four defenders to one side.

We refer to the man side as the Gilligan side, because we feel they are on an island. The running back is part of that side of the protection. He handles any type of linemen games that occur between the two defensive linemen.

The other side is the gapside, which we refer to as the trio side. The term trio refers to the three-gap protection scheme to that side.

We teach this to the quarterback and he can flip the protection from one direction to the other. We utilize the tight end and involve him in the protection scheme. We give him check-release rules.

The offensive line and running back must understand the three- and four-down-linemen fronts. They have to understand the shade fronts and double-eagle package. We have slight adjustments in rules against various fronts and looks, based on the game plan.

To the gap or trio side, the protection could be A/B/C, A/B/D, A/C/D, or B/C/D. All those letter combinations refer to gap responsibilities for the gapside linemen. The linemen have to read the gouge set and the triangle as to whether it is hard or soft. I will explain that later.

I teach my linemen to recognize hard gaps with someone in them or soft gaps with no one in them. They have to know and react to linemen or a linebacker spiking or blitzing into those soft gaps.

The backside tackle will make one of three calls based on the five-by-five overhang area. That is the immediate area outside his alignment. The tackle calls "alert," "clear," or "watch it."

The running back reads inside to outside to the man or Gilligan side. He will only block to the opposite side if the quarterback checks the protection. If the quarterback reads four coming from the zone side, he checks opposite. The running back reads from the center going inside-out to his side.

The quarterback's drop is a three- to five-step drop. If he is in the shotgun, it is a three-step drop. If he is under the center, his pass drop is five steps. The launch point of the football is five to seven yards behind the center. The guards are responsible for the depth of the pocket and the tackles are responsible for the width of it.

The combat zone for the center and guards is two to three yards from the line of scrimmage. I am a big believer in being aggressive in our pass protection. In the offensive line, we teach our linemen how to deal with a linebacker in a tough position. If the linebacker walks up on the line of scrimmage, we never set and take him on. In that situation, the offensive linemen get depth off the line before attempting to take on the linebacker.

If the linebacker walks up on the line, the defense wants the offensive linemen to set on him. I want all my offensive linemen to set on the same level. We have to be aware and recognize one- or two-gap spikers. I will show that situation to you and the way we zone off those games.

When the linebacker aligns on the line of scrimmage, most of the time he will not blitz. I teach my linemen not to chase ghosts. If the linebacker disappears, they sit back, reposition, and wait for the twist to come to them.

Any time we face a double-eagle defense, we treat it as a five-for-five concept. When we have all the offensive linemen covered, even with linebackers, we block five for five. If we have trouble with a linebacker blitz in the A gap, we squeeze with the offensive guard and tackle.

If the Mike linebacker walks up in a tough position on the center, we treat that the same as a double eagle. Any time the playside gets spiking defensive linemen, they must reposition themselves to pick up the linebacker or looper.

We have pass-blocking rules for our six-man protection. The playside guard and tackle are on the Gilligan side of the protection. They are on the island.

The playside tackle always uses a two-step vertical set on all dropback passes, except against a wide-aligned defensive end. In that case, he uses a slight angle set. I believe in vertical setting and staying square. That allows the linemen to reposition and move in any direction. The tackle sets to a spot two yards straight back from his alignment. He has to beat the defender to that spot. He has to intersect the path of the rusher to the set of the quarterback. You have to train your players to get to that spot.

If the defense is a three- or four-man front, the tackle blocks the number 2 lineman on or outside the center. If his blocking assignment spies to the outside, he looks for the overhang or repositions to the inside. That means he has to be aware of an outside blitzer coming or an inside spike from a defensive lineman. An overhang defender is one not aligned on an offensive lineman to the outside. He never blocks a tough linebacker unless the squeeze scheme is in the game plan. You have to teach them to react properly and handle the stunt.

The playside guard uses a vertical or angle set. If the defense is a four-man front, he blocks the number 1 defensive linemen on or outside the center. If the defensive lineman does not charge, he looks for the linebacker or safety. We want him to be more aggressive against 3 techniques, because it keeps them off the other offensive linemen for a longer period.

He never blocks a tough linebacker unless a squeeze scheme is in the game plan. If the defense is a three-man front, he reads the noseguard. Our gaps are 18 inches in width and I do not want the guards to overset on a noseguard. We have a half-gap set that is a slight nine-inch inside set to use on the noseguard. If the noseguard spikes toward him, he blocks him. If he goes away, the guard looks outside to help on the tackle block or some stunt.

The center has a vertical set and stays square to the line of scrimmage. Against the three- or four-man front, his responsibility is the backside A gap. He listens to the backside tackle for alert calls as to possible blitzes.

If the center has a playside 1-technique defender or a noseguard aligned on him, he keys the near knee of the defender. If the front is a four-man scheme and the noseguard spikes to the man-protection side, he travels with him. If the defense is a three-man front, he keys the direction of the noseguard. If he spikes to the man-protection side, he reads the defensive end to the backside of the formation.

The backside guard uses the two-step vertical set. He is responsible for the B gap when facing a three- or four-man front. He listens for the call of the backside tackle.

If the backside guard has an A-gap defender to his inside, he keys his near knee. In the four-man front, the guard travels with the defensive end if he spikes one or two gaps to the inside. In the three-man front, the guard passes the defensive end to the center, if he spikes two gaps inside. He passes him to the center and steps outside to block the linebacker.

The backside tackle is responsible for the C gap to the backside in a three- or four-man defense. He makes his calls for the backside guard and center. He calls "alert," "clear," or "watch it." He blocks the overhang on the backside. The overhang is the defender not aligned on anyone to the backside. If there are two defenders outside the tackle, he makes a wide alert call.

The backside tackle makes his calls based on what he sees in the five–by-five area. That area is five yards outside of his alignment by five yards deep from his alignment. He has to see any linebacker, safeties, or corners moving into that area that could be a blitz threat. If he gives a call, the center and backside guard know that they are responsible for the two defensive linemen.

An alert call does not mean that we change blocking rules. It alerts the guard and center to a possible stunt from the outside. A clear call means there is no outside threat of a blitz, and the center, guard, and tackle are responsible for the two down linemen and the weakside linebacker.

I am a believer in the triangle read for the offensive lineman. His vision should travel from the inside defensive lineman to the linebacker to the outside defensive lineman. He can see all these defenders by using the corners of the eyes. Any defensive linemen moving or spiking from his original alignment will tell the offensive lineman how to react. I believe in looking opposite first in the vision scan. The right tackle will scan to the left side first and look at his side last. That gives him the whole picture and keeps him from having tunnel vision.

We set in both a two-point and three-point stance. Our favorite is the two-point stance. I want my post or inside foot straight downfield. I want my stagger foot slightly turned outside. I want my center of gravity stationary between my two feet.

We have to key the near knee in so many of our alignments, I need to talk about that.

If the center has an A-gap responsibility with a defender aligned in that gap, he keys the near knee. He wants to set head up on the A-gap defender. The guard has the outside B gap, but does not forget about the A-gap defender. As he sets, he jams inside with his inside hand and gets it on the A-gap player. His eyes are outside, looking at the defensive end.

He gets his hand on the inside defender to feel any spike coming in his direction. He never sits and pulls his hand back. He feels inside and looks outside. The offensive tackle has to look past the defender aligned on him. He has to see into the five- by five-yard area to his outside. Every offensive lineman with a gap defender to his inside and a blocking responsibility to his outside applies the same technique. It helps in passing off stunts and allows the inside blocker to set squarely on the defender.

The next diagrams are examples of how we block various fronts using the six-man protection scheme. The first front is a 3-4 defense with the man protection left (Diagram #1). The defense slants to the offensive left. The center keys the noseguard and comes to the right, looking for the linebacker blitz. The left guard takes the noseguard slanting toward him, as he is the number 1 defensive lineman on or past the center. The trio side is to the right and blocks an A, B, C, pattern.

3-4

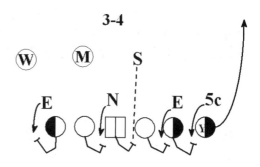

Diagram #1. 3-4 Man Left

The next defense is a 3-3 defense with the slant toward the offensive left (Diagram #2). The blocking is the same, except the center on his A-gap read has to key the Mike and Sam linebackers.

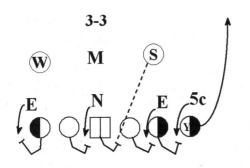

Diagram #2. 3-3 Man Left

The next defense is the 4-3 wide alignment (Diagram #3). We block the man side to the right and the zone side to the left. Notice the center is gapping to his left, but on his set he gets his right hand out on the tackle in the hard A gap to his right.

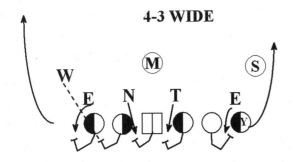

Diagram #3. 4-3 Wide

The 4-2 and 4-4 defenses are almost alike in their alignments (Diagram #4). In the diagram, we man to the left and zone to the right. As the center and guard to the trio side fan out, they have a secondary key coming from the tackle to that side. He gives an alert call because of the strong safety's alignment.

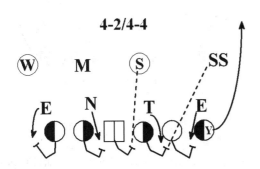

Diagram #4. 4-2/4-4 Defense

The last defense is the bear front (Diagram #5).

In this diagram, we apply the double-eagle rule and block the five-for-five principle. The five offensive linemen are blocking the five down linemen on the defensive front. In this alignment, we could squeeze from the outside and let the back block off the edge.

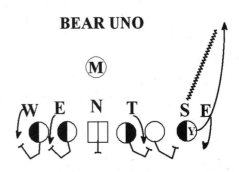

Diagram #5. Bear Front

In our offense, we run options, draws, zones, traps, and powers. In our passing game, we run sprint-out and dropback passes. We have play-action, naked, and bootlegs. We have the full gambit of offense in our scheme. We are effective at running the screen game. I want to show you the tunnel screen we run.

The tunnel screen has been a great play for us. You want to find ways to attack defenses that are attacking you. When you run the spread offense, you will know early on what the game plan of the defense is designed to do. They are going to blitz you or play defense against you. We like to throw the screen game against pressure.

The tunnel screen is a wide-receiver screen that we run to the field or into the boundary. We run it to a two-receiver set or a three-receiver set. We run it with the tight end attached or detached and to the playside or backside.

It is an effective play against any defensive alignment. It is very effective against pressure defenses and line stunts. The quarterback has the ability to check into this play at the line of scrimmage.

The quarterback can be under the center or in the shotgun set. We prefer the play from the shotgun set. His launch point is initially behind the center. If pressured, he should stay on the move toward the screenside. The throw is a medium-fast ball thrown outside the playside tackle area. The ball must be thrown behind the line of scrimmage.

The running back either aligns in the home position, opposite the call, to the call, or in the empty set. We base his assignment on where he aligns. This gives you more versatility in the spread offense. It gives you a way to confuse defenses that try to attack you according to the alignment of the running back. It allows you to put the running back in multiple spots.

The wide receiver receiving the ball must sell the three-step vertical release. He plants on the third step and retraces his steps. We call it coming down the vertical stem. After he retraces his steps, he works toward the quarterback. The wide receiver is responsible for the line of scrimmage. He has to get behind the line of scrimmage. He stays on the move, catches the ball, and comes underneath the kick-out block by the guard. After he comes inside the kick-out block, he gets vertical and bursts back outside.

We assign the offensive line to a specific gap. They will be downfield on their blocks, so the ball must be caught behind the line of scrimmage. When the offensive linemen get downfield on defenders in space, they must never measure up on them. The offensive linemen do not break down on a defensive back. They run right through him or utilize cut blocking.

The playside tackle is responsible for the C gap. He blocks his man upfield as far as he can take him. He wants to be aggressive so the defender does not knock the ball down. If the defensive end spikes inside and no one comes out to the C gap, he gets out into the screen. If the defensive end spies out and does not rush, he goes out to block him. If there is an overhang defender outside the defensive end, he make an alert call to the center and guard.

The coaching point for the offensive tackle is to not change his demeanor on the play. Make it look exactly like any other pass protection.

The playside guard quick-vertical sets to the B gap. He uses a number of escapes to get out on the screen. He uses a club-n-go, punch-n-go, shoulder/bump-n-go, or a snap down-n-go. Different linemen use different techniques, which is fine with us. He uses the one so he can get a free release down the line. He releases flat to the line of scrimmage and kicks out the alley defender. If the alley defender blitzes, he works up to the safety.

The center uses the quick-vertical set and executes a clubbing move to release down the line of scrimmage. He sprints down the line and seals the inside linebacker. If the linebacker blitzes, he blocks the low-hole player or safety.

The backside guard quick sets on the backside A gap or the number 1 defender past the center. In the four-man front, he oversets on the A-gap player. On the three-man front, he reads the noseguard. He has a flat release down the line of scrimmage to the width of the playside tackle area. He cuts any defenders retracing their steps after recognizing the screen. There is the chance of a squeeze call if the A and B gaps are threatened by a blitz.

The backside tackle vertical sets on the backside B gap or the number 2 defensive lineman past the center. He is the man that stays on the backside. If the defensive end spikes inside, he torques him out.

The receivers' rules in a 2 X 2, or double, set are standard (Diagram #6). The outside receiver to the playside receives the ball. The playside number 2 receiver blocks the defender over the outside receiver. To the backside, the number 1 receiver

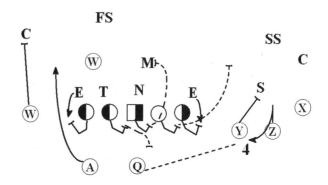

Diagram #6. Tunnel From a 2 X 2 Tight-End Set

blocks the man over him. The number 2 receiver blocks the alley to the safety.

If there is a tight end to the playside, he has a free release and kicks out the man over the number 1 receiver. He never blocks an overhang blitz from the outside. If he has a defensive end aligned on his feet, he takes an outside release. If the defensive end is widened or in a loose alignment, he takes an inside release. If there is man coverage on him, he drives upfield, breaks off his pattern, and gets to his assignment quickly. If the tight end is on the backside of the formation, he takes an inside or outside release and blocks the nearest safety.

If the set is a 3 X 1 set, the blocking for the line stays the same (Diagram #7). The wide receiver to the trips side blocks the man over him. The number 2 receiver catches the ball. The number 3 receiver blocks the man over the number 2 receiver. The backside receiver blocks the man over him.

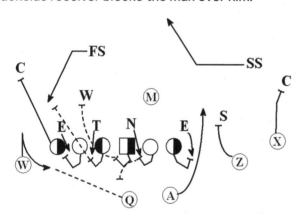

Diagram #7. Tunnel Screen From a 3 X 1 Set

I want to show you some defensive fronts and show the way we block them on the tunnel screen. The first front is the 3-3 defense (Diagram #8). The

3-3

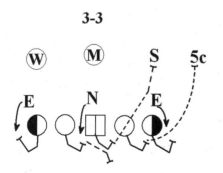

Diagram #8. Tunnel Screen Against a 3-3 Set

playside guard pulls outside the tackle's block and the center pulls inside the tackle. The backside guard pulls and picks up the defender pursuing from the inside.

The next defense is the 4-2/4-4 defense (Diagram #9). The blocking is primarily the same. On the 4/4 defense, the pulls from the frontside are trying to find the quickest route to the linebackers.

4-2/4-4

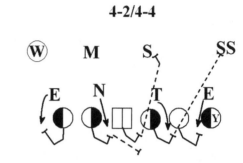

Diagram #9. Tunnel Screen Against a 4/4 Set

The last front is the bear front (Diagram #10). The playside tackle may have a wide rusher coming off the edge if we have a tight end to that side. The playside guard has a direct path to the outside linebacker. The center takes the nearest angle to block the Mike linebacker.

BEAR UNO

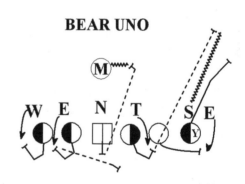

Diagram #10. Tunnel Screen Against Bear

This play has been an effective play for us. I have some film of the tunnel screen. Are there any questions before I go to the film?

I gave you a little of what we do in those particular parts of our offense. Any time you want to come up to the University of Central Michigan, I will be happy to spend the time with you. Thank you.

CLOCK MANAGEMENT AND THE TWO-MINUTE OFFENSE

University of Georgia

Thank you very much. It is good to be here. My topic today is clock management. In addition, I will cover our two-minute offense. I am no expert, but I am not sure if anyone is an expert on that part of the game. The clock is always moving and situations always change. No matter how much time you spend preparing for things, you tend to make a mistake, because something comes up you never thought you would have to deal with.

Before I get started, I want to say I understand you play great football in this state and the surrounding area. The reputation of the high school coaches in this area is phenomenal. I recruited this area when I was at Florida State. Since I have been at Georgia, we have not recruited this area very much, although we have a couple of players from the Maryland area.

I was at Florida State for 15 years and called the plays for nine years. We won most of our games while I was there and we won most of them by a bunch of points. I did not have to worry about clock management much. I did not know much about it at that time.

At Florida State, we did play Miami and Florida and were more evenly matched with them. When the games got close, the more opportunities you had to deal with the clock. When you get beat badly or beat someone badly the clock does not mean much.

At Georgia, there were many close games. My first year as head coach, I made many mistakes while trying to learn how to be a head coach. The thing that probably got the most attention was our Auburn game at Georgia. I botched the end of the game against Auburn. We were behind in the game and needed a touchdown to win the game. The field goal would not win the game. We had a game-winning drive going at the end of the game.

We hit a long pass or run, I do not remember which, but it ended on the one-yard line. We were out of time-outs. We had 10 to 12 seconds on the clock, but it stopped on the first down. I called a running play and we were stuffed. We had no time-outs and the clock ran out. I could have thrown the ball and gotten at least two plays.

When the game was over, I went into the locker room and apologized to the team for not giving them a good enough chance to win the game. I apologized to the coaches, and I had to go to the press conference after the game. The first thing I did was to tell them how stupid I was and how many bad decisions I made. They were licking their chops getting ready to blast me. I blasted myself. They looked at me rather dumbfounded and the press conference was over. I had blasted myself and they had nothing to ask.

That was my first experience with clock management and I handled it poorly. That one game probably cost us a big bowl game. We played in the Music City Bowl that year instead of the Capitol One Bowl, which is the highest paid bowl outside of the BCS bowls. When you make mistakes like that during the season, in the off-season you go get help.

I went to see a coach by the name of Homer Smith. In my opinion, he is the smartest man in football. He is tremendously cerebral and thinks everything through. Everything you can think of in football, he has already thought it. He is in the process of writing a book called *Clock Management*.

The clock does not know about the reputation of the coach. It does not care how many games or championships you have won. It is cruel to everyone if you are not prepared. Learning clock management is an ongoing process. We spent two days with Homer Smith and learned many things from him.

Clock management takes on many forms and I will cover a bunch of them. If you feel you are better than the team you are playing, should you speed up play? You may want to slow the game. That keeps the ball away from the other team's offense. Your time-out pattern is different from the first half to the second half. The first two time-outs are not as important as the third time-out.

If you are about to get the ball, you need to know if you can run out the clock without getting a first down. If you cannot, it changes your way of thinking. You need to know when and if you should spike the ball. You must consider running off excess time before a score. It takes nerve to run the clock down and depend on a kick winning the game for you. That is particularly true if you are inside the five-yard line.

Another thing in the clock-management decisions, which was new to me, was letting a team score. That situation occurred in our Auburn game this year. We were up by six points and had them in a fourth-and-13 yards for the first down. They hit a big pass play and got the ball to the one-yard line with one minute and 15 seconds to go in the game. If we tried to make a goal-line stand and it took them more than two plays to score, we had no time left on the clock. Should we let them score and try to drive for the winning field goal? That is a tough decision to make. We tried to make the goal-line stand. They scored on third down with virtually no time left on the clock.

Clock management in the two-minute offense is tremendously important. The first thing you have to teach your quarterback and players is when the clock stops. The clock stops until the ball is snapped in certain situations. Those situations are a time-out, an incomplete pass, when the ball goes out of bounds, or a time-out called by the official to control the crowd.

There are situations in a game where the clock stops temporarily. After each situation, the ball is marked ready and the clock starts. On a made first down, the clock stops to allow the officials to move the chains. If there is an injury, the clock will stop. Once the injured player is removed from the field, the clock starts. A measurement for a first down stops the clock. After the measurement, the ball is marked ready for play and the clock starts. The last two are a TV time-out or an official's time-out.

In a penalty situation, if the play preceding the penalty was a clock-stopping play, the clock does not start until the snap. If the preceding play was a live play, the clock starts after the penalty is enforced or after a declaration of refusal.

In the two-minute offense, the quarterback acts immediately after the play. He either calls a time-out or signals the formation. We want to run the two-minute offense with the same personnel grouping and, hopefully, with the same formation. As soon as the play is over, the quarterback looks directly at the coaches on the sideline. He gets the play or a time-out signal.

Running to the spot of the ball, the quarterback calls the direction of the formation and signals that direction to the receivers coming back to the line from downfield. We want to keep the formation to the field. If the ball is in the middle of the field, we align in the formation from the prior play.

If the quarterback gets a play, he immediately calls it and snaps the ball. He never slows the pace of play unless the coach calls it. The coach decides if he wants to go no-huddle and speed up, or huddle and slow down. If we are trying to get in field-goal position, we want no time left on the clock after we kick the field goal.

If we are backed up in our own territory before the half, we go with our regular offense. On the first play, we could break a big play. That takes us out of our regular offense and puts us in the two-minute offense. That takes us from a slow tempo to a fast tempo all in one play. You do not want to call time-out to do that. You have to be organized and be ready to go with the two-minute offensive personnel when the situation changes.

The reverse situation occurs if the offense takes a big loss right before the half. We want to slow our offense and run out the clock.

On a temporary stoppage of the clock, the offense has to be on the line ready to snap the ball when it is marked ready for play. At Georgia, we do not huddle after an incomplete pass. We go back to the line of scrimmage and we hand signal the next play into the game.

After the ball is marked ready for play, the offense should have the play and be aligned. The officials in our league take 13 seconds from the time the player is down until the ball is marked ready for play. If we get in the no-huddle offense, the officials have a tendency to speed up their marking of the ball.

The quarterback never takes a sack, if possible. Throw the ball away to stop the clock. You can complete one of four passes and still win the game. If the quarterback takes a sack, we have to waste a time-out or it kills the drive. It you have no time-outs left, the clock could run out.

The ballcarrier has a role to play in the clock-management routine. He has to give the football to the referee quickly after the play. We want the running back to work the sideline. He cannot turn back into the field unless he is sure he can make the first down.

In the two-minute situation, the back should not struggle for extra yards. If the defense has one tackler on him and more coming, he cannot struggle for the extra one or two yards unless it means a first down. Get on the ground, give the ball to the official, and get ready for the next play.

We instruct the quarterback when he can use a time-out in the two-minute offense. If the situation is before the half, we may tell him not to take a time-out after a sack. In that situation, we get into a slow tempo so we do not have to punt the ball before halftime.

At the end of the game, we tell the quarterback to take the time-out immediately if the defense sacks him. The quarterback must have his eyes on the coach at all times while he is preparing the offense for the next play. That way you do not lose any time in calling a time-out.

The type of passes to use in the two-minute offense is where I learned a lot from Coach Smith. In the two-minute offense, there are certain types of passes for different situations. The first type of pass is the boundary throw. A boundary pass will be incomplete or the receiver will catch the ball and get out of bounds. Nothing else should happen on that play.

The next type of pass is the first-down pass. That is a pass thrown to achieve the first down. The depth of the first-down pass has to be in front of the first-down marker. If the quarterback completes that pass, we have a first down. The quarterback cannot throw to a checkdown receiver. He gets the first down or the ball is incomplete. Do not dump the ball to someone who has to run to get the first down.

The yardage pass is the best play the defense gives you. That comes from studying the film. You throw this type of play to gain yardage, even if it does not stop the clock. You throw this type of play if you have time and time-outs.

The touchdown pass is designed to do just that. It is a pass thrown into the end zone. If the receiver catches the ball, it is a touchdown. Either you score or the clock will stop. It could be a play right before half, when you are in field-goal range. You want the touchdown, but a field will be all right. You throw the touchdown pass and the ball is a score, or you line up and kick the field goal. If you throw the ball short of the end zone and run out of time, you look like a dummy because did not get the field goal.

We design the clock play to stop the clock by spiking the ball. To avoid the penalty, everyone has to be onside and still. The receivers simply have to align on the line of scrimmage. It does not matter if he is the flanker or split end. The formation does not matter; you need at least seven bodies on the line of scrimmage.

The bull's-eye play is a play to position the ball in the middle of the field. This is the play before we kick the field goal. If we have to go right to get to the middle of the field, the quarterback calls bull's-eye right. All the receivers align right and the entire line reach blocks to the right on the snap of the ball. The quarterback scrambles to the right and takes a knee in the middle of the field.

If we give him the bull's-eye and a time-out signal, he runs the play and immediately calls time-out. If we call the play and give him no time-out signal, he runs the play and milks the clock before he calls time-out. We could also call the bull's-eye and the clock play. That means we have no time-outs and we want to center the ball and kill the clock. On first down, the quarterback runs the bull's-eye play. Everyone resets quickly, the quarterback spikes the ball, and we kick the field goal.

We use the Mayday play when we are in trouble. The field-goal team has to run on the field and kick the ball with the clock running. We hope we have 20 seconds when this situation occurs. An example of that situation is third-and-25 yards for the first down from the 40-yard line. You throw the ball and gain 20 yards. You are in field-goal range, but the clock is not going to stop. When we make the Mayday call, everyone on that team knows the situation. They sprint on the field and get down. Everyone on the field who is not on the field-goal team has to get off the field with the same urgency as the team coming on the field.

This year, we played Tennessee at their field and had 25 seconds to go in the half. We had third-and-three to go from the three-yard line. We had no time-outs left in the half. We called what we thought was a touchdown pass. In this situation, we ran a double fade by the outside receivers and a four-step speed out by the inside receivers. Our All-American tight end ran a two-step speed out. He was in the end zone at one time, but caught the ball outside the end zone at the one-inch line. We used the Mayday call and kicked the field before the clock ran out for the half.

The first type of pass I want to show you are our boundary passes (Diagram #1). Our personnel group in the two-minute offense is three wide receivers, a tight end, and one back. We call the group eagle personnel. We align in the shotgun set. This is red gun right. The formation is a wide slot right by the Y- and Z-receivers with a tight end and X-receiver to the backside. We call the tight end Ted. The H back sets to the wide slotside in the shotgun.

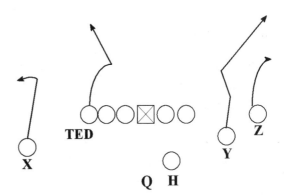

Diagram #1. Crush

We do flip our receivers in the two-minute offense. When we call right, our receivers have to be in particular positions. We call the pattern crush. In the huddle, we call 560-crush, which means we run 560 protection and the crush route. At the line, we give one call that means the protection scheme of the line as well as the routes for the receivers. The route is a five- to six-yard speed out for both outside receivers and flag routes by the inside receivers. In both of these routes, if we catch the ball we can get out of bounds. The play may not get the first down, but it gets the clock stopped.

Our protection is a basic slide protection for the line and a dual read for the H back blocking away from the slide. We can fan the back and dual read with the line as a change-up.

Another boundary pass is thunder (Diagram #2). In the regular offense, we motion the X-receiver into the wide slotside. In the two-minute offense, he aligns as the inside slot in the triple set. The outside receiver runs the go route, the outside slot runs a deep out at 12 yards, and the inside slot runs an arrow route to the sideline. The H back blocks the first defender off the edge and the quarterback sprints to the outside.

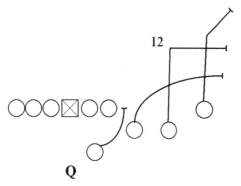

Diagram #2. Thunder

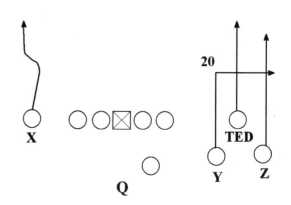

Diagram #4. Berlin Out

The receiver catches the pass and gets out of bounds or it is an incomplete pass.

Another boundary pass is corner/arrow (Diagram #3). This goes into the boundary. The set is a pro formation shotgun with the Y and H back in the backfield. The X-receiver runs the post-corner and the Y-receiver runs an arrow from his backfield set. The Ted stays in to block and the Z-receiver runs a deep post down the middle. The Z-receiver's pattern does not fit into a boundary-type play, but it is a home run ball if we complete it.

The next two plays are touchdown plays. This is our Berlin pass (Diagram #5). The middle receiver is our 6'8" tight end. We align him on the hash mark and he goes straight up the hash and sits down five yards deep in the end zone. The inside slot sprints down the field and ends up three yards past the tight end in the end zone. The outside receiver sprints down the field and ends up three yards in front of, and outside of, the tight end. The backside receiver sprints down the field to a point three to five yards inside the tight end.

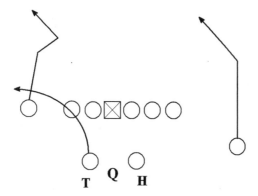

Diagram #3. Corner/Arrow

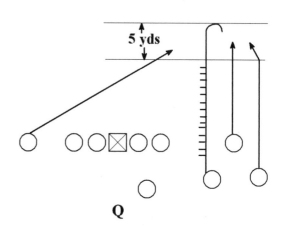

Diagram #5. Berlin

Those patterns are the boundary plays. I have one more play, but I do not have film on it. It is Berlin out (Diagram #4). We run our Hail Mary pass from this set. We align in a triple set with the receivers bunched right and a split end left. Everyone runs as deep as he can go, except the inside slot receiver. He runs a 20-yard out route. This makes the defense think you are going deep with everyone. We break the single receiver out and we may have a chance to get in field-goal range. This is a good pass at the end of a half, when the situation fits itself to it.

The quarterback throws the ball high and five yards deep in the end zone on the hash mark. The tight end is going up to make the catch. The other three receivers have built a triangle around him. If the tight end cannot catch the ball, there is a chance for the ball to ricochet to one of the other receivers. They have to be alert and alive when the tight end and defensive backs go up for the ball.

The next touchdown pass is Mayday (Diagram #6). We ran this pass when I talked about the Mayday field goal. We run double fade routes by the outside receivers and double four-step speed outs by the inside receivers. If the pass is complete, in most cases it is a touchdown.

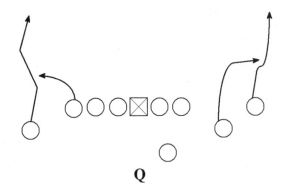

Diagram #6. Mayday

This is the play against Tennessee on national TV when the tight end ran the wrong pattern. Fortunately, we had enough time to run the field-goal team on the field and get the field goal.

This next group of plays is our first-down plays. If we complete this pass, it will be a first down. If we catch the pass, the clock stops and the chains move. If we do not catch it, the clock stops and we run another play. We call this play stick (Diagram #7). Into the field, we run a 10- to 12-yard out by the outside receiver. If the corner plays soft on this receiver, we take the pattern. The inside receiver runs a flag route toward the sideline. If we have more than 10 yards to go for the first down, we do not call this play.

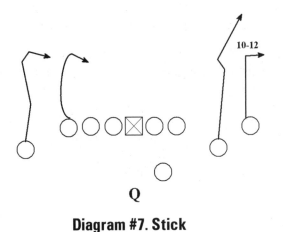

Diagram #7. Stick

To the boundary side, the tight end and X-receiver run a stick route. This is a double dig route. They run their pattern two yards past the yardage needed for the first down and run a dig. They are eight to 10 yards apart in their routes.

The next play is delta (Diagram #8). This play is the same play as the stick. The difference is the boundary outside receiver runs the bench, or 10- to 12-yard out pattern. The field receivers run the dig routes. They get two yards past the sticks and run their stick routes.

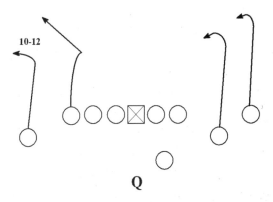

Diagram #8. Delta

The Berlin in runs off the Hail Mary set (Diagram #9). The receivers to the wide side take off on go routes. The outside receiver runs a 20-yard in route. The backside receiver runs a bench route.

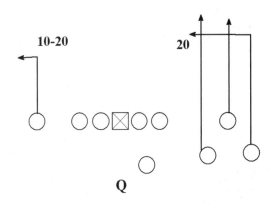

Diagram #9. Berlin In

I have one more play, called prison rebel (Diagram #10). We trade the tight end from the left to the right. Both the wide receivers to that side come off the line of scrimmage. The single receiver is never in the read. We tell the quarterback that he will never throw the ball to the backside.

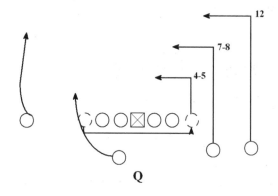

Diagram #10. Prison Rebel

The tight end runs a three-step dig pattern. The slot receiver runs a five-step dig pattern. The outside receiver runs a seven- to nine-step dig pattern. The tight end's pattern is four to five yards deep, the pattern of the slot is seven to eight yards deep, and the outside receiver is 12 yards deep. If I call prison rebel and the tight end cannot get the first down, I made the mistake.

Against Tennessee two years ago, we had 11 seconds remaining in the game. We were trailing 19-14. We were on the 39-yard line. We could throw the Hail Mary or the Berlin out play. We decided to throw this pattern. It can be risky. We felt we had time for two plays. We wanted to get closer with the rebel play.

Tennessee covered the first and second options, but the third receiver caught the ball and almost scored. However, he almost ran us out of time also. He got out of bounds and we had two seconds to go in the game. We got the second play, but it was incomplete and we lost the game.

Quickly let us go over and review what I have covered. When you get into the two-minute offense, you need to get into a personnel group that you will not have to change.

You want to line up in a formation you can call in the two-minute offense, without a huddle, and without taking too much time at the line of scrimmage. For us to call the formation and play, we say right crush.

You must have a plan to get into the two-minute offense and a plan to get out of it. You also want a plan to start in the regular offense and get into the two-minute offense if you hit a big play.

You need the right tools to run the two-minute offense. You need boundary passes. We design them to get receivers the ball and get them out of bounds. You need first-down passes. The receivers must know that if they catch the ball, they have enough yardage for the first down.

On the touchdown passes, if you catch the ball it is a touchdown. If you do not complete the pass, it is incomplete and the clock is stopped.

Bull's-eye is the ability to get the ball into the middle of the field for a field-goal attempt. We never give the bull's-eye signal without another signal with it. We call bull's-eye with the clock play, time-out, or milk to time-out.

You never know what is going to happen to you. The one time you get your rear end embarrassed in front of your fans, they never seem to forget it. My time happened to be on national TV in my first year as head coach. People wanted to know if I knew what I was doing. I wondered myself. I had to walk into our locker room, apologize to my team, and tell them I blew it. You do not want to do that to your players.

I could have handled the situation differently. We had a player miss a block on that one-yard plunge and we did not score. I could have come into the locker room ranting and raving about the poor job on the goal line. However, when I took the blame, that meant a lot to those players and my assistant coaches. That made a big difference down the road for our football team. If you make a mistake, admit it. I appreciate your attention. Thank you.

DEFENSIVE FUNDAMENTALS AND DRILLS

University of Miami

Thank you for the applause. We always give the high school coaches a round of applause every chance we get. We have two of our assistant coaches with us tonight. First is Tim Walton, our defensive backs coach. Tim has been with us for the past three years and he does a great job. After I finish with this session, Tim will go to another room for a breakout session on defensive back techniques and drills.

Also with us is Coach Clint Hurtt, our defensive line coach. He was at FIU last year. Two years ago, he was a grad assistant for us. He is a Miami graduate. He has a lot of knowledge of what we want to do with our defensive scheme. He will have a breakout session as well on defensive line play.

One thing I want to do tonight is give you something to take back to your program. After I cover some of the basic things we do, we will have the three breakout sessions: defensive backs, defensive line, and linebackers. You can ask me anything you want about our defense team-wise, or about linebacker play.

At the University of Miami, we will not accept anything less than speed. The way we train speed all the time is by power. We base everything we do on speed and power. We never stress schemes over fundamentals. We are always going to go with fundamentals over schemes. If you do not have strong fundamentals, it matters little what scheme you run.

We have a number of things in our defensive package. We blitz and get after people, but we base the schemes we teach on concepts. Those concepts are deeply rooted in techniques. We teach them every day, we practice them every day, and our players play fast because they understand those fundamentals.

One thing coaches like to use to make excuses is that speed is hard to teach. If you have a scheme you believe in and trust, you can teach it to your team. Defensive football is about getting off blocks, releasing outside, and reading base blocks. The one thing that always gets the young coach is thinking about schemes and forgetting about fundamentals. It got me a couple of times two years ago. We lost two or three games that year. I started thinking about schemes and stopped coaching the fundamentals. Coach Walton reminded me that we needed to get back to our fundamentals. We did much better after we went back to the fundamentals.

What I am going to show you tonight is what we do every day to teach our players to chase the ball. The drills we do in practice, you can see in the games. I will show you how we set up the drills and show you the tapes of us running those drills. After that, I will show you some game tapes, where you can see the drills pay off in good play in those games.

It is all about repetition. I learned that one point in the coaching business. The more reps you get in practice, the better your players perform in the games.

In practice, we do the Pursuit Drill every day (Diagram #1). In the drill, we line up two ballcarriers. We align them on the uprights of the goal post on the five-yard line and put cones five yards from the hash mark on each side. We place another cone down the field outside the numbers on each side. We huddle our defense and break the huddle. We line up in the defense called in the huddle.

Everyone aligns in the defense and coverage called in the huddle. The key to this drill is to make

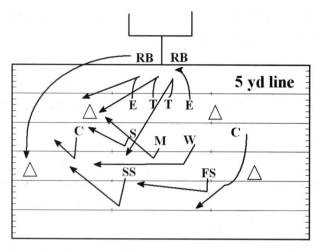

Diagram #1. Pursuit Drill

sure the defenders pursuing the football are not following the same-colored jersey. We tell our players every day not to follow their teammate's jersey on the pursuit drill. When we get to the ballcarrier, we want to arrive in a frenzy.

In the drill, you coach the fundamentals of football. We want to get off the ball, get in a good football position, and run to the ball. We constantly remind the players to bend their knees.

We have three ways to do the drill. We pursue the run going left. Then we come back and pursue going to the right. We pursue the ball on a screen. The best thing we do is our pursuit-interception phase of the drill. In the last six years, we have returned more interceptions for touchdowns then anyone in the country.

If we get a pursuit interception, we treat it like a punt return (Diagram #2). We want to get to the

nearest sideline to form a wall on the hash to get to the end zone. If we get an interception, we try to score with it. If the defensive back gets his hands on the ball, he has to catch it.

When we intercept the ball, the defenders become the offense. You must emphasize to them to block upfield and not behind the ball. The nearest defensive back to the ball blocks the intended receiver. The defensive end to the side of the interception has the quarterback. Everyone else gets to the near sideline and forms the wall. On an interception, we always emphasize getting into the end zone.

Everyone must come back and block. In the films, we find loafers all the time not doing what they should be doing. We have typical defensive linemen. All they want is the sack. When we find them loafing, we remind them in practice what it takes to score on defense.

We do not have specific pursuit lanes. We found that if we put players in pursuit lanes, the faster players outran the slower ones. We never got that true staggered line of tacklers coming in an orderly fashion, one after the other. That is when we adjusted our rules on pursuit and told our players not to follow the same-colored jersey to the ball. That means your faster players arrive at the proper position in their pursuit. The slower players take deeper angles to get to the ball.

The next drill we do is the Bag Drill (Diagram #3). I got this drill from Bill Belichick of the New England Patriots. I went up to their camp and watched the drill. I asked him why he did the drill. He told me that this was a quick drill and it got the players' motors going fast. You do the drill fast, and get them moving and flying around in practice. This gets the players breaking a sweat.

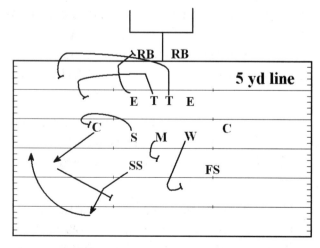

Diagram #2. Pursuit Interception

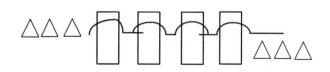

Diagram #3. Bag Drill

In the Bag Drill, we do a number of different things. We run over the bags going one way and come back over them going the other way. We backpedal, and we shuffle in and out of the bags. As they go through the bags shuffling, they touch the end of the bags. This makes them bend their knees and stay down. That keeps their pad level low. They start in the first chute and sprint forward. At the end of the chute, they change direction and shuffle over to the next chute. They backpedal through that chute, change direction, pop the end of the bag, and shuffle to the next chute. They repeat the same exercise in each chute.

In the drill, we emphasize speed, quickness, and accelerating upfield. In football, the defense makes most of their plays going upfield. We do not want to go east and west.

The next drill we do is an old-fashioned string-out drill. We have done this drill at the University of Miami for as long as I can remember. I played for Jimmy Johnson and he started this drill. He did this drill when he was the head coach. I played for him in Dallas and he did it down there.

It is a drill in which the defender has to bend his knees, get off blocks, explode, and run through the ballcarrier. To set up the drill, you need a ballcarrier, two offensive blockers, and one defender. The offensive blockers are defensive linemen or linebackers. We want the other defensive players to make our man work on the drill.

On our Shed Drill, the offensive blocker aligns down on the hash mark (Diagram #4). The second blocker is five yards behind him. The defender aligns on the blocker on the hash mark. The ballcarrier

aligns on the upright of the goal post, five yards behind the second blocker.

The first blocker has one shot to get the defender blocked. The drill is set up like a get-off block. It is not a continuous effort by the blocker. He tries to take the defender off his feet with one cut. The key to this drill is the offensive blockers. They have to make the defender work. It cannot be a brother-in-law drill, where the offense tries to make the defender look good. If they do not go hard, it does not work in the games.

The defender takes on the first blocker. He gets off the blocker and attacks the next blocker. The key is to not let the defender run laterally. If he does that, he is running away from the pressure instead of penetrating upfield.

The defender wants to come off low with bent knees, use good hand placement, rip through the blocker's outside shoulder, and get upfield. The thing you want to do is get up the field and not run laterally to the outside. If they run laterally, the defender opens a big gap for the runner to cutback.

He uses good techniques to defeat the first block, plays the second block the way he did the first, and gets upfield for the ballcarrier. When he gets to the ballcarrier, he explodes and runs through the tackle. He does not put the ballcarrier on the ground. He makes good contact using proper tackling techniques. One thing we do in this drill is to shoot the hips all the time on a tackle.

We make sure the ballcarrier is running downhill. We do not want to make the arc wide to encourage the defender to widen. He wants to come downhill from the hash mark, aiming at the corner cone on the goal line. The dummy players in the drill are what make the defender improve his techniques.

If the defender does not play in a hurry, his angle to the ballcarrier is not good and he is behind him. He has to stay low, play with his hands, and bend his knees.

The next drill is an important drill, particularly for freshmen coming into our program. This form drill emphasizes shooting the hips. We treat the tackle

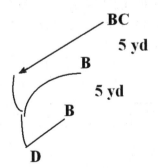

Diagram #4. Shed Drill

just as you treat the power clean used in high school. You must bring the hips into the tackle and bring the butt through on the tackle. We use a tackling circuit using the fit principles and the fundamentals of tackling. The chief emphasis at each station is rolling the hips and maximizing the hits.

If defensive linemen penetrate, they can make more tackles than anyone in the defense. When we practice low block drills, everyone on the defense practices them. The defensive line, linebackers, and defensive backs all, at one time or another, have to play against that kind of block.

The fumbles you will see in the film do not just pop out. We practice ripping the ball away from ballcarriers every day in practice. We club and punch the ball when we tackle. If we are in the open field, we try to scoop the ball up and score. (Film)

Every Thursday in practice, we go over the two-minute drill. In that drill, we walk through the practice of what to do if a turnover occurs in the last two minutes of the game. If you have an opportunity to recover a fumble, get on the ball. Do not attempt to pick it up and score. If you intercept a pass, get to the ground at the first sign of a tackler.

If the defense gains possession of the ball in the last two minutes of a game, the game is over. If the turnover occurs, make sure we keep possession of the ball. Too many times during an interception return, the defender gets the ball stripped and the offense regains possession.

As I said earlier, fundamentals are the keys to everything we do. When we try to outscheme teams, that is when we screw up. We teach fundamentals over schemes. Then we can become a great defense.

Coach Randy Shannon—Linebackers

Let me get started again by asking this question: Would you prefer that we talk about linebacker play or go over drills for linebackers? You want me to talk about coaching linebackers.

The most important thing in coaching linebackers is to teach the basics of what you want to accomplish. You have to be careful of how you say certain things. When I worked with the Dolphins, I told Zach Thomas to keep his outside arm free. He played the technique alright, but the other players were having trouble playing the technique the way we wanted them to play. I had to change my verbiage and say, stay head up and keep your outside arm free.

By saying exactly what we wanted them to do, we got the desired technique. We wanted them to play with the outside arm free and not open the gap. For every instruction you give the linebackers, give them one more detail to define what you want. When you say attack the blocker in the V of his neck, take it one more step. Tell him to attack the V of the neck and keep the outside arm free.

If you tell a 6-technique end not to be reached, the first thing he does is run outside. When he runs outside, he opens the C gap and puts the pressure on someone else to fill it. What you should tell them is, do not worry about being reached. If the tight end reaches the 6 technique, the first thing he has to do is not panic. He works upfield and continues to work his outside arm. He will eventually work back outside. Even if we never get back outside, if the play has to hump to get to the outside, we did our job. We got penetration so the play could not hit to the outside quickly.

We play a 4-3 defense and our linebacker reads vary as to the teams we play. As you watch film, you will find every coach has mannerisms in the way he teaches backs to run plays. When we play certain teams, as soon as the running back takes his first step, we know the play. In our defense, it is hard to teach the linebacker to react off the movement he sees in the offensive line.

We read the action of the backs and follow the scouting report. Learning the mannerisms of the backs will lead the linebacker to the play quicker. When teams run the trap play, what do they do with the tailback? They flare him off to one side. When I tried to teach the linebacker to read the blocking scheme of everyone instead of the mannerisms of the back, it was hard. When I taught them the mannerisms of the backs, it was easy. Now they knew what play was coming and who would block them right away.

I will take any questions you may have at this time.

Question: Whom do the linebackers key against in the wing-T?

Wing-T football is similar to playing the option. The thing about playing wing-T teams is this. There is always a runner and always a cross runner. That is how they set the plays up in the wing-T.

You must always have a man that will split the wing, and you must have a backside player against the pro scheme. This is the way we teach it. The middle linebacker has the fullback and the Will and Sam linebackers have to cross key. When you see a wing-T team, you can look at their films and see that they are similar to some of the old wishbone teams such as Arkansas and Oklahoma. You can look at any backs you want to look at, but the cross key will get the linebacker to the play a little faster. You need the extra linebacker to be the cutback player. If the play cuts back, the Mike linebacker may make the stop, but the backside linebacker must make the play.

Question: What do you teach the linebacker to do on runners coming out of the backfield?

I teach them to do whatever the running back does. If a receiver takes a step outside, the linebacker should be taking the same step. If the back runs the counter trey play, the linebacker should make the counter step, and then come back to his starting position when the back cuts back on the counter. We want to mirror whatever he does. For example, if it is a pass, the back opens to get on his route. The linebacker should open as the back opens and he reads the path of the back.

On a draw play, when that back takes a counter step, the linebacker takes that same counter step. When the back goes downhill on the draw play, the linebacker goes downhill with him. That is what I mean by reading the mannerisms of the back. If you can do that, the back will take you to the ball. Pro football is so fast now. Because there is so much

speed in the game, you cannot afford to come up short by one step. There is a lot of speed in high school football today.

Question: How do keep the linebackers from taking false steps?

We teach a drill to prevent the linebackers from taking a false step. We set up two cones side by side and one yard apart. We set up another cone for the back, so the linebacker can get his read. We have the back simulate his first step. The linebacker gets his read on the back. The back must take a direct step on his path. A lot of linebackers like to shuffle their feet in two quick steps. When they do that, they have taken a false step on a false read. Now the question is, can he get around the blocking scheme and accelerate upfield?

For the middle linebacker, we set up a shield dummy and force him to go inside-out on the dummy and then work upfield. For the outside linebackers, they have to come around the shield dummy and then work upfield. We take the shield and stand the linebackers up as they come on their track upfield. If the linebackers are not coming around the dummy and getting upfield, we give a good shot with the shield. For the middle linebacker, they must get inside the shield. If they are not doing it right, we give them a good, hard shot with the shield. We use this drill a lot when we have linebackers that are taking a false step.

When the linebacker sees the path of the back, he must recognize who is going to block him. He must know the tight end or tackle is going to try to control him. Once he makes the read on the back, his eyes must go to the man that is going to block him. He cannot run in there like a wild dog in a meat house.

My time is up. I will be around if you have additional questions. Thank you.

WHY COVER 4

Waynesburg College

Thank you. It is a pleasure to be here with you representing Waynesburg College. We are talking about cover 4 today, which I have always loved since the time when I first started coaching.

Cover 4 gets the secondary into an aggressive mode of behavior. It gets players into a position to stop the run.

Why Cover 4?

- Align/adjust: Basic four-across alignment allows the secondary to adjust to formation, personnel grouping, and motion.

- Support vs. the run: Depending on formation and backfield set, cover 4 will allow eight or nine defenders in the box versus the run.

- Flexibility vs. play-action passes: Cover 4 enables us to handle full- and split-flow play-action pass variations with four deep defenders.

- Coverage disguise: With safeties aligned at funnel depth, it makes it easy to match routes in coverage, use robber concepts to both strong and weaksides, as well as play both odd and even coverages

- Handle four verticals: Cover 4 allows us to handle balanced one-back sets by matching four defensive backs on four vertical threats.

Here is our base alignment versus pro (Diagram #1). I am showing an eagle front here, but you can play it out of a 4-3 just as well. I used to play a lot of over front with an eagle concept, putting the 3 technique on the tight-end side and the Sam up on the line of scrimmage.

In any case, what I like to do with the corners is pretty simple. I like the corners to play that inside technique. I think that is important for me.

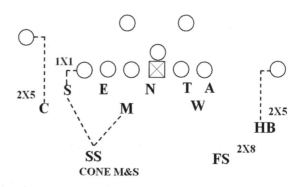

Diagram #1. Base Alignment/Pro

The rules in this situation are simple and I will talk a little more about them later. Even though we are a cover 4 secondary, I like to play a lot of match and robber coverages with them. In that case, we will be reading routes as much as we can, and that is why I go back to practicing several plays against the play-action pass game. It is very important along with the run fits.

Now, this next slide shows a single-width alignment (Diagram #2). Against this formation, a decision must be made about handling the tight-end side, where there is a strong run opportunity, and still defending the open-end side with the threat of two verticals or a quick pass.

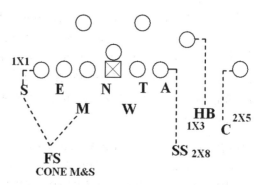

Diagram #2. Base Alignment/Twins

Okay, let us look at the next slide (Diagram #3). This diagram shows our run supports and the fits for our secondary. If we get a full-flow support, this is what we really have to rep, and it has to fit the way we will handle the play-action game.

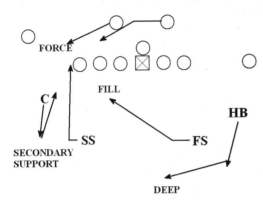

Diagram #3. Run Support/Flow

The corner has inside shade. He will take his normal read steps and read inside through the number 2 receiver. We are almost ignoring number 1 and the wider he lines up, the more I want to ignore him. We are almost going to get into some basketball concepts when we talk about how we will defend the pass. Then it becomes how good the quarterback is, which will determine whether we stay in cover 4 or use it in a disguise situation.

The strong safety will get a downhill fit off of the hat read of the tight end. Because our Sam plays aggressively, that will more than likely be right off of the hip of the Sam. The backer supports are not shown, but I trust you know how they fit.

The weak safety is our "hole checker." He plays flat and slow to the hole. Ball on the line of scrimmage, he comes down. Ball off the line of scrimmage, he is back zoning the deep third. The weakside corner HB is already playing inside leverage, so he goes "backpedal, run, run, run," and stays high over top of the post. Once again, we are going to rep the fits, rep the fits, and rep the fits in a 5-on-3 shell, which I will show you, and we are leery of the throwback post.

If you play cover 4, you have to commit to it, especially if you are going to match patterns, and you have to rep those things out or you could be in trouble. I actually love to attack cover 4 as much as I like to play it on defense.

I want to show a little bit of our weakside support (Diagram #4). Almost everything is the same here in the fit. We show backer support here, we show secondary contain. We are just showing the same thing.

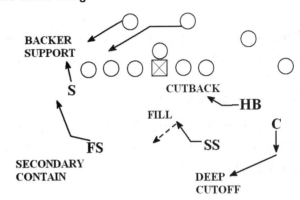

Diagram #4. Run Support/Flow

Now, this slide shows the weakside fit and where the force is coming from (Diagram #5). Now, again this is going to need to be repped up, because we are bringing the free safety into the fit. We have the Sam to the tight-end side, so he becomes the fold player and will check the cutback windows on his pursuit angle. That will allow the strong safety to be more aggressive, and in this situation against flow weak, he is almost in a situation where he can replace the Mike linebacker. Then, we will give our Mike linebacker a lot of freedom to get in the run-through, take the open window, and go from there.

Against play-action pass here, Sam is slow to go. If the ball is on the line, safeties are in the fit, but

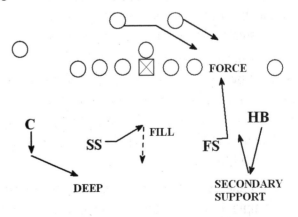

Diagram #5. Run Support/Webb

if ball is off the line, the strong safety had better bust his tail to get back.

If run, the free safety fits off the edge of the anchor. We have a color fit here with the Will linebacker. If he gets a closed window, he will scrape over the top of that and the safety will fit off of the Will's hip, but if he gets an open window, the safety fits off of the anchor's hip. Of course, the halfback on the weakside has secondary run support, and we have deep cutoff with the backside corner.

Originally, how I started getting into cover 4 and liking it came about because our corners were always overly aggressive on inside routes. Corners get very nosy on inside routes, which means they are susceptible to curl-flat wheel, to double moves, and also to playing the run. I wanted to make it simpler for them and that his how I got started with this.

This next slide shows run support versus split flow (Diagram #6). I want to talk about the keys now. We already talked about the hat read for the safety coming over the tight end, but if we want a quick key, I would put the strong safety through the tight end to the near back, the linebackers will play the depth of the backs, and the weak safety is on the tailback.

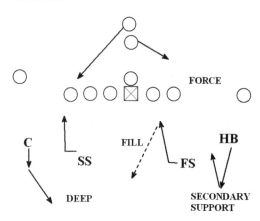

Diagram #6. Run Support/Split

That is "no matter what." If we get stretch zone or whatever, it is going to make it easier for us, especially on the backside, to get into our fits and get into the cutback lane. In this case, if we see stretch zone, we have the fill, and we have the safety up in the hole replacing the backer. Of course, if the ball is off the line of scrimmage, he gets out of there.

Now, I want to go to the next slide and look at pass-defense assignments (Diagram #7). The corner takes his read steps, staying deeper than the deepest in his quarter of the field, and sees number 2. The Sam linebacker covers windows and has a 2-to-1 read.

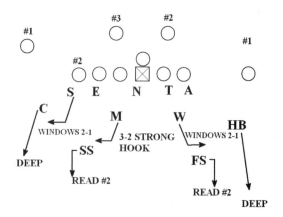

Diagram #7. Pass Assignments

The safety is reading number 2. If number 1 releases outside right now to the strongside of the field, the safety robs number 1. We will talk more about that, but if number 2 is out, we will look immediately for number 1 coming in. We are going to rob any in route and we will get under the post with a man turn.

In the hook to curl area, Mike works 3 to 2. Mike, Sam, and the safety are really going to work together in the pass game. No matter what happens outside, these three guys together work inside 2 to 3 off of the fit. Obviously, if 2 goes out we expect 1 to come in.

Let me talk for a minute about a defensive back drill progression.

Defensive Back Drill Progression

- Footwork/pedal
- Pedal turn
- Read pedal with man turn
- Weave drill
- W drill
- Four square
  - ✓ Incorporate W progression with breaks
  - ✓ Angle sticks at 45 to zero/45 to 90/45 to 45 high

- Boundary corner funnel
- Crack replace

We like to pedal and turn into the receiver, kind of reroute him, use the boundary, and do a little NASCAR technique on him. We teach the defensive backs that it is okay to engage the wide receivers. In most cases, the receivers do not want that kind of contact and can be rerouted. We are very tactful in how we play the coverage and how we use our hands when we are running with these guys in phase, and maybe bumping them some. All you need is a little bit.

Our Weave Drill is pretty simple. We partner up, weave, and maintain our leverage point. In our case, we will play inside leverage in cover 4, so as we weave we maintain inside leverage and reduce to the ball.

Of course, everybody does a W Drill, but out of this Four Square Drill we will do pedals, turns, 45-degree breaks, and incorporate our W Drill into it so we are also working on breaking on the ball. We are going to do a bunch of things in this drill.

Now, we will rep a lot of this boundary corner funnel, because we like to take our most aggressive corner HB and play him in some press alignments. When I say press, it depends on how good our guy is as to how physical we can be. Some coaches say you cannot take a defensive back and play him off a receiver at four yards, that it defeats the purpose. They believe that if you are going to press, you should go up and get in his face, play the hip and trail, play the leverage point, or, if not, just play him from back off the line of scrimmage.

We will explore that concept, but if we can reroute a guy and be up in there to deter some of the short throws, bubble throws, arcs, and flat routes, just by alignment, we will do it. We will not play contact from that position at all. We will reroute by alignment and play the concept from there. I am still going to stick with that, even though some coaches do not want their guys lunging. We just will not lunge. We will just play that imaginary line, that leverage point, so we reroute our guys without making any contact whatsoever.

This crack replace drill is important for the corners, and you need to rep this a ton, because one of the weaknesses of playing cover 4 is getting cracked by the wide receivers. The great running teams will come out and stalk two or three times, and then they will bring their wideouts up the field five yards, turn inside, and crack back on the safety. If the corner is sleeping, they will break the big play.

There is a lot of theory on coming up with the combination routes that you need to defend. The four basic patterns for us include the curl-flat combination, the fork route where number 1 runs post and number 2 bends out under it, the high-low concept, and the four verticals. We defend those instead of going out every day in practice and repping every single route. Rep those four basic concepts every day, because every route is pretty much built off of those concepts anyway. When you see a particular route, you can go back and refer to the basic concept.

Now I want to talk about rules for cornerbacks.

Fundamental Rules for Corners

- Maintain inside leverage
- See number 2 to number 1 (check vertical)
- No curl/no dig/high on post
- Break on anything in your quarter
  - ✓ Quick out
  - ✓ Deep out
  - ✓ Corner
  - ✓ Late on hitch
  - ✓ Man turn on vertical (play basketball—ball/me/man)

This is why I wanted to get into quarters coverage and why I wanted to know more about it. I wanted to make things as easy as I possibly could for every position. Now, I know the corners are secondary on most run supports, but I did not want them to get too nosy. I did not want them getting beat by double moves and I did not want to get beat by wheel routes. What I ended up saying to the corners was this: You have a vertical plane on the field. You are going to play on a vertical plane, and you have anything that breaks to the out. Now, we are obviously going to be a little late on the out, and we may be a little late on the dig route. We know that because of the leverage point, we will hold, but at the same time, if we take away the window inside, that quarterback has to throw it outside on time, and he has to make a perfect throw.

Cover 4 takes a lot of thinking off of the corners. They do not have to worry about as much stuff, it makes them relax a little more, and it allows them to play a little more aggressively. They have no curl responsibility, no dig responsibility. They play high over the post and high over the dig. Now, if we can do a good job of playing the underneath windows and taking away the first-down look, many quarterbacks will stay with the first read too long and we get a coverage sack.

We do not "spot drop" our linebackers. When teaching match coverage, especially in the underneath zones, it becomes a lot easier for everyone if you take windows away. We teach our linebackers about spacing and about where that first window is going to break to the interior. We have to play the windows and take away that inside throw.

So we want our corners to maintain inside leverage, see number 2 to number 1, be leery of the verticals, and be ready to squeeze them. No curl, no dig, be high on the post, and break on anything in your quarter. Be late on the hitch and man turn on the vertical. Saying to stay deeper than the deepest is okay, and if the backers can play the windows correctly, they will get some tipped balls and the corners will get some steals.

Now, let us get to the drills for the safeties.

Safety Drill Progression

- Work flat to pedal
- Work flat break alley/support
- Work flat check hole/zone/middle
- Streamer Drill
  - ✓ Deeper than the deepest
- W Drill
- Four Square Drill
  - ✓ Incorporate W progression with breaks
  - ✓ Angle sticks at 45 to zero/45 to 90/45 to 45 high
- Vertical
  - ✓ Eight- to 10-yard vertical rule
  - ✓ Lock man after eight yards

Safeties are not working deep as much. They are working flatter, so you can play with their alignment. You can put them at 10, you can put them at eight, at nine, or even at seven. It depends on the kind of athlete you have, and how experienced he may be.

They should "work flat break alley," always conscious of what their support is and where their fits are, and knowing where help is. We are always going to work flat and then do our breaks. We are going to do a lot of "checking the hole" in our shell drill, working with our safeties, and then zoning up the middle of the field.

In the Streamer Drill, we put a safety at 10 yards and we run two receivers down the field that are five yards on either side of him. We just want them in a good solid backpedal and getting high over the top of the break.

We will still do some W Drills and the same Four Square Drill, where we incorporate the W progression with all the angle breaks, but the biggest thing is going to be the vertical rule and that is the toughest thing to teach. As a high school coach, the rule was always five yards for me. With a five-yard vertical rule, I could tell the safeties the quickest way to identify when number 2 ran an out route, as opposed to holding him in a vertical read. At the college level, we will say that if he gets to eight yards, just carry the seam and at 10 it becomes man, beyond eight to 10 yards. In high school, I just wanted to make it simple—get the quickest read, get the next move, and get into position. That vertical rule is going to be a pretty key thing—that and the way you adjust to double sets—but we are locking man after eight yards.

Fundamental Rules for Safeties

- Hat read for support
- Key near or deepest back for flow
- Play flat before you commit
- Play number 2 out vs. pass
  - ✓ Strong number 2 out, look to number 1
  - ✓ Strong number 2 vertical, carry the seam eight to 10, lock past 10
  - ✓ Weakside play number 2 out (tackle box rule)
    - ❍ Number 2 stays, double number 1 weak
    - ❍ Number 2 out, play release
    - ❍ Number 2 flat rob curl/slant by number 1
    - ❍ Number 2 vertical, carry seam eight to 10, lock at 10

When we say to read hat for run support, the weak safety should key the near lineman through to the back, whether he is near or in the I set. I cannot say it enough that our safeties are to play flat before they commit. We will teach patience and we will rep out that play-action. Everyone knows we want to stop the run, so when we get against a running team they will run, run, run, lull you to sleep, play-action pass, and you get hit. You have to respect your other teammates and be where you need to be at all times.

"Strong number 2 out, look to number 1" is obviously speaking to the tight-end side, and if 2 goes vertical, carry the seam and lock past 10 yards. The Sam, Mike, and safety to the tight-end side will work 2 to 3 off of that configuration.

On the weakside, we will play "number 2 out" using a tackle box rule. If number 2 stays, we are doubling number 1. We do not have another receiver in the flat, so we are in the "bonus" position, and that takes away one of the weaknesses of the cover 4 configuration.

Now, in the second scenario, number 2 is out, so we play the release. If number 2 goes flat, we will rob number 1. If number 2 goes vertical, carry the seam as if he was removed to the flank as an H in a double set. If the back releases through the tackle box, the safety lets the underneath coverage deal with him, because he is up in the mix.

Now, let us talk about our shell drill.

Shell Drill Progression

- 5-on-3 (Fit Drill)
  - ✓ Run fits vs. flow
  - ✓ Play-action
  - ✓ Match patterns
- Split skelly (no help, quarter, quarter, half)
- Split line match-up skelly
- Combination quarter coverage vs. double sets
- Crack replace
- Option period

We will talk about these 5-on-3 fits versus run and versus flow, some 5-on-3 Drill versus play-action, and then we will talk about our basic pattern matches out of a 5-on-3 shell without the corners.

While we are working the 5-on-3 Drill, we have a bunch of things going on with the corners. We are teaching the Funnel Drill, we are teaching crack replace, we are working against stalk blocks, and all those things we do in our practice plan and in our progression.

We are going to talk about split skelly, and what is "no help," what is "quarter-quarter-half," "split line match-up" where we just break it down and work the combination coverages, combination quarter coverage versus double sets, the crack replacement, and assignments versus option.

Now let us go to the next slide and look at the 5-on-3 Drill (Diagram #8). Here is the way the drill is going to look, but in many cases that will be a coach instead of a center, on one knee snapping the ball. He will be coaching the quarterback on his fakes,

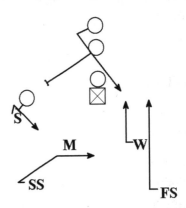

Diagram #8. 5-on-3 Run Fit

the running backs on their steps, and talking to them about what they are doing. On defense, we are coaching linebackers and safeties working their fits, and talking to them about where they need to be. This is a run fit drill.

On this next slide, we are looking at 5-on-3 versus the play-action pass (Diagram #9). We get the counter action fake and obviously, we are going to respect the play fake. The strong safety is going to get his hat read and the tight end comes out high. The strong safety is going to stay flat, the ball is off the line of scrimmage, and we go to our coverage responsibilities. We will play 2 to 3 with the Sam in the underneath, and we want the quarterback to throw that flat route to the fullback. Initially, we want to take away what looks to be the inside window.

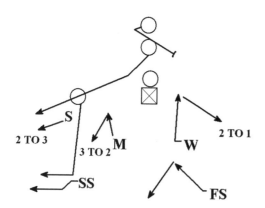

Diagram #9. 5-on-3 Play-Action Pass

In this case, it is a play-action pass, so Sam is slow to go anyway. He really has to take a good angle to take away that first window, so he will be very high over top of the fullback in the flat. The free safety is checking cutback and then must be leery of the post, from either the tight end or the X on the backside, because he is leaving on the hard play fake.

You have all seen those counter post throwbacks where you fake counter and throw a double-post throwback. The inside number 2 takes the safety, the cross-field safety takes the low post route, so they open up the deep post behind it, and they just read off the safety. You have to rep those things.

In the next slide, this is a Shell Pass Drill where we made it easy and put the quarterback in the gun (Diagram #10). This is a tough play to defend and, quite honestly, it exposes the weakness of the coverage. We have already talked about number 2 backside releasing outside to the flat. The Will linebacker will push, and the safety is looking to rob number 1. Our strong safety will lock the tight end and should get some help from the weak corner, who will play high on the split end vertical with inside leverage. We have to really rep this one out and get our guys used to seeing this concept.

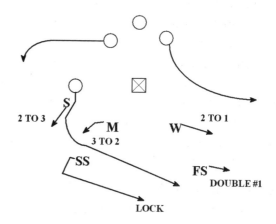

Diagram #10. 5-on-3 Shell Pass

At any rate, this NCAA route is tough to defend when you are in quarters coverage against a two-back set. It would be a lot easier to defend if number 2 stays in or comes up the seam. Now, if he comes up the seam, we lose our Will linebacker from the flat area but you still have the safety getting some depth and the corner playing high.

This is a foundation drill for us, this 5-on-3 shell. We practice fits on both sides of the ball, offense and defense. It is a very important drill and we are in it every practice that we are out on the field.

Now, let us talk about split skelly (Diagram #11). Under normal circumstance, there would be an offensive coach here snapping two balls, with a quarterback and a back working strongside to two receivers and a quarterback and a back working weakside with a single receiver. We will show you the weakside part of the drill in the next slide.

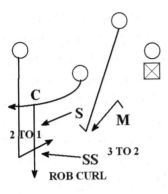

Diagram #11. Split Skelly

Anyway, in the split-line skelly, we are going to start working some of our progression reads, or pattern-read situations. We are going to play with half the coverage, take our time with it, and rep it out. When you guys have your seven-on-sevens in the summer, that is a great time to teach your guys where you want them to be, and even though there are weaknesses in every coverage, you can compensate with time spent, and build a secondary that communicates well together.

Again, in this drill, the cornerback stays high and the backers are getting in windows. This is really the time when you get on your underneath coverage guys and talk to them about getting in those window areas, as opposed to just dropping and being worried about the quarterback throwing the ball so quickly. Get them to run to their areas and force the quarterback to his next read.

Okay, on the splitside again (Diagram #12). As we go through these, we can add our formations in accordingly. We can work the strongside out of one back looking at a three-by-one set. We will look at

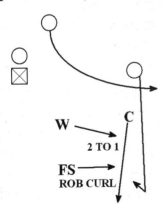

Diagram #12. Split Skelly

three-by-one double-width, three-by-one single-width, and go through all of the formations we are going to see. We will work against two out in the flank on the backside and work our true quarters concept, where we are reading two verticals challenging the weakside of the football.

Now, in the next slide we are looking at split-line skelly versus twins and I want to show you what I like about our adjustments to this set (Diagram #13). I like it when we want to kick our front and we are running some blitzes, and we want to get back over to the tight-end side to defend the football. That is something a lot of people worry about against the two-back twins set.

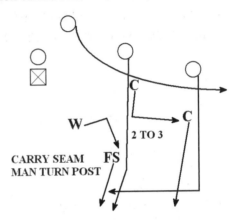

Diagram #13. Split Skelly Twins

In this case, we are going to rep this out. We are almost going to go hard outside with our inside corner and just look right at the quarterback. We want to see the triangle and really make it hard for number 2 to get outside of us. Then, we want to make it simple from that point.

If it is a run coming this way, we are going to flat-out press number 2 until we get where we need to be. It would be where the Sam would be if he was on that side of the ball. Then we will be over the top and it will be a true corner force, physical fit.

If number 2 releases inside and we press him until 3 comes, the corner is over the top of number 1 with inside leverage, and the rest of us play our fits.

Now, I want to look at the key points for our defense.

Key Points

- Wide corner rules (KISS)
- Eight-to-10 yard vertical rule
- Take away windows with basketball concepts
- Crack replace
- Need to rep play-action pass vs. play-action throwbacks
- Route recognition

The key points for us, before we go to tape here, have to do with wide corner alignment rules, and with "keep it simple, stupid." We cannot ask more of a player than he can reasonably learn to do. We are not going to teach any more than four techniques at one position. Of course, the better a player is, the less you would want to do anyway, but the more you add the more you make him think, and that may slow his reactions.

The eight-to-10 yard vertical rule is obviously significant, but you make it what you wish for the level you are on. Take away the windows in the underneath coverage using basketball concepts. When I say "ball-me-man," I am saying to make the quarterback throw through the defender. Take away his first down throw, his first look.

You cannot neglect the "crack replace" concept of your cover 4 coverage or you will surely suffer for it sooner or later. You also absolutely must rep the play-action stuff and the play-action throwbacks, or they will find the weaknesses of cover 4, because we are going to always be aggressive against the run.

Finally, you should identify four basic route concepts and rep those routes every day. Every combination you will see will be built off them, so when you see a particular route you can go back and refer to the basic concept.

Now, let us look at some game film, and see how we play our cover 4. (Film)

TEACHING ZONE-BLITZ CONCEPTS

Marshall University

I was on the same crappy-type flight that Urban Meyer was on today. I was reading the paper as the plane was going up and down. I saw that Coach Dick LeBeau of the Steelers was on the front page of the sports section. Here is what he was saying in the paper. "Because zone blitzes are so common today, and so easy to copy, I can see high school teams running them all over the country very soon."

I am going to talk to you today about the zone-blitz package. I have been running this package for about 12 years. Dick LeBeau is a graduate of Ohio State University. When I was at Ohio State, Dick was kind enough to allow me and Mark Dantonio to visit with him. He went over the techniques in how to teach the zone blitz in a very simple fashion. It was not something we memorized.

We had been teaching the zone blitz all along. Today I am going to share with you three or four thoughts that you can take back with you and possibly implement into your program. As Urban Meyer said, I would not recommend this package against a team that likes to run the option. I highly recommend it against a team that has a quarterback that can run. The reason for this is because everyone has their eyes on the quarterback. None of our defenders has their back turned as you do in man coverage.

We actually had been teaching the zone blitz wrong. We were talking about the zone blitz up front. We wanted to know where we could send people and what gaps we should attack. We told Coach LeBeau this and he said, "Whoa! Stop! You must teach the secondary coverage first. Teach the coverage first!"

We were calling what we were doing an all fire zone coverage. To us, it was fire zone coverage. For every blitz we drew up, it was fire zone coverage to us. Dick LeBeau told us that if we did it that way, our secondary had to memorize coverages. He advised us to give the four defensive backs specific calls to play in the secondary.

In teaching the defense, we start with this premise. If you do not write anything down from this lecture beside this point, it will be worthwhile. You must have a wall-to-flat player to the field, a hook- to-free player, and a wall-to-flat player to the boundary (Diagram #1). We are in a three-deep and three-under set. The defensive backs are obviously playing three-deep coverage. Again, we were calling this all fire coverage. We learned that we needed to name the secondary coverage, because most of the time those three under players can be different players. It all depends on what you are doing up front.

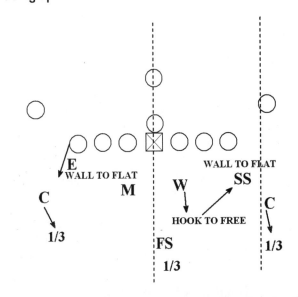

Diagram #1. Three Deep, Three Under Look—Fire

In setting up our defense, we kept the play when a defensive back came "down to the field."

We called that fire coverage. One of the two inside linebackers was our hook-to-free players. Our defensive end to the boundary was our wall-to-flat player weak. We called this fire coverage. This told us who our hook-to-free player was going to be, and most of the time the defensive end is going to be the wall-to-flat player to the boundary.

We are going to change some things this spring. We just did not have time to put everything in our defensive package because I was hired late at Marshall.

The fire zone coverage for us, if the ball is on the hash mark, is this. The safetyman to the field is going to be the wall-to-flat player to the field. One of the two linebackers, either Mike or Will, will be the hook-to-free player. The defensive end is going to be the wall-to-flat player weak.

Here is where we started learning about this defense from Dick LeBeau. We play a MOP coverage in this package. Coach LeBeau and Ohio State called it magic coverage (Diagram #2). For whatever reason, at Marshall we call it MOP coverage. The same principle still applies. We have wall-to-flat players to the field, a free-to-hook player in the middle, and a wall-to-flat player to the boundary. The ball is on the left hash mark.

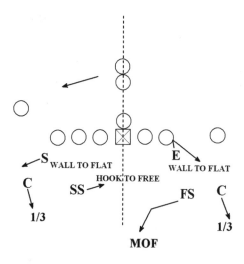

Diagram #2. MOP Coverage

The Sam linebacker becomes the wall-to-flat player to the field. The strong safety comes down

and plays the hook-to-free player, and the defensive end still plays the wall-to-flat player to the boundary. We call that MOP coverage. We are talking about the pass coverage here. We will get to the run defense later.

The one thing we do not have in our package at Marshall at this time is the Zorro coverage (Diagram #3). Again, we did not have enough time to put this in because I was hired late at Marshall. We will add Zorro this spring. Zorro is when we take the free safety and drop him down to the weakside to be the flat-to-wall player to the weakside, take a linebacker and make him a hook-to-free player, and take the other linebacker and make him a wall-to-flat player to the field. The strong safety is in the middle of the field and we are playing three deep.

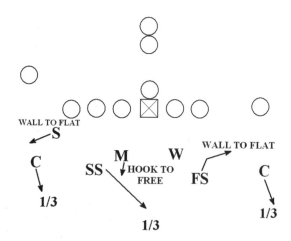

Diagram #3. Zorro Coverage

For the first six years we used this defense, we called this fire coverage. We had to memorize a lot of calls such as field fire, bomb field, and bazooka MOP. The defensive backs had to remember where they had to come down on the defense. Dick LeBeau made it very simple for us by giving it three different terms. On fire, we come down to the field. On MOP, we have a hook between the linebackers. On Zorro, we are bringing the free safety down on the weakside. The rest of the defensive backs are playing three deep.

What are the liabilities for fire zone coverage? The seam to the field is one area where your wall-to-flat players cannot mess up. The other area of concerned is with the quick out passes. The offense is going to throw the hitch route a lot against this defense. We do have one bastardized coverage that allows us to roll up to the field and still use zone pressure.

At Marshall, we call this 2-Z (Diagram #4). It is simply a cover 2. The number 2 tells us that the corner to the field is no longer playing one-thirds coverage. He is going to roll up and play a soft squat technique to the field. We are still able to use our zone pressure. He is looking to make the interception on the quick hitch route. What is his technique? I really do not know. I have run these a million different ways. We have eased outside and we have squirmed inside.

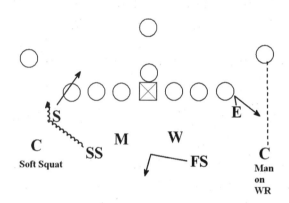

Diagram #4. Strong Shoot 2-Z Coverage

We are playing a three-deep secondary on this coverage. The offensive coordinators see that coverage and want to get the ball outside to the wide receiver on the short hitch route for five yards. This is where we want to have that corner play soft and squat on that outside receiver. That sends a message to the quarterback and the offensive coordinator. We are going to roll up on the play and take that pass away from the offense. On the backside, the corner is man-to-man on the outside man. The free safety comes to the middle of the field and plays one-half of the field.

This is what it looks like to the other side (Diagram #5). Here we have the other corner playing the soft squat technique. The free safety is coming hard and the strong safety is playing one-half of the

field. The backside corner has the outside receiver man-to-man.

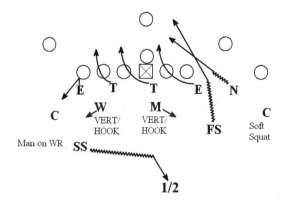

Diagram #5. Strong Shoot 2-Z Coverage

So, we have field coverage, which means that we are coming down to the fieldside. We have MOP or magic, or whatever you want to call it. This is where the strong safety is the hook-to-free player. Then we have Zorro, where the free safety is the wall-to-flat player to the weakside. Now I can take my two safeties and I can make them a wall-to-flat player weak, a hook-to-3 player, or a wall-to-flat player to the field. Again, we are playing three-deep coverage behind those calls.

Next, we look at the field inside MOP. Again, we are telling the safeties what to do on the plays. We give them names to make it easier for them to remember what to do.

Now we are in a field inside MOP look. We want the free safety covering the middle of the field. The corners are covering one-thirds (Diagram #6). The

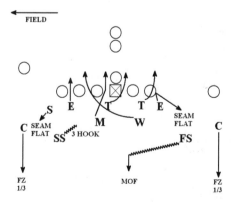

Diagram #6. Field Inside MOP

strong safety comes down and plays the 3-hook area between the two linebackers. We run the stunt inside with the Mike and Will linebackers.

Now we can get to the defense against the run. When you think about fire zone or zone blitz, as long as you have a wall-to-flat, a hook-to-3, and a wall-to-flat player, you can do whatever you want to do on defense. We see the NFL teams take their noseguard and drop him back and he plays the hook-to-3 area. They bring in another player to play the safety position. They will run him through the A gap. You can come up with any combination you want, as long as you understand how to teach the coverage. You have to teach the coverage first. The secondary coaches must know how to teach this first.

After you teach the secondary how to cover, you take the linebacker coach and the line coach and let their minds run wild. You can come up with any combination stunts you want. The ones I will cover today are very simple, meat-and-potatoes-type stunts. Everyone in America runs these stunts. They may be boring. The trickle-down effect has been unbelievable for the last eight years.

This is what we call field fox fire strong. The ball is on the right hash now. The field is to the left. We are in fire coverage. Here are the paths we run on the stunt (Diagram #7). We take the end on the wide side off the field and tell him he is a big stick player. He is going to slant inside all the way to the A gap on his side. The Mike linebacker runs off the hills of the end and goes through the B gap. We bring the Sam linebacker off the tail of the end's butt. The nose man

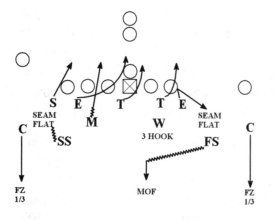

Diagram #7. Field Fox Fire Strong Vs. Pro Set

does an over technique to the A gap. The 3-technique tackle does a loop technique. That is our field fox fire look. I call this the NCAA blitz, because everyone runs this. This is what it looks like against the pro set.

If we run it against two tight ends or against the one-back set, we run it the same way (Diagram #8). Nothing really changes. It is still field fox fire strong.

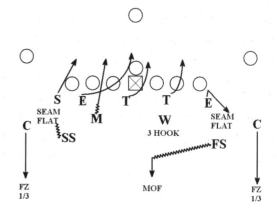

Diagram #8. Field Fox Fire Strong Vs. One-Back Set

If you want to send the Mike linebacker first, you can. He can walk up into the B gap and go first and the end comes off the heels of the Mike linebacker. Sam still comes off the edge. It is still field fox fire because no one else changed. We call that Bama, but you can call it what ever you want to call it.

With those two blitz plays, you have given the offense a lot to work on and you did not have to do a lot of teaching. All you have done is taught the Mike to go first and the end to go second. That is a change-up from the end going first and the Mike going second.

You can take those same two blitz plays and put a nickel back on the field. That would be our nickel field fox fire strong. Now you are in a four-man front and you are in the nickel set. You can run the same blitz out of the four-man front as you ran out of the five-man front. Now you have two blitz plays from the four-man front and two blitz plays from the five-man front. You can actually get to the point where you run the blitzes with three down linemen. Now, that would be the 3-4 defense. You are running the same two zone pressures.

If you are an offensive line coach, you must teach the blocking against the five-man look with the two blitz plays. You must teach the four-man line with two blitzes, and the three-man line with two blitzes. The defensive coach has not taught anything. Why? Because we have taught fire coverage. You have six defenses the offensive line coach must deal with and the defensive coach has not done much of anything except teach fire coverage and those two stunts. When we teach the two stunts, all we are doing is switching the Mike and the end. For the offense, the defense has become very, very complex. They look at the films and they say, "Damn, these guys run a lot of defense." Really, you are not doing a lot of different things. You are just doing them out of the three-man, four-man, and five-man looks. Why? Because you were able to teach fire coverage. Those principles are in place and work with all of those calls.

Let me move on to MOP coverage. This is our field bazooka MOP look (Diagram #9). You can call it whatever you want to call it. Again, the field is to the left. We use the same blitz as we did before, except we have changed the tracks. We loop the noseguard to the B gap. We send the Mike linebacker to the backside A gap first, and we send the Will linebacker to the playside A gap. The 3-technique tackle is still looping. The defensive end has wall-to-flat. The Sam linebacker has wall-to-flat. The strong safety is the hook-to-3 player.

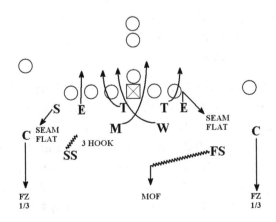

Diagram #9. Field Bazooka MOP

You can do whatever you want to do with those two linebackers with MOP coverage. We have sent

Will first and Mike second. We set the noseguard in a 3 technique and send both Mike and Will through the two A gaps. You can do whatever you want to do with those two linebackers with MOP coverage. You can come up with a lot of different combinations on this look. We want to make sure we have every gap covered on the stunts.

Because you have taught MOP coverage, you can run a lot of combinations with the under players. You can take the end, nose tackle, loop tackle, the Mike linebacker, and the Will linebacker and let them do whatever they want to do on the play. You can have four different zone pressures with these players. Why? Because we have taught MOP coverage.

We can run these looks out of a five-man front, a four-man front, and a three-man front. You have six different looks with only two different tracks. That is a total of 12 defenses that we have put into our package because you understand MOP coverage.

We are going to run these stunts out of the five-man, four-man, and three-man looks, but we are only going to teach two different blitz paths. For example, when we run fire, we let the Mike go first and the end come off his heels. Next, we let the end go first and the Mike come off his heels. That is all we use on that call. However, we run it out of a five-man, four-man, and three-man path.

This gives the offensive line coach a lot more to work against. This gives him more problems than it would if we stayed in a five-man look and were running all kinds of junk. We never run more than two paths on the stunts. You can carry any two stunts you want. You can send the linebackers straight ahead in the A gap and B gap. You can cross the two linebackers. Anytime you cross linebackers, it gives the offensive line coach a lot of problems. That is why we cross fire the linebackers.

This past year, we did send the Mike linebacker first in the A gap and then wrapped the Will linebacker around him. I like this stunt if we are facing a lot of two-back offenses. It is good against teams that run the isolation play. The bazooka MOP is good against the pass, but not bad against the run.

In the spring, we will come up with a completely new set of paths for the linebackers. In Conference USA, we see a lot of one-back offenses. We will come up with new paths for those linebackers.

We have been looking at these stunts all from the field. However, we always want to have the ability to come from the field, the middle, and the boundary. If we call cowboy, we are running the stunt to the boundary. All we are going to do is to bring the corner on that side. We are still in a three-deep look. All of the principles still apply.

If you want to change cowboy up, you can run rodeo. I am not showing these looks, but all you do is to take the Will linebacker, walk him up on the edge, and bring him on the rush instead of the corner. You must have something in your package where you come from the boundary.

With all of that side, we have two zone blitzes from the field and out of a five-man, four-man, and three-man set. We have two stunts where we can puncture the middle of the formation, and we have our sister blitz where we come off the edge on the boundary side. This is a total of 15 different defenses, but really all we had to teach is about five or six. We think this is a big advantage for our players and coaches, in that we do not have to teach a great deal. The offensive coordinator must prepare for 16 different looks. The odds are in our favor with this set-up.

When you are going through this defense, I would advise you to start slowly and add later. We started with one stunt to the field and one to the middle. We tried to get good at those two stunts before we added a great deal. After you get good on those two stunts, then you can bring the full complement of stunts.

On the 2-Z call, if anyone has a different stunt on this look, I want to know about it. I only know of one zone dog that we can use here and play 2-Z coverage. The only stunt I know of where we can play 2-Z is to bring the Sam linebacker and strong safety off the edge (Diagram #10). It is a lot like fox fire, but we are bringing two players off the edge. We want the quarterback to see immediate pressure in his face. It is good versus the option, any tight-end running game, or the passing game.

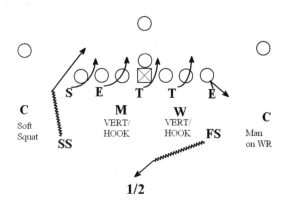

Diagram #10. Strong Shoot 2-Z

We have flirted with trying to incorporate the Mike linebacker on the stunt. We have kept the strong safety out of the blitz and used the Sam and Mike linebackers. We walked up the Mike linebacker next to Sam and sent him on the rush, so we could keep the strong safety back and play cover 2. We did not do well on the play, so we quit using the play. We wanted to get the strong safety involved in the stunt.

If we want to apply pressure to the slot formation, we can run our nickel field hawk fire (Diagram #11). We bring the free safety off the tail of the defensive tackle. The Will linebacker shoots the B gap and the end loops into the A gap. The nickel has the seam-to-flat, and we play three deep with the secondary.

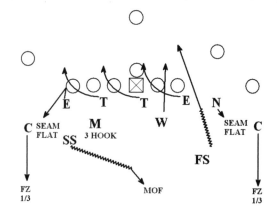

Diagram #11. Nickel Field Hawk Fire

A change-up on the hawk fire would be our odd whiskey fire weak (Diagram #12). We are still in our three-deep coverage, but we are bringing the Will linebacker in the C gap and the end is in the B gap.

We insert the X player and he shoots the A gap. This gives us an opportunity to put the pressure on the offense from the tight-end side of the formation.

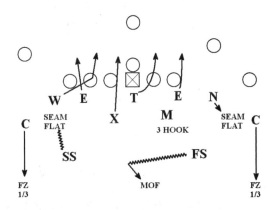

Diagram #12. Odd Whiskey Fire Weak

The question is what type of drills we use in teaching this defense. We have walk-throughs. We walk through the defense over and over. When we get to the nine-on-seven drills, and just before we go to the team drills, our first six plays are all zone calls. We bring one from the field, one from the middle, and one from the boundary. We are going to get six of these on film and then we are going back to our base defense. I tell our offense to run the best plays they have against our defense.

I will tell you what is great about the zone blitz. I probably should not admit this, but it great for the defensive coordinator. It is good against the run, it is gap sound, and it is good against the pass. You are playing an eight-man front with pressure. We are all playing the eight-man fronts to stop the run. The question is if the offense is going to throw the ball, or if they are going to run the ball. This defense gives you a chance to be right on the call. (Film)

Let me recap for you, because I have a tight schedule and have to make that next flight back home. Let me get moving with the defense.

Fire is down to the wide side of the field. MOP means you are the hook-to-3 player. Zorro means you are the wall-to-flat player to the weakside. You must use your imagination in how you want to bring the linebackers. You can do it out of a five-man, four-man, or three-man look. When you do that, you have 15 defenses to run against the offense, because you can teach fire, MOP, and Zorro. Plus you have the two complements to the backside on cowboy and rodeo. You have 17 defenses and all you had to teach was six tracks. This is because the secondary coach teaches our three coverages. We teach three concepts: down to the strongside, hook-to-3, and down to the weakside.

I want you to know I really appreciate the high school coaches. We are glad to work with you. We would love to have you visit with us. Thank you for having me here today.

THE 4-3 RUN DEFENSE

University of Michigan

In my career, I have been at Minnesota, Indiana, Louisville, Michigan State, and Michigan. I have been at four Big Ten schools and that primarily is my background. I played in the offensive line and started out as an offensive line coach. I went to the defensive side of the ball, coached the defensive line, and later coached the linebackers for several years. I went back to the defensive line and this past year that has been my assignment at Michigan.

To start off, I want to talk about the run defense at University of Michigan. The first thing we talk to our players about is understanding the defensive-front philosophy. They must understand that every defensive front has strengths and weaknesses.

In the seven-man front, we want our players to know that we play cover 2 behind it and use seven men to defend the box. A seven-and-a-half front is a three-deep type of scheme. In that scheme, we have someone from the secondary involved in run support, but we cannot count on him to fill the box.

We want them to know that an eight- or nine-man front has secondary support. In that scheme, there are secondary players assigned run responsibility who will show up in the box. They have gap assignments in the run game. I want them to understand those fronts and the strengths and weaknesses of them.

Terminology is an important thing for us in the structure of our defense. We are very particular with the words we use. We have two new coaches at Michigan who are going through the process of learning our terminology. That allows them to get on the same page with everyone else. We never want to use the same word for two particular cases.

For instance, the term "read support" is the safety reading the tight end's block on our outside linebacker. If we ask the outside linebacker what his technique is called, we do not want him to say read. Read is related to support. We define our words and put them in the playbooks before spring football practice. When we ask our players the meanings of words, we want them to know exactly what they are. We make sure we are on the same page with all our players and coaches.

We try to develop trust among our players. The player knows what his job is and trusts his teammates to know their jobs.

In our teaching, we want to teach aggressive techniques. That starts in your tackling. Tackling is not a natural act. Imagine being told to keep your head up and eyes open. Running at full speed toward a ballcarrier who weighs 200 pounds and who is running at full speed toward you is not a natural act. We have to teach that kind of aggressiveness.

I coach the defensive linemen. We base everything we do with this group on keeping it simple. We do not play a double-eagle type of defense. We play 3-technique alignments in our defense all the time. However, the 3 techniques played in the double eagle require a different teaching. That equates to additional teaching and learning for the defensive line. Therefore, we do not play that type of defensive adjustment. You cannot be aggressive if you are thinking too much. I call the way we play a foxhole mentality. Each defensive linemen and linebacker has a foxhole. That is represented by his gap responsibility. The gap can be a foot to three feet wide. If everyone on the defense defends his foxhole, the defense will be very effective.

We teach soundness in our defensive philosophy. We want everyone to know what to do and how to do it. One of the essential things when we grade our players is "critical errors." The worst thing a player can get on his grade sheet is one or more critical errors. A critical error is letting the football outside or behind the defense. If an end was supposed to contain the football and it got outside of him, that is a critical error. If the corner in his coverage let the ball get behind him, that is a critical error.

One of the worst things I can hear a player say is, "My bad." That means the player thinks the mistake is okay. It is not okay to make a mistake. It does not go away just because you say, "My bad." I do not allow my players to use that expression. All that pertains to being sound.

We teach presnap awareness, which is extremely important in defensive line play.

Presnap Awareness

- Down and distance
- Formation/backfield set
- Field position/yard and hash
- Stance
- Splits
- Eye contact
- Listen

We consider these things in our presnap reads of the offense.

Of all the items mentioned in the list, I think down and distance is the worst one of them. I think they understand first-and-10 and third-and-eight situations. However, if you tell your players on second-and-eight, the offense runs the influence trap, that does not sink in to them. They do not know it on the field.

The only place I have been where we did an effective job was a job I had at a particular school. We had sideline chains as part of every drill we ran. During the drill, the head coach blew his whistle and questioned players and coaches as to the down and distance. If the player or coaches did not know, there was hell to pay. That was a point of emphasis in his practices.

I think one of the most important presnap reads is formation and backfield sets. We have our players going through what we call formation school. They have to recognize the formations and be able to draw them on a blackboard. I think that is a great teaching tool. Getting the players to draw the formations is a key to their understanding. If they can draw a trips-open set, they increase their terminology and visual understanding of formations.

If you follow what goes on in the NFL combines, you know that has become a point of emphasis with NFL teams. Instead of simply interviewing the players, they are asking them to draw sets and formations to test their knowledge of football.

Formations are important, but backfield sets are more important. We want the defensive line to know every time what the backfield set is. We do not just want the linemen to know the quarterback is in the shotgun rather than under center. We want him to know where all the backs are in that set. In a two-back set, if the fullback sets weak, the offense only has a few plays. However, if the fullback sets strong, the offense has a bunch of plays to the tight-end side.

In our terminology, a fullback to the tight-end side is "king." If he is set away from the tight end, we call that "queen." If he sets in a wing toward the tight end, that is "Jack." If he is in the slot away from the tight end, we call that "Jill." We try to come up with words our players remember and visualize.

We identify field position as zones on the field. Everyone knows what a red zone refers to in football. We call the midfield area the free-wheeling zone, because everything in the offense is available to be run. We also have a black zone, which is the coming-out area for the offense.

When our players come on the field with the offense backed up to their goal line, they know this is the black zone. In that area, the offense is more limited as to what they can do. They also are more likely to try and get the defense to jump offside by using a long count. That alerts our defensive linemen to hold and react to the movement, not the cadence. The offense looks to get cheap yardage when they are backed up.

The hash marks to me are very important. I want our defensive front aware of the wide side of the field and the openside of the formation. If the open set with two wide receivers is to the wide side, 75 percent of the passes are thrown into that area. If the 3 technique is into the boundary, he has to be aware that 75 percent of the throws are made away from him. On his pass rush, he wants to go inside the guard's block instead of outside to rush the quarterback. They need to be aware of where they are on the football field.

The defensive linemen look at the offensive linemen's stance. When you listen to a secondary coach as they start to teach, the first thing they mention is eye progression. The first thing the defensive linemen should see is the stance of the offense. When he sees the stance, what can he see? He sees the distribution of weight either on the hands or on back in his stance. Talk to your linemen about offensive linemen stances and tell him what to look for.

The splits of the offensive linemen will vary from week to week. The more disciplined the offensive linemen are, the better it is for us. They widen the splits on the runs and tighten down on the passes. The teams that are difficult for us are the ones that take the same split every time.

We do not huddle on defense, so eye contact is an area we work. When the offensive lineman comes out of the huddle and begins looking at the defender, he probably is going to block him. If he is looking to the outside and all around, he probably is pass blocking or going to pull.

This last one drives me nuts. We tell our players to listen. It happens every game. About the middle of the second quarter, I ask the defense, what is the offense's snap count. Most of them cannot tell you. They have to learn how to listen for the snap count and line calls.

As I just mentioned, we do not huddle on defense. That has become the way to coach against the spread no-huddle offenses. More colleges are going to the no-huddle concept on defense. That makes communication very important. Each player has to see the signal. We also rely on a buddy system. You probably did the same thing last night. You probably asked someone to make sure you were up this morning. Having a buddy to take care of you is the kind of system we talk about.

We do a tremendous amount of substituting at Michigan. When we have players running onto the field, they will not see the signal the coach gives. It is up to their buddy to relay that signal to them. We are in the process of breaking down our cut-ups of last season. When there is a long run, most of the time we trace the breakdown to communication. The linebackers were playing one coverage and the secondary was playing another one.

When you coach your players, make sure you teach aggressive techniques, soundness, presnap awareness, and communication. Those things are tremendously important.

Our coaching staff is going to be demanding of the players. We let them know exactly what we want them to do and how to do it. We want our players to have toughness. I use the word "strain" a lot in dealing with the players.

It is like getting your car stuck in the mud on a date with your girlfriend. She has to be home by midnight and you have to push the car out of the mud. When he is pushing that car out of the mud, he will strain and make a noise while he is doing it. He will grunt as he strains to get the car out.

That is what I want from my players. When a player is tough, he knows how to strain. He is not just holding off somebody, he is straining and making some noise. That is one of my favorite words on the practice field. I tell them they have to strain more.

Another thing I think is important in the concept of toughness is being able to "suck it up." I have been in coaching for a long time and I have always heard that expression. I have a good friend who has a five-year-old son. He took him to a basketball game the other day. The kid did not feel well, ran into the bathroom, and threw up a little. When he came out, my friend asked him if he wanted to go home and watch the game on TV. The child told him, "Dad, sometimes when you make a decision you just have to suck it up. Let's go to the game."

I have a saying that I use all the time, particularly in a game situation. I ask them if they are hurt or injured. I tell them if they are hurt, that is part of football. Get back on the field and into the lineup. If the player is injured, he is the one who knows. I do not know if he is injured. If he is injured, he takes himself out of the game and we substitute for him.

It is a quick way to identify toughness and a quick way to eliminate mistakes. What you do not want to happen is an injured player trying to play. All he does is hurt the team. If he is injured, get him out of the game. If he is hurt, suck it up and be tough.

As a coaching staff, we demand effort. You have to demand effort and you have to define it. We define effort by telling our players what loafing is. We define this for our players so they understand exactly what a loaf is.

The following chart tells our players what we look for on the playing field.

What is a Loaf?

- No change of speed
- Not turning and going to the ball
- Getting passed by another player
- Laying on the ground
- Turning down a hit

When we talk about no change of speed, this idea is different from what other coaches feel. Most coaches say they want no change of speed. The defender should go hell bent for election all the time. As a defensive lineman, we place our hands, defend the gap, and find the football. Once the defensive lineman finds the ball, I want to see a change of speed. I want them in an all-out sprint to the ball. If I do not see that burst of speed, that is a loaf.

The second one is not turning and going to the ball. If we rush the quarterback and he throws the ball, the normal player will turn and look to see if the ball is complete or incomplete. I do not want that. When the quarterback throws the ball, they turn and sprint to the ball. If they turn and look, that is a loaf.

Getting passed by another player on the way to the ball is a loaf. I do not care how fast the player is.

I really hate to see this in a defensive football player. The offensive lineman chops the defender down and he lays on the ground. If they knock you down, do not lay there. Get up and get back into the play. Pursue the football. Do not let your friends do the dirty work.

The last one does not occur very much in defensive football. In fact, the other extreme is more prevalent. They do not turn down the hit, they continue to go after the whistle. However, turning down a hit does occur and that is a loaf.

When my players get their grade sheets, I want them to look at how many loafs they have and how many critical errors. I put those items in red on their grade sheet. That defines it for them and they can understand what we are talking about.

Drill work is important to the overall learning of your players. There are some things you must do in your drill work. There has to be a purpose for every drill you do. Do not do a drill just to be doing a drill. Drilling is like conditioning. I do not like the coach that just runs sprints. That is not drilling with a purpose. You need to design some drill that conditions as you do the drill. Make the drills football-related. Do something that produces football skills that carry over to the game field.

Do not ask players to do something they cannot do. If the first five or six players through the drill cannot do it, you are probably doing something they cannot do. If that happens, change the drill and do something different.

Make sure there is variety in your drill work. When you have variety in your drill work, it improves the purpose for the players. They are able to stay locked in on the drill. When you have variety, it makes you a creative coach. Make up your own drills and try them out. In all my agility drills, I have a football that I constantly toss to the players. It teaches them to catch, scoop the ball off the ground, and improves their agility.

When you do your drill work, be organized. The worst mistakes I see on practice fields come from the coach that is not organized in his drill work. If you are not organized, you waste valuable time. If you only have 15 minutes for the individual period, do not waste any of it setting up a drill. The times you spend in your individual drills are precious minutes you cannot afford to lose.

At Michigan, I have the four down linemen. I may have 16 to 18 players I am coaching at one time. I will tell you a couple of things that have really helped me as a defensive line coach. If I want my players to partner up, I call, "right on right." That means they face each other with their right foot on their partner's right foot. I stand on one side or the other. The side I stand on is designated the defensive side.

In one simple command, I have organized 16 players into eight pairs and they know which player is the defensive player. That eliminates all the confusion and answers all the questions.

I use players as the coach. If we do a drill with four lines, the second player in the line becomes the coach. I cannot watch all four lines at the same time. If we are doing stance work, he critiques the man in front of him. He knows the coaching points and applies them as if he were the coach. We want to make them coaches on the field.

In your drill work, you must get the tempo that fits the drill. If the drill is a live contact drill, the tempo of the drill is full speed. We have a blitz drill that requires the blitz runner to touch the runner or quarterback. That drill has a throttled tempo, where the player is holding back at the end. You cannot have full-tempo drills in everything you do. There are too many injuries that occur in those types of drills.

Our philosophy for our down linemen is "attack and react." Miami and Florida defenses are full-blown attack defenses. They teach their defensive linemen to penetrate and get up the football field.

Read defenses play defense by reacting to the offensive lineman in front of them. Our defensive philosophy is in the middle of those two extremes.

We attack the line of scrimmage and react. If our players know what to do and how to do it, they are aggressive and confident football players. That is what we strive to do.

The next part of the philosophy deals with alignment and stance. In general terms, our defensive tackles play with their foot inside the offensive blocker foot. The defensive ends play with their foot outside the foot of the offensive blocker. We number our alignments just like everyone else. The shade alignments are 1, 3, 5, 7, and 9.

In our stance, we step to pressure. If the defensive tackle aligns on the outside shoulder, his inside foot is back in his stance. When the offense snaps the ball, the tackle steps to the pressure of his technique. If he aligns on the inside shoulder of the blocker, his inside foot is back. That allows him to step to the pressure of the blocker. That means we must align in left- and right-handed stances. The hand on the ground and the stagger foot are on the same side of the player.

Some coaches do not like switching the stance because they think it is too hard to teach. I do it each year in our high school camps. By the third day, all the linemen master this skill. It can definitely help your players if they can be comfortable in that stance.

The most critical part of the attacking defense is the take-off. This area at Michigan is a little different than most coaches talk about. Before I talk about the take-off, let me talk about the stance.

The width of the stance generally is underneath the armpits. We get into a toe-to-heel relationship with our feet. The feet in the stance are straight ahead with the heels slightly out. When the player bends down to put his elbows on his knees, his heels will turn slightly inside. To correct the inward movement of the heels, we align with them slightly outside. Therefore, when the player put his elbows on his knees, his feet will be straight down the field.

He drops the hand on the side of the stagger down to the ground with about 50 percent of the weight on the hand. If I kicked the player's hand out from under him, he falls forward.

When we teach the stance, we do it by the numbers. One is to position the feet straight down the field with the heel slightly outside. On two, we squat over and put our elbows on our knees. On three, we drop our ground hand down to the ground. If I call "up" and the player can get off the ground without stepping forward, he does not have enough weight on his hand. When we do this part of the teaching, the second man in line is being the coach and correcting all the mistakes.

In the take-off, we have to get out of the stance. The first thing we have to do is key the football and react to the movement of the ball. The most important thing in the take-off is "throwing our pads." That means the utilization of the hips. If the player steps, he is negating the large muscles in the hips.

In the take-off, the first things to move are the shoulder pads going forward, because he is exploding from his hips. He is not stepping, he is throwing his pads. He places his hands and locates his eyes.

In the hand placement, the down hand is jammed on the chest with the thumb up. The outside hand is on the cuff of his jersey with the thumb inside. If the thumbs are out, that is a weak position. With the thumbs up, that is a position of strength. The eyes are staring at the chest of the blocker. In the first part of the take-off, the defender throws his pads, places his hands, and locks his eyes.

The keying the ball, throwing of the pads, and exploding from the hips are the attacking parts of the take-off. The placement of the hands and seeing what the blocker is doing are the reaction parts of the take-off.

Defensive linemen do all kinds of hand drills in today's football. We juggle and do tennis ball drills to improve our hand agility and strength. We have to do that because offensive linemen cheat. They hold and do everything they can to a defensive lineman.

The last part of the take-off is the first step. That step depends on what is happening in front of the defender. The defense has to play with their thumbs up, elbow in, and locking out for separation. As the defender comes off the ball, he throws his pads, places his hands on the chest, and takes his first step. He reacts as he comes off to what the offensive blocker does. If the charge is a low hat, his first step is short. If the coach listens for the smack of the hand on the chest and the stomp of the first step coming down, the pattern is a rhythm of two thuds a fraction of a second apart. He can tell by listening whether the take-off was right.

The hands are in front of the foot as they contact the blocker. If the defender concentrates on his punch with his hands, the feet will follow in correct time. If the blocker moves outside, the foot goes that way if the hand placement is correct.

Some players pick up that concept in one practice. It takes others longer, but they eventually learn the technique. This allows the defender to utilize his larger muscle groups. If you came to our practice, all you hear me say is hands and eyes.

If we do the same technique in the take-off and the blocker retreats, the first step becomes a three-foot step. We did not change anything except the block goes away from the defender instead of coming toward him. The result is a short step in the run game and a long step in the pass rush. In both situations, that is the reaction we want. By using this system, the defender is not running up the field on run or taking a short step on pass.

The next part of the progression is to get into a fitted drill. We put the both defender and the blocker in a two-point stance. The defender explodes and places his hands on the blocker. The next part puts the defender in a three-point stance with the partner in a two-point stance. He explodes and places the hands. The next sequence puts both players in a three-point and he does the same thing.

That is the offensive line coach in me. I teach everything in a progression and sequence. The next part after the fit position is the block reactions.

Six things can happen to a defensive lineman. There are five run reactions and a pass set. Every block will fit into one of the following categories.

The first block reaction is the base block (Diagram #1). If I ask my players what they do to a base block, their answers are short and simple. The reactions to the base block are press out and defend their gap. It does not matter the technique the defender plays. He plays it the same way. He gains separation by locking out, places his head in his gap, and defends the gap. I do not ask him to knock the blocker into the backfield.

Diagram #1. Base Block

On the reach block (Diagram #2), we anchor the defense at 2x2. The defender anchors his defensive position two yards outside the blocker and two yards up the field. On this block, we want to penetrate. If the defender stays on the line of scrimmage with the ball coming toward him, the blocker is in control. The ball can go outside or inside of the defender.

Diagram #2. Reach Block

If the defender continues to widen with the reach block, he may be in his gap, but he makes it tough on his teammates. The inside gap becomes too wide for the inside defender to cover. That is why the defender anchors at two yards wide. By getting two yards of penetration, the ball may get outside of the block, but the ballcarrier makes a declaration. He turns up with the ball or he goes outside with it. In both cases, the ball goes one way. If it goes outside, the ballcarrier has to give ground to get there.

The blocker may reach the defender, but to reach him the ballcarrier has to declare. The gap is tight for the linebacker tracking the hip of the ballcarrier, and to get wide the ballcarrier has to bubble back with one direction to go.

The take-off is the same for any block reaction. As the head of the blocker goes to the outside of the defender, he is not reached. The defender has his first step in the ground and on the second step of the blocker, he presses with his outside arm and grabs cloth with the inside hand. He turns the blocker, gets two yards upfield, and anchors his position. The only time the defender is reached is when the ball runs through his gap.

The next block reaction is a combination of two situations. This reaction is the veer/cutoff block (Diagram #3). The veer block is the blocker going inside the defender, trying not to make contact. The cutoff block is the same thing, except the blocker hits the defender. Our block reaction is squeeze and close. Squeeze to us means to keep the shoulder parallel to the line of scrimmage. Our reaction off the blocker leads us to the trap. We squeeze to the next gap. If the ball continues away, he turns and closes to the ball.

Diagram #3. Veer/Cutoff Block

In our block reaction, part of the close is the spill. If we close to the ball, we spill or wrong arm everything to the outside. Close to us means go to the ball.

Here is a coaching point for the cutoff block. There is a low and high block in the cutoff. We tell our players, if the block is below our waist, there is no chance of a cutback run by the running back. The defender can run his feet as fast as possible to get away from the block. If the block is high and above the waist, that tells the defender to slow down and play for the cutback run.

The next block is the down block with a guard pulling across the gap (Diagram #4). The essential phase to defend this block is secure the gap and pursue. There are two examples in the diagram. The first one is a 3-technique tackle and the second is a 5-technique end. If the 3 technique can beat the block of the tackle coming down, he moves through his gap and pursues the ball outside. By going through his gap he secures it.

Diagram #4. Down Block

However, the tackle performing the down block is on scholarship too. He reduces his split and makes sure the 3 technique does not get through that gap. In that case, the 3 technique secures his gap and makes sure the ball is not in his gap. Once the ball passes, he cross-faces the offensive tackle and gets outside. We cross-face about 80 percent of the time and 20 percent go through the gap.

Question: If the 3 technique throws his pads at the guard, how does he get contact on the tackle coming down on him?

The tackle throws his pads. If the tackle's down block hits the defender behind the shoulder pads, he dips his outside shoulder and continues to pursue the ball through his gap. When the tackle dips his shoulder, we call that reducing the blocking surface.

In our presnap read, the 3-technique tackle reads the pull of the guard and expects the down block from the tackle. Presnap reads work, but it takes coaching to make them useful in games. Our call for the pull at Michigan is a yellow call. If you play Michigan and they call yellow, we know you are pulling.

The defensive tackle reads the guard as he comes out of the huddle. The guard is looking outside and the tackle is looking at the defender. On the snap of the ball, the defensive tackle steps into the down block and plays across his face. The biggest problem we have is getting the tackle to stay in his gap before the ball crosses to the outside.

This block is the one that gets a little hairy and is the hardest for our defenders to play. It is what we call double pressure (Diagram #5). It is not a double-team block because one of the blockers wants to get to the second level and block a linebacker. They want to knock the down defender off the ball, then slip to a linebacker. The catchphrase is get low and react to the blockers. A double pressure block converts to a base, cutoff, or down block.

Diagram #5. Double Pressure

The defender takes on his primary key with his hands and eyes. When he feels the pressure from the second blocker, he tilts his shoulders and reduces the blocking surface. He gets lower to lower his center of gravity. He does not turn sideways or pull down. We get lower and tilt the shoulders. If the outside blocker comes off the block, we face a base block on the original blocker. In the base block we press out and defend our gap.

If the double pressure comes, the defender gets low and tilts his shoulders. If the inside blocker comes off to the inside, that is the cutoff block. The defensive tackle on the cutoff block squeezes and closes to the inside.

The last one is the hardest to read. The 5 technique gets a double-pressure block from the tackle and tight end. He plays his base-block technique on the tackle, tilts his shoulder, and plays football. When the tackle comes off the block to get inside, the 5 technique originally reads that as a cutoff block. However, when he sees the guard pull, he knows the play is a down block from the outside. He secures his gap and pursues the ball. That is all the defensive linemen at Michigan know.

If we can every do anything for you at Michigan, do not hesitate to call. Thanks for coming out. It was a great morning. Come see us at Michigan.

EXECUTING THE BASIC FOOTBALL FUNDAMENTALS

University of Washington

Thank you. I am delighted to be here. I am delighted to spend some time with you guys and talk a little football, and some important things that I like to talk about. Tonight I will start with an area that I think we all do a poor job in and that is, very simply, the fundamentals of the game. I am only going to take a couple of them, but I think they are absolutely critical to success.

If you are like we are, we have 20 hours per week to take our guys and work with them, so we are all cut down by time. In addition, some of you probably do not have all of your coaches in the school, and they come from various parts of the community to help coach the football team. So sometimes, under these circumstances, some of the fundamentals are lacking. With the various backgrounds of your coaches, and their inability to look at it all the time, sometimes the fundamentals are missing.

In view of that, I want to start with a couple of basic fundamentals—things that I believe we all do a poor job of. I believe that because I study film. The simple question we all have to ask ourselves is, "Is what I see on film consistent with what I am teaching?" How many of us can say that we see on film exactly what we are teaching? The truth is, teaching the fundamentals of the game is something that we have to do a better job of.

I want to start by talking about simply holding the football. In 2004, prior to my arrival at the University of Washington, that program led the country in turnovers with 42. Men, you and I both know, with that many turnovers, it is difficult to win a football game. In fact, it is virtually impossible.

We cut that down by two-thirds in 2005, and we only had eight fumbles. Holding the football is a key ingredient. I suspect that there are coaches here today who lost a game last year because of a fumble. It happens. If you could have avoided that one, you already would have made your season better.

I just happened to bring a football with me. We try to teach our guys basic common sense, and we stay after them. Almost every drill our running back coach does has some kind of ball security involved in it. Every time we scrimmage, we expect our defensive players to try to dislodge the ball from our offensive guys in order to force them to concentrate on holding on to the football.

We start with finger placement relative to the point of the ball. I hope you do not coach your players to put their fingers on the point. I hope you are telling your guys to take their fingers and extend them *beyond* the point. I am a short guy, but as short as my arms are, this ball does not even get to my elbow with my fingers on the point. Not even close. We teach our guys to extend the fingers over the point.

Then we teach them to place the ball high in the armpit, on the ribcage, and under the bicep, in this manner. We ask them to squeeze the ball and work across the body.

One of the worst things that has happened to us, in terms of carrying the ball, is what they teach in track, and yet every football coach knows that we need track. The faster your kids are, the more of a problem they become for your opponent. You want them to have track speed, but in track they teach the arm swing straight up and down, as opposed to any cross-body action. That is counterproductive to what you want from a ballcarrier.

There is no question about it. If I take this ball and swing it up and down instead of across the body, it is exposed to the defense. You do not want that.

We try to get our guys to put fingers across the point, back end high in the armpit, on the ribcage, under the bicep, and then work the ball across the chest. Never down. If you work it down, just like you are running for speed, you are going to expose the football. It should never be exposed. It should be right here on this chest all the time. It is pretty simple.

Do you see that when you look at your film? Or, do you see your guys, like I see my guys sometimes, with the ball out when they are trying to maintain balance, and the ball gets away from them? The key is that you have to be on them all the time about ball leverage. We are, and that is why we think we went from that horrendous number of 42 turnovers down to 13 or 14.

We are on it all the time. It gives you a chance. It is part of our philosophy of saying, "If we will not beat ourselves, you are going to have a hard time beating us." All other things being equal, you will not be able to beat us.

Holding the football, in my opinion, is something that is not taught or emphasized enough. Some of you may have seen this year that Tiki Barber of the New York Giants had problems holding the ball. He has gone to a unique approach to carrying it. He has clearly got it right here, up on his chest, so that any hit that he takes on the ball goes against the body. So, maybe he has got something there, and maybe that is what will be taught next.

One of the other things I think you have to look at when you are teaching ballhandling is the notion of the angles of the body. I have always been one to believe that a 45-degree angle is one of the muscle's best places to execute. That 45-degree angle right here at the elbow is a better position for your arm because of leverage. It gives you maximum muscle involvement.

Which muscles are involved when you hold a football in this position? Chest muscles, agreed? Obviously, arm muscles. Also, the back muscles are involved. Now, I am willing to bet that most of us are stronger curling from a 45-degree angle than we are with our arms extended, simply because of the number of muscles involved.

So, I am not telling you something that I think has just limited value. When you look at it from a scientific standpoint, you are going to be much stronger holding the ball in this position, having it put away, having it not exposed. Defenders can club it from underneath or club it from on top and it is just going right into the body. They do not have a chance.

The first running back in the NFL who gained 1000 yards rushing and 1000 yards passing in the same year was a great back named Roger Craig. I remember that Roger Craig had a critical fumble in a playoff game. He was heading down the left side of the field with the ball in the correct position. When he started to cut back, a guy grabbed his arm and the ball came out. I knew when I saw it that something was wrong with his technique in traffic.

What happened was that his body worked against itself. When the guy pulled his arm, the other arm reacted and the ball was exposed. At that time, I was running backs coach at Stanford and I went right to my players and changed the way we protected the ball in traffic. Instead of covering both points, as Roger had, and as most people teach, I asked my players to place the opposite hand over the belly of the ball when they got into traffic. Then, if someone grabbed their off arm, they are not working against themselves, and they still have the ball protected.

It also puts me in a much more powerful position when I am in traffic. Coaches tell ballcarriers to split two defenders by narrowing their surface. Placing the opposite hand over the belly of the ball will reduce my surface, keep the ball away from the defender, and give me something that will rattle his dental work. That is what I now teach our guys.

Next, I want to talk about switching the football. I tell our guys that they can switch the ball in the open field if they need to, but to never switch the ball in traffic. One of the all-time great runners in the NFL, Emmitt Smith, always carried the ball in his left arm and he never switched. He never fumbled because he had great security on it and it was in the right place. When he needed to protect it, he put his body over it and protected it. Now, I believe you switch, but I believe you only switch when you are not in traffic.

Our players are taught to switch by reaching over the top and sliding the ball across their body from a secure position under one arm to a secure position under the other. We do not reach under, because we want to keep the ball in the same level position, and it seems like the natural way to do it. We also do not want to risk exposing the point of the ball by the tilt that might occur if we reached under.

Next, I want to talk about catching the football. When I played baseball, we were all told that we could not hit what we could not see. You have to see the ball to hit it. Well, there is a parallel example for pass receivers in football and that is you have to see the ball to catch it.

Our players today are marvelous athletes, and they have timing and rhythm that is unbelievable. However, big-time quarterbacks throw the football between 50 and 70 miles per hour, and if you think that is not fast, just stick your head out of the window of your car at 60 miles an hour when you are going past a telephone pole.

Today, we see a lot of pass receivers catching the ball near their body and not looking it in. I think they lose just a split second when they do that. Their timing is good and they may make the catch, but they put themselves in a more difficult position to catch the football.

We teach our receivers that a ball above the waist is caught "thumbs together," while a ball below the waist is caught "pinkies together," but we try to make sure that they get their hands out in front of their body. If they will do that, they will see the ball caught, and they do not lose that extra fraction of a second that could be the difference in their timing in catching the football. I think you are a better receiver when you catch the ball with your hands in front of your body and you see it caught.

I used to work with a guy named Chris Carter, who was a great receiver with the Vikings. I had been a quarterback in high school and college, and I could throw the ball fairly well, so he asked me to throw to him every day after practice. He would put himself behind one of the goalposts, place his hands on either side of the post, and catch passes. He had a designated number that he caught each day, so he got used to having his hands out in front of his body catching the ball.

Then, he would move away from the goalposts and catch the ball one-handed. He caught a designated number up high, a designated number waist high, and a designated number down low. Then, he would reach across his body and catch a designated number, all one-handed. That was his drill work every day. It is no wonder that some of those catches he made on Sundays and Monday nights looked spectacular, but to him it was everyday work.

Getting back to my original point about pass receiving, I think it is important that we teach our guys to see the ball hit their hands, and not that flash coming in. I think they sometimes miss it. I think that is all timing and I do not think they always see the ball hit their hands.

We also tell them to keep their elbows within the framework of their body. I once coached defensive backs and I loved it when receivers spread their elbows. They are not in a position of strength. That arm would fly on contact, and so would the ball.

Think about the position of the elbows in the bench press. Elbows outside is not a strong position, but elbows within the frame of the body is. Well, I want to catch this ball within the framework of my body and have strength.

The next fundamental I want to discuss is the plant and drive. A clear description of the technique depends upon the language you use. When you see a defensive back in his backpedal, and the receiver makes his break on an out cut, the defensive back will try to plant right here and his next step will be some type of "gather." The important thing for him is to keep his base up under him.

So we go "step, slide in, and step." Now, it does not quite look like a "slide in" when you are doing it.

It has kind of a "run" to it, kind of a "Bang! Bang! Bang!" tempo. We are trying to get our guys so they do not get caught overextended, because then they lose time, weight distribution, and ultimately the battle. In short, if they get overextended, they are screwed up.

When I coached defensive backs, I taught the plant and drive like an old dance we all used to do. You young guys would not know it, but it has a rhythm just like the cha-cha—bang, bang, and go. I like our technique because it allows the defender to drive in any direction off of any foot.

Let us say the receiver is running an out. The defender's left foot goes back and hits, then he slides with his right foot, and with that base he can still cross and drive on him without having the right foot be his lead foot. If you can establish that foot pattern, it allows you to drive in any direction off of any foot. It is just timing. Bang, bang, and go! Bang, bang, and go! Crossover does not matter. Any direction, you can do it.

My favorite fundamental is the basic stance. It is my favorite because I believe that, in a lot of places, we are teaching mistakes. Many years ago, the halfbacks would get in their three-point stances, take their lead steps, and away they would go. Now, tell me a halfback that you see in the I who does not start with a drop-step on everything he does. Our response to that as coaches was just to start teaching the drop-step instead of correcting it.

I have seen some quarterbacks today in stances with one foot under and one foot trying to get to the fullback, and the first thing they do is bring the foot back to get started.

It is so simple, men, to teach basic stance. I had a great coach in college named Andy McDonald. He taught the quarterbacks a very simple stance. He said to put feet shoulder-width apart, using armpits as a gauge, and bend at the knees and waist. Then, roll your knees in so that your weight goes to the balls of your feet. Extend the arms up under the center wrist-deep, place one thumb into the curvature of the other thumb, and press both hands up on the center. Of course, we expect the center to press his behind down onto the quarterback's hands.

Those two pressures form a sort of glue, so that if the elbows are flexed, the hands will move with the center. That is a key point—the elbows must be flexed. The quarterback is moving with the snap to get to the handoff on that stretch play, and the center is moving to his block. If we have that glue, and if the quarterback has some slack in his elbows, there will be no bad snaps, and the play will time out.

If there is a differential in pressure, the quarterback will stay in there too long, because his first responsibility is to get the ball. We have all seen quarterbacks get stepped on by the center or the guard because they stayed under center too long. If it is coached right, it should never happen.

The problems of getting good fundamentals taught are not limited to the skill positions, because we now have offensive linemen that are amazingly big. Pretty soon, there will be offensive linemen weighing 400 pounds who can move. It is coming, and they will be able to move. On the zone play, they get into that stance with their feet awfully wide to support those 300 or 400 pounds. If it is zone right, that guard or tackle will pick that right foot up and basically put it down in the same place. You want him to take that step because it coordinates the timing of the play, but it also puts him in position to put his head where you want it to be on that defensive player.

One of the mistakes I think we make, even with our big guys, is that we allow them to have their stances too wide. They cannot take a step if they are already spread out. In most cases, they are going to try to get themselves into a position where they can gather, and then go take a step.

Think about what you are teaching. Are you getting on video what you are teaching? That is the same question we ask ourselves all of the time. "Are we getting what we are teaching?"

I want to show some cut-ups that illustrate what I have been talking about. The first two should be fumbles. (Video)

I love words and I love quotes and I love to think them through.

One of my favorite quotes is by Dr. Martin Luther King: "The ultimate measure of a man is not where he stands in moments of comfort, but where he stands at times of challenge and controversy."

I want our team, when challenge and controversy comes, which is usually in the fourth quarter, I want them to step up. I want them to have the thought that this is the measure of a man.

The other quote came from when I was defensive secondary coach at Michigan State. Sherman Lewis was the defensive coordinator and he asked each coach to put up in his office his favorite quote. This one was my favorite, author unknown. "You judge a man by what he does when no one is watching."

To me, that is critical. It is critical from a leadership point, and it is critical from the one simple word that will gain you more closeness with your players. The simple word of "honesty."

For me, the first thing I talked to our guys about when I got the University of Washington job was the word "hypocrite," as it involves leadership. We all have players that are fantastic when the coach is around and do everything you ask them to do. But as soon as that coach is not there, they are killing the team in the locker room and killing the team with their habits.

We want to make sure that in our program, that in our coaches, we have no hypocrites. That our leadership is judged by what a man does when no one is watching. That it is not a program that says, "Do as I say." We are simply about, "Do as I do."

I make it clear to our players that anything I ask them to do, I have done it or I am willing to do it right now. That is clear, and I expect every coach to work that way. That is the way we coach—not by what we say, but by what we do.

Our players have to feel our energy and they have to feel our sacrifice. They have to feel our effort in making this a winning football team.

Here are some "words to ponder." Now, I want to talk about our defensive personnel. What I am looking for is someone who wants to be a great player—coachable attitude—consistency. I am looking for that guy who wants to come out every day and bring that coachable attitude. He cannot wait for you to put your arms around him, hands on him, instructing him on how he can get better. We are looking for guys who know their assignments.

Knowing assignments seems like such a simple thing, but it involves so much. You do not just look at a sheet of paper and know your assignment, with all of the adjustments you have today. You might have done that 30 years ago when I played. As a quarterback then, you had two coverages, cover 3 and man free, that you had to recognize. No one would risk blitzing their safeties. Everyone kept a man in deep middle in case somebody broke loose.

All of a sudden, cover 2 started to come into the picture. Now, think of all the things a quarterback faces today. He may see cover 1, cover zero, cover 3, cover 4, cover 6, cover 8, or combinations of those. It is a different game now, and guys have to be willing to pay a price. That is a commitment they have to make.

We are expecting our guys to run and hit, and that is our style of play. We want guys who want to run and smack it around.

We want to make sure in our defense that we limit the big plays. That is nothing new and everybody believes that. You have to cut down on the big plays. Do not give your opponent those explosive plays that can change the momentum of a game.

We are looking to create turnovers and we are looking to score on defense. When I was with the Minnesota Vikings some years ago, we had a man on the staff who was a Ph.D. in statistics, and all he did was follow the numbers of football. He took the numbers and showed us that throughout an NFL season, if you scored off of a turnover, 97 percent of the time you won the football game. That caught our attention. That is the reason so many people practice trying to create turnovers today. They that it leads to success and winning the ball game. Creating a turnover, and creating a ... off of that turnover, is critical.

We want to be a defense that is "three and out." ... want to give our offense that ball in great field ... sition.

We want to shut out our opponents in the fourth quarter. We think that the fourth quarter is a different ball game, so last year we graded our kids as always, but then we gave them a separate grade for just the fourth quarter. The fourth quarter is an independent entity that we grade. We want to know how each player performs in the fourth quarter. We are looking for those guys who are willing to step up and handle the big-time pressure of football.

Our number-one defensive goal is to win. Now, that one takes some work because that one has to come from the head coach. In my final year at Stanford, we averaged 31 points per game on offense, but we gave up 26 points per game on defense. Not once did we have a conflict with our offense and our defense, because the head coach said that there is one thing that is important in this program and that is winning.

Stats are fine, and it is nice to have great stats, but I really did not care as long as we won. If we score 50, which we did four times that year, and our opponent scores 20 or even 30, we still win. We will come back and work and look at the things we need to do to get better, but the number-one thing in our football program is winning. The offense will have that listed as their number-one goal—win. If they only score seven but we win, we are upset, they are not sleeping very well, but it still looks good when you watch ESPN say that you won the game.

That is our number-one defensive goal. Let me give you our other ones quickly:

- Allow 19 or fewer points per game
- Shut out the opponent in the fourth quarter
- Get a "three and out" 40 percent of the time
- Stop all third-down conversions

- Create three turnovers per game
- Allow no run over 20 yards
- Allow no pass over 30 yards
- Allow three yards or less in 65 percent of all runs
- Allow seven yards or less per pass attempt
- Score, and set up a score
- Win the sudden change
- Play smart—be the most aggressive, least penalized team in the league
- Be a great tackling team

We work on tackling every day. Every day we do something with tackling. Now, I am a little different in that we practice in shorts as much as we do in pads. This spring we will alternate pads, shorts, or shells, and we will essentially be in pads only four of the first eight practices, but we will work on tackling on all eight days.

First, we are going to recruit only tough guys, so I do not have to test their manhood. If we watch a high school player on film and see that he is not tough, then I do not recruit him. I do not care if he is big and fast. If he is not tough, I do not want him.

Give me tough guys. Tough guys will find a way to win. They can be undersized, but they will find a way to win. So, the key for us is that we do not have to test our players' courage, because we are only recruiting guys who are tough enough to play for us.

What I have to do is teach them to get their feet in the right position. I have spent this entire lecture talking about basic fundamentals and, except for holding the football, everything else I have talked about involves feet. If you get your feet in the right place, you will make the tackle. If the quarterback has his feet in the right place, he will make an accurate throw. Feet are the key.

I do not think that you need pads on to get your feet in the right place. I think you are more likely to get your feet in the right place when you do not have pads. The first thing that happens when we start saying "thud" and "tackle" and we put our pads on, is we start lunging.

We work hard on getting our guys to get themselves in the right position. If they are in the right position, they will make the tackle. If my backs put their feet in the right position, they will make the block. If my linemen get their feet in the right position, they will make the block. The feet, to me, are the key. We want to work to get our feet in the right position. If we do that, we think we are going to be a great tackling team.

We have one more defensive goal that I have not mentioned yet and it is the most difficult one for me as a coach. It is to have fun. This is my toughest one because I am kind of "old school," and guys who consider themselves in that way are "grinders." We just want to go out and grind, and grind, and grind, but the fact is, we do not have grind and grind kinds of kids today.

Football today must have some element of fun to it. You have to find a way to make it be fun. For us, one of the things we do to make it a little more fun is to give awards for everything. We will award the most interceptions in two-a-day camp, the most fumble recoveries in camp, the most caused fumbles in camp, and we will give an award to the guy who hustles on every play in two-a-day camp.

We will have all of these things so that the competition is not exactly a grind, but we are still getting all of the things that we want done. Find a way to make it competitive, so the kids can have fun. A T-shirt is a wonderful thing. I have seen pro athletes fight for T-shirts when they could buy the T-shirt factory, but they will fight for someone giving them a T-shirt. For me that is a tough one, but we have to find ways to make it fun.

I want to talk about the spread offense and what it offers that is unique. The spread offers us the read play by the quarterback, which is basically an extension of the option. So, in my mind, the first thing our coaches will look at when we talk about defending the spread offense is our ability to handle the option and the read play. We are going to go right back and make sure we have those fundamentals in place.

The change in offensive football today is the combination of the option play with a sophisticated passing game. It used to be the option p[...] attack was simply to fake the option and thr[...] post or vertical route. It was probably a one[...] route, not any more.

You have to be able to defend the option fir[...] and then defend a sophisticated passing attack. It[...] a problem. Our defensive coordinator, Kent Baer, is [...] good defensive coordinator. In the last four years, he has been up for the Frank Broyles Award for the assistant coach of the year three times, so he knows what he is doing. He has had defenses that have led the country in various statistical categories. We always start our game plan with stopping the run.

That is the first consideration. We are not going to think pass until we have figured out how to stop the run.

To me it is simple math. Most of the quarterbacks we see are very talented and if you let them stand back there by themselves, they will complete 70 percent of their passes. If we put a defense out there, we might get that down to 60 percent, and if we play good defense we could keep it around 50 percent. Fifty percent means that you have a chance to get off of the field. If you do not give up the big pass, you have a chance to get off the field.

But if you do not stop the run, any good running back will put together first downs on you, and you will not get off of the field. We better figure out a way to stop him from doing that, so the first thing we talk about is being able to stop the run.

So, the first thought I have when I think about the spread offense is stopping the run. The first thing we make sure we have in place is all of our option responsibilities. Taking care of those responsibilities should put us in position to take care of the read zone. We want everything matched up. That is the first thing, to identify the run and stop it.

Question: How do you get recruiting information on prospects?

You want to trust his high school coach. The main thing I do is look at film. You can tell if a player ough by the way he plays. We get guys from winning teams and guys from teams that have not been as successful. If a player is on an unsuccessful team, how does he play? What kind of player is he when his team is down and getting kicked? On a championship team, you assume players are better, they understand leadership, and understand how to win.

There are other things to look for that are important. I ask our coaches to go in and look at a young man's attendance. It is not easy to go to work every day and it is not easy to go to school every day. The kids who are there every day usually have some kind of special quality about them, so you find those little things that are not just what they do on the football field.

That should be a big indicator, but we want to find those other things that will tell us that this is a tough kid. Maybe he is the football player who is also a wrestler. It takes a little bit of toughness to wrestle, to sacrifice and drop all that weight, so we look at all of those things that tell us this is a tough kid. We do not just look at football alone.

Let me go back to the things we look for in a player to tell us about his toughness. We look at his commitment, his ability to communicate, his ability to focus, and his ability to listen. We look for passion. Find guys who are passionate about the game. Great coaches and great leaders are passionate about the game.

We look for positive attitudes, and I apply this one to our coaching staff as well. I will not hire a guy who does not have a positive attitude. It just sucks the life right out of you to spend the day around a guy who is negative, and we have all been around them. We want people with positive attitudes.

We want people who will take responsibility—people who have the ability to point the finger at themselves and not at somebody else.

We are looking for guys who are self-disciplined. Great leaders are self-disciplined. Great players are also self-disciplined.

The last quality we look for is selflessness, which I believe is the most important quality of any great person. You have to have ego, no question about that, but if you are selfless, you will stand above. Great parents are selfless, and will do everything for their children to be successful. Great generals are selfless and will put themselves on the front of the battle line with their soldiers. I think great coaches are the same way. It is not about them; it is about their team.

Finally, men, I always bring this up when I speak. I am an ambassador for the Jason Foundation, which is dedicated to the prevention of teenage suicide. It is all around us.

I was asked some time ago about coaching today's players, and if they are different. Well, they are different. Whether they have more information or more pressures I do not know, but they are different.

I spend more "couch time" now than I did 11 years ago as a head coach, and I suspect that you do too. Players today are different and the pressures are different, and we need to make sure, if we can, that we help some of these kids. It is all around us.

The signs are there, so be alert to them. If nothing else, just remember the number, so you can contact someone if you think there is a kid in trouble. You know what they say: "The kid you save may be your own."

When Coach Tony Dungy of the Indianapolis Colts lost his son, I immediately thought of my son. I think I may have done a better job of raising everybody else's children as opposed to my child, because I spend more time with my players than I do in my own home sometimes. We work from 6:30 in the morning until near midnight, men. We are not seeing our kids or our families. The kid you save could be your own.

I see my time is up. Thank you.